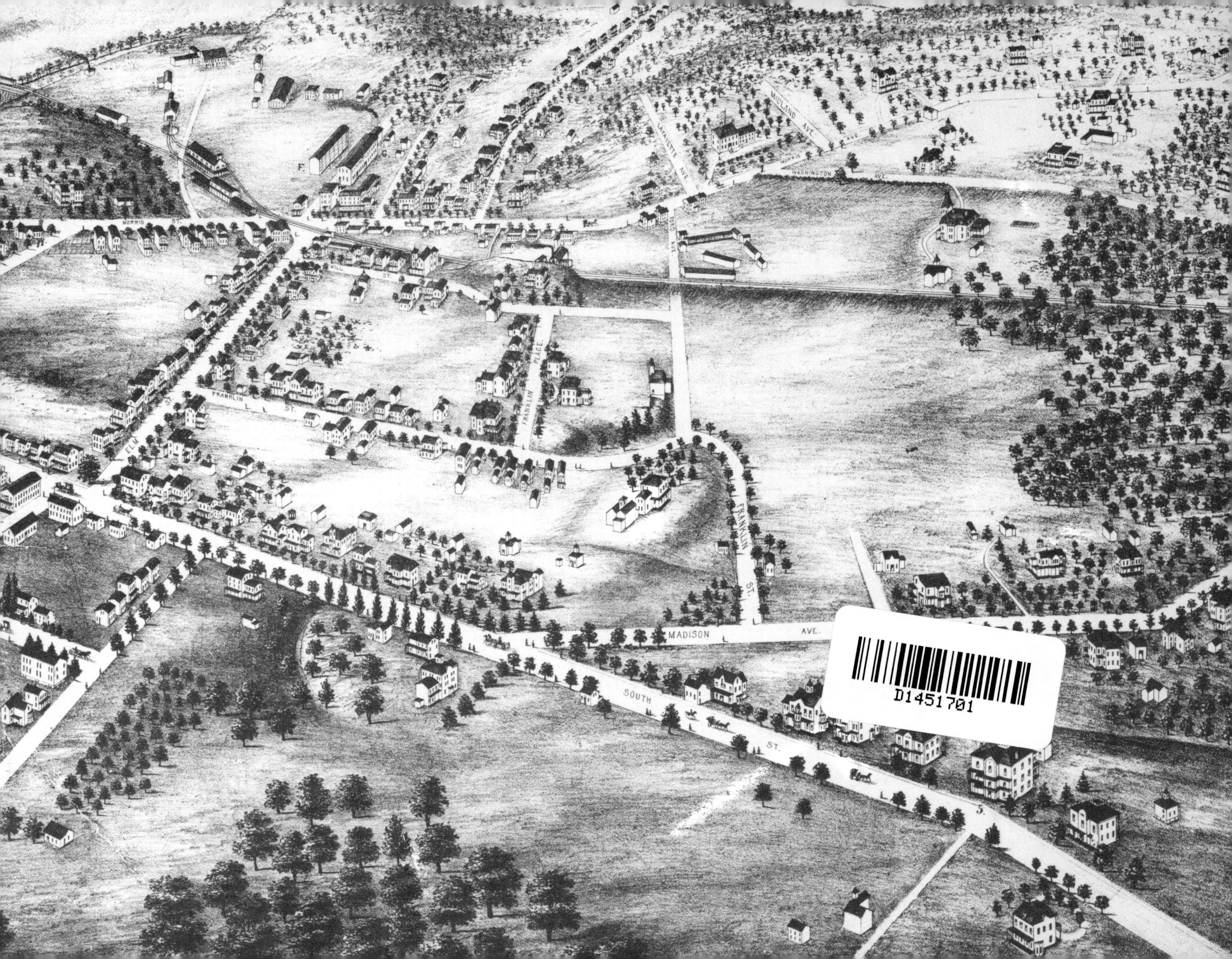
MORRIS ST.
HILL ST.
FRANKLIN ST.
FRANKLIN PLACE
ELM ST.
FRANKLIN ST.
MADISON AVE.
SOUTH ST.
WASHINGTON AVE.
MIDLAND AVE.
LAFAYETTE AVE.
F.
G.
5.

In Lights and Shadows

Photograph by James L. Grabow/TJFPLMMT

The 1871 Civil War Monument on the Morristown Green, 1983.

In Lights and Shadows

Morristown in Three Centuries

Cam Cavanaugh

The Joint Free Public Library of Morristown and Morris Township
Morristown, New Jersey

Photograph by George Goodwin/TJFPLMMT

Fosterfields, from the corner of Mendham and Kahdena Roads, Morris Township, 1985.

To
Barbara Hoskins,
whose love and knowledge of history
have inspired and helped so many.

If this book is not available
at your local bookstore, please
write to The Joint Free Public
Library of Morristown and Morris
Township, One Miller Road,
Morristown, NJ 07960.

ISBN 0-940631-02-4

Contents

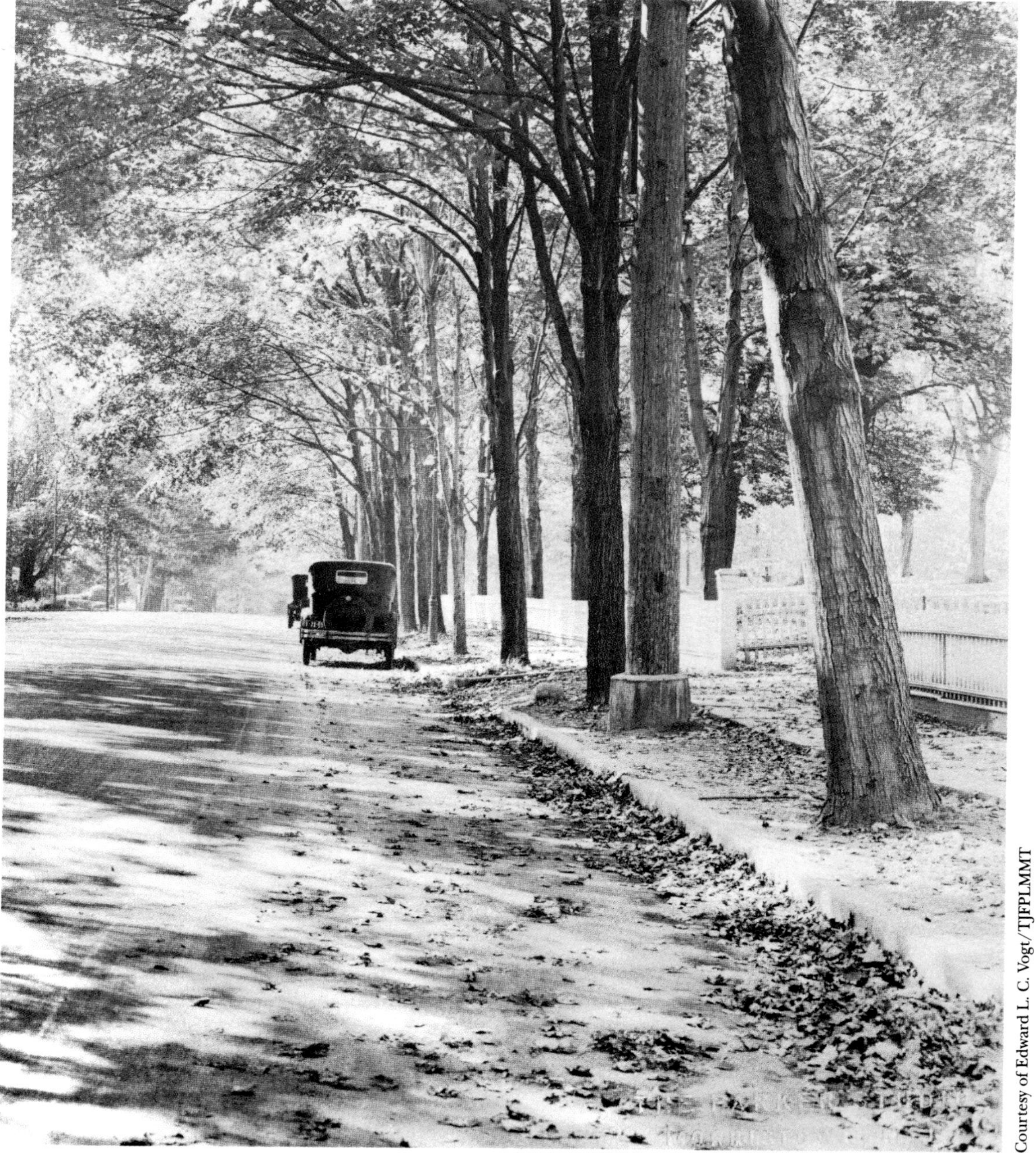

Courtesy of Edward L. C. Vogt/TJFPLMMT

Morris Avenue in front of Washington's Headquarters, Morristown, late 1920s.

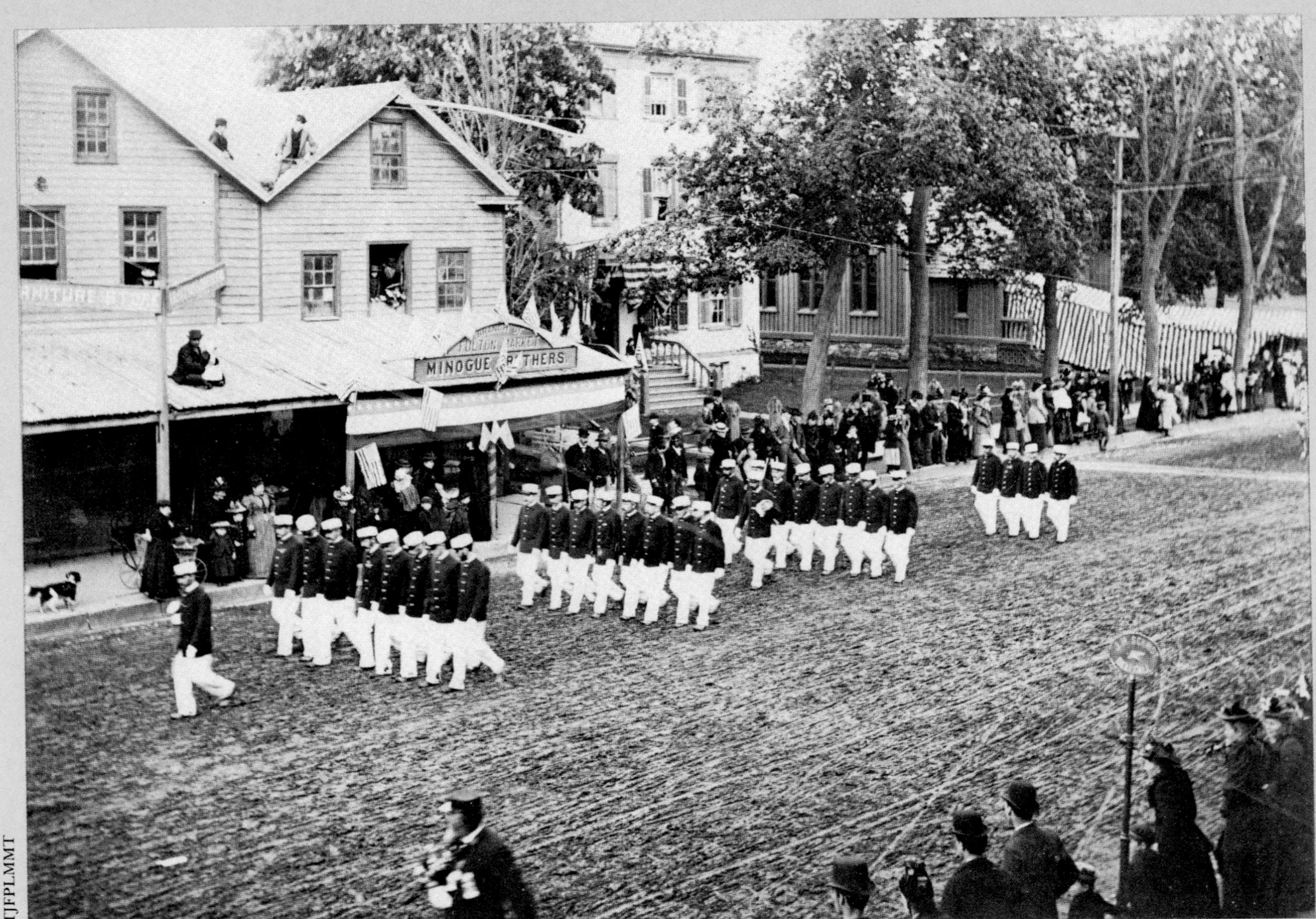

TJFPLMMT

The 1898 parade in honor of the State Exempt Firemen on South Street at the corner of DeHart Street, Morristown. The old Church of the Redeemer is on the right.

Foreword

Given only modest imagination, Morristown could be one of the major centers of America's history, as magnetic as Williamsburg, as vital as Valley Forge, as contrasting as Newport, playground of 19th-century millionaires.

Ford Mansion, where Washington spent the dreadful winter of 1779-80, is more authentic than anything at reconstructed Williamsburg. Jockey Hollow is as worthy of remembrance and visitation as Valley Forge.

And then, a century after the American Revolution, Morristown was reborn in an opulence and self-indulgence that contrasted sharply with the meagerness and sacrifice at Jockey Hollow. The millionaires came, in such droves that by 1890 the Morristown area had the nation's highest concentration of the super-rich.

Such things are part of the story that Cam Cavanaugh tells so impellingly in this book. This is the Morristown that so many of us know and cherish.

This is the story that Morristown should be telling — and showing — to the world. For now our introduction must be *In Lights and Shadows*, this saga of Morristown and of Morris Township, the "doughnut" that surrounds the town. As far as history is concerned, the two are one.

Longtime residents and admirers of Morristown, such as I, find much in this book that we have known — but only in a hazy way. Revisiting through these pages is a special privilege.

Morristown is special. It was so when Washington first strode across the Green in the winter of 1777. It was so when some of us as children roller-skated where he had walked. It was so when grandes dames patronized (in more ways than one) the local merchants ranged around the Green. It was so when automobiles circled the square in two directions, a seeming impossibility in today's one-way traffic.

Sadly, much of the area's story can be found only in this book, unless a visitor wants to spend as much time and effort as Cam Cavanaugh expended in digging through the splendid files of The Joint Free Public Library of Morristown and Morris Township.

She estimates four years of constant research. That doesn't count the hours, the days, the weeks, and finally the years of walking through Morristown or driving through the area to get a sense of what it might have been like for Washington or for one of the millionaires, or for those who come here today to train with their Seeing Eye dogs.

Inevitably she felt regret at the loss of much of the past. Gone are Arnold's Tavern, where Washington spent the winter of 1777; Dickerson's Tavern, where Benedict Arnold was tried in the waning days of 1779, and many of the mini-palaces where the area's millionaires flaunted their wealth.

The joy of what has survived, even if only in these pages, partially balances the sense of loss.

After all, Morristown still has its colonial green, a rarity in Middle Atlantic states. It has the splendid Ford Mansion, Washington's Headquarters in the winter of 1779-80; Macculloch Hall, where the idea of the hill-climbing Morris Canal was conceived; and the private home on Macculloch Avenue where the brilliant cartoonist Thomas Nast lived. It has the stately courthouse, opened in 1827; and Acorn Hall, as fine a Victorian home as can be found anywhere and now the home of the Morris County Historical Society.

Outward from the Green are The Willows, a remarkable "country lodge" at Fosterfields; the 100-room Twombly mansion, now the home of Fairleigh Dickinson University; and Historic Speedwell, where the telegraph instrument and the "Morse Code" were perfected by a "local boy," Alfred Vail.

Cam Cavanaugh has frozen in time much beyond the obvious. In these "lights and shadows" are the comfortable Morristown that existed long before the millionaires discovered it, the parades, the social life, the trains, the trolleys, the automobiles, people like us, and all those who have gone before or have yet to arrive. She takes due note of change, linking it with continuity.

Now let us travel through time and place with Cam Cavanaugh as Morristown and Morris Township come vividly to life — for appraisal, for judgement, and ultimately, for appreciation.

John T. Cunningham
August 1994

Introduction

I had a fantasy I thought others might share. I would spend a day in the library seeking the answer to this quesiton: *What was the Morristown area like* — in colonial times, during the Revolution, in the bustling days of the new country, in the Golden Age, during the sometimes shaky moments of the early 20th century? On that day I would be alone except for all the librarians at The Joint Free Public Library of Morristown and Morris Township crowding around to help only me.

I wanted this experience to be interesting, even fun. I didn't expect or even want to learn everything, but I would pore over photographs, paintings and sketches, absorb the thoughts in diaries and memoirs, delve into contemporary books and newspapers, study the ancient maps and marvel at the accomplishments of men and women that still shine today. In short, on this fanciful day I would learn much of the "look and feel" of an exciting place.

When I left in the evening, traveling through the streets of Morristown and Morris Township, I would feel a great communion with what I saw . . . Oh, yes, Washington rode on this street many times . . . five generations of a remarkable family lived here . . . that's the oldest building standing on the Green . . . this used to be a beautiful mansion where the most elegant parties were given. Images of the past that blend with the present make a scene alive in a special way.

That "day" happened, although it took four-and-a-half years. This book is my way of sharing the experience with you.

Cam Cavanaugh
August 1986

The Maple Avenue School, near Market Street, shortly after it was built in 1869. In 1956, the building was torn down to make room for the Morristown Municipal Parking Plaza.

TJFPLMMT

Photograph by James L. Grabow/TJFPLMMT

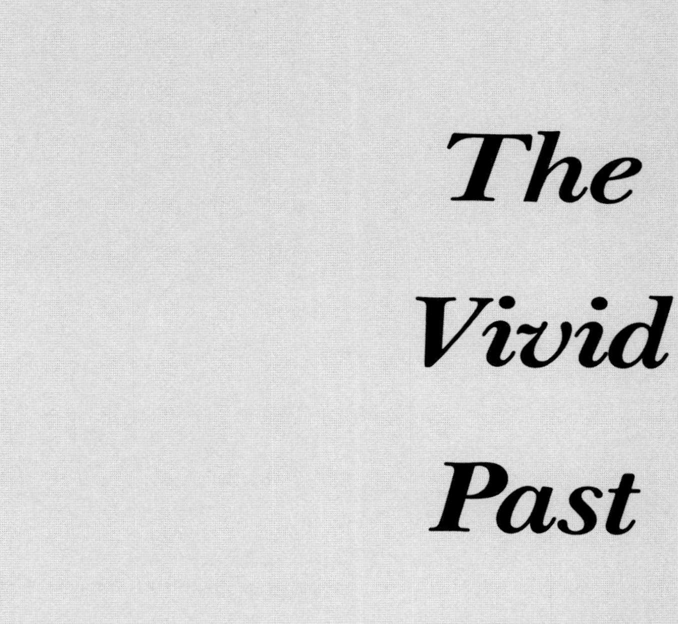

The Vivid Past

Overleaf The 1750 Wick House in light snow from the old Mendham-Elizabethtown Road in the Jockey Hollow Area of the Morristown National Historical Park, 1982.

NO ONE KNOWS EXACTLY WHEN the first white men settled in the area known as Morristown and Morris Township. That shadowy date remains ever elusive. Some historians guess it was 1715 because of the number of land surveys made that year. Others place the settlement years as early as 1710. There is agreement, however, that as late as 1738 Morristown, then called West Hanover or New Hanover, was small and difficult to reach. "Roads were scarecely known," wrote the Rev. Jacob Green, third pastor of the Hanover Presbyterian Church, where these settlers first worshipped. "The bridle path or Indian trail was all that conducted the occasional traveler [through Morristown] to Mendham." Determined men on widely scattered homesteads struggled to clear the woods and tame the land.

Two separate events, however, made certain the area would swiftly grow in significance.

In 1738, the settlers were permitted their own Presbyterian Church. Not only would members no longer have to walk or ride the long distance to Hanover (now Whippany) every Sunday, but also church affairs would be in local hands.

In 1739, Morris County was set off from Hunterdon County, and on March 25, 1740, about half the new county became the Town-

Photograph by James L. Grabow/TJFPLMM

Log huts on Sugar Loaf Hill in Jockey Hollow, reconstructions typical of the single-door enlisted men's huts and two-door officers' huts built during the winter of 1779-80, 1982.

ship of Morris. As the most promising village in that county, Morristown became the county seat.

Twice during the Revolutionary War Morristown was chosen as George Washington's winter headquarters. The name now was known through the 13 colonies and in the courts of Europe. Most of the famous military heroes of the war visited here; the bitterest and coldest winter of the war was endured here; a famous treason trial and a celebrated courtship were played out here.

After the War of Independence, farming remained of primary importance but emphasis also turned to producing the goods previously bought from Great Britain. By 1815, Stephen Vail was operating the highly successful Speedwell Iron Works. One of its early successes was the building and assembling of most of the machinery for the *S. S. Savannah,* the first steam-powered vessel to cross the Atlantic, in 1819. Less than 20 years later, Alfred Vail, the older son, became the partner of Samuel F. B. Morse in perfecting the electromagnetic telegraph that would revolutionize communication. Then came the Morris Canal in 1831 and the Morris & Essex Railroad in 1838, dramatically altering land transportation.

It was an exciting, crowded past. □

The Village That Washington Found

Photograph by James L. Grabow/TJFPLMMT

Door handle, Wick House.

MORRISTOWN WAS A CROSSROADS long before the Revolution. Still today some of the most traveled streets follow closely the colonial roads. Morris Street and Morris Avenue are part of the old "Road to New Arck thro Hanover"; Washington Avenue was the beginning of the Road to Elizabethtown; South Street and James Street follow the "Road to New Vernon." Other old roads are Bank Street and Mount Kemble Avenue, "Roads to Basker Ridge and Vealtown [Bernardsville]"; Western Avenue, "Road to Jockey Hollow"; and Mendham Road, "Road to Roxiticus." Then as now, there was a route to every point of the compass.

A few hardy settlers built small dwellings — probably no more than log huts — in "The Hollow" section (Spring Street and the old Water Street, now Martin Luther King Avenue). Once established as the county seat, the little village expanded out of "The Hollow." Houses were built on the present Morris Street and on the way up "Town Hill" to the church-owned commons. It was the Presbyterian church that donated one acre on the Green for the first Morris County Court House.

The first Presbyterian church stood where the Presbyterian church stands today at East Park Place. The Trustees owned all the land south and east from the Green to the present Pine Street, known as the Parsonage Land. Gradually, some of this land was sold off. According to church records: "May the 1 1761 the Trustees [Benjamin Hathaway, President] met on the Green but Capt [Joseph] Stiles absent and agread to Lay out with Lots and Sell Some Part of the Pairsonag Land Lying before the meeting house Dore." Three lots at the beginning of Morris Street were soon sold. The first on June 8, 1761, "Conveyed to Joseph King was Sixteen Pound ten Shilling and Sealed the Conveyeand with the Shape of a mans head." The second lot was sold on August 26 to Daniel Cooper for the same price over the same seal. The corner lot went for 25 pounds on April 6, 1782, to Isaac Bobbet sealed "with the Seign of a Sheaf and that same Day Agreed and bought that Same Seal for the use of the [Church] Charter."

By the beginning of the Revolution, there were about 250 inhabitants in the town and an unknown number, probably not exceeding that amount, in the rest of the township. (The one "census" that survived and the 1778 tax roll are incomplete.) In addition to the two churches and the Court House, the town had two taverns, two schoolhouses and several stores.

Within a three-mile radius, there were five iron forges, two sawmills, three gristmills, one fulling mill, and the newly built Ford's Powder Mill, the only gunpowder mill in New Jersey. □

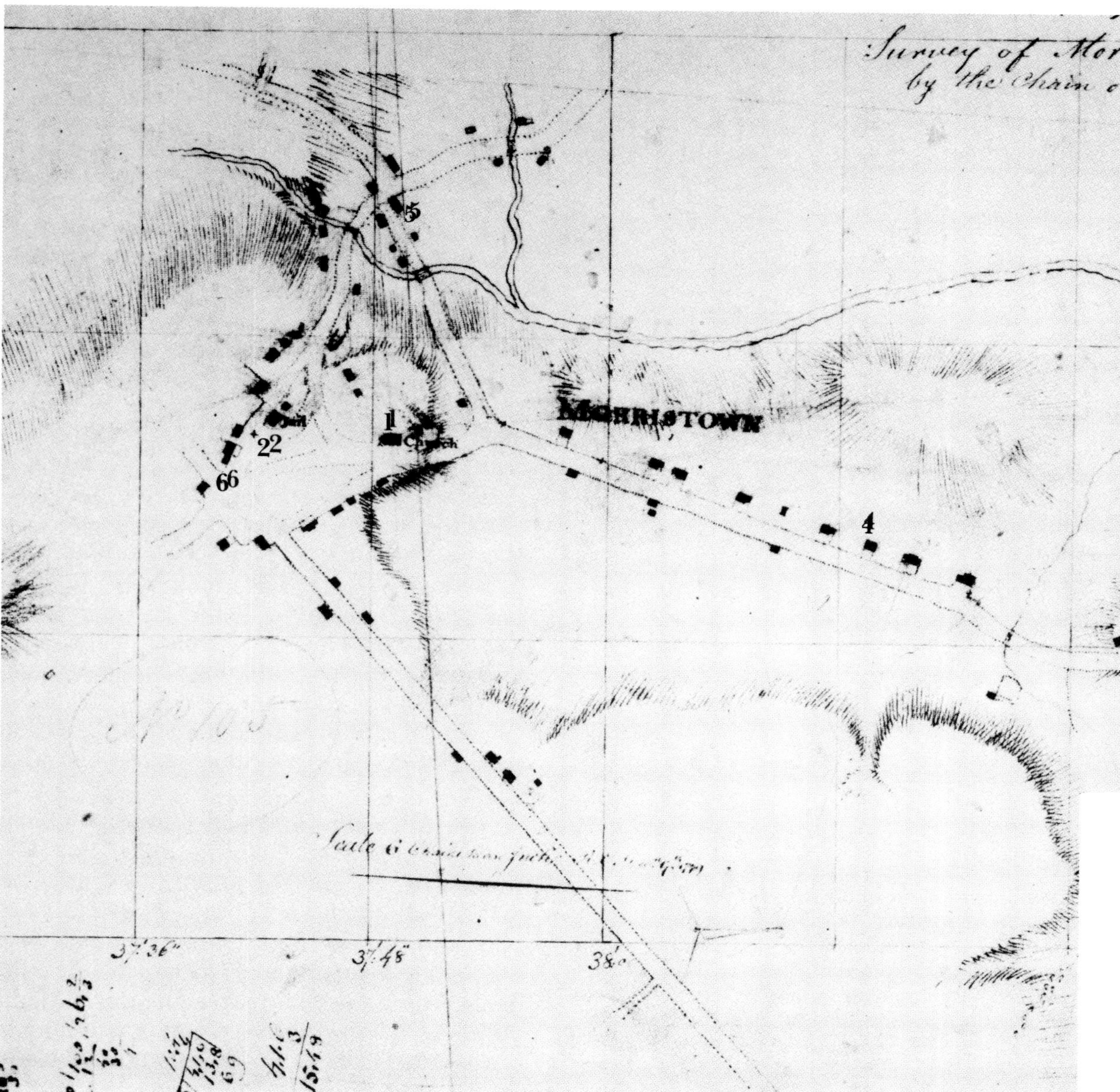

Courtesy of The New-York Historical Society

"Survey of Morristown by the chain only, December 12, 1779"

This map shows the layout of the colonial town and its principal streets from the Green to the Jacob Ford Mansion, then considered on the outskirts of town.

This is one of six maps Col. Robert Erskine, geographer and surveyor to the army, drew of the Morristown area at George Washington's request. Unfortunately for future historians, Erskine marked only the Presbyterian Church (1) and the Jail (2), which was part of the courthouse — although he did this, no doubt, for security reasons should the map fall into enemy hands. However, it is possible to locate a number of buildings important to early Morristown, including the Ford Mansion (3); Dr. Jabez Campfield's house, original site (4); Dickerson's Tavern in "The Hollow" (5); and Arnold's Tavern on the Green (6).

Curtiss Collection/TJFPLMMT

The Presbyterian Church on the Green

The first meeting house, as it appeared just before the Revolution, had already been enlarged twice. It faced Morris Street and was located about where the present Manse is.

The original wooden church was built in 1738-40 on land donated by Benjamin Hathaway and Jonathan Lindsley. It had a square, barn-like appearance. According to Rev. David Irving in *The Record*, "It was stated by some who seceded from Hanover that when the frame was raised, a small platform of boards, with a chair and small table served for a pulpit and the congregation were seated on the sills and on other timbers."

In 1760, the building was cut in half and the western part moved about 25 feet toward the Green. The space was then enclosed and the building completely renovated. "A spacious gallery was raised on the front and each end," continued Dr. Irving, although he placed the year as 1774. "The pulpit [was] high and cup like in the centre of the north side, the main entrance door on the S. side in front of the pulpit. Two other entrances, one at each end, were provided." In 1764, the tower with a spire about 125 feet high was erected on the west end with a bell, traditionally believed the gift of King George II. The first school in Morristown was probably held in the steeple.

George Washington knew this church and its remarkable pastor, Rev. Timothy Johnes. It became a hospital for the troops in 1777-78.

Colonial Beginnings

The Presbyterian Church dominated the religious, social and political activities of the colonial village and the surrounding township. This was true not only because most residents were Presbyterians but because of a remarkable and much admired minister.

In 1730 enough families from the Hanover (now Whippany) Presbyterian Church had moved west along the Whippanong River to discuss the organization of a new church nearer their homes. The idea was not greeted with joy — quite the opposite — and the majority of the congregation voted against allowing these families to form their own church. Despite this, they began to hold their own services and, in 1733, received permission from the Philadelphia Synod to form a new church in West Hanover. This they did with 20 founding members, although official recognition did not come until 1738. Under John Cleverly, the Harvard graduate who served as unofficial pastor, the number of members soon rose to 55.

In 1742, the Reverend Timothy Johnes (1717-1794) took firm charge of a flock that now numbered 100. In one of his first acts, he demanded a confession from every man who had gone against the Hanover church's vote and beside the name was written, "confest for disregarding the lot," in church records for all to know in centuries to come. A graduate of Yale, he came from Southampton, Long Island, on August 13, 1742, to serve 52 years, keeping a faithful record of births, marriages, deaths and conversions to the faith and careful minutes of the decision of the Elders of the Session and the Trustees, the spiritual and temporal leaders of the Church.

A later Presbyterian minister, Albert Barnes, summarized his influence this way: "As a preacher he is said to have been clear, plain, practical and persuasive. He aimed rather to bring men to the practice of religion rather to terrify and denounce them [unusual in those days!] yet he suffered no public vice to escape without reproof."

During his ministry, he supervised three church revivals — in 1764, 1774 and 1790 — and he received into the church 600 members and 572 half-way members, officiated at 2,827 baptisms and 948 marriages, and disciplined 170 members. Some of his admonitions were connected with disputes over property. Intemperance was often involved. Three cases are extracted from his notes:

"January 3, 1760, Mr. ——— and wife for partaking of a stolen watermelon."

"July 26, 1766, ——— for a premeditated fist quarrel."

"January 1, 1772, ——— for taking hold of an antient man & member of ye ch., and shaking him in an unchristian & threatening."

There were plenty of cases left over for the court, however. A church-dominated town did not mean a crime-free one, despite the threat of hanging, brutal flogging or standing in the public pillory to be ridiculed for minor crimes. Even debtors were jailed.

Counterfeiting was a crime that carried the death penalty, yet the most sensational trial in colonial Morristown involved counterfeiters — all but one of whom was well connected. The ringleader was Samuel Ford, a cousin of Jacob Ford and only blot on that family name. Samuel learned his villany in Ireland and in 1772 he established his "money-making business" of printing bills of Maryland, Pennsylvania, New York and New Jersey in a secluded place called the "Hummock" (near the present Morristown Airport). With him in this venture were Dr.

Curtiss Collection/TJFPLMMT

The Baptist Church on the Green

Built in 1771, this church stood on the northwest side of the Green on land about where 10 Park Place is located.

The Baptist congregation, organized in 1752, had first worshipped at a meeting house on the west side of Mount Kemble Avenue almost opposite the entrance to Sand Spring Road. However, in 1770, many Baptists had moved closer to Morristown and services were held in the new Morris County Court House (page 19).

On the second Sunday in May 1771, the new church was dedicated with a sermon by Rev. John Gano, the first pastor, of whom Henry Clay is reported to have said: "Of all the preachers I have ever listened to, he made me feel the most that religion was a divine reality." "The Baptist meetinghouse, when completed, was about forty feet in length by thirty feet in depth and stood on a slight elevation back from what is now Speedwell Avenue," wrote Rev. Andrew Sherman in *Historic Morristown.* "The first pastor of the Baptist Church on 'Morris Green' was the Rev. Reune Runyon [who] was ordained to the Baptist ministry in the month of June, in the year 1771. Mr. Runyon was the pastor of the Morristown Baptist Church during the Revolution; and he is said to have been an ardent patriot, brave and true."

Like the Presbyterian Church, this building was used as an army hospital in 1777-78, and many soldiers were buried in its churchyard.

At a Court of Oyer and Terminer and General
Gaol Delivery holden for the County of Morris,
on Monday, the Second of July, 1750.

Present

The Honble Samuel Nevill, Esq Second Judge.

Your County is also, by his Majesty's New Ordinance, taken into the Western Circuit, and a Supreme Court of Judicature is now established amongst you, for the Tryal of Causes brought to Issue in the same County [illegible]. These are some of the inestimable Blessings you enjoy under the Happiest Constitution in the World! Not to have Justice denyed you; but to have it brought in a free and clear [illegible] even to your own Door; ye how happy, &c.

The Charge to the Grand Jury.

Gentlemen of the Grand Jury,

Your County is now honoured with his Majesty's Special Commission of Oyer and Terminer and General Gaol Delivery for the first Time, which hath been publickly read; and by which his Majesty hath delegated to his Judges, and their Associates, the Power of Life and Death, and of hearing, trying, and determining, according to the Laws of the Land, all Criminal Causes what-soever, from Treason to Trespass. [And I cannot help saying, That this Court of Judicature was extremely wanted in the County of Morris, to which Publick Offenders seem to retreat, as to an Asylum, or Place of Refuge from the Laws. But though Justice hath [illegible]

Leaden

This Court of Judicature was extremely wanted in the County of Morris, to which Publick offenders seem to retreat, as to an Asylum, or Place of Refuge from the Laws.
Judge Samuel Nevill, July 2, 1756

Charge to the first Grand Jury in Morris County, July 2, 1750

This event probably took place at the tavern of Jacob Ford, Sr., who was a judge. From this first page, it is clear Judge Samuel Nevill did not have a high opinion of Morris County colonists, 20 of whom were bound over for "such divers crimes" as unlawful assembly, inciting a riot, felony and assault, escape from prison and — a thriving business — counterfeiting.

Bern Budd, a leading Morristown physician; Benjamin Cooper of Hibernia, son of the judge who later tried the case; Samuel Haynes and one Ayers of Sussex County — all justices of the peace — and David Reynolds, the one "common" man without connections. In some way, suspicion fell on Samuel Ford and on July 16, 1773, he was lodged in the county jail on the Green. Late that night or early the next day, however, he disappeared, probably aided by a former sheriff. Sheriff Thomas Kinney was himself accused of negligence in office. He had led his posse to the hiding place in Hibernia so slowly that Samuel had already fled to Virginia, never to return.

Cooper, Budd, Haynes and Reynolds were arraigned on August 19th; Ayers was tried in Sussex. "A thousand people were thought to be within the walls with scarcely an eye which did not exhibit some tokens of sympathetic sorrow," wrote the historian Rev. Rufus S. Green. But a death sentence was passed. "The day fixed for the execution arrived," continued the Rev. Green, "and Reynolds, who seems to have been really the least guilty of the lot, but who alone unfortunately for himself, had no influential friends, suffered the ignominious death to which he had been sentenced; while the other three were remanded, and finally in December, after a number of respites, William Franklin [Benjamin Franklin's son and last colonial governor of New Jersey] gave them a full pardon."

There are not many colonial stories as well documented as this one. Those few who could write had little leisure time to tell tales, and there were no newspapers in New Jersey before the Revolution. Therefore, it is from church records, legal documents and the occasional notices in the New York or Pennsylvania newspapers that we can capture a glimpse of life in the early beginnings. □

Curtiss Collection/TJFPLMMT

Photograph by James L. Grabow/TJFPLMMT

Courtesy of Morristown National Historical Park

The 1770 Morris County Court House on the Green

This building replaced a log cabin built in 1755 on the same site almost opposite the Baptist Church. In addition to the common rooms for the prisoners, there was a slightly more comfortable debtors' room and an apartment for the "goaler." Prisoners stood at the pillory for even minor crimes until that punishment was outlawed in 1796. Hangings took place on the Green until 1833. Less dangerous prisoners got their water at the town well at the rear of the building.

Conditions were always overcrowded and unhealthy but became particularly bad when suspected Tories also were lodged in the jail. A monument stone commemorates the approximate location of both courthouses.

Old 1755 weathervane (above, right) that also sat on top of the 1770 court house, although this is not clear in the 19th century rendering. It is in the Morristown National Historical Park museum.

Glimpses into the Colonial Past

Early Newspaper Notices

1750. Run away on the 5th Day of August Inst. from Jacob Ford [Sr.] of Morris-Town and County, East New Jersey, a Negro Boy, named Ishmael, aged about 16 Years, short and thick, full Faced, has a very large Foot, born in the Country, and has a sly Look: Had when he went away, a Flannel Jacket, dyed with Logwood of a purple Colour, two woolen Shirts, one Tow Shirt, and a Dowles Shirt, a new Felt Hat, Leather Breeches, and Oznabrigs Trowsers.

Whoever takes up and secures said Boy so that his Master may have him again, shall have Three Pounds Reward, and all reasonable Charges paid by me JACOB FORD

N.B. He went away with a Negro Fellow already advertised by Shadreck Hatheway.

[*New Jersey Archives* (NJA), 1st Series, Vol. XII, Newspaper Extracts, Vol. II, 1740-50, pages 665-66.]

February 29, 1768. THREE POUNDS REWARD.
Run-away about the 6th of January last, an indented servant man named Siles Palmer, born in New-England and is supposed to have gone that way . . . . He is about 25 years old, 5 feet 6 or 7 inches high, light hair, blue eyes, adicted to drinking, and when in liquor, talkative and impertinent: Had on when he went away, a small bound felt hat, leather breeches, and a blue jacket, but it is likely he may change his dress. Whoever takes up said servant, and commits him to any of his Majesty's goals, shall have the above reward, by applying to the subscriber living in Morris-Town, East New Jersey. MARY MOORE

[*NJA*, 1st Series, Vol. XXVI, Newspaper Extracts, Vol. VII, 1768-69, page 62.]

Jacob Ford Esqr Presenting a Petition to the Court Pursuant to a Late Act of the General Assembly of this Province for the Granting him a Licence to Keep a Publick house and Inn in Morris Town where he Now Lives the Court on reading the Same Ordered the Same to be filed he having Entred into a Recognizance pursuant to said Act the Court grants said Jacob Ford said License for one Year Now next Ensuing Jacob Ford Joseph Howard & David Wheeler Entred into recognizance Pursuant to the Directions of said Act.

TJFPLMMT

License to keep a tavern in 1740, probably on Spring Street, granted to Jacob Ford, Sr. Since 1668, every town had to provide an "ordinary" (tavern or inn) for the "relief and entertainment of strangers." Ford ran his tavern from 1738 to 1758. Court sessions were held there until the first courthouse was built in 1755.

Timothy Mills marks [cattle] with two half pennys underside of right Eare and a half penny underside of the Left.
Town Book, 1745

1769. We hear from Morris-Town, that on the 11th Ult. as one Peter Berry was riding down a Hill, his Horse stumbled, by which he was thrown down, and the Horse falling on him instantly killed him. — He was on the point of going to Ireland, where it was said he had 1000£ Sterling lately bequested to him.

And on the 18th, which was the Saturday following, as David Correy was driving his Team, the Horses ran with Violence down the aforesaid Hill, and by the Waggon giving a Jolt over a Stone, pitched him out, when the Wheels run over his Head. He continued in great Misery till the Morning, when he died.
[*NJA*, 1st Series, Vol. XXVI, Newspaper Extracts, Vol. VII, 1768-69, page 376.]

New-York, December 11, 1769. We are desired to let the Public know, that the New-Jersey Men will not be out done by those of New-England, in so virtuous an Act as the killing of those destructive Vermin called Squirrels. For it is said a whole Town of the latter assembled, and killed about 1600; whereas about thirty eight Men of the former, from the Towns of Morris and Mendem, (not one Quarter of either) in one Day killed 840.
[*NJA*, 1st Series, Vol. XXVI, Newspaper Extracts, Vol. VII, 1768-69, pages 581-82.]

Historic American Buildings Survey/TJFPLMMT

The 1740 Timothy Mills House

This house at 27 Mills Street is the oldest one still standing in Morristown on its original site, as it appeared in the 1940s.

The builder came from Long Island, like so many early Morristown settlers. Large by Colonial standards, the farm house is sturdily built, with chimneys on both sides. Teams of oxen moved the thick stones in place to build the foundation. The house was surrounded by 50 acres, which he farmed and used for a tannery — highly odoriferous profession that was properly carried on at the edge of town. Mills was a communicant in the Presbyterian Church before Parson Johnes arrived and it was probably through the church that he met his wife, Phebe Lindsley of New Vernon. They had nine children. In 1761, he was elected a church elder, a member of the Session. Between 1754 and 1785, he also held many official town positions, including overseer and surveyor of highways and roads, and collector and overseer of the poor.

TO BE RUN FOR, round the course at Morris-Town, and to be won by the best of three two-mile heats; a SILVER TANKARD OF TWENTY POUNDS value, on the fifth day of November next, free for any horse, mare, or gelding, not exceeding three-quarter blood, carrying weight for age and blood.
From *The New York Gazette; and the Weekly Mercury,* No. 1041, October 7, 1771

January 11, 1771. TO BE SOLD at public Vendue, on Wednesday, the 13th day of February next, at 10 o'clock. The Plantation belonging to me the Subscriber, containing about 400 Acres, near one-third Part of it is extraordinary good Meadow, whereon is cut yearly, upwards of 100 Tons of good Hay, a good Part of it is English and Timothy; and can, with a little Expence, be cut as much more yearly; there is near 40 Acres of it the best sort of Bog Meadow, ready ditch'd, fit for raising Hemp or Corn; the Upland is very good for all sorts of Grain, in good Fence, and 400 bearing Apple Trees, and a large Number of other Fruit Trees; well water'd and timber'd; there is on the Premises, a good Dwelling House, four Rooms on a Floor, with four Fire-places, a good Kitchen, Barn and Barracks, and can easily be divided into two Farms; the Title indisputable. There will also be sold on the Premises the same Day, a Negro Man and Boy, and a Negro Wench, if not sold at private Sale before said Day; together with all sorts of farming Utensils, and Household Furniture, and Horses, Cattle, Sheep and Hogs; and many other Things too tedious to mention: A reasonable Time of Payment will be given for the whole, and Conditions made known on the Day of Sale, by me. JOSEPH TUTTEL
[*NJA*, 1st Series, Vol. XXVII, Newspaper Extracts, Vol. VIII, 1770-71, pages 347-48.]

1771. WANTED, Some Person who well understands Water rotting Hemp. Such a one, by applying to Jacob Ford, Junior, at his Farm near Morris Town, in Morris County (about the First of August next) will meet with Encouragement well worth his Notice.
[*NJA*, 1st Series, Vol. XXVII, Newspaper Extracts, Vol. VIII, 1770-71, page 523.]

November 3, 1771. WHEREAS the Shop of Hubert Burke, Taylor, was broke open on Thursday, the 31st of October last, and the following Articles feloniously taken from thence, viz. About 8 or 9 Yards of Homespun mixed Cloth, white and Sheep's grey, 4 Yards of Coarse Blue Cloth, about 2 Yards Scarlet Cloth, 4 Yards Durant same Colour, 4 Yards black Homespun, ¼ wide Cloth, 2 Yards blue Plush and a round Piece of the same like the seat of a Woman's Saddle, about three yards Fustian, 2 Yards Homespun Linnen. Supposed to be taken away by a Fellow that has come into town and sold a bald faced Sorrel Horse, 14 Hands high, he called his name John Hughs, born in Chester-County, Pennsylvania, he is about 5 Feet 6 Inches high, short blackish Hair, blue and white mixed Coat, bound Holes, Flaps and Sleeves, he is very round made, very hairy on the Breast, small Legs, it is supposed he stole a Horse at the same Time, as there is a Bridle and Saddle missing the same Night. Whoever takes up said Thief, and secures him, so as the Cloths may be found, shall have five Dollars Reward, and all reasonable Charges paid by the above named. HUBERT BURKE
[*NJA*, 1st Series, Vol. XXVII, Newspaper Extracts, Vol. VIII, 1770-71, pages 644-45.]

1772. THE STAGE WAGGON. Lately erected by the subscriber, which he intends to keep going between Morris Town, in New-Jersey, and Powles Hook [Jersey City] ferry, once every week, will perform as follows. To set out from Mr. Samuel Haines's tavern, in Morris Town, every Monday, weather permitting, at sun-rising, and proceed to Christopher Wood's tavern, in Hanover, at which place he will make about a quarter of an hour's halt, to take in what passengers may happen to be waiting there for him; from thence to Mr. Ellis Cook's tavern [also in Hanover] where he likewise purposes to halt; and from thence to Mr. Munn's, at Newark Mountains; and to halt there for the same purpose; then proceed to Powles Hook ferry. All of which he can perform in the same day with ease, and to return the next, and be at Morris Town that night. The fare for a passenger is half a dollar going, and half a dollar coming, and at the rate of four shillings per hundred weight, for any kind of lumber or produce, suitable for a stage to carry. DANIEL BURNETT

[*NJA*, 1st Series, Vol. XXVIII, Newspaper Extracts, Vol. IX, 1772-73, pages 235-36.]

1773. THIRTY POUNDS REWARD.
Broke goal, a certain Samuel Ford, accused of counterfeiting money: He is a tall well built fellow, about 30 years of age, 5 feet 10 inches high; he had on when he went away, a nankeen jaket and breeches, and a brown coat, plain brown thread stockings, a handsome pair of shoes, and silver twist buckles; has brown curl'd hair, red cheecks, and a remarkable dimple in his chin. — Whoever takes up said Samuel Ford, and secures him in any of his majesty's goals, so that he may be had again, shall receive the above sum of 30£ and all reasonable charges, from THOMAS KENNY, High Sheriff of the County of Morris.

[*NJA*, 1st Series, Vol. XXVIII, Newspaper Extracts, Vol. IX, 1772-73, page 565.]

March 4, 1775. Last Wednesday at three o'clock, P.M., departed this Life, Phoebe, the wife of James M'Bride, who left her distressed and afflicted husband with three small helpless Children to bewail her loss. She is much lamented by her relations, neighbours, and all who had the pleasure of being acquainted with her virtuous life and conversation.

[*NJA*, 1st Series, Vol. XXXI, Newspaper Extracts, Vol. XI, 1775, page 81.]

A true and Exact Inventory of the Estate of Peter Condict Dec.d as apprized by Eben.r Condict & Benoni Hathaway July 28. 1776

	£	s	d
one horse £18..10 two Cows £10 four sheep 48/	30	18	0
one Swine 35/ two Beds 45/ bedsted 10/ four pillowcases & bolster 9/	4	19	0
two Coverleds 50/ Rugg 25/ bedquilt 40/ Curtains 80/	9	15	0
five flannel Sheets 53/ five pair Sheets 62/ Do pillowcases 10/	6	5	0
one Cupboard 70/ two Tables 42/ Warming pan 16/6	6	8	6
Six chairs 15/ Chest 40/. 8 pewter platters 11/. 6 plates 10/	3	16	0
Tea pot 4/ Cups 3/6 two knotbowls 6/ two Trays & pan 2/10	—	16	4
three pewter Basons 6/ Bedsted 4/ Lookingglass 2.8/	1	18	0
two Stone pots 5/ Trenchers & jugg 2/8 Smoothing Irons 5/	—	12	8
fryingpan 1/9 Brasskittle 25/0 Ironpot 7/ hand Irons 8/	2	1	9
Trammels & Tongs 9/. churn 5/. two pails 3/. wash tub 5/0	1	2	0
Saddle 70/ Box 1/6 Sundry old Irons 18/1	4	9	7
three Calves 68/1 Tub and Sundrys 27/0	4	15	1
Two Calves 60/ Trays 5/4 Coverled & Sundrys 11/6	3	17	0
Horse 79/11 Cydermill 21/0 Cow 112/ Sundrys 1/4	10	14	3
Watch £6..10..2. 15 Sheep £8..18..6 one Swine 49/7	17	18	3
Cow £6..11. Ram 30/ Sundry Irons 26/5	9	6	5
two bedticks 35/1 Sythe 12/2 Leather 15/8 Sundrys 52/7	5	15	1
grass £23..18..2 Cow £6..10..6 gun 25/1 Sundrys 36/2	33	9	11
Desk 57/ Meat 33/10 foxtraps 12/3 Sundrys 17/11	6	1	0
Corn house 60/ pair of Steers 90/ Bull 52/11 Heifer 85/6	14	8	5
Waggon £7..5. Meat 17/10 Barral of vinegar 11/6	8	14	4
Sundry old Barrals and Lumber 71/7	3	11	7
Sundry Farming utensils & Smiths Tools 120/	6	0	0
three Heifers £7..13 bed 94/6 one heifer 52/0	14	19	6
Corn & purtatoes in the field 89/ Chest 80/	5	19	0
Wheel 6/1 waterpot 6/3 Case & bottles 16/0	1	8	4
Swine 25/0 Bedstead 10/ Sundrys 90/ Sundry notes £28..2..8	34	7	8
anvil Bellows & Beckiron £18..9 Sundrys 48/5 Wheat £22.13.2	38	10	7
	£292	18	3
Wearing apparrel £7..8..7 Wheat £6..10..3	13	18	10
	306	17	1

TJFPLMMT

Inventory of the possessions of Peter Condict, 3rd.

Curtiss Collection/TJFPLMMT

The Dickerson, or Norris, Tavern

The tavern stood at the corner of Spring and Water streets (Martin Luther King Avenue), Morristown. An advertisement in 1775 described the tavern as a "large two-story house with six fireplaces and a good cellar under it, 5 acres of good land adjoining, a good barn, stables, and outhouses, a good well of water at the door and the best garden in town." Inside, the lower floor was divided into two parts with a wide hall in the center and a winding stairway at the rear. On the right was a large room with a bar extending across the back. This was used for the trial of Benedict Arnold in 1779-80 (page 57). Peter Dickerson, a member of the Provincial Congress in New Jersey in 1775, served in the 2nd company, 3d regiment of the New Jersey Brigade. During the war, his tavern was leased to Robert Norris, whose patriotic sympathies were suspect; nevertheless, it continued to be an important patriot meeting place. Sometime around the beginning of the 20th century, the tavern burned and was rebuilt and called The Yellow House. It no longer exists. Capt. Dickerson died in May of 1790 at age 56. Mrs. Dickerson ran the tavern for some years after his death. A grandson, Mahlon Dickerson, became the first New Jersey governor from Morris County.

A Center of Patriots

How dare he? The loyal subjects of George II were turning into the rebellious subjects of George III. The words of Patrick Henry and the writings of Thomas Paine fanned the fires already started in the talk at the inns and taverns.

The Revolution was soundly backed by the influential leaders and large property owners of Morris Township — including the Hathaway and Johnes families to the north of the village, the Ford family to the east, General John Doughty to the south, and Silas Condict and his brothers to the west.

On June 27, 1774, a Monday, "a respectable body of freeholders and inhabitants" of Morris County met at the Court House on the Green. Jacob Ford, Sr., was chairman of a meeting that met to protest "oppressive and arbitrary taxes" and "the unconstitutional and injurious" closing of Boston harbor and to elect delegates to a proposed General Congress and form a committee of correspondence with other counties. Of nine delegates, four were from Morristown — Jacob Ford; his prominent son-in-law Samuel Tuttle, who after the war became a clerk of the county and judge of the county court; William DeHart, the lawyer; and Jonathan Stiles, a former county judge and sheriff.

Ford was again chairman and DeHart clerk at a meeting on May 1, at "Morristown, New Jersie 1775 Arnold Tavern," when nine delegates to the Provincial Congress were about to meet in Trenton. In addition to Ford and DeHart were Silas Condict and Peter Dickerson of Morristown; William Winds of Rockaway, who became a much respected colonel in the Continental Army and general in the militia; Jacob Drake, Ellis Cook, David Thompson and Abraham Kitchell. The following notes, attributed to DeHart, show the excitement of the meeting:

"Their [sic] was on that day a great many people assembled at Morristown from all parts of the county. Col. Hathaway had a small cannon which he had brought from Newark which was bought from Captain Samuel's by publike subscription, and was to be used on patriotic occasions. The cannon was used at one time by the Sloop Liberty owned by Mr. Stevens of Newark, and had a very interesting history — after this meeting had adjourned the crowd having been well supplied with apple brandy — were all for fighting and tar and feathering all the Torys that were suspected living in the town. However, after much talking, threats, as to what they would do — and the Colonel had burnt up the powder which had been bought by other people's money — and was to be used for the defence of the town — and not for a drinking celebration — after a great deal of howling and a few punches, order was restored. Mr. David Thompson addressed the crowd which was on the Green and told them what the delegates were going to do at Trenton on the twenty third day of May — it was to be liberty and self-government or all would fight to a man. There was one patriotic woman in the crowd who yelled out 'I say judge, don't yu'ins figger on any of us wyems we are just as good as a lot of no account men!'

"William Wind[s] was in the crowd and Mr. Thompson called upon him for a few remarks but there being so much disturbance it was impossible for anybody to hear him whereupon he said his name was Wind but that he could not make enough of it to be heard by that crowd, so he guessed he would hold it for Trenton."

Morris County was one of the first to raise "Minute Men" — men in constant readiness on the shortest notice to march wherever assistance was required. On August 16, 1775, the Provincial Congress passed a regulation providing for two regiments and a battalion of militia for Morris County. These two regiments were divided into the Eastern and Western Battalions. Col. Jacob Ford, Jr., became the commander of the Eastern Battalion, and was detailed to cover Washington's retreat across New Jersey after the evacuation of New York in 1776. He participated in the first battle of Springfield. In that same year, Ford petitioned and won approval to build a gunpowder mill, the only such mill to operate during the Revolution in New Jersey. There is no doubt he would have been an invaluable officer and patriot but fate decreed otherwise. Riding in a military parade on the Morristown Green, he became delirious and was carried by fellow officers to his newly built mansion, where he died of pneumonia on January 11, 1777. □

Curtiss Collection/TJFPLMMT

The Silas Condict House

A prominent patriot, Silas Condict lived in this house surrounded by a 98-acre farm off Sussex Avenue near the present Lake Valley Road in Morris Township with Abigail, his wife, and Elizabeth, his daughter, and the slaves John Cezar, Zenas, Cato and Chloe, two of whom died of smallpox in 1777.

The secluded location of the house made it an ideal meeting place for the Council of Safety, established in 1776 to investigate Tory activities and take appropriate action. George Washington, as a member of the council, met there when he was in Morristown.

In 1901, the building was torn down to make way for a golf course. Its exact location is unknown.

Some Who Were Ready

Barbara Hoskins

ALEXANDER CARMICHAEL, ESQ. (1734-1808) was described by his contemporaries as a "warm and active supporter of the principles of the American Revolution and a firm friend to our Republican form and administration of government." Born in Scotland, he settled first Hanover Township about 1755; then in Morristown where he lived in a large house on the corner of the Green and the present South Street with his wife, Mary Elizabeth, ten children and slaves Matt, Will, Frank and Bill.

He was sheriff of Morris County during the years 1776-1779 and also served as second lieutenant in the Morris County militia. As an ironmaster, he suffered heavy losses when soldiers in the Continental Army destroyed his forge and carried away 20 loads of charcoal and 500 lbs. of iron from his bloomery, Morristown Old Forge, located on the Whippany River in Morristown.

In addition to his many other duties, he was chairman of the Morristown Committee of Safety and a member of the State Assembly in 1779.

In 1778, he was taxed on 200 acres, six horses, 12 cows and one pig. His granddaughter, Caroline Carmichael, married Millard Fillmore, 13th President of the United States.

SILAS CONDICT (1738-1801), one of Morris County's outstanding patriots, was a delegate to the Provincial Congress in 1775 with power to draft men, money and arms for the common defense and, the following year, helped to draft the new State Constitution. He was a member of the Committee (later Council) of Safety formed to investigate Tory sympathizers and take appropriate action against them. From 1781 to 1784, he was a member of the Continental Congress in Philadelphia and later served for several terms as speaker of the New Jersey Legislature and as deputy surveyor general of East Jersey, a director of the Morris County Freeholders and a commissioner to obtain back pay for Revoluntionary War veterans.

COL. WILLIAM DEHART 1746-1801) was a "Gentleman of the Bar," a lawyer residing on the street later named for him in Morristown. He was a son of Dr. Matthias DeHart and had two brothers killed in the war. In 1775, at age 28, he was appointed as clerk to the Committee of Correspondence and later was a delegate to the Provincial Congress. From 1775 to 1781 he served as major and then lieutenant colonel in the New Jersey line, Eastern Division. He died of consumption at age 54; his wife, Elizabeth, surviving him by many years continued living in the house.

JACOB FORD, SR. (1704-1777) was probably the most important citizen of Morris Township and one of its largest landowners, owning 200 acres where Morristown now stands as well as other land inherited from John Ford, his father. From 1738 to 1758, he operated a tavern in town in which it is believed the early court was held prior to the building of the Court House. Iron must have been the primary source of the family's wealth for he was one of the most successful iron masters in Morris County owning the Burnt Meadow, Middle and Mount Pleasant forges. The first two forges as well as other property were later owned by Jacob Ford, Jr. The elder Ford was one of the original members of the First Presbyterian Church as well as a ruling Elder. His civic duties included justice of the peace for almost 50 years; judge in the Court of Common Pleas; member of the Assembly in 1772; and member of the Committee of Grievances in 1775.

Mrs. Hoskins was the librarian for the Local History and Genealogy Department of The Joint Free Public Library of Morristown and Morris Township from 1968 to 1979. She is the author of *Men of Morris County, New Jersey, Who Served in the American Revolution* and *Morris Township: A Glimpse into the Past* and co-author of *Washington Valley, Morris County, New Jersey: An Informal History* and *At Speedwell in the Nineteenth Century.* She also prepared for the library many research papers, bibliographies and indexes on historical subjects.

He married Hannah Baldwin at age 38 and had eight children. Both Jacob and Hannah died in 1777, he from fever and she from dysentery.

JACOB FORD, JR. (1738-1777) was their son, builder of Washington's Headquarters and Ford Powder Mill, whose patriotic career was cut short by an early death (page 25).

He was married to Theodosia, daughter of Parson Johnes. She outlived him by many years, dying in 1824 at the age of 83. They had five children. Timothy Gabriel, Elizabeth, Jacob and little Phoebe, who died at the age of 2 in 1777, the same year as her father and paternal grandparents.

Timothy took part in a skirmish against the enemy and was wounded. The second son, Gabriel, however, was the source of many of the stories about the Ford Mansion during Washington's stay in 1779-80.

LT. COL. BENONI HATHAWAY (1743-1823) has been described as "bustling" because of his many roles in the cause of freedom, both at home and in the field of battle. At the outbreak of the Revolution, he enlisted at the age of 32 in the Morris County militia, Eastern Battalion, serving first as captain and then as colonel. He also served in the State Troops and at the battle of Springfield, he is said to have received a severe wound in the neck.

TJFPLMMT

Ford's Powder Mill and Maj. Joseph Lindsley's House

The gunpowder mill, the only such mill operating in New Jersey during the Revolution, was in Morristown in a dense thicket on the banks of the Whippany River (behind Acorn Hall). The house was on Lindsley property nearby (near the present Governor Morris Inn).

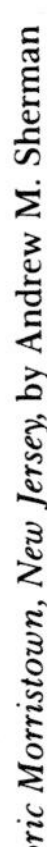
Historic Morristown, New Jersey, by Andrew M. Sherman

Joseph Lewis (1748-1814). When Washington came to Morristown, Lewis, a prominent merchant and lawyer, served as assistant quartermaster and had the unenviable task of finding provisions and horses for the Revolutionary soldiers. He was married to Anne, a daughter of Parson Johnes, and lived on Morris Street next door to his father-in-law, "Daddy Johnes," whom he greatly revered. He was also a brother-in-law of Jacob Ford, Jr.

After the Revolution, he served two terms as justice of the peace and kept a diary that described not only his own busy life but those of the many town and township residents he knew.

This miniature oil portrait was loaned to Andrew Sherman by General Lewis's granddaughter, Mrs. E. Anna Dickerson of Bloomfield, N.J.

His role in the Ford Powder Mill has been in some dispute but it is believed that he converted gunpowder manufactured in the Mill into cartridges and then transported them, under camouflage, from the Mill to storage in the Continental House on the Green (page 51).

The son of Benjamin Hathaway, president of the trustees of the Presbyterian Church, Benoni was one of the largest of the early landowners, including the Morristown Green. In 1778, tax records show he owned 130 acres of land, most of it inherited from his father and much of it in the "Hollow" area. His house was on or near the site of the present Neighborhood House on Flagler Street. Here he lived with his wife, Ruth, and six children. Tradition says that he always had a horseshoe nailed over his door to keep away evil spirits. Despite this, in 1788, he was one of the Morristown residents, written about in *The Morristown Ghost* (page 95), deluded by schoolmaster Ransford Rogers into believing that wealthy Tories had buried treasure at Schooley's Mountain.

After the war, Benoni became one of Morristown's early developers. Flagler Street was cut across Hathaway lands and he sold lots there and as far east as Speedwell Avenue.

MAJOR JOSEPH LINDSLEY (1736-1822), carpenter, millwright and part owner of a sawmill lived on a 70-acre farm east of Jacob Ford, Jr.'s on the present Morris Avenue. At the outbreak of the Revolution, he joined the militia at age 40 and within a year was made captain of a company of artificers (carpenters) in the Continental Army, which served in both New York City and Canada. Upon returning to Morristown in 1778, he continued in the militia, serving as a second major in the Eastern Battalion. He also became part owner with Jonas Phillips of the Ford Powder Mill originally built by Jacob Ford in the spring of 1776 for the manufacture of gunpowder for Washington's Army.

When the second edifice of the Presbyterian Church on the Green was built in 1791, Joseph Lindsley was head carpenter. In 1792, he became totally blind and remained so for the remainder of his life, some 27 years later. He had two wives and eleven children and is buried in the Presbyterian churchyard.

I —, have this day voluntarily enlisted myself as a soldier in the American Continental army for one year, unless sooner discharged, and do bind myself to conform in all instances to such rules and regulations as are or shall be established for the government of the said army.

Form of enlistment used at the first call from Congress for New Jersey troops, October 9, 1775

Courtesy of Morristown National Historical Park

Historic Morristown, New Jersey, by Andrew M. Sherman

The Joshua Guerin House (left), built shortly before the Revolution on the corner of Jockey Hollow and Sugar Loaf roads, Morris Township. Joshua (1737-1808), a wagoner and a sergeant in the Militia, lived in the smaller section on the right with his wife Susanna and seven children. A blacksmith shop, carriage factory and orchards were nearby. This house is now part of the Morristown National Historical Park.

The Col. Benoni Hathaway House (above), originally on Flagler Street, Morristown. It is no longer in existence.

Curtiss Collection/TJFPLMMT

How Different the Morris County of 1776

Rev. Joseph F. Tuttle, D.D., *The Revolutionary Forefathers of Morris County*, Address at Morristown, July 4, 1876

It is true its mountains then as now were grand to look at, the conspicuous watch-towers whence our fathers saw the enemy and gave the alarm, and yet these mountains then stood in the midst of a sparsely settled wilderness in which were scattered a few towns and villages with far fewer acres under cultivation than in our day. The Presbyterian churches are at Morristown, Hanover, Bottle Hill, Rockaway, Mendham, Black River (or Chester), Parsippany, Succassunna, the Congregational Church at Chester, the Baptist church at Morristown, and the Dutch churches at Old Boonton and Pompton Plains. Its schools were few. The late Dr. Condit says that the majority of those who learned the most common English branches did so in night schools taught either by the preacher or some itinerant Irish scholar. The roads were bad and the wheeled vehicles so scarce that at the funeral of a light horseman on Morris Plains after the war, as an eye witness once told me, there was only a single wagon of any sort present, that being the one that carried the remains to the grave. Dr. Johnes, the pastor, the attending physician, the bearers, the mourners, and the friends were either afoot or on horseback . . . .

The manners and occupations of the people were simple. The fleece, the flax, the spinning wheel and the houseloom were found in every mansion, and the most eloquent men at the bar and in the pulpit, as also the most women, and brave men who this county so glorious in those days, wore garments which the women had made of cloth which themselves had manufactured. They were hardy, simple, frugal, brave and good, and when the conflict came it required as little to keep both men and women in fighting condition as it did the soldiers of the Great Frederic.

Tempe Wick Road, Jockey Hollow, still looking much like an 18th-century path in this photograph taken in 1938.

A Position Little Understood at the Time

Memoirs of General James Wilkinson, January 3-6, 1777

Pressed as we were for time, it was the desire of the commander in chief, and the inclination of every officer, to make a stroke at Brunswick, which had been left with a small garrison, in charge of General Matthews; but our physical force could not bear us out; the men had been under arms eighteen hours, and had suffered much from cold and hunger. The commander and several general officers halted at the forks of the road in Kingston, whilst our troops were filing off to Rocky Hill, when the exclamation was general. "O that we had 500 fresh men to beat up their quarters at Brunswick." But the measure was found to be impracticable, and therefore we proceeded down Millstone river, and halted at Somerset court-house, where many of the militia, whose baggage had been sent to Burlington, lay in the open air without blankets. We marched the next day to Pluckamin, and halted until the 5th. It had been previously determined by the General, on the advice of General St. Clair, after the plan of visiting Brunswick had been abandoned, to take quarters at Morristown; but the troops were so much exhausted, that they required a short respite from fatigue.

We reached Morristown the sixth, and the troops were cantoned in the vicinity. This position, little understood at the time, was afterwards discovered to be a most safe one for the winter quarters of an army of observation, and such was General Washington's; the approach to it from the sea-board is rendered difficult and dangerous by a chain of sharp hills, which extend from Pluckamin by Bound brook and Springfield to the vicinity of the Passaic river; it is situate in the heart of a country abounding with forage and provisions, and is nearly equidistant from New York and Amboy, and also from Newark and New Brunswick, with defiles in rear to cover a retreat should circumstances render it necessary.

Curtiss Collection/TJFPLMMT

Stone at the New Vernon crossroads placed by the Daughters of the American Revolution in 1933 to mark an army route from Princeton to Morristown.

Twice Military Capital of the Revolution

Historical Collections of the State of New Jersey by John Warner Barber and Henry Howe, 1844

General George Washington at Trenton, January 2, 1777.

GENERALS, SOLDIERS, FOREIGN dignitaries, ardent patriots, Tory sympathizers, and spies crossed and recrossed the Green during the Revolution. Continental soldiers, supported by local militia, were in the Morristown area from 1776 to 1782. And during two crucial encampments — January to May 1777 and December 1779 to June 1780 — George Washington established his headquarters here. It was the only place to have this honor.

Officers whose names are engraved in Revolutionary War history came to Morristown with their Commander in Chief: Nathanael Greene, Henry Knox, Alexander Hamilton, "Light Horse" Harry Lee, Israel Putnam, Daniel Morgan, John Cochran, Philip Schuyler, Lord Stirling, Friedrich von Steuben, Marquis de Lafayette, Casimir Pulaski, Thaddeus Kosciuszko — even the traitorous Benedict Arnold.

Eighteenth-century warfare slowed down in winter, although never stopped if weather permitted. Winter encampment was a vital period to train and build military strength, replenish supplies and plan strategy.

Morristown was an excellent position. From here Washington could move freely from the Hudson Highlands and West Point to Philadelphia without crossing enemy lines. The two Watchung ranges and the vast, impenetrable Great Swamp offered protection from the British in New York. Furthermore, Morris County had proven its loyalty. Wood and water in the area were plentiful. As to subsistence for the troops, Washington was philosophical: "I very well know that a supply of Forage will be difficult at this post, and so it will be wherever the Bulk of the Army shall sit down."

The two encampments were very different in character but some problems were similar. There was the matter of maintaining troop strength. In both the first months of 1777 and 1780, Washington faced the end of enlistment periods. Thus, in a few short months, a largely new army had to be formed into an efficient fighting force ready for whatever was to come.

Supplies of food, clothing and powder were always desperately low. A galloping inflation rate made farmers unwilling to sell at the fixed prices offered by the Army. Provisional state governments failed to come through with promised supplies for their Continental soldiers. Congress debated and bickered.

As to forming future plans, grand strategy was almost impossible when facing an enemy of superior strength. Courage, cunning, determination and, unquestionably, great luck were needed. Only one thing seemed sure. Morristown could one day be the target of an attack. □

Painting by John Ward Dunsmore/Courtesy of The New York Historical Society

"The Petition," depicting the first Convention Lodge of Freemasons in America on St. John the Evangelist Day, December 27, 1779, at the Arnold Tavern on the Green

Masons of the Connecticut Line invited freemasons from the Pennsylvania, Rhode Island, New Hampshire, Massachusetts, Maryland, New York and New Jersey Lines, a group of more than 100, "to take into consideration some matters respecting the good of masonry." The petition is being read to the Lodge by Brig. Gen. Mordecai Gist of Maryland. Capt., later Col., Jonathan Heart of the 3d Connecticut Regiment, who had been installed recently as Worshipful Master, is on the raised platform. The visitors included Gen. George Washington (on the left, leaning on a cane); Col. Alexander Hamilton (next to him) and Maj. Caleb Gibbs, both aide-de-camps; and Col. Robert Erskine, surveyor-general. From New Jersey were Gen. William Maxwell, Gen. Elias Dayton, and Gen. Anthony Walton White. Morristown residents included Col. Thomas Kinney, tavern keeper Col. Jacob Arnold, Maj. Jeremiah Bruen and surgeon Dr. Jabez Campfield. From nearby Mendham came Capt. John Armstrong. In honor of this unusual event, the general orders of the day listed "St. John's — masons" as the sign and countersign.

Benedict Arnold's trial, then in session at Dickerson's Tavern, was adjourned for the day so it would not interfere with the celebration, which included a parade to and from the Presbyterian meeting house, a church service and a reception at the Arnold Tavern before the meeting got underway.

Curtiss Collection/TJFPL.MMT

Arnold Tavern, north side of the Green,
Washington's Headquarters from January 6 to May 28, 1777

According to a newspaper advertisement in the *Genius of Liberty*, January 30, 1807: "The house is large and commodious and contains thirteen rooms and thirteen fireplaces, one of which is fifty by twenty feet and is one of the best in the State for public assembly room. There are on the premises a large barn with very commodious stables — several sheds — a good well of water near the door together with an aqueduct and an ice house well filled with ice — an excellent garden and every other convenience necessary for a public stand." In November 1780, the Marquis de Chastellux admired the dining room "adorned with looking glasses and handsome mahogany furniture."

The tavern was owned by Col. Jacob Arnold (1749-1827), whose father, Samuel, was believed to have built it sometime before 1764. Before the Revolution, in defiance of British law, Jacob Arnold and his brother-in-law, Thomas Kinney, operated a slitting mill at Speedwell, second in the county, although such activity was prohibited in the colonies. During the Revolution, Arnold was commander of Morris County's light-horse militia — succeeding Kinney — and was promoted to lieutenant colonel in the Continental Army. He later served as county sheriff in 1780 and 1786 and assemblyman in 1784-85 and 1789-90. He built a house in Washington Valley (page 149) that still stands.

This building remained a tavern until the middle of the 19th century, when it was turned into stores with apartments above them (page 281). At the insistence of Julia Keese Colles, George's historian wife, it was moved to Mount Kemble Avenue, Morris Township, in 1886 and burned in 1918.

The Winter of 1777

Can you imagine the excitement? On January 6, 1777, at sunset, General George Washington rode up to the Morristown Green and entered Jacob Arnold's Tavern to establish winter headquarters. It was his third winter as Commander in Chief and almost six months since the Declaration of Independence, yet the war was just heating up.

He arrived in triumph. A month before, Britain had control of virtually the entire state, but thanks to his victories at Trenton and Princeton, he had pinned down the enemy troops to a small part. He would have liked to push them out of New Jersey entirely. However, he explained to the President of Congress on January 7, 1777, the "Severity of the Season has made our Troops, especially the Militia, extremely impatient, and has reduced the number very considerably, their complaints and the great fatigues they have undergone, induced me to come to this place, as best calculated of any in this Quarter, to accommodate and refresh them."

To this end, the officers and men were quartered in every house and barn in the vicinity, including Hanover, Whippany, Chatham and Madison. A good-sized encampment is believed to have pitched tents in the Loantaka (Spring) Valley where there was gently sloping, protected land and a steady water supply from the Loantaka Brook and several large springs.

Washington made three far-reaching moves in his first month in Morristown. First, he set about the perfect spy system; intelligence work became one of Hamilton's first duties. Not only did he want to keep track of British movements, but he decided to send false intimidating

From Trenton onwards, Washington was recognized as a far-sighted and skilful general all Europe over — by the great military nobles in the Empress Catherine's court, by French Marshals and Ministers, in the King's cabinet at Potsdam, at Madrid, at Vienna, and in London. [His] march through the British lines was allowed to be a prodigy of leadership.
Sir George Otto Trevelyan in
***The American Revolution*, London, 1903**

The enemy, by two lucky strokes, at Trenton and Princeton, have been obliged to Abandon every part of Jersey except Brunswic and Amboy, and the small tract of country between them, which is so entirely exhausted of supplies of every kind, that I hope, by preventing them from sending their foraging parties to any great distance, to reduce them to the utmost distress, in the course of this winter.
Washington to General Philip Schuyler, January 18, 1777

messages of his strength to confuse the enemy. Each commander was instructed to write a report greatly exaggerating the number of men and supplies available.

There are several versions of this story, but each makes the same point of the success of this scheme. (This version comes from "Washington at Morristown," *Harper's New Monthly Magazine*, 1859.)

"It is said that a certain man was employed by Washington as a spy to gain information concerning the enemy, but it was suspected that he carried more news to the enemy than he brought to those in whose employ he was. General [Nathanael] Greene, who acted as Quarter-Master General, occupied a small office [on the southeast corner of the Green]. One day Colonel Hamilton was in this office when the suspected spy made his appearance. The Colonel had made out what purported to be a careful statement of the condition of the army as to numbers and munitions, making the numbers much more flattering than the actual facts. Leaving this statement on the table apparently by mistake, Colonel Hamilton left the office saying he would return in a few minutes. The spy instantly seized the paper as a very authentic document, and left with it for parts unknown! It was supposed that this trick did much to preserve the army of Morristown from attack that winter."

Second, Washington issued a proclamation requiring an oath of loyalty for the entire "United States." Up to this time, his attitude toward civilian British sympathizers had been lenient compared to the British treatment of "insurgents." Tories who did not cause trouble were left pretty much alone or were allowed to leave with all their possessions. Now, even though Morris County was faithful to the American cause, it was too dangerous to lead troops through countryside untested for loyalty.

Third, Washington ordered the first mass inoculation of the Army against smallpox. This affected not only the troops in New Jersey but those in Philadelphia. This inoculation — unlike vaccination — produced immunity by causing a slight case of the disease. His gamble worked for the Army; relatively few died of the disease if they had not previously contracted it. Unfortunately, this was not true for the militia and the townspeople. Despite the urgings of Parson Johnes, many refused to go along with the "experiment" and died of the disease.

Early in March, Washington fell so seriously ill with the quinsy, a throat ailment, there was need to think about the possibility of a successor. Tradition says Washington's unhesitating choice was his friend Nathanael Greene. It is also believed that this illness was the major reason that Martha Washington ventured on her longest — perhaps first — trip out of Virginia to nurse him back to health. Mrs. Washington (who had been inoculated in Philadelphia the previous year) stayed until early May, when Washington sent her back to Mount Vernon escorted by her son, John Parke Custis. He wanted her well past Philadelphia before the British could move on the city.

On May 28, Washington left Morristown for Middlebrook Valley. There had been no major fighting, just minor skirmishes, but now the war would start up again. □

Loantaka Campground (right). The white cross marks the approximate center of the camp, according to the Rev. Andrew M. Sherman, the historian who commissioned this photograph looking north on Treadwell Avenue on the border of Morris and Chatham Townships, November 1919. In the 19th century, the Rev. Samuel L. Tuttle wrote that a flagpole stood there in the middle of the principal street that served as a parade ground and was lined with officers' cabins. So far, archaeological evidence has not corroborated the large number of buildings, "probably as many as three hundred," Tuttle described.

TJFPLMMT

Old Presbyterian Church Burying Ground (left). In the foreground, the stones date back to the 1750s. On January 10, 1777, Washington would have walked this way from the First Church to the burial service of Jacob Ford, Jr., whose death was a severe blow to the General. Ford's grave is just to the right of this photograph taken in 1983. Also in 1777, the Bill of Mortality of the Presbyterian Church lists 68 deaths from smallpox, where there were none in the two years before and after. By contrast, 20 died of consumption, the usual leading killer.

Peter Dickerson's grave is marked with the small flag. A number of American and French Revolutionary soldiers are buried nearby. The Spanish envoy Don Juan Miralles was temporarily buried here after he died of a high fever in April 1780. Washington and two French ministers, Chevalier de la Luzerne and Barbe Marbois, led the procession from the Ford Mansion to the church for the most elaborate service the village had seen. Miralles was dressed in a scarlet coat embroidered heavily with lace, a gold watch and diamond rings, necessitating a guard over the grave!

First sermon after smallpox (opposite), May 4, 1777, first of four pages. Actually, few heard Pastor Johnes's words, since the epidemic did not abate until September. As he noted elsewhere, "some confined at homes were contagioned — some afraid to catch it, and others fearful lest they communicate it."

Photograph by George Goodwin/TJFPLMMT

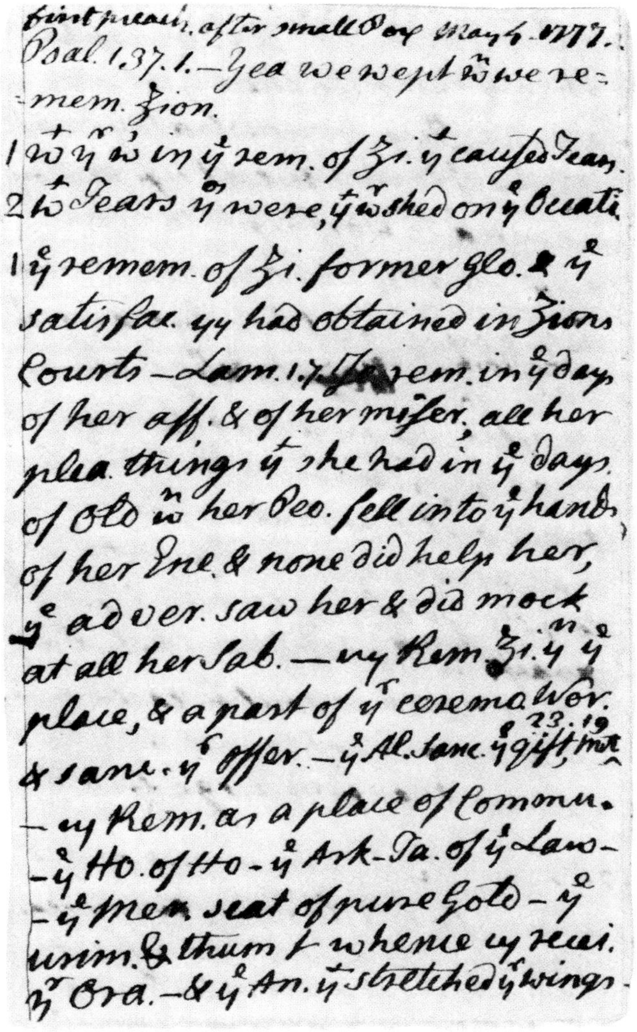

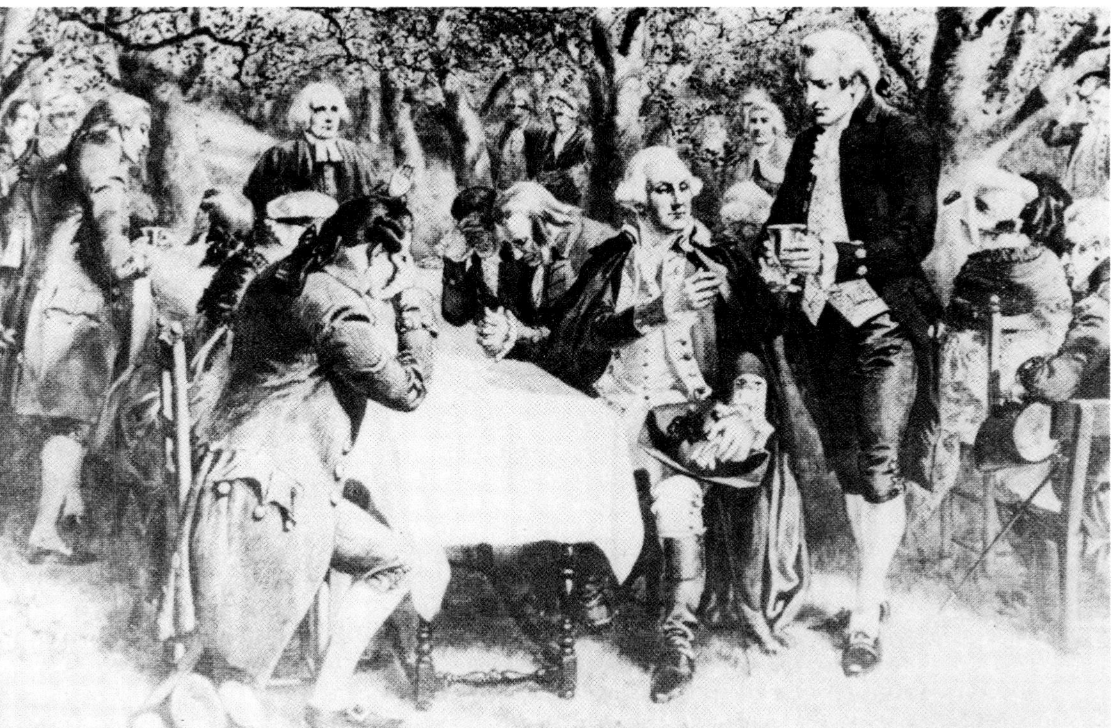

first preach. after small Pox May 4. 1777.
Psal. 137.1.—Yea we wept when we re-
-mem. Zion.
1 wt ye wh in ye rem. of Zi. yt caused Tears.
2 wt Tears yt were, yt wr shed on ye Occasi
1 ye remem. of Zi. former Glo. & ye
satisfac. yy had obtained in Zions
Courts—Lam. 1.7 Jer. rem. in ye days
of her aff. & of her miser. all her
plea. things yt she had in ye days
of Old wn her Peo. fell into ye hands
of her Ene. & none did help her,
ye adver. saw her & did mock
at all her Sab.—my Rem. Zi. 4 ye
place, & a part of ye cerema Wor.
& sanc. ye offer.—ye Al. sanc. ye gifts,
—my Rem. as a place of Commun.
—ye Ho. of Ho—ye Ark—Ta. of ye Laws—
—ye mer. seat of pure Gold—ye
urim & thum whence my recei.
ye Ora.—& ye An. yt stretched ye wings—

TJFPLMMT

TJFPLMMT

TJFPLMMT

Washington taking communion (above, right) in the Rev. Timothy Johnes's orchard behind his parsonage, spring of 1777. Tradition says when Washington asked if a person of another denomination would be welcome at the service, the parson told him that "ours is not the Presbyterian but the Lord's table."

Johnes parsonage (right), Morris Street, built about 1750, as it appeared in 1893 when it became the first Morristown Memorial Hospital building. The site is now a mall. The house was moved across the street and later torn down.

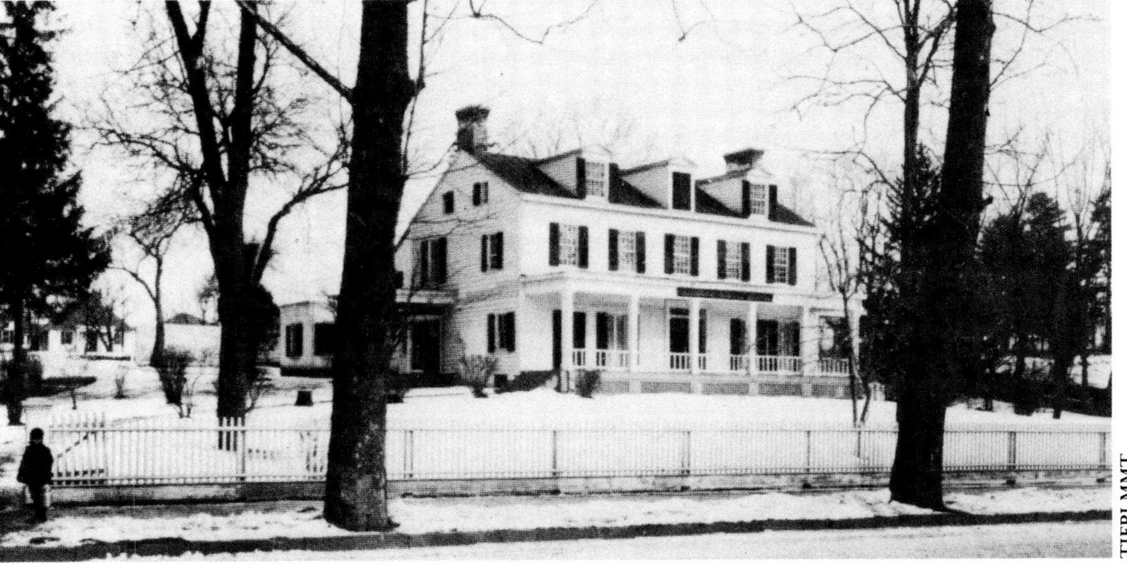

Letters from Camp, 1777

General George Washington's letters from Morristown, reflecting some of the difficulties faced in the first month

To Doctor William Shippen, Junior, January 6. Finding the small pox to be spreading much and fearing that no precaution can prevent it from running thro' the whole of our Army, I have determined that the Troops shall be inoculated . . . . Necessity not only authorizes but seems to require the measure, for should the disorder infect the Army, in the natural way, and rage with its usual Virulence, we should have more to dread from it, than from the Sword of the Enemy.

To Congress, January 7. The Severity of the Season has made our Troops, especially the Militia, extremely impatient, and has reduced the number very considerably. Every day more or less leave us. Their complaints and the great fatigues they have undergone induced me to come to this place, as the best calculated of any in this Quarter, to accommodate and refresh them.

To James E. Mauran, January 12. Instructions, Recruiting Orders and a Warrant for 6000 Dollars to Recruit with are now Inclosed to you. Copies of the Recruiting Orders are to be given to the Officers so soon as they are nominated, & I should think if only part of the bounty was given to the Men at the time of enlisting them and the residue when they join their Regt. it might be a means of preventing Desertion.

The short time allowed us for the most Vigorous Exertions which I am persuaded Render Arguments unnecessary to stimulate you to the speedy Completion of your Regiment and preparing it for the Field.

To Colonel Joseph Reed, January 12. The order you sent to Colonel Winds has interfered with a plan, concerted by Generals Sullivan and Maxwell. Whenever you have occasion to order a movement of any part of the army, it will be best to apply to the Commanding officer, lest it may, as it has in the present instance, interfered with some other object.

To William Duer, January 14. I some time ago received advice, that a large parcel of Cloathing was forwarded from New England to Peekskill, with an intent to come on to this Army.

I could not account for its being delayed there, until I was just now informed by the Quarter Master General, that the Convention of your State had appropriated 26. Bales of it to their own use, without consulting him in the least. This I look upon as a most extraordinary piece of Conduct, and what involves me just at this time in the greatest difficulties; for depending upon that Cloathing, I have not applied elsewhere and the Troops in the Field are now absolutely perishing for want of it.

To Joseph J. Cooke, January 15. The enclosed was intended to have gone by the Express who brought me your last Letter. He came in the Evening of the 13th, was desired to call early next morning, & I have never seen or heard of him since.

Many days ago I wrote to Genl. Putnam supposing him to be at Princeton to have the stores rescued from the hands of the Militia who had borne them off, and had no doubt but he had done it. What in the name of Heaven he can be doing at Crosswicks I know not, after my repeated wishes to hear of him at Princeton.

To Colonel Joseph Reed, January 19. The Morris County light horse have disbanded themselves I believe, for I have seen none of them for some time. A strict scrutiny will, I hope, be made into the conduct of Col. Chambers and his officers, and proper examples made. Genl. Putnam was directed long ago by me to have the arms collected from the Country I hope he has done it. I have no objection to his allowing some compensation.

To John Parke Custis, January 22. The misfortune of short enlistments, and an unhappy dependence upon militia, have shown their baneful influence at every period, and almost upon every occasion, throughout the whole course of this war. At no time, nor upon no occasion, were they ever more exemplified than since Christmas; for if we could but have got in the militia in time, or prevailed upon those troops whose times expired (as they generally did) on the first of this instant, to have continued (not more than a thousand or twelve hundred agreeing to stay) we might, I am persuaded, have cleared the Jerseys of the enemy.

By his Excellency *GEORGE WASHINGTON*, Esq; General and Commander in Chief of all the forces of the United States of America.

PROCLAMATION.

WHEREAS several persons, inhabitants of the United States of America, influenced by inimical motives, intimidated by the threats of the enemy, or deluded by a Proclamation issued the 30th of November last, by Lord and General Howe, stiled the King's Commissioners for granting pardons, &c. (now at open war and invading these states) have been so lost to the interest and welfare of their country, as to repair to the enemy, sign a declaration of fidelity, and, in some instances, have been compelled to take oaths of allegiance, and to engage not to take up arms, or encourage others so to do, against the King of Great-Britain. And whereas it has become necessary to distinguish between the friends of America and those of Great-Britain, inhabitants of these States, and that every man who receives a protection from and is a subject of any State (not being conscientiously scrupulous against bearing arms) should stand ready to defend the same against every hostile invasion, I do therefore, in behalf of the United States, by virtue of the powers committed to me by Congress, hereby strictly command and require every person, having subscribed such declaration, taken such oaths, and accepted protection and certificates from Lord or General Howe, or any person acting under their authority, forthwith to repair to Head-Quarters, or to the quarters of the nearest general officer of the Continental Army or Militia (until farther provision can be made by the civil authority) and there deliver up such protections, certificates, and passports, and take the oath of allegiance to the United States of America. Nevertheless, hereby granting full liberty to all such as prefer the interest and protection of Great-Britain to the freedom and happiness of their country, forthwith to withdraw themselves and families within the enemy's lines. And I do hereby declare that all and every person, who may neglect or refuse to comply with this order, within thirty days from the date hereof, will be deemed adherents to the King of Great-Britain, and treated as common enemies of the American States.

Given at Head-Quarters, Morris-Town, January 25, 1777.

GEORGE WASHINGTON.

By his Excellency's command,
ROBERT H. HARRISON, *Secretary.*

Courtesy of Morristown National Historical Park

First proclamation against British sympathizers, issued in Morristown, January 27, 1777. Persons who had taken oaths of allegiance or "accepted protections and certificates from Lord General Howe" were given 30 days to deliver them to Washington's Headquarters or "the nearest general officer of the Continental Army or Militia" and pledge allegiance to the United States or to withdraw behind the British lines.

Form used by the Council of Safety (right) to subpoena witnesses against suspected Tories, in the handwriting of Silas Condict.

Sufferings in the Goal of Morris have been exceedingly grievous. Sometimes upwards of 50 have been confined with them in one room not exceeding 18 Feet Square; frequently Water was not to be had from the Failure of the Public Pump; often very often have they been obliged to fast 48 hours & not been able to procure for Money Provisions to subsist upon; & finally unless relieved by the Charity of some Familys in the Neighbourhood they must have starved to death.

Petition to Council of Safety to transfer three Essex County men accused of treason out of Morris County jail, July 1777

Subpena

Morris County } ss. The State of N. jersey

To — greeting you are hereby Required Personally to be and appear before the governor and Council of Safety for this State at — on — next at — oclock in the — noon of the same day to Testify the truth and Evidence in behalf of the said State against — and this you are in nowise to omit under the penalty of one hundred pounds. by order of the said governor & Council of Safety the — day of — 1777

Cutler Collection/TJFPL.MMT

I Found Morris a Very Clever Little Village

Martha Daingerfield Bland, wife of Colonel Theodorick Bland, to her sister-in-law Frances Bland Randolph, in Virginia, May 12, 1777

It was my dear Fanny, with great pleasure that I read your agreeable letter & heard of all your healths, but it is so long since the date that you may be all married or dead by this time. Four months may bring many unforseen things to light. I have wrote to you three letters, two to my sister Banister & one to Mr. Banister. Many to Miss Portty Carloss (who so kindly took charge of my family) relative to domestick matters but no doubt many of them are loss'd or never got to hand — As yours have been of a quarter of a year traviling this distance. I got well of the smallpox in Feb^r^ but was for four weeks very ill & had them severely for innoculation I had many pocks on my face all of which are at present visible & I shall be pitied with them. Your Brother used to laugh at my poor forehead and says the de—l throa'd homineyburs upon it. and now as the sailors' phrase is the D—l has thrash'd black eyed peas upon it — so with the two threshings it is a jumbled piece of work. However every face almost keeps me in countenance here are few smooth faces. & no beautys so that one does very well to pass. I left Philadelphia last month (the first day) & came to Morristown where Genl Washington keeps Headquarters. Mrs. Washington had arrived three weeks before me, so that I could with a good face make a visit to Camp. I had been from Jany to Ap^rl^ from your Brother & you may suppose we were very glad to meet. I had many Qualms of consiance about visiting a camp however a very agreeable Gentleman and Lady was coming to Morristown on their way to Boston and with them I left my winter quarters. I found Morris a very clever little village, situated in a most beautiful valley at the foot of 5 mountains. It has three houses with steeples which give it a consequential look — and is something larger than Blandford. it has two familys — refugees from New York in it otherwise it is inhabited by the errentest rusticks you ever beheld — you cannot travil three miles without passing through one of these villages all of them having meeting houses and court houses etc. etc. decorated with steeples which gives them a pretty Airy look & the farmes between the mountains are the most rural sweet spots in nature, their medows of a fine luxuriant grass which looks like a bed of velvet interspersed with yellow blue and white flowers. They represent us with just such scenes as the poets paint Arcadia purling rills mossy beds etc. but not crying swains & lovely nymphs tho there are some exceding pretty girls but they appear to have souls form'd for the distaff rather than the tender passions and realy I never met with such pleasant looking creatures. & the most inhospitable mortals breathing you can get nothing from them but "dreadful good water" as they term everything that is good desperate and dreadfull are their favorite words you'd laugh to hear them talk . . . . Ascending from small to great things — now let me speak of *our* Noble and Agreable Commander (for he commands both Sexes) one by his Excellent Skill in Military Matters the other by his ability politeness and attention we visit them twice or three times a week by particular invitation — Ev'ry day frequently from Inclination — he is generally busy in the forenoon — but from dinner till night he is free for all company his Worthy Lady seems to be in perfect felicity while she is by the side of her *Old Man* as she calls him, we often make partys on Horse Back the Genl his lady Miss Livingstone & his Aid de Camps who are Col^o^ Fitz Gerald and agreable broad shouldered Irishman — Col^o^ Johnson Brother of Mrs Malone who is exceedingly witty at everybody's expense but cant allow other people to be so at his own, tho they often take the liberty. Col^o^ Hamilton a sensable Genteel polite young fellow a West indian — Col^o^ Meade — Col^o^ Tillman a modest worthy man who from his attachment to the Genl vollenterly lives in his family and acts in any capacity that is uppermost without fee or reward — Col^o^ Harrison Brother of Billy Harrison that kept store in Petersburg & as much like him as possible a worthy man — Capt Gibbs of the Genl^s^ Guard a good natured Yankee who makes a thousand Blunders in the Yankee stile and keeps the Dinner table in constant Laugh — These are the Genl^s^ family all polite sociable gentlemen who make the day pass with a great deal of satisfaction to the Visitors — but I had forgot my subject almost, this is our riding party Generly — at which time General Washington throws of the Hero — and takes on the chatty agreable companion — he can be down right impudent sometimes — such impudence, Fanny, as you and I like — and realy I have wished often for you — it is a life that is calculated for one of your temper . . . .

Fort Nonsense

When Ebenezer Hazard, surveyor for the post office, traveled through New Jersey, August 8-10, 1777, he noted: "At Morristown, This is a very pleasant Village, surrounded with Hills, it is situated partly on a Hill & partly in a Valley. On the Top of a Mountain at the Back of it we have a Breast Work and a Guard House from thence there is a beautiful and extensive Prospect."

Tradition gives two reasons for building Fort Nonsense. The first is that Washington planned to mount cannons there from which to command all the entrances to Morristown in case of enemy attack. Both troops and townspeople would be able to go there for protection. The second reason given is that Washington wanted to keep his troops busy, for their health and to keep them out of mischief. This tradition continues that, after it was completed, Washington asked a friend what to name it, to which the friend replied, "Fort Nonsense."

A Morristown resident, Francis E. Woodruff, saved Fort Nonsense. At his death in 1914, he left the Town of Morristown a legacy of $50,000 to purchase acreage on Fort Nonsense hill and maintain it as a historic park. On July 4, 1933, the Town turned over the land to the Morristown National Historical Park. On October 4, 1991, Fort Nonsense was rededicated as part of the celebration to mark the Park's 75th Anniversary. □

The Quarter Master General [is] to have a Guard-house, in the upper Redoubt, on the hill adjoining this place, erected with dispatch and sufficient to contain 30 Men — This building to be slight, and attended with little expence.
General Orders about Fort Nonsense, May 14, 1777

TJFPLMMT

Fort Nonsense, earthworks or redoubt, begun in 1777. The plan (above) shows its considerable size. The modern photograph gives an idea of its prominent position 230 feet above the Green.

Courtesy of Morristown National Historical Park

Photograph by James L. Grabow/TJFPLMMT

The Ford Mansion, Washington Headquarters, 1779-80

The house was built probably in 1774 by Joseph Lindsley for Col. Jacob Ford, Jr., on land acquired by his father. Both father and son died in 1777 and the house was unfinished when Washington chose it as his headquarters. He used six rooms as sleeping quarters and office space. The widow Theodosia Ford kept two downstairs rooms and the use of the kitchen on the east side of the house for herself and four surviving children.

Martha Washington spent most of the time there with the General, as did his nephew, George Augustine Washington, who served as civilian aide until he was commissioned as "ensign." Staff members who lived at the house probably included the General's personal secretary, Lt. Col. Robert Hanson Harrison, and aides Lt. Col. Alexander Hamilton, Tench Tilghman, and Richard Kidder Meade and Capt. James McHenry. Other staff officers lived nearby and spent much of their time at the house. Maj. Caleb Gibbs, commander of the General's Life Guard, was across the street with his men, who had built 11 enlisted men's and three officers' huts.

Five generations lived in this house, but in 1873 the house was put up for sale by the heirs of Henry A. Ford. It was purchased by four men: Ex-Governor Theodore Randolph, whose holdings in Morristown included most of what is now Madison Avenue; William van Vleck Lidgerwood, the stepson of Judge Stephen Vail who lived in London but had returned to visit his brother John in his boyhood home at Speedwell (page 88); and George A. Halsey and Nathaniel N. Halsted of Newark. These four men, together with prominent men of Morristown, formed the Washington Association in 1874 and preserved the house as a museum until it was turned over to the Morristown National Historical Park in 1933. The house is also a National Historic Landmark.

The photographs on both pages were taken in the early 1980s.

The Winter of 1779-80

When Washington returned to Morristown two-and-a-half years later, there had been changes. The war was dragging wearily on in a deadlock.

The British had captured but later abandoned Philadelphia; Burgoyne's army had surrendered at Saratoga; France and Spain had entered the war against Great Britain. However, the enemy held Savannah; Sir Henry Clinton, Howe's successor, was expected to leave New York soon by sea to attack Charleston; and the French alliance had not yet provided the hoped-for benefits.

Washington arrived at the Ford Mansion on December 1, 1779, during a "very severe storm of hail & snow all day." It was a bad omen. The main part of his army, camping in Jockey Hollow (page 46), was to endure the most bitter cold and prolonged winter of the war — 28 snowfalls from November to April.

Officers, however, fared better than the men in an encampment and the senior officers fared considerably better. As soon as Martha Washington arrived on or about December 31st, social life began for the Washingtons' military family. Lord Stirling and his wife lived nearby in Basking Ridge. Sarah Stirling was the sister of New Jersey Governor William Livingston who with his wife, Susannah French, had a home in Parsippany as well as in Elizabethtown. Major General Greene and his wife, Catherine Littlefield, and Surgeon General Dr. John Cochran and Mrs. Cochran participated in many social events, as did Mrs. Cochran's brother, Major General Philip Schuyler, and his wife when they arrived for a visit.

On May 10, Lafayette arrived in Morristown for four days with the welcome news that

I certify that the Commander in Chief took up his quarters at Mrs. Ford's at Morris Town the first day of December 1779, that he left them the 23d of June 1780, and that he occupied two Rooms below; all the upper floor, Kitchen, Cellar, and Stable. The Stable was built and the two Rooms above Stairs finished at public expence, and a well, which was entirely useless and filled up before, put in thorough repair by walling &c.
Letter requested by Mrs. Theodosia Ford, from Washington's Headquarters "near Passaick," July 26, 1780

A Ride to Headquarters

From *Thankful Blossom* by Bret Harte*

The rising wind, which had ridden much faster than Mistress Thankful, had increased to a gale by the time it reached Morristown. It swept through the leafless maples, and rattled the dry bones of the elms. It whistled through the quiet Presbyterian churchyard, as if trying to arouse the sleepers it had known in days gone by. It shook the blank, lustreless windows of the Assembly Rooms over the Freemason's Tavern, and wrought in their gusty curtains moving shadows of those amply petticoated dames and tightly hosed cavaliers who had swung in "Sir Roger," or jigged in "Money Musk," the night before.

But I fancy it was around the isolated "Ford Mansion," better known as the "Headquarters," that the wind wreaked its grotesque rage. It howled under its scant eaves, it sang under its bleak porch, it tweaked the peak of its front gable, it whistled through every chink and cranny of its square, solid, unpicturesque structure. Situated on a hill-side that descended rapidly to the Whippany River, every summer zephyr that whispered through the porches of the Morristown farm houses charged as a stiff breeze upon the swinging half doors and windows of the "Ford Mansion"; every wintry wind became a gale that threatened its security. The sentinel who paced before its front porch knew from experience when to linger under its lee, and adjust his threadbare outer coat to the bitter North wind.

*The author gathered material for this novel while spending the summer at The Willows (page 151) in Morris Township.

Photograph by James L. Grabow/TJFPLMMT

Kitchen of Ford Mansion. This was a very crowded place for several months after Washington arrived. On January 22, 1780, he wrote to Gen. Greene: "I have been in my Prest. quarters from the first day of Decr. and have not a Kitchen to Cook a Dinner in, altho' the Logs have been put together some considerable time by my own Guard: nor is there a place at this moment in which a servant can lodge with the smallest degree of comfort. Eighteen belonging to my family and all Mrs. Ford's are crowded together in her Kitchen and scarce one of them able to speak for Colds they have caught . . . ."

Morristown's Joseph Lewis, assistant quartermaster, eventually came to the rescue. "I have been Ransackking this part of the world for a few [about 2,000 feet] of White pine boards to finish the Room for His Excellency," wrote Lewis and apparently shortly after a kitchen-dining building was completed.

A New Year Commences But Brings No Relief

Military Journal of James Thacher, M.D., January 1, 1780

A new year commences, but brings no relief to the sufferings and privations of our army. Our canvass covering affords but a miserable security from storms of rain and snow, and a great scarcity of provision still prevails, and its effects are felt even at head quarters, as appears by the following anecdote. "We have nothing but the rations to cook, Sir," said Mrs. Thomson, a very worthy Irish woman and housekeeper to General Washington. "Well, Mrs. Thomson, you must then cook the rations, for I have not a farthing to give you." "If you please, Sir, let one of the gentlemen give me an order for six bushels of salt." "Six bushels of salt, for what?" "To preserve the fresh beef, Sir." One of the aids gave the order, and the next day his Excellency's table was amply provided. Mrs. Thomson was sent for, and told that she had done very wrong to expend her own money, for it was not known when she could be repaid. "I owe you," said his Excellency, "too much already to permit the debt being increased, and our situation is not at this moment such as to induce very sanguine hope." "Dear Sir," said the good old lady, "it is always darkest just before daylight, and I hope your Excellency will forgive me for bartering the salt for other necessaries which are now on the table." Salt was eight dollars a bushel, and it might always be exchanged with the country people for articles of provision.

The weather for several days has been remarkably cold and stormy. On the 3d instant, we experienced one of the most tremendous snow storms ever remembered; no man could endure its violence many minutes without danger of his life. Several marquees were torn asunder and blown down over the officers' heads in the night, and some of the soldiers were actually covered while in their tents, and buried like sheep under the snow. My comrades and myself were roused from sleep by the calls of some officers for assistance; their marquee had blown down, and they were almost smothered in the storm, before they could reach our marquee, only a few yards, and their blankets and baggage were nearly buried in the snow. We are greatly favored in having a supply of straw for bedding, over this we spread all our blankets, and with our clothes and large fires at our feet, while four or five are crowded together, preserve ourselves from freezing. But the sufferings of the poor soldiers can scarcely be described; while on duty they are unavoidably exposed to all the inclemency of storms and severe cold; at night they now have a bed of straw on the ground, and a single blanket to each man; they are badly clad, and some are destitute of shoes. We have contrived a kind of stone chimney outside, and an opening at one end of our tents gives us the benefit of the fire within. The snow is now from four to six feet deep, which so obstructs the roads as to prevent our receiving a supply of provisions. For the last ten days we have received but two pounds of meat a man, and we are frequently for six or eight days entirely destitute of meat, and then as long without bread. The consequence is, the soldiers are so enfeebled from hunger and cold, as to be almost unable to perform their military duty, or labor in constructing their huts. It is well known that General Washington experiences the greatest solicitude for the sufferings of his army, and is sensible that they in general conduct with heroic patience and fortitude. His Excellency, it is understood, despairing of supplies from the Commissary General, has made application to the magistrates of the state of New Jersey for assistance in procuring provisions. This expedient has been attended with the happiest success. It is honorable to the magistrates and people of Jersey, that they have cheerfully complied with the requisition, and furnished for the present an ample supply, and have thus probably saved the army from destruction.

French frigates and troops would be arriving soon. A huge cloud must have lifted from Washington's mind. But in less than a month there would be two stiff battles to protect the Morristown area.

The enemy Hessian General Knyphausen had heard reports of the dreadful conditions and low morale of the troops at Jockey Hollow and chose this time to strike. On June 6, 5,000 British and Hessian troops crossed over from Staten Island to Elizabethtown Point to begin an advance on Morristown. The New Jersey Brigade which was guarding American outposts took the brunt of the attack, but local militia soon swarmed to the scene to assist in the heavy fighting. In the all-day battle, Knyphausen burned Connecticut Farms (Union) and came within a half mile of Springfield. Then he retreated in a thunderstorm to Elizabethtown Point.

The six brigades of the Continental Army still encamped in Jockey Hollow — Hand's, Stark's, 1st and 2nd Connecticut, 1st and 2nd Pennsylvania — were marched to Short Hills but held in reserve for any further advances closer to Morristown. For about two weeks, there was no significant change until June 23, the very day that Washington planned to depart. This time two columns, under Generals Matthew and Knyphausen, succeeded in getting through Springfield, where they burned every building but two. However, under Greene's command, the Americans fought with determination and skill and forced the enemy to retreat all the way back to Staten Island. Never again would there be a major invasion of New Jersey. ☐

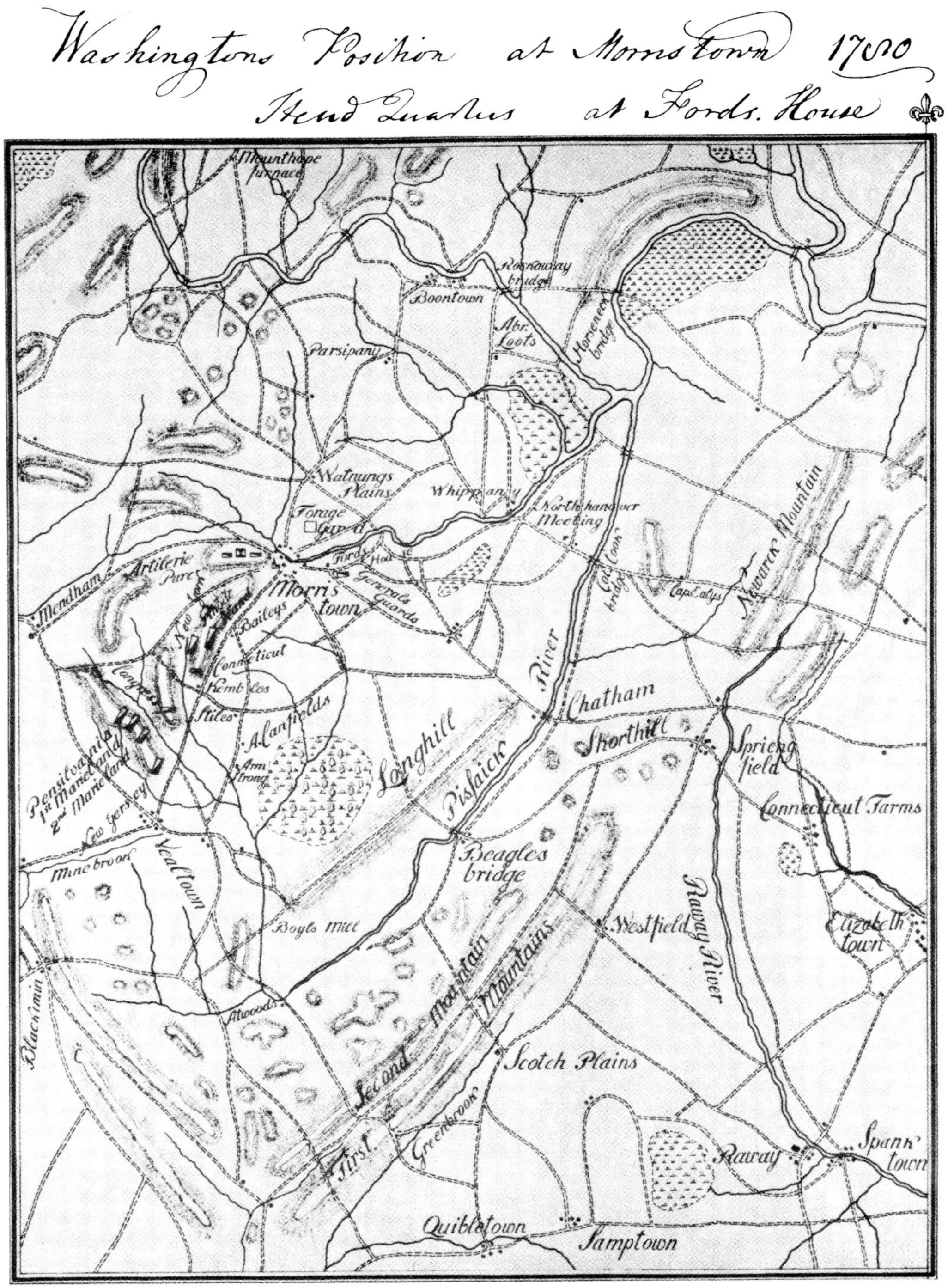

Washington's position at Morristown, February 20, 1780. This map was drawn by a British officer in New York who never saw the area but obviously had good information. Note, however, he did not learn the location of the Powder Mill.

Courtesy of the William L. Clemens Library, University of Michigan, Ann Arbor

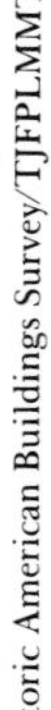

Peter Kemble House

When Gen. Washington chose "the position back of Mr. Kemble's," he was referring to Peter Kemble, once a loyal servant of the Crown. One of the most eminent men of colonial New Jersey, he lived in what was then Morris (now Harding) Township on the corner of the present Mount Kemble Avenue and Tempe Wick Road. The Hon. Peter Kemble built this house between 1750 and 1765 and lived in comfort and style with fine furnishings and a valuable library; many slaves cultivated his extensive holdings on the mountain that bears his name.

He took great interest in his property, as this entry from his diary reveals: "On or abt ye year 1754, I took out of my garden at Brunswick a May Duke Cherry tree in diameter about an inch & a half & planted it in my garden at Morris. I measured it ye 5th day of May 1781 & it was four feet in the girth."

Kemble had been a member of the Royal Council since 1745 and acted as president in the colonial Governor's absence. In December 1758, his daughter Margaret married Gen. Thomas Gage, commander in chief of the British Army in America and governor of Massachusetts during the Battle of Bunker Hill. Kemble's eldest son, Samuel, joined the British Army but left it in 1773 to accept the post of collector of the Port of New York. Kemble himself was accused of circulating British General Howe's pardons and oaths of allegiance to the Crown but somehow was saved from prosecution, probably partly because of his advanced age and the fact that his second son, Richard, took the oath of allegiance to the United States.

For the rest of the Revolution, Peter Kemble wisely kept his opinions to himself and invited American officers including Washington to enjoy his hospitality and fine table. He died there in 1789.

The house was headquarters for Gen. William Smallwood, commander of the 1st Maryland Brigade, 1779-80, and for "Mad" Anthony Wayne the following winter. When the French ministers Luzerne and Marbois and visiting congressmen were escorted in brilliant cavalcade to Jockey Hollow, April 25, 1780, the party visited this house.

In 1840, the house was moved slightly north on Mount Kemble Avenue and the front porch and a wing were added. It is still a private residence and looks very much like the 1940 photograph.

Jockey Hollow Encampment

There is only one word to describe the winter of 1779-80 in Jockey Hollow: Misery. When the army straggled in to their assigned places, at least four snowstorms had already taken place. It was the common bond between the farmers, laborers, landowners, craftsmen, tradesmen and frontier hunters who made up the Continental Line.

On November 30, 1779, Washington had informed Quartermaster General Greene he had decided "upon the position back of Mt. Kembles" in a somewhat mountainous area about three miles southwest of Morristown. He later wrote to Congress it was the nearest place available that seemed "compatible with any security which could also supply water and wood for covering and fuel." Dr. James Thacher, a surgeon of Stark's Brigade, looked at it and called it "wilderness." The site encompassed part of Peter Kemble's property and the farms of Henry Wick and Joshua Guerin.

There were perhaps 10,000 to 12,000 men at one time or another. Eight infantry brigades — Hand's, New York, 1st and 2nd Maryland, 1st and 2nd Connecticut, and 1st and 2nd Pennsylvania — were in Jockey Hollow proper. Two additional infantry brigades were nearby: Stark's Brigade on the east slope of Mount Kemble and New Jersey Brigade at "Eyer's Forge" on the Passaic River.

A "log-house city" of about 1,000 huts was built under incredibly severe conditions. "Notwithstanding large fires we can hardly keep from freezing," wrote Dr. Thacher. Major Ebenezer Huntington of Webb's Regiment, who like Thacher was part of Stark's Brigade, noted that "the men have suffer'd much without shoes and stockings and working half leg deep in snow." Despite this, huts went up built of oak, walnut and chestnut timber at hand, the logs notched together at the corners and chinked with clay. Soldiers' huts, with 12 bunks, were ordered to be 14 feet wide and 15 or 16 feet long, 6½ feet high at the eaves, with a chimney at one end and a door in front. Officers' cabins, accommodating two to four, were larger, with usually two chimneys and sometimes two doors.

In an attempt to get supplies, a daring plan was hatched at Headquarters. Major General William Alexander, Lord Stirling, was to lead a commando raid on Staten Island, January 14-15. Five hundred sleighs were obtained on the pretense of going west for provisions. Instead, the secret plan was to cross over the ice at Elizabethtown Point on the night of the 14th with cannons and about 3,000 troops "with the determination," to quote Quartermaster Lewis, "to remove all Staten Island bagg and Baggage to Morris Town."

Unfortunately, this expedition failed because the British had been forewarned and retired behind their posts to defy attack. The Americans lingered 24 hours in the terrible cold in snow four feet deep before returning with only a handful of prisoners and some blankets and stores.

Morale seemed high at first. "I am in hopes the army will be kept together till we have gained the point we have been contending for," wrote a soldier named Stanton on February 10, 1780. "I could wish I had two lives to lose in defense of so glorious a cause." The dreadful winter dragged on, however, to chill the stoutest heart. A constant round of inspections, drills, work details and guard duty did not keep starving, half-clothed soldiers from stealing to survive. Desertions were so common they were ignored the first few days. Frequent floggings did little to subdue crime. It was indeed the hardest of times. □

Photograph by James L. Grabow/TJFPLMMT

The Henry, or Tempe, Wick House

This 1983 photograph shows the restored house in Jockey Hollow with closed shutters as it would have been most of the bitter winter of 1779-80 when troops were camped on the farm.

Henry Wick, unlike his neighbor Peter Kemble, was a proven patriot, serving in the Morris County militia and cavalry and as a guard of Governor Livingston until he died on December 21, 1780.

A prosperous farmer owning 1,400 acres of timberland and open fields, he built his house about 1750. Having come from a part of Long Island strongly influenced by New England, he built this house in Cape Cod style, featuring a central chimney with three fireplaces and a large "keeping room" or kitchen. The windows had real glass panes. The fact that the house became known as Wick Hall suggests it was considered much more than just a farmhouse.

The Wicks grew typical 18th-century New Jersey crops: corn, winter wheat, buckwheat, oats and rye. Orchards were maintained for apples. Cows, horses, swine, geese, chickens, and other livestock occupied the barnyard. Near the house was a smokehouse and a well. A garden supplied fresh vegetables, fruits and herbs.

During the winter of 1779-80, it was the headquarters of Gen. Arthur St. Clair, commander of the Pennsylvania Regiments. He used the small spare, or spinning, room, while his aides probably slept in the dining room or parlor.

During the encampment, Tempe Wick was the only child still at home and a romantic tradition surrounds her and this house. The most popular version is that on January 1, 1781, when soldiers of the Pennsylvania Line were in mutiny (page 65), she had gone to her brother-in-law, Dr. Leddell (on the present Tempe Wick Road), to fetch medicine for her ailing mother. She was stopped by a roving band of mutineers who demanded her horse. It is said she feigned giving up the horse, but while the soldiers were off guard, turned the animal around and escaped. She rode swiftly home and hid the horse in her bedroom until the soldiers departed the area. Hoof marks were supposedly visible for many years after the Revolutionary War.

The house is part of Morristown National Historical Park.

I am just down from dinner about half Drunk, all dined together upon good roast & boiled, but in a Cold hut, however grog enough will keep out cold for which there is no Desiring, tomorrow we all dine at one with the Colonel, which will be another excellent dinner and I think you may call that fair living, but Ah! I am afraid it wont last many days.

Erkuries Beatty to Reading Beatty, December 25, 1779

Courtesy of Morristown National Historical Park

FIRE! A 1981 re-enactment of musket practice in Jockey Hollow. Actually, powder was too scarce — and too dangerous — to distribute in camp. The Revolutionary soldiers would have practiced all the loading procedures up to firing.

The Greatest Trouble I Believe I Was Ever In

Erkuries Beatty in the Jockey Hollow Encampment to his brother, Reading, also in the Continental Army, January 25, 1780

Your Favour of the 9th Instant came to hand a few Days ago, and obliged to answer it from Camp, which is very Disagreeable to me, but how can I help it — I must tell that I have lately involved myself in the greatest trouble I believe I was ever in, which is this, after we came off the expedition there was no Pay Master to the Reg[t]. the officers thought proper to appoint me, when we join'd the Army I found I had to do the Duty of Regiment Clothier to, which is the Cause of all my trouble, for I have lately drew Cloathing for the Reg[t] & it is almost all to make up from the Cloth all which I must oversee, which keeps me very Close confined — If you was just now to step into my Hutt (which is only a very small Room if it ever got finished) I will tell you just how you would find me, for to give you a small scrap of my trouble — You'll find me sitting on a Chest, in the Center of Six or Eight Taylors, with my Book, Pen & Ink on one side and the Buttons and thread on the other — the Taylors yo'll find some A Cutting out, others sewing, outside of the taylors you will see maybe half Dozen Men naked as Lazarus, begging for Cloathing, all about the Room you will see nothing but Cloth & Cloathing, on the floor you'll find it about knee deep with Snips of Cloth & Dirt — If you stay any time you'll hear every Minute knock-knock at the door & I calling walk in, others going out, which makes a Continual Bussle — presently I begin to swear, sometimes have to jump up blundering over two or three taylors to whip somebody out of the house — othertimes Tudor and my Mess Mates they begin to swear, & with our Swearing, and the taylors singing (as you know they must), and the Men a grumbling . . . . makes pretty Music for your Ear, and thats the way from morning to night, & from Weeks End to weeks end, & I am sure I need not complain for want of Company as you do such as it is — & what makes it a good Deal worse I think of nothing but getting a Change which makes me a good Deal fretfull . . . .

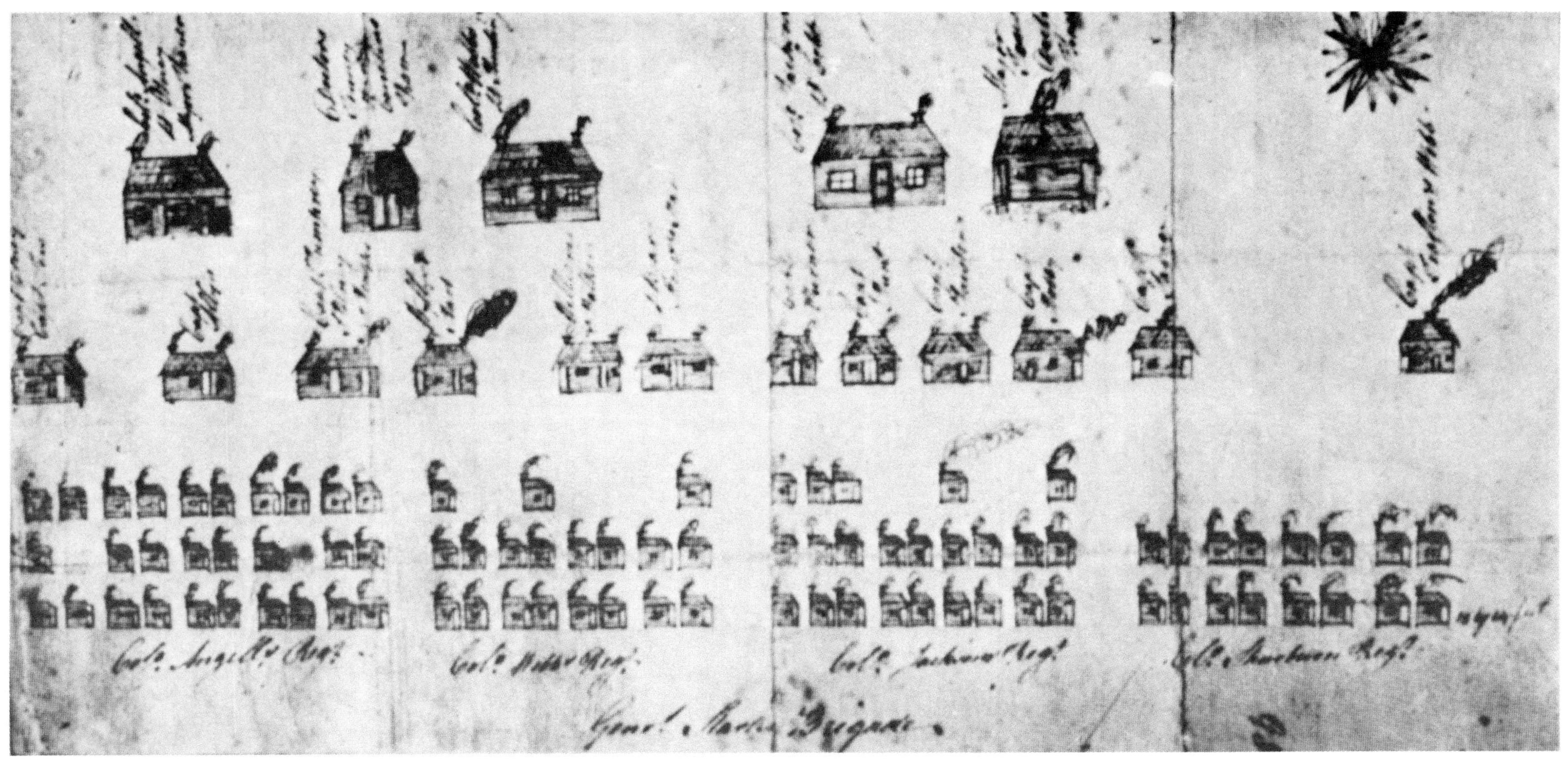

Hutting arrangement for General Stark's Brigade, 1779-80, on the east slope of Mount Kemble

This contemporary drawing illustrates a typical arrangement. Each brigade occupied a hillside area of about 320 yards long and 200 yards deep facing a parade ground 40 yards deep. Above the parade ground were the soldiers' huts, eight in a row and three or four deep. Behind them were the officers, with the senior field officers in the highest position. Note that James Thacher was assigned to the "Doctors" hut, smallest in the top row. This drawing is from an original manuscript once owned by Erskine Hewitt of Ringwood, N.J.

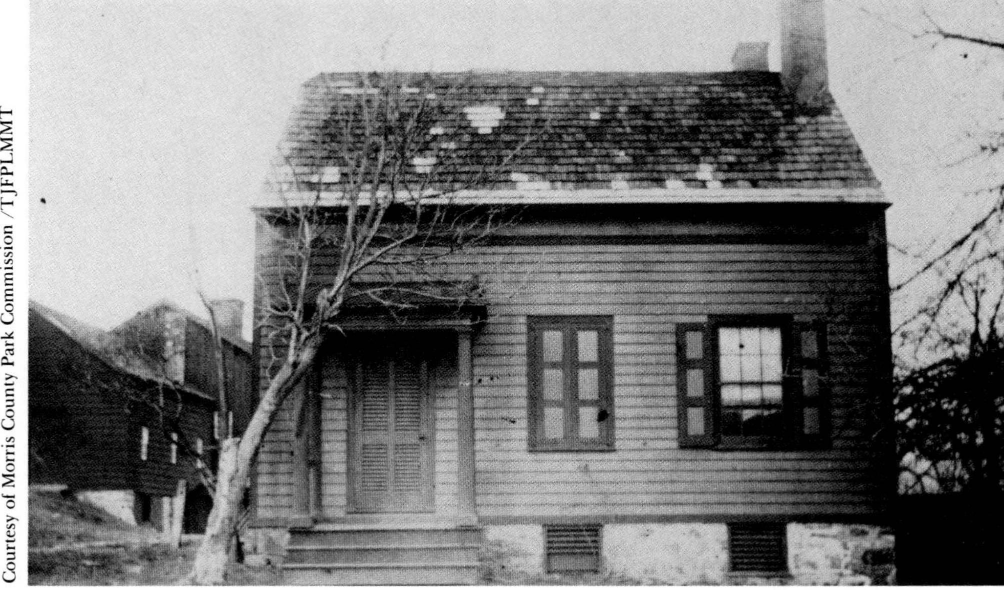

Courtesy of Morris County Park Commission/TJFPLMMT

The Jonathan Ogden House, built about 1774, believed to be the quarters of Gen. Knox. It was on the **road to Jacob Arnold's** (below), the old road to Washington Valley in Morris Township, now part of Fosterfields (page 151). This house burned and was rebuilt with three stories, as can be seen in the photograph.

Photograph by George Goodwin/TJFPLMMT

The Artillery Park

About a mile west from the Green, General Henry Knox encamped with four artillery battalions and Colonel Baldwin's Regiment of Artificers.

An "Artillery Park" was formed of huts drawn up by battalion in a line along the old Mendham Road (map) on the north slope between the present Egbert Hill and Kadhena Roads facing Burnham Park. Here were stored heavy guns and field pieces, and here also were constructed forges and machine shops. On the south side of Mendham Road, in the meadow that is now Burnham Park, the artillery horses grazed when spring came.

Baldwin's artificers provided the artillery battalions with a master carpenter (the company commander) and other carpenters, wheelwrights, blacksmiths, tinmen, turners, coopers, harness-makers, nailers and farriers to supervise the maintenance and repair of weapons and vehicles. This regiment was actually part of the Quartermaster Department and served the entire army at Morristown that winter.

Some of the officers probably occupied huts in the Park while others secured quarters at houses in the neighborhood. General Knox took up quarters at a house less than one-half mile west, generally believed to be the newly built home of Jonathan Ogden.

Quartermaster General Nathanael Greene quartered in the Jacob Arnold House in Washington Valley, on the corner of the present Washington Valley and Gaston Roads (page 149).

The site of the "Park of Artillery" is commemorated by a boulder with a bronze plaque, which was placed on Mendham Road by the Morristown Post Number 59, American Legion, on November 11, 1932 (page 263). □

Courtesy of The New-York Historical Society

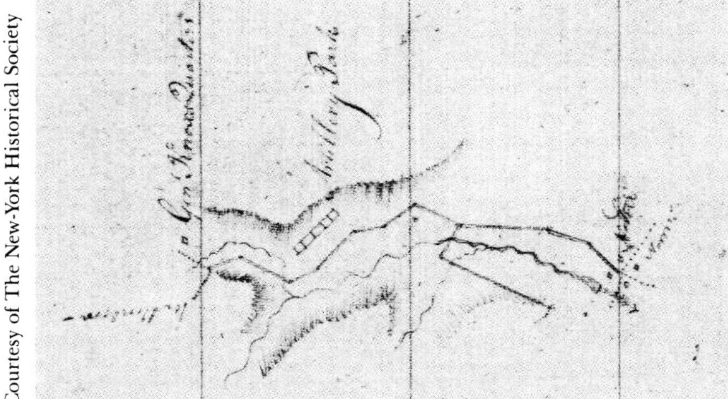

The Artillery Park. "Road from Norris's [Dickerson's] Tavern in Morristown past the Park of Artillery to Genl Knox's Quarters," drawn by Col. Robert Erskine, December 17, 1779. **Continental Store House on the Green** (right), later O'Hara's Tavern, west side of the Green. (Part of M. Epstein is on the site.) In addition to its military use, this building was the scene of at least two dancing assemblies. It was also the scene of a brilliant ball honoring Luzerne and Marbois, the French ministers who arrived in Morristown from Philadelphia on April 19, 1780, in a "closed carriage drawn by four horses & guarded by forty light dragoons in beautiful uniform."

Curtiss Collection/TJFPLMMT

The Assembly Balls of 1780

From *Annals of Morris County* by the Rev. Joseph F. Tuttle, D.D.

From documents, not very important in themselves, we sometimes derive impressive lessons. The original of the following subscriptions for Assembly Balls in Morristown, that winter, is still in possession of the Biddle family, on the Delaware: "The subscribers [Nath. Greene, H. Knox, John Lawrence, J. Wilkinson, Clement Biddle, Robt. H. Harrison, R. K. Meade, Alex. Hamilton, Tench Tilghman, C. Gibbs, Jno. Pierce, The Baron de Kalb, Jno. Moylan, Le Ch. Dulingsley, Geo. Washington, R. Clairborne, Lord Sterling, Col. Hazen, Asa Worthington, Benj. Brown, Major Stagg, James Thompson, H. Jackson, Col. Thomas Proctor, J. B. Cutting, Edward Hand, William Little, Thos. Woolford, Geo. Olney, Jas. Abeel, Robert Erskine, Jno. Cochran, Geo. Draper, J. Burnet] agree to pay the sums [$400] annexed to their respective names and an equal quota of any further expence which may be incurred in the promotion and support of a dancing Assembly to be held in Morristown, the present winter of 1780 . . . . The amounts thus paid constitute the somewhat imposing sum of thirteen thousand, six hundred dollars . . . . Now I frankly confess that this paper produced an uncomfortable sensation in my mind, by the somewhat harsh contrast between the dancing of the well-housed officers, at O'Hara tavern, and the "hungry ruin" at Kimbal-hill. The Assembly was not so well set off with gas-lights and fashionable splendor as many a Ball in our day. No doubt it was rather a plain affair, of its kind; and yet it reminds one that, while these distinguished men were tripping "the light fantastic toe," in well-warmed rooms there were at that very time, as Captain William Tuttle often told it, a great many tents in which there were soldiers without coats . . . [and] real blood [was] expressed from the cracked and frozen feet of soldiers who had no shoes!

TJFPLMMT

The Schuyler-Hamilton House, home of Dr. Jabez Campfield, where the courtship of Alexander Hamilton and Elizabeth Schuyler took place in 1780

It also served as the quarters for Dr. John Cochran, chief physician and surgeon of the Army and later Director General of Military Hospitals. This comfortable house at 5 Olyphant Place, Morristown, originally faced on Morris Street and was closer to Washington's headquarters in the Ford Mansion.

In 1923, the Morristown chapter of the Daughters of the American Revolution purchased the house as its headquarters and museum.

In 1964, the Home Garden Club of Morristown planted a colonial garden of flowers and cooking and medicinal herbs similar to the ones known to Dr. Campfield and his guests.

A Love Story

In the winter of 1779-80, Dr. John Cochran, then Chief Physician and Surgeon, and later Director General of Military Hospital, was quartered in the home of Dr. Jabez Campfield. Dr. Cochran was accompanied by Mrs. Cochran and was soon joined by her niece, Elizabeth, daughter of General Philip Schuyler, who recently resigned from the army and now was a member of Congress. In April, accompanied by Mrs. Schuyler, he arrived with two other Congressmen on a "fact-finding" mission. It must have been a crowded house but nevertheless a happy one. With the arrival of "Betsy," the youthful members of Washington's staff led by Alexander Hamilton began frequent visits to the cozy corner fireplaces of the Campfield house. Betsy had known Hamilton before and the renewed acquaintance quickly blossomed into a serious romance.

Hamilton was still the pampered Prince Charming of the military, with the fair skin and deep blue, almost violet eyes inherited from his Scottish father. Betsy was "a Brunette with the most good natured, dark, lovely eyes that I ever saw," according to Tench Tilghman, who also noted Hamilton was "a gone man."

An amusing incident is told to illustrate the point. The originator was, no doubt, the little boy in the story. One evening when Hamilton returned from the Campfield house thinking of his love, he was challenged by a guard at Headquarters who did not recognize him. Preoccupied, he could not remember the countersign. The incident could have resulted in his being shot as a presumed spy. Fortunately, young Gabriel Ford overheard the incident and was able to supply the necessary word.

Hamilton pursued his courtship with characteristic energy and enthusiasm. By April, they were betrothed and were married in December of that year. Philip Schuyler gave his heartiest approval. "You cannot, my dear Sir, be more happy at the connection than I am . . . . I shall therefore only entreat you to consider me as one who wishes in every way to promote your happiness, and I shall." And this he did, not only as father-in-law, parent and grandparent to their seven children, but as friend and politically influential advisor.

Hamilton is perhaps best known as the first Secretary of the Treasury and a major writer of the Federalist Papers. However, he was also a brilliant military strategist as he proved at Yorktown, a successful lawyer, a member of Congress and the head of the Federalist Party after Washington's death. It was partly because of the latter role that he accepted the challenge to a duel by Aaron Burr, a leader of the opposition Republican Party after Jefferson's death. He died as a result on July 13, 1804.

Elizabeth Hamilton's thoughts must have turned thousands of times to the happy days of Morristown. A grandson, Allan McLane Hamilton, wrote in *The Intimate Life of Alexander Hamilton* that "I have in my possession a little verse which was found in a tiny bag hanging from his wife's neck after her death [at 97] . . . probably given to her when they were together this winter." Apparently a sonnet, it was on yellow and torn paper, fragments sewn together with thread.

ANSWER TO THE INQUIRY WHY I SIGHED

Before no mortal ever knew
A love like mine so tender — true —
Completely wretched — you away —
And but half blessed e'en while you stay.

If present love [illegible] face
Deny you to my fond embrace
No joy unmixed by bosom warms
But when my angel's in my arms.

TJFPLMMT

Dr. Jabez Campfield (1737-1821)

A highly respected surgeon in the Continental Army, he was a personal friend of George Washington and became a member of the Society of Cincinnati. The Marquis de Lafayette gave him the gift of a sword. In 1780, having just returned from a four-month campaign against Indians under Gen. Sullivan, he was home in Morristown serving with Gen. Oliver Spencer's regiment. Dr. Campfield was a graduate of the College of New Jersey (Princeton) and continued to practice medicine and benefit his community in many other ways after the Revolution.

TJFPLMMT

Interior of the Schuyler-Hamilton House

As it appeared in the 1920s, the **living room** has a portrait of Dr. Cochran over the desk. This was originally two rooms, as shown by the low dividing beam in the center, each room having a corner fireplace.

The **dining room** (opposite) has a portrait of Elizabeth's father, Gen. Philip Schuyler.

TJFPLMMT

Curtiss Collection/TJFPLMMT

Courtship of Alexander Hamilton and Elizabeth Schuyler (left), who were married in Albany in December 1780. This panel is on the bronze doors of the Vail Mansion, later the Morristown Municipal Building, 110 South Street (page 174).

A Lover's Confession

Lt. Colonel Alexander Hamilton to one of Elizabeth Schuyler's sisters, February, 1780

I have already confessed the influence your sister has gained over me; yet nothwithstanding this, I have some things of a very serious and heinous nature to lay to her charge. She is most unmercifully handsome and so perverse that she has none of those pretty affectations which are the prerogatives of beauty. Her good sense is destitute of that happy mixture of vanity and ostentation which would make it conspicuous to the whole tribe of fools and foplings as well as to men of understanding so that as the matter now stands it is very little known beyond the circle of these. She has good nature affability and vivacity unembellished with that charming frivolousness which is justly deemed one of the principal accomplishments of a *belle*. In short she is so strange a creature that she possesses all the beauties virtues and graces of her sex without any of those amiable defects which from their general prevalence are esteemed by connoisseurs necessary shades in the character of a fine woman.

Mr. Washington is Much More Agreeable Than His Portraits Represent

Unpublished Memoirs of Comte de Broglie,* 1782

He is tall, nobly formed and very well proportioned; his face is much more agreeable than his portraits represent it; three years ago he was still very handsome, and although persons who have not left him since that time say that he seems to have aged a great deal, there is no question that the general is still as fresh and active as a young man.

His physiognomy is mild and open; his manner is cold, though polite; his thoughtful eyes seem attentive rather than sparkling; but his look is gentle, noble and assured. In his private conduct he maintains that refined and attentive propriety which satisfies everyone, and that reserved dignity which does not offend. He is an enemy of ostentation and vain-glory. His disposition is always even; he has never shown the least ill-humor. Modest, even to the point of humility, he does not seem to esteem himself at his true worth. He receives the homage paid to him with good grace; but he shuns rather than seeks it. His society is agreeable and pleasing. Always serious, never absent-minded, always simple, always free and affable without being familiar, the respect that he inspires never becomes painful. Generally he speaks little and in a very low tone; but he is so attentive to what is said to him that you would almost dispense with a reply, being persuaded that he understands you. This course of conduct has been very useful to him on several occasions. No one has needed more than he to be circumspect and to weigh his words.

He combines to an unalterable tranquility of mind an exquisite judgment, and you cannot reproach him with anything except a little slowness in coming to a decision and even in acting. When he has made up his mind, his courage is calm and brilliant. But to appreciate to a certainty the extent of his talents, and to give him the name of a great warrior, I believe that it would be necessary to have seen him at the head of a larger army, with more resources at his command, and opposed to a less overwhelming enemy. We can at least give him the title of an excellent patriot and of a wise and virtuous man, and we are greatly tempted to give him all the good qualities, even those which circumstances have not allowed him to develop.

He was unanimously called to the command of the army. Never was there a man better suited to command the Americans, or who has exhibited in his conduct more order, wisdom, constancy and reason.

Mr. Washington receives no pay as general. He always refused it as not needing it. Only the outlay of his table is at the expense of the State. Every day he has some thirty persons to dinner, maintains very good military fare, and is very attentive to all the officers whom he admits to his table. This is generally the time when he is most lively. During dessert, he consumes an enormous quantity of nuts, and, when the conversation amuses him, he eats them for hours, proposing, according to English and American usage, numerous healths (*Santés*). This is what they call "toaster." They always begin by drinking to the United States of America, then to the King of France, to the Queen, to the success of the combined armies. Then they sometimes give what is called a "sentiment": for instance, to our success over the enemy and the fair sex; to our good luck in war and love. I have also frequently drunk toasts with General Washington. Among others I proposed to him to drink to the Marquis de La Fayette, whom he looks on as his own child. He agreed with a pleasant smile, and had the politeness to propose to me in return, the health of my father and my wife.

Mr. Washington seemed to me to maintain a perfect deportment towards the officers of his army. He treats them very politely, but they are very far from being familiar with him. On the contrary, they all maintain, in the presence of this general, an air of respect, confidence, and admiration.

*Comte de Broglie's assessment is interesting because it was rumored at one time he had hoped to supersede Washington. He was Lafayette's former commander in France. The family was related to the French king and suffered heavily during that country's revolution.

Courtesy of Morristown National Historical Park

General Orders

From the Orderly Book kept by General Washington in Morristown from December 3, 1779, to May 29, 1780

HEAD QRS. MORRIS TOWN, DECEMBER 3RD, 1779. All the regimental officers are to hut with their respective Regts., the Regimental and Brigade Staff are also to be with their Respective Corps, & the Brigadiers if they do not Hutt with their Brigades are to be as Convenient to them as possible.

The auditors of Accts & the D[eputy] Pay Master are to take Quarters in Houses Contiguous to each other and as Convenient to H. Quarters as they can be procured.

Officers of every Rank are requested to exhort themselves in getting their Corps Covered with Hutts so soon as possible and that they may be built agreable to order allready Issued for uniformity and Regularity. Each Brigadier or Officer Commanding a Brigade will be pleased to appoint a Superintendent who is to see the orders for this purpose strictly attended to.

The Brigade Q[uarter] Masters are to apply to the QMG [General] for their allowance of Straw and have it Issued as soon as the troops Come to their ground.

5TH. A Trusty Sergt with a Sufficient Number of Men are to be Sent from the Difft Brigades to drive the Waggon Horses belonging to them Respectively to such places as the F[orage] M[aster] G[eneral] shall point out.

7TH. The Honble. the Board of War being desirious to furnish as soon as possible a Register of the Army the Brigadiers & officers Commanding Brigades are desired to Cause Returns to be made Immediately to the Adjt. Genl. of all vacancies that have hapned in their Respective Commands since the late arrangement of the Army.

13TH. The men warned for Detachment tomorrow to be inspected by the Compy officers this Day and an Inventory to be taken of their Arms Accoutrements & Ammunition and of every article of Cloathing in their possession which they have recd since the 1st

Secretary George Washington used in the Ford Mansion.

day of November 1779 — Musquets, Bayonets, Bayonets Belts, Scabbards, Cartouch Boxes, Cartridges, Flints, Brushes and Pricks, Turn Screws, Gun Works &c &c &c. The officers of the Brigades are to meet this Eveng at Capt Bleckers Markee between 4 & 5 o clock at the Beat of the Drum.

16TH. By a Brigade of G[eneral] C[ourt] M[artial] whereof Lt. Colo. Conndt Weisinfells was Presdt Coonvadt Hyde Thos Davenport Frederick Myers & Jno Smith of the 3rd Regt was tryed for desertion found guilty and sentenced to receive 100 lashes each.

Henry Speigler and Joseph Cornwall also of the 3r Regt. was tryd for desertion & theft found guilty & sentenced Cornwall to receive 100 lashes & Speigler to receive 100 lashes and pay Mr. Bowen on whose property the theft was committed for the shirts that were stolen.

Andw. Vanpenny of the 5th Regt was tryd for desertion & sentenced to receive 100 lashes.

The Commanding Officer of the Brigade approves of the above sentences & orders the Corporal punishment to be inflicted tomorrow morning on the parade to which the Delinquents respectively belong.

17TH. The following is to be considered as our Genl. Order of Battles, the Army to form in two lines — the 1st Composed of three division, the second of two. The 1st line to form right to left, thus 1st Maryland, 2nd Maryland, Hands, Maxwells, 1st Connecticut, 2nd Connecticut. Second Line from right to left, thus First Pensylvania, 2nd Pensylvania, Clintons and Starks.

The firing of 2 pieces of Cannon from the spot pointed out in the orders of the 4th inst will be the Signal of Alarm. The Several Brigades are then to form on their Respective Parades and when marched to their Alarm Post to take their place in the line in the foregoing Order.

The Regimental Surgeons to make returns to the Director Genl. of the Flying Hosptl next monday at Doctor Campfields where they may Draw the necessary stores.

21ST. It has been represented that some officers Quartered in neighborhood of the camp draw the wood for their own use from the encamping ground of the Corps to which they belong. This practice not only increases the inconvenience of the proprietors of the land in which the army is quartered butt will tend to distress the Service by consuming the wood on the spot for the use of the Troops and oblidg them hereafter to draw their supplies from a distance.

25TH. In passing thru the Camp the Genl. observed with pain that there is a shamefull waste of forrage. The High price of this Article & the Difficulty in procuring it if no other reason Exists ought to Induce all possible Economy.

29TH. It having been represented that the property of the Inhabitants in the Vicinity of the Camp is a prey to the plundering Spirit of the Soldiers in so much that they can neither keep poultry stock or any other article on their farms, the Genl. most earnestly exorts the officers to use their utmost Exertion to put an effectual Stop to the practice.

JANUARY 18TH, 1780. A pound of Soft or hard bread & 1 quarter of a pound of Indian Meal & one pound of flour, a pound of Beef or fourteen ounces of Pork be the Daily Ration till further orders.

19TH. The Honble. the Congress have been pleased to pass the following resolution. Resolved, That every officer in the Army of the United States whose duties requires them being on horseback in time of action being allowed a sum not exceeding the average price given at that time in the Departmen & place where the action shall happen for horses purchased for private Draggoons as a compensation for any horse he shall have killed in battle.

25TH. The Regmtl. Paymasters will Bring in their Pay Rolls & abstracts for Decr. to the Paymaster Genl. for examination as there is money arriving for the payment of Novr. and Decr. The Troops will receive the same Immediately after the Examination of the Abstracts. To Preserve uniformity in the Accts the Rolls & abstracts are to be made out for the future in Dollars & 90ths. The whole Army to be supplyd with two Days Privision which is to be Cookd & the Troops to be held in perfect order.

28TH. The Genl. is astonished & Mortified that notwithstanding the order issued on the 29th of last month & this exhortation to the officers to prevent it that the Inhabitants in the Vicinity of the Camp are absolutely a prey to the Plundering & licentious spirit of the Soldiers. From the Daily Complaints & the formal representation of the Magistrates on the Subject, a night scarcely passes without a gang of Soldiers going out of Camp & committing every Species of Robbery, Depredation & the grossest personal Insults. This conduct is intollerable & a disgrace to the Army & if anything can aggravate it it is that these violences are committed on the property and persons of those who on a very late & alarming occasion for the want of Provision manifested the warmest attachment to the Army by affording it the most generous & most plentiful relief. It has also been reported that when Detachments are relieved & are returning to Camp the Soldiers straggle & plunder in the most shamefull injurious manner. The Genl. Trusts and entreats that the Officers will exort themselves to take Effectual measures to prevent such practices in future.

31ST. The Genl observes with great concern that to many offrs. are absent from Camp by which the Discipline of their Respective Corps must necessarily be much neglected & many disorders ensue. To this in a great measure is to be attributed the shocking spirit of Licentiousness now prevailing among the Soldiers. The late Capture of some Officers on the Lines who were not there on Duty ought to be a Caution against the like practice. In future Gentlemen taken in this manner may assure themselves that they will not be exchanged in turn but will be postponed.

FEBRUARY 16TH. When it rains or snows [the only mention of snow!] the Camp Guard may be excused from assembling on the Grand Parade but they are to be visited as usual at the respective Posts by the Offr. of the Day. Where Hutts have been built on the Declivity of Hills and are sunk in the ground particular Care is to be taken to have Snow Removed & Trenches Dug round to Carry off the water without which the Soldiers will sleep amidst a Continual Damp & their health will consequently be injured. This must be done Immediately.

20TH. Dead Carcasses in and about Camp are to be buried by fatigue partys from the Brigade near which they lay . . . .

At the particular intercession of Ensign Baggly and the Officers of the 3rd N York Regt the Commr in Chief is pleased to remit the sentence against Edmund Burke of the same Corps he is therefore to be released from Confinement. The Case of Burke ought to be a striking example to the Soldiers of the Dangerous excess & the fatal Consequences into which the pernicious Crime of Drunkeness will frequently Betray them.

MARCH 7TH. No Furlough to be given till further Orders . . . .

8TH. From the Great Scarcity of Forrage & Difficulty of Obtaining the necessary Supplies the Genl. Calls for a strict attention to the Order of the Eighth day of December last for sending away as many Horses from Camp as possible when Hay Cannot be had & the Supplies of Grain will admit of it. Eight Qts. of Grain is to be issued for each Horse & when Hay is Issued 4 Qts.

16TH. The Genl. Congratulates the Army on the very interesting proceedings of The Parliament of Ireland & of the Inhabitants of that Country which have been lately Communicated not only as they appear Calculated to remove those heavy & tyranical oppressions on their trade but to restore to a Brave & generous people their Ancient Rights & freedom & by their opperation to promote the cause of America.

Desirious of impressing on the minds of the Army transactions so important in their nature the Genl. directs that all fatigue & working parties Cease for tomorrow the 17th, a day held in particular regard by the people of that Nation. At the same time he orders this as a mark of the pleasure he feels on the Occasion persuades himself that the Celebration of the Day will not be attended with the least Rioting or Disorder . . . .

26TH. Lt. Theophilus Park was tryd for defrauding his men of their Pay & Bounty & pleads not Guilty . . . . The Court unanimously find Capt. Lt. Park Guilty & not only of fraud but repeated forgeries & sentence him to be cashiered with Infamy by having his Sword broke over his Head on the Publick Parade in the Front of the Regt. to which he belongs by the Adjt. of the Regt & it is the opinion of the Court from the Scandalous

Infamous & Vilainous Conduct of Capt. Lt. Park that he is unworthy of ever holding any Post Civil or Mility in the Service of the United States.

APRIL 1ST. The State Clothiers & Regimental Clothiers of Additional Regts. are desired to Call on the Clothier Genl. tomorrow for their respective proportions of shoes.

2ND. Corpl. Roberts of the Delaware Regt was tryd for promoting & encouraging Desertion among the Men & declaring that he intended to Desert himself the first fair opportunity & advising others to go off with him & pleads not guilty. The Court after duly Considering the Charge against him & the Evidence are of opinion he is guilty of a Breach of the 3d Article second section of the Articles of War & Sentence him to suffer Death.

6TH. The Genl being in want of a person who understands the Care & Management of Horses will thank any Officer who will recommend any Soldier engaged for the War to him for this purpose. Sobriety, fidelity & good temper are Essentially necessary as are Cleanliness in Dress, Genteel Shape & small size — Saturday at eight O'Clock in the morng such as Can be recommended are to attend at H Qrs.

10TH. The Commr in Chief being informd that sevl. suspicious persons are frequently seen lurking in & about Camp directs that offrs. in genl. more especially those of the Guards would take up & examine all straglers who are found in Camp or the Vicinity . . . . The Importance of surpressing Spies demands the strictest Attention.

12TH. The men warnd for Duty are to be Closely Shaved previously to their Comeing on the Brigade Parade with their Hands, faces, neat & Clean their Arms to be in such order as to bear the most Strictest inspection those who appear in Contrary Order will not merit but actually receive Immediate punishment.

25TH. The Commander in Chief at the request of the Minister of France has the pleasure to inform Major Genl Baron De Stuben [von Steuben] & the Officers & Men of the four Battalions that the appearance and Manovours of the troops yesterday met his entire approbation & afforded him the highest Satisfaction.

His Excellency the Minister of France was pleased to express in the warmest Terms his approbation of the Troops in the Review of Yesterday, applause so Honorable cannot but prove a new motive to the emulous exortions of the Army.
General Orders, April 26, 1780

30TH. The Honble. the Congress having been pleased to pass the following resolution on Apl 10th 1780. Resolved, That when Congress shall be furnished with proper documents to Liquidate the Depreciation of the Continental Bills of Credit they will hereafter as soon as the state of the Public Finance will admit make good to the line of the Army & the Independence Corps thereof the Deficiencies of their Original pay occasional by such Depreciation.

MAY 12TH. On Monday next the Troops will begin to Exercise every day Friday & Sunday excepted in the following manner. At 6 O Clock in the M each Regt. will parade & the Rolls be Calld, the Commanding Officers takeing particular Care that none of the Officers or men be absent except those on Guard or those on other Military Duty & Immediately after the Rolls are Calld each Regt. will begin to Exercise by Companies in the Manner prescribed in the 6th Chapter of Regulations . . . .

13TH. Benjamin Quackenbos Soldier in the 3d N Y Regt. was tryd for attempting to Desert to the Enemy with his Arms & Accoutrements being a Breach of Article the 1st Section the 6th of the Articles of War & Sentenced to run the Gauntlope twice thro the Brigade with fixd Bayonets at his breast to regulate his pace.

15TH. The Commissary is to deliver 40 lbs of Tallow or 60 lbs of fat to each Regt for the purpose of makeing soap.

28TH. The Brigade to be in readiness to march tomorrow Morng at 6 O Clock. All Men in the Countrey on small Detatchd Duties to be Calld in Immediately. Returns to be made witht Delay of the Number of Tents & Camp Equipage in the Sevl Regts.

29TH. The Brigade to move by the left by Regts. As soon as the Teams arrive the Regts will move off. The Rout is through Pompton & Ramepough to Kings ferry.

I left the General about the middle of June — The last I heard of him he was going up the North River — I got home on Fryday — and find myself so much fatigue with my ride that I shall not be able to come down to see you this summer . . . We were sorry that we did not see you at the Camp — there was not much pleasure there the distress of the army and other difficultys that I did not know the cause, the pore General was so unhappy that it distressed me exceedingly.

Martha Washington, on her return to Mount Vernon, to her brother-in-law, Colonel Burwell Bassett, July 15, 1780

Courtesy of Morristown National Historical Park

Courtesy of Morristown National Historical Park

Courtesy of Morristown National Historical Park

Leaving Times and Mutiny

End of the second encampment, June 1780 (opposite, left), a 1980 re-enactment. Later, other troops returned to Jockey Hollow.

The New Jersey Brigade (opposite, right), a re-enactment. From December 1781 to August 1782, about 700 men of the 1st and 2nd Regiments under Col. Elias Dayton camped 1½ miles southwest of the Wick House on Hardscrabble Road.

Mutiny in the Pennsylvania Line, January 1, 1781 (above). "It is with inexpressible pain that I now inform your Excellency of the general mutiny and defection which suddenly took place in the Pennsylvania Line, between the hours of nine and ten o'clock last evening," wrote Maj. Gen. Anthony Wayne, commander of the Line to Washington on January 2, 1780. The soldiers, led by their sergeants, had not been paid for nearly a year, and promised food and clothing had not been supplied. Most important, most of the soldiers considered that their enlistments were up on January 1. Many considered that their original enlistments "for three years or during the War" entitled them to be discharged at the end of three years, or sooner if the war had ended earlier — not later since the war continued — and felt their officers were unjustly holding them. Still another major irritation was the generous enlistment bounty given to late joiners, while three-year veterans received a mere shadow of that compensation.

Deciding to rebel and take their grievances directly to Congress in Philadelphia, the soldiers seized guns and ammunition and stole horses and oxen from the local farmers to pull the cannons and wagons out of camp. One officer, Capt. Adam Bettin, was killed and two others wounded in attempts to restore order. Even Wayne could not get the men to lay down their arms.

This mutiny had barely subsided when the New Jersey troops at Pompton revolted. Although a comparatively mild affair, Washington took no chances and condemned the three ringleaders to be shot by 12 of their partners, although only two were actually executed. On February 7, this chastened New Jersey Brigade was sent to Jockey Hollow to take up quarters "in the Huts, lately occupied by the Pennsylvanians." New Jersey troops were posted there until July 8, 1781.

The Illustrious GENERAL GEORGE WASHINGTON IS DEAD !!!—Columbia Mou[rns]

MORRIS-TOWN:

THURSDAY, DECEMBER, 26, 1799.

Never since we have been in the capacity of recording and communica[ti]ng public events, has our task been so painful, as at this present time; nor [nev]er shall we, again, in all probability, have to announce a circumstance, [s]o universally interesting to the feelings of American Citizens, as that which [d]ictates, and occasions the sable garb, in which this paper is clothed; and [w]hich, as a tribute of veneration from us, it shall, in some measure, continue [t]o wear, until the 22nd of February next.—

THE ILLUSTRIOUS

General George Washington,

COMMANDER IN CHIEF

Of the Armies, and late President, of the United States of America,

DIED

MATURE IN YEARS—COVERED WITH GLORY, AND

Rich in the Affections of the American People,

[A]t his seat at Mount-Vernon, on Saturday the 14th instant, of an [in]flammatory Quinzey, in 24 hours after he was attacked. He retained the [p]erfect use of his senses until the moment of his dissolution; just before which [h]e mentioned to those about him, that he had made his will—that all his private [a]ffairs were in good order—that his public business was but two days behind [h]and, and that he was perfectly resigned to the dispensations of providence.

We shall not exaggerate when we say, that the death of this great man must be [c]onsidered, by every American, as an irreparable loss to the U. States: It is a [c]alamity, which, tho inevitable in the order of nature, and tho deferred until [h]e was nigh the goal of *Seventy Years*, will clothe millions in deep mourn[in]g: groans, and tears will attend the solemn tidings through the wide terri[t]ories of the American people. Our *Independence*, which is a true record, [a]nd recent monument of his labors, reminds us of that eventful war, which [h]e conducted with such ability, and terminated with such glory. Whether [w]e view him in the field, or cabinet—in the shade of retirement, or chair of [st]ate, he is ever the same:—great, and powerful in command—a lion in the [d]ay of battle—in victory, mild, and merciful—in policy, uniting perfection [o]f system, with grandeur of design—firm, and unshaken in the face of dan[g]er, and storm of adversity—uniting and blending, with all, gentleness and [s]implicity of manners, with pure and bright morality; and thus forming a [c]haracter as well calculated to inspire confidence—command respect, and be[n]efit mankind, as ever was exhibited by a mortal man.

He was born February 11, 1732—Appointed Member of Congress un[d]er the Confederation in 1774—made Commander in Chief of the Ameri[c]an Armies in 1775—Resigned that Command in 1783—Was elected Pre[s]ident of the United States in 1789—Resigned that office in 1797—and in [1]798, was appointed Lieutenant General of the American Armies. For near[l]y *Fifty Years*, he was employed in a series of great actions, thro all which, [h]e passed without a stain, moving sublimely towards the grand climax. His [s]erene and tranquil genius often dissipated the storms which were gathering [r]ound him, and he had the uncommon felicity to enjoy Fortune's highest fa[v]ors, without her painful vicissitudes:—But, alas! *he is Gone Forever!!!*—He is torn from the bleeding bosom of his country!—He sleeps in death!!! Then let love and gratitude enroll his name amongst the Wise—the Honora[b]le, and virtuous of every age; and the People of America, to the latest

dolence of this mournful event.

"*Resolved*, That the Speaker's chair [be] shrouded with black, and that the members and officers of the House wear bl[ack du]ring the session.

"*Resolved*, That a comm[ittee, in con]junction with one from [the Senate, be ap]pointed to consider o[f a suitable] manner of paying ho[nor to the memory] of the man, first in [war, first in peace], and first in the [hearts of his countrymen] ... when it ad[journs] ... unanimously a[greed to] ... [memb]ers were appoint[ed] ...

... the President was recei[ved] ... a letter from Tobias [Lear], ... secretary to GENERAL [WASHIN]GTON.

President's Message.

Gentlemen of the Senate, and
Gentlemen of the House of Representatives,

The letter herewith transmitted will inform you, that it has pleased Divine Providence to remove from this life, our excellent fellow-citizen, GEORGE WASHINGTON, by the purity of his character, and a long series of services to his country, rendered illustrious through the world.—It remains for an affectionate and grateful people, in whose hearts he can never die, to pay suitable honor to his memory.

JOHN ADAMS.

Mount Vernon, Dec. 15, 1799.

SIR,

It is with inexpressible grief, that I have to announce to you the death of the great and good General Washington. He died last evening, between 10 and 11 o'clock, after a short illness of about 24 hours. His disorder was an inflammatory sore-throat, which proceeded from a cold, of which he made but little complaint on Friday. On Saturday morning, about 3 o'clock, he became ill. Dr. Craik attended him in the morning, and Dr. Dick, of Alexandria, and Dr. Brown, of Port Tobacco, were soon after called in. Every medical assistance was offered, but without the desired effect. His last scene corresponded with the whole tenor of his life. Not a groan, nor a complaint escaped him, in extreme distress.—With perfect resignation, and a full possession of his reason, he closed his well spent life. I have the honor to be, &c.

TOBIAS LEAR.

On motion of Mr. Otis, the message of the President, and letter accompanying it, were referred to the joint-committee appointed this day, in pursuance of the third resolution moved by Mr. Marshall.

The hour having arrived which the President had appointed, the House proceeded to wait on him; and having returned, Mr. Speaker read the following address of the House, and the President's reply thereto:

CONGRESS.

HOUSE OF REPRESENTATIVES.

Thurſday, December 19.

Mr. Marſhall addreſſed the chair as follows:

Mr. Speaker,

The melancholy event which was yesterday announced with doubt, has been rendered but too certain. Our WASHINGTON IS NO MORE! The Hero, the Sage, and the Patriot of America—the Man on whom, in times of danger, every eye was turned, and all hopes were placed, lives now only in his own great actions, and in the hearts of an affectionate and afflicted people.

If, Sir, it had not been unuſual, openly to teſtify reſpect for the memory of those whom Heaven had ſelected as its inſtruments for diſpenſing good to men, yet ſuch has been the uncommon worth, and ſuch the extraordinary incidents which have marked the life of him whoſe loſs we all deplore, that the whole American nation, impelled by the ſame feelings, would call with one voice for a public manifeſtation of that ſorrow which is ſo deep and ſo univerſal.

More than any individual, and as much as to one individual was poſſible, has he contributed to found this our wide-ſpread-ing empire ... were diſſolving, we have ſeen him the chief of thoſe patriots who formed for us a conſtitution, which, by preſerving the Union, will, I truſt, ſubſtantiate and perpetuate thoſe bleſſings our revolution has promiſed to beſtow.

In obedience to the general voice of his country, calling on him to preſide over a great people, we have ſeen him once more quit the retirement he loved, and, in a ſeaſon more ſtormy and tempeſtuous than war itſelf, with calm and wiſe determination, purſue the true intereſts of the nation, and contribute, more than any other could contribute, to the eſtabliſhment of that ſyſtem of policy which will, I truſt, yet preſerve our peace, our honor, and our independence. Having been twice unanimouſly choſen the chief magiſtrate of a free people, we ſee him, at a time when his re-election with the univerſal ſuffrage could not have been doubted, affording the world a rare inſtance of moderation, by withdrawing from his high ſtation to the peaceful walks of a private life.

However the public confidence may change, and the public affections fluctuate with reſpect to others, yet with reſpect to him, they have, in war and peace, in public and private life, been as ſteady as his own firm mind, and as conſtant as his own exalted virtues.

Let us then, Mr. Speaker, pay the laſt tribute of reſpect and affection to our departed friend. Let the grand council of ... tained by the Nation, by the death of that great and good man, the illuſtrious and beloved WASHINGTON, wait on you, Sir, to expreſs their condolence on this melancholy and diſtreſſing event.

To which the Preſident made the following

REPLY:

Gentlemen of the Houſe of Repreſentatives,

I receive, with great reſpect & affection, the condolence of the Houſe of Repreſentatives, on the melancholy and afflicting event, in the death of the moſt illuſtrious and beloved perſonage which this country ever produced. I ſympathize with you—with the Nation, and with good men, through the world, in this irreparable loſs, ſuſtained by us all.

JOHN ADAMS.

A meſſage from the Senate announced their concurrence to the reſolution appointing a joint-committee, paſſed this day—and that ſeven members had been appointed on their part. Sixteen were appointed on the part of this houſe; and then the houſe adjourned till Monday morning, 11 o'clock.

WAR-OFFICE, Dec. 19, 1799.

The Preſident, with deep regret, announces to the army the death of its beloved Chief, General GEORGE WASHINGTON. Sharing in the grief, which every heart muſt feel for ſo heavy and afflicting a public loſs, and deſirous to expreſs his high ſenſe of the vaſt debt of gratitude, which is due to the virtues, talents,

TJFPLMMT

I went to meeting at Morristown where a funural Sermon was Dillivered by the Rev. James Richards on the Death of **GENERAL GEORGE WASHINGTON** *who Died the 14th Inst. Saturday evening with an inflamatory affection of the throat wich put a period to his existince in 23 hours. The Colours were half Displayed on the flagstaff the pulpit Dressed in morning and the greatest part of the Citizens paraded before the Acadamy. The horseman Dressed in uniform march before followed by the reverend Clergy and magistrates next the preceptors and scholars & then Citizens to the house of worship and the horsemen opened and formed. Then the Clergy marched, in the bell tolled for half an hour. He died in the 68th year of his age.*

Diary of Stephen Youngs, December 29, 1799

The sorrowful news of George Washington's death on December 14, 1799, as reported in Morristown's only paper, *The Genius of Liberty,* on December 26. The paper was owned by Caleb Russell and run at that time by Jacob Mann (page 92). Washington had died of the "Inflammatory Quinzey" that had brought him so close to death in Morristown 22 years before.

Fruits of Peace

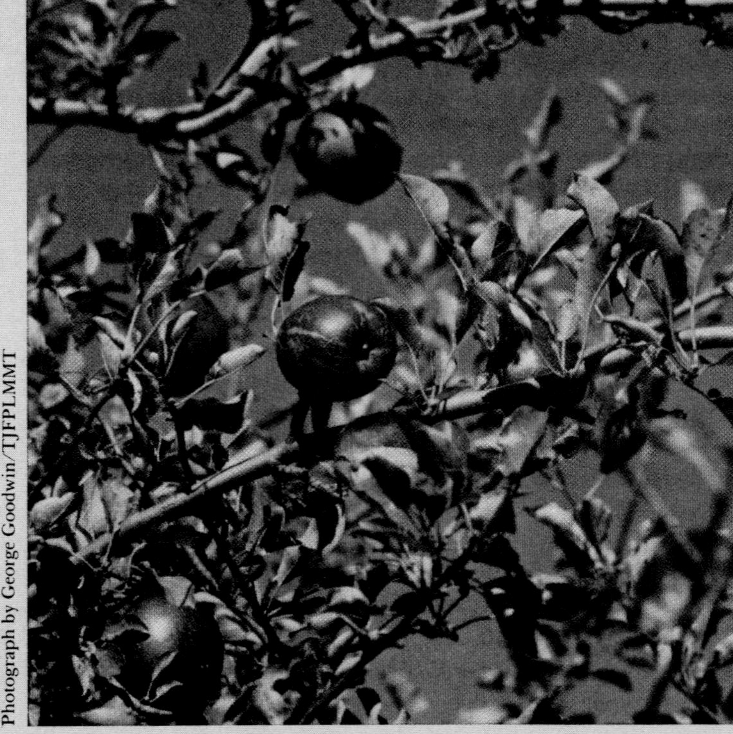

Photograph by George Goodwin/TJFPLMMT

Apple Harvest.

The Polish traveler Julian Niemcewicz, who dined with Gabriel Ford in November 1799, noted in his diary: "In Morys Tow[n] one can see proof of public intent, the sentiment through which a citizen (in the success, the advantages, the splendors of the city in which he was born) finds an internal joy and satisfaction." He marveled at one of the guests, an 86-year-old Miss Carny, who "remembers this country in the hands of the Indians, remembers the founding of a large number of the cities; in a word, she remembers the transformation of a wilderness into a cultivated land inhabited by industrious and enlightened people."

A Massachusetts visitor, Elbridge Gerry, Jr., son of the U.S. Vice President under James Madison, also noted Morristown's energetic quality when he traveled through in 1813: "It is some like a seaport town and much business is transacted."

By the end of the 18th century, these earnest citizens had established a library, printing press, newspaper, fire company, waterworks, charitable organization and an academy whose graduates could enter the second year of college.

Transportation as well as communication improved. In 1798 — possibly a year earlier — Benjamin Freeman, new owner of the Arnold Tavern, and John Halsey ran a stage line to Paulus Hook (Jersey City) using a coach pulled by four horses. In 1799, Matthias Crane started a rival stage and soon there were other competitors following various routes, most to Paulus Hook but some to Newark and Elizabethtown Points, where passengers also could cross the river to New York. One stage arranged its schedule to meet the Long Island stage the same day.

The old roads were never the best and several turnpike were chartered. The first to include Morristown was the Morris Turnpike Company, chartered March 9, 1801. The highway entered Morris County at Chatham and passed to Madison in a straight line (paralleling Route 24) then ran to a point opposite Washington Headquarters, then west on Morris and Spring Street and out Sussex Avenue, where it eventually ended in Newton.

The Washington Turnpike from Morristown to Phillipsburg, chartered March 3, 1806, began at the present Washington Street and Western Avenue, followed Mendham Road (Route 24 west) to Chester, German (Long) Valley and up Schooley's Mountain. While a spur went north to Hackettstown, the main line continued to Phillipsburg.

Soon the transportation network would include a canal and a railroad.

The population of the town and township was small — in 1810 (the first year such figures were available), the total population was 3,753 — but the quality if not the quantity of its citizens kept the area vigorously moving ahead. □

TJFPLMMT

Morristown about 1820

The general impression in this painting by Charles Jeremiah Wetmore is of a thriving town with comfortable houses, large gardens and orchards, and tree-lined streets.

The "Road to Baskinridge" (Mount Kemble Avenue, Route 202) is in the foreground. Prominent on the Green are the new 1795 Presbyterian Church and the 1819 Session House and the cupola of the 1770 courthouse. Although other buildings are difficult to identify, the map on the following pages also documents the town of this period.

Two foreign visitors left these impressions of Morristown after the Revolution: "The houses are of wood, neat and well painted. The town lots each cost from 80 to 120 dollars," observed the French social reformer La Rochefoucauld about 1797. "A square of houses is off a huge open common; at the sides the houses are a furlong from each," noticed the Polish writer Niemcewicz in 1799. "[The inhabitants] have plenty of land; they occupy and fence as much as need requires or greed tempts."

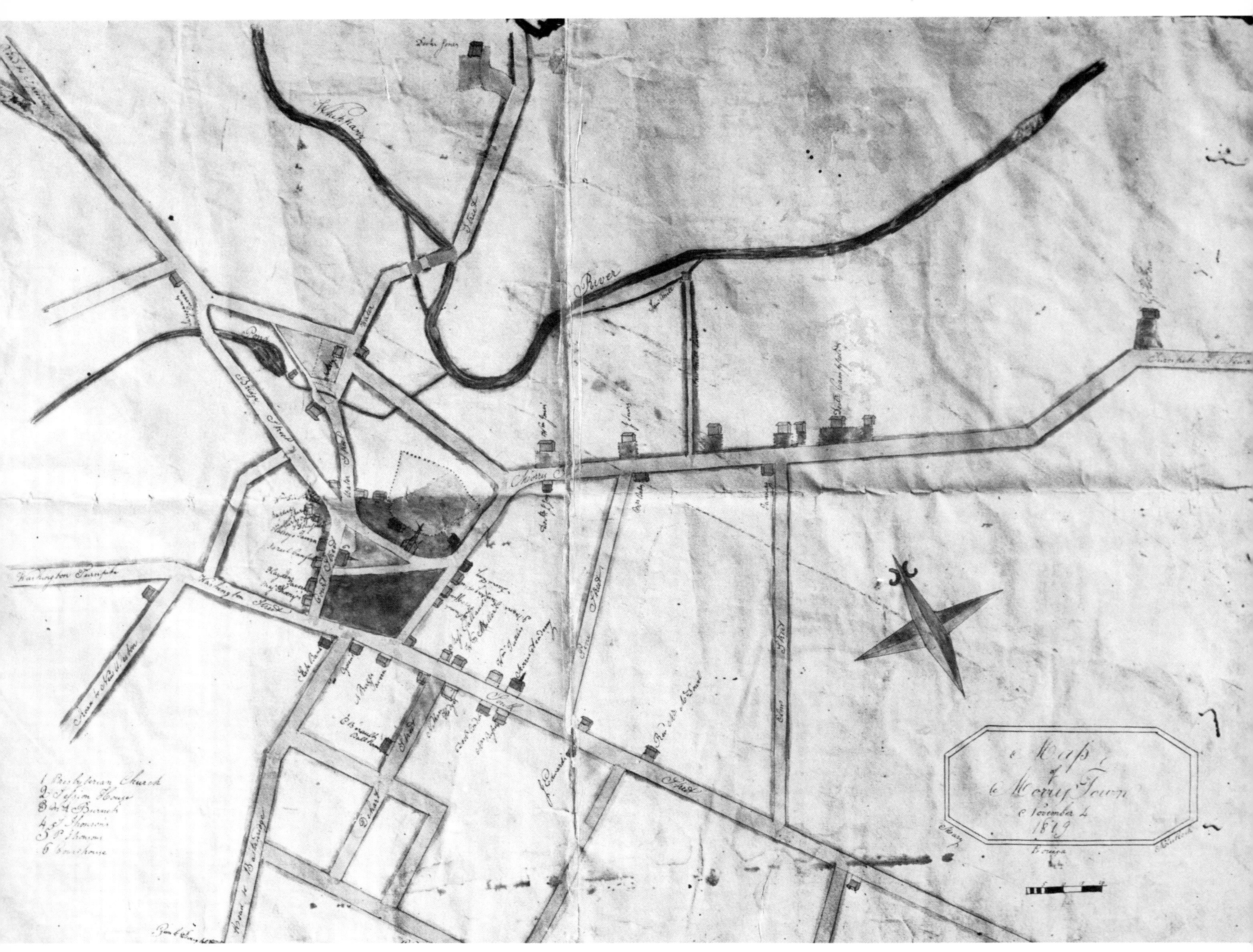
Map
of
Morris Town
November 4
1819
River
Washington Turnpike
Washington Street
Court Street
Water Street
Bridge Street
Pine Street
Elm Street
Dehart Street
Road to Baskinridge
Road to New Vernon
1 Presbyterian Church
2 Session House
3 Dr. L Burnet
4 J Thomson's
5 P Thomson
6 Courthouse

Macculloch Map of November 4, 1819

Mary Louisa Macculloch made this 18- by 34-inch watercolor map when she was only 15. She was the daughter of George P. Macculloch, influential Morristown citizen and promoter of the Morris Canal (pages 101, 124).

Since the Revolution, many new buildings have been added and there are a number of new streets — Washington Turnpike; Bridge Street (Speedwell Avenue); Elm, Pine, Market and DeHart Streets; and the unnamed Maple and Macculloch Avenues and Miller Road. One curiosity is the omission of Bank Street, which was an old Colonial road, at the beginning of the "Road to Baskinridge" while she included the newer road, later called Market Street, which only was put through in 1804 or 1805.

Of Revolutionary landmarks on the Green, the Baptist church and the court house are still standing. The Arnold Tavern is now Hayden's and the Continental Store House, later George O'Hara's Tavern, is now Nathaniel Bull's. The late Col. DeHart's house on the corner of South and DeHart Streets is occupied by Nathan Hedges. On Morris Street, the parsonage of the Rev. Timothy Johnes, which belonged to him and not the church, has passed to his son William. A grandson, Dr. John, son of Dr. Timothy, lives across the street. A son-in-law, Joseph Lewis, lives in the house next door. Dr. Jabez Campfield still occupies his house on Morris Street, but the Ford Mansion is now owned by Gabriel Ford, who bought out the interests of his brother and two sisters about 1805.

Among the post-Revolutionary buildings are the Presbyterian church on the Green and the Morris Academy on South Street and the homes of Dr. Lewis Condict, South Street; Gen. John Doughty, Mount Kemble Avenue; Moses Estey, Water Street; and M. Louis Sansay, DeHart Street, which on this map is identified as "C. Barrault Ballroom."

At the bottom of the map near the edge of town is the Macculloch home.

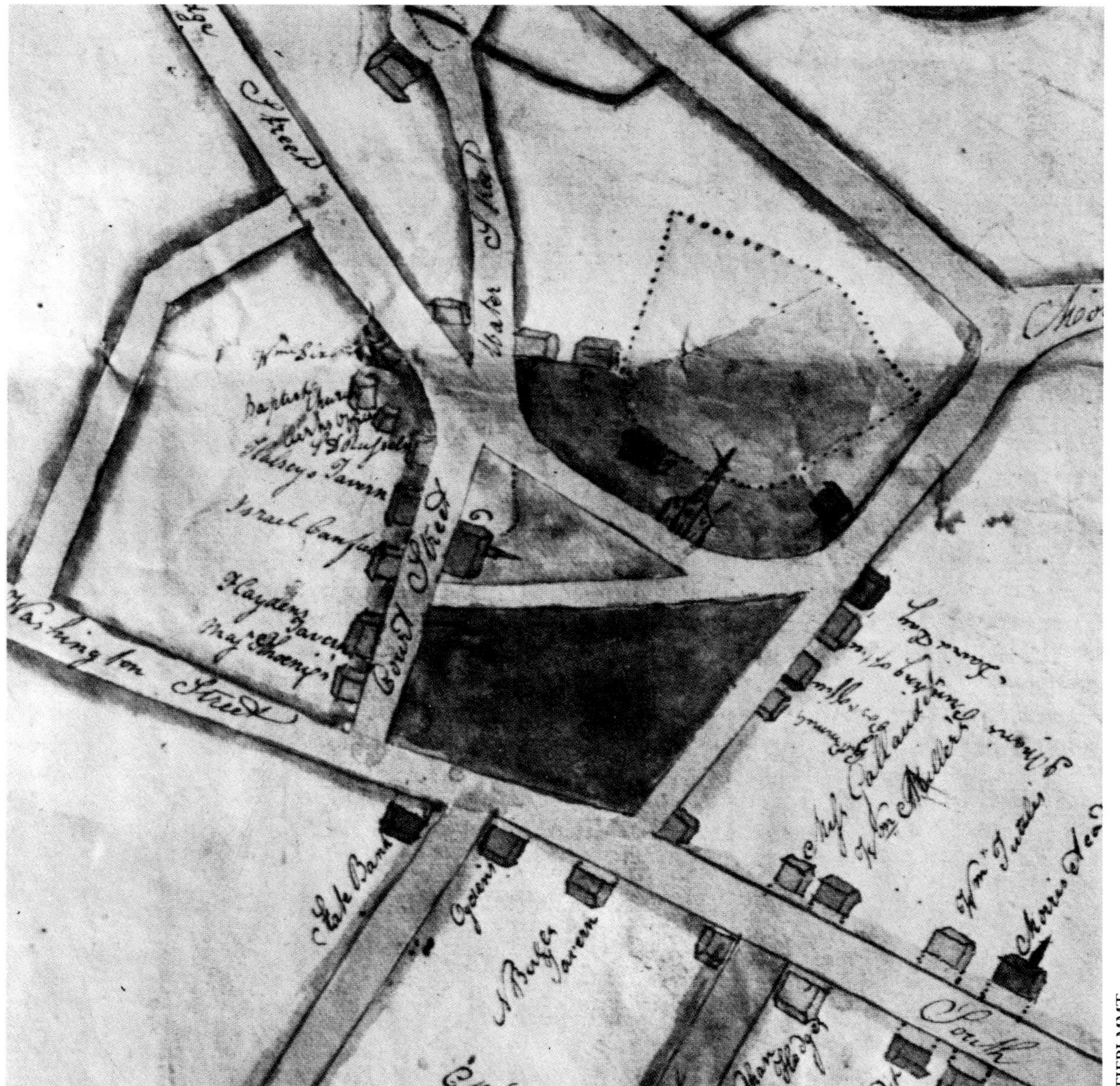

TJFPLMMT

Around the Green (full size detail, right), moving clockwise beginning at the Presbyterian church with its burying ground indicated with a dotted line: house of David Day; printing office of Jacob Mann, now publishing *The Palladium of Liberty*; post office; house and store of George Emmel, a former Hessian soldier; building used as an office by Gen. Green during the Revolution; Nathaniel Bull's (O'Hara's) Tavern; Charles Ogden's house, in front of which Lafayette spoke to the welcoming crowd on the Green in 1825; State Bank, first known bank in Morristown; home of Maj. Phoenix; Hayden's (Arnold's) Tavern; house and store of Israel Canfield; Halsey Tavern; house and office of Sylvester Russell, son of Caleb, who served four terms as Morris County Clerk; the 1770 court house; and the Session House.

"Plan of Morristown, Morris County, N.J.," 1868/TJFPLMMT

ALEXANDER & STEVENS PHOTOGRAPHERS

Men of Mettle

The old-fashioned expression "men of mettle" applies perfectly to the men who shaped Morristown after the Revolution. A man with mettle is strong and purposeful, a believer in what is right, with the spirit to do it. Early Morristown was fortunate in having a number of men with this quality. Many were extraordinarily farseeing, not only about the town but about the state and the nation. Their lives reveal a courage, fortitude, even ardor which led to remarkable achievements. In a real sense, these leaders carried high the torch of their Revolutionary forebears.

Adversity after the Revolution, such as the serious drain on the economy and runaway inflation, did not seem to threaten them. Lack of materials, a poor communication system, the hazards of travel were not the hindrances we would expect.

Some sons traveled alone on horseback to the western territories newly opening up. But

The Presbyterian Church on the Green

This second edifice, begun in 1791 and completed in 1795, was built in New England style by Maj. Joseph Lindsley, assisted by Gilbert Allen, both church elders, to resemble a church in Elizabethtown. In an old memorandum book, this entry was found: "Timber to be all white oak, cut in old moon of Dec., Jan'y or Feb'y, and delivered on the Green by the — day of — next, Nov. 1790." The church stood until 1893 when a third edifice was built on the same site (pages 287, 300). The steeple was preserved and can be seen in the burying ground.

Went to Morristown to Cellebrate the Anniversiry of our Independence procession was formed about 12 oclock and proceed to Church after Seated vocal musick then prayer by the Rev James Richards then the Declaration of Independence read by Mr. Stevens then musick then Oration by Henry Mills then musick all performed harmoniously then procession was formed and marched to George O'Hara's where them that pleased dined and partook of the Joys of the day.
Diary of Stephen Young, July 4, 1805

This day was observed by the members of the Congregation, as a day of humiliation, fasting & Prayer, instead of the 15th as recommended by Presbytery, in consequence of the review of drafted troops, which is to take place tomorrow on Morris Green (Collection for the poor, $28.93).
Minutes of the Session, First Presbyterian Church, May 14, 1812, concerning the parade of Capt. Carter's 250 "well-disciplined, handsome" militia with Capt. Halliday's Morris rangers and Capt. Britain's fusiliers in the War of 1812.

most stayed behind — indeed were joined by many others — to build a strong town and township, county and state.

There seemed to be a collective energy arising from the knowledge that a new nation offers opportunities that may never come again. □

TJFPLMMT

The 1816 Session House

This building was constructed for the Presbyterian Church elders, one of whom was ordered in that year to express public remorse and ask God's forgiveness for allowing his men to cut buckwheat on a Sunday. The fence around the burying ground kept out the farm animals that roamed freely on the Green. Also in this year, the church trustees deeded the Green to a group of private citizens with the stipulation that no stores, homes, shops or barns be permitted there. The present Chapel replaced this building in 1869 (page 286).

Two Men of Adventure: John Cleves Symmes and John Doughty

They knew each other and probably did not like each other, but they both served their country well during the Revolution and made significant contributions to the growth of the nation.

John Cleves Symmes (1742-1814), a lawyer, was also a school teacher, surveyor, judge and land speculator. He served as a member of the Provincial Congress (1776), the Legislative Counsel (1776-77, 1780-85) and the Confederation Congress (1785-86). He was a colonel in the Third Battalion from Sussex County (1775-77) and Associate Justice of the Supreme Court of New Jersey (1777-83). In 1782, he presided at the trial of James Morgan for the murder of the Reverend James Caldwell of Springfield and over many trials of British sympathizers.

Symmes probably moved to "Solitude" (Wheatsheaf Farms), his large property near Sussex Avenue in Morris Township about 1777-78, where he became a neighbor of Silas Condict. He brought with him his wife, Anna Tuttle, but she died shortly after, leaving him with two small daughters. Little Anna grew up to marry President William Henry Harrison.

While serving in Congress, Symmes became interested in the opening of the Northwest Territories. With Elias Boudinot and others, he purchased two million acres in the Territory of Ohio, known as the "Miami Purchase." He sold shares of land in this "city proposed to be built" — the future North Bend — to his friends back in Morristown. Everything was not as successful as he hoped because, tradition says, of another Morristonian, John Doughty (1754-1826). But this anticipates the story.

John Doughty owned extensive woodland and farmland on both sides of Mount Kemble Avenue, a total of 400 acres. Macculloch Avenue, Doughty Street, Colles and Wetmore Avenues, and Farragut and Ogden Places were all part of his property.

Doughty enlisted in the Army in Morristown in 1776 as a captain and remained in the Army after the war. From 1785 to 1791, Doughty, now a major, spent most of his time in the western frontier. His bravery was legendary. On one occasion, Major Doughty was attacked by a large party of Indians while he was surveying the Tennessee River in a barge, manned by 16 soldiers. Eventually, when 11 of his men had been killed or disabled, the Major decided to take drastic action. He stood up in the stern of the boat, presenting himself as a perfect target and took deliberate aim at the Indian chief. As the leader fell, his followers fled at this show of expert marksmanship.

Now to the story of the "disagreement," surely too mild a word from Symmes's point of view. Part of Doughty's job was choosing and building forts in the new territory, and he went to North Bend to select an appropriate site there. While inspecting, it is said, the Major — who never married but had an appreciative eye for women — met the beautiful blackeyed wife of one of the residents. The officer's attentions were not lost on the husband, who hastily moved his wife to the little village of Losantiville (the future Cincinnati). When Doughty heard of this, so the story continues, he decided to visit this other village and soon concluded the fort should be constructed there — which was immediately done. This story may well have

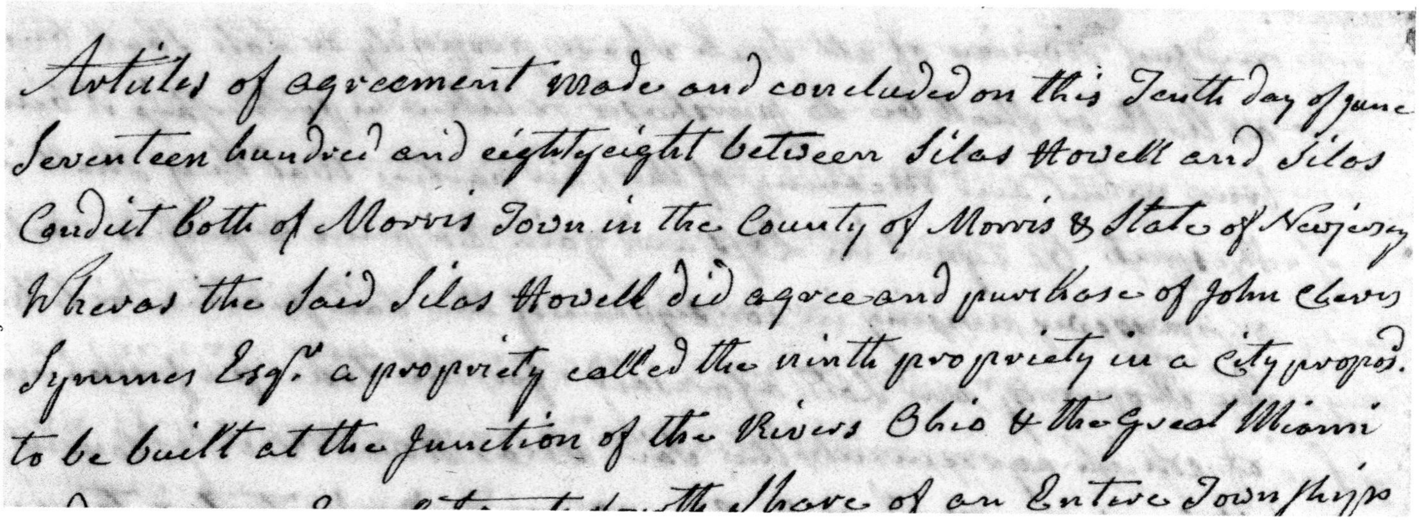
Articles of agreement made and concluded on this Tenth day of June
Seventeen hundred and eighty eight between Silas Howell and Silas
Condict both of Morris Town in the County of Morris & State of New Jersey
Whereas the said Silas Howell did agree and purchase of John Cleves
Symmes Esqr. a propriety called the ninth propriety in a City propos.
to be built at the junction of the Rivers Ohio & the Great Miami

Cutler Collection/TJFPLMMT

A share in the Territory of Ohio

This agreement was signed on June 10, 1788, for land and development rights in what later became North Bend.

been malicious gossip spread by the greatly disappointed investors and residents of North Bend. His reputation for honor was never questioned in Morristown. However, it is true Doughty built a fine fort in Cincinnati, and that location prospered at North Bend's expense.

Doughty returned to Morristown in his later years to enjoy his fine house and to pursue his interests in agriculture and literature. His extensive library was worth $1,500, an enormous sum then. His name appears in connection with many public ceremonies and subscriptions.

On September 16, 1826, he died and is buried in the Presbyterian churchyard beside his mother and father. In his will, he remembered his "old slave Sussex" with an annuity of $50 a year for the remainder of his life. He directed that his slaves "Jacob, Peter, and Abraham shall be free and emancipated in one year after my decease" and given a legacy. To Jacob and Peter he left land; to Abraham a mortgage which he held against another's property. Doughty was one of the first slave-owners in the township to release his slaves — a very forward-looking man. □

Historic Morristown, New Jersey, by Andrew M. Sherman

U.S. Army Recruiting News, Aug. 1, 1935

John Doughty as General-in-Chief of the United States Army, 1784

He was third commander in chief after Washington and Knox but held the position only three months because of a change in Congressional policy. He was a loyal soldier and served the Army in some capacity between 1776 and 1800. He was a general again in 1793 with the New Jersey artillery.

His house (left) on Mount Kemble near Colles Avenue. Torn down in the 1930s, it is now the site of apartment buildings.

TJFPLMMT

Photograph by Timothy G. Cutler

Dr. Lewis Condict House

This 1797 house at 51 South Street is one of the few Federal style buildings remaining in the Morristown Historic District. The center dormer and rear half of the building were added in the 19th century. The above photograph shows the house before Community Place was put through from Maple Avenue. The porch in the 1970s photographs on the left was added after 1922.

Lewis bought the property for the house, some 11 acres, from his uncle, Silas Condict. He later gave part of the back of the property to the Morris and Essex Railroad for the first train station (page 103).

The building is now the headquarters of The Woman's Club of Morristown.

Hon. Lewis Condict, M.D.

Lewis Condict went to the western frontier to explore but decided his prospects were better back in Morristown (box, opposite page). When Lewis was two, his father, Peter Condict 3rd, died (1774 inventory, page 17) and he was brought up by his patriot uncle Silas Condict. At 14, he began to study medicine under Dr. Timothy Johnes, a son of the Parson, and lived with the doctor as an apprentice five or six years, judging from bills submitted to Peter Condict's estate for new clothes — a great coat, suits, breeches, overalls, shirts, stockings, handkerchiefs, a set of buckles and a new pair of shoes each year — and for washing and mending, and for books (the last year). Then he went to the University of Pennsylvania, where the famous Dr. Benjamin Rush, a signer of the Declaration of Independence, signed his medical diploma.

The young doctor began his practice in Morristown in 1794. Whether he went to the Ohio Territory just before or just after this date is not clear, but as he wrote his friend Daniel Cooper, he built his Federal-style, white clapboard house with stone foundation in 1797, on 11 acres of land bought from Silas Condict for £1400. The original building was considerably smaller than it is today, probably 50 feet deep, but it had two floors, an attic and a large basement kitchen.

Despite his apparent determination to remain a bachelor, on October 6, 1798, he married Martha Woodhull. Three sons, Silas L., Nathan W. and Lewis, became physicians. Martha died in 1820 and on December 20, 1824, Dr. Condict married Martina Elmindorf, who died in 1851.

Dr. Condict was always a forward-looking man in his profession. He was largely responsible for an Act of Congress that permitted a

I Have Compleated My House and Find My Prospects Flattering

Lewis Condict from Morristown, December 30, 1797, to Daniel C. Cooper, Cincinnati, North Western Territory

Dear Sir: — I rec'd your's of the 18th Sept. in about one month from its date, and at that time did not imagine I should have delayed answering it so long, but unavoidable circumstances have prevented till now.

It affords me infinite satisfaction to hear of your prosperity in that Country which though young and uncultivated is rendered by nature one of the finest in the world in points of fertility, and climate. With propriety it may be termed the "Land of Canaan," if not the "Garden of Eden" or ancient paradise of which we read. Had I settled my affairs in Jersey before I set out on my journey, I am convinced, I should not have returned, but have remained there to this day. The distance is so great and my friends here were so opposed to my settling there, that I was induced to pitch my tent in Jersey, where perhaps I shall spend my days. I have compleated my house, and find my prospects flattering. I am yet free from matrimonial shackles, and at present do not see much prospect of being encumbered with them. The married folks tell me I want nothing but a *wife* to compleat my happiness, and I in return, remind them of the fox that lost his tail in a trap, and wished it to become fashionable to go without tails. [Actually, he married the following year.] Parson Richards [of the Presbyterian Church] and his family live in the house with me, and I board with him. I endeavor to enjoy myself as I pass through life, as well as circumstances will admit, remembering that we cannot take the world with us when we die . . . .

No remarkable occurences have happened among your acquaintances here since your departure, except the marriage of Samuel Arnold to Miss Jackson of Rockaway. They have moved to Albany and are doing very well. Sylvester Russell is now practising law and lives next door to me . . . .

I saw Judge Symmes in the beginning of the fall or latter end of summer when passing through this Town on his way to Detroit . . . .

As to news we have none worth communicating. Political parties and disputes run high and apprehensions have been entertained that we should be involved in war with France but I hope we shall avoid it by prudent measures. Insults are more easily pocketed than bloody noses, though neither of them are very desirable. Do you ever visit Judge Symmes and family? If you do, please to present my respects to Mrs. Symmes and Mrs. Harrison [Anna Symmes, wife of future U.S. President William Henry Harrison*], with whom I had some acquaintance in Jersey and Miami . . . .

With best wishes for your health and prosperity I remain Dear Sir your sincere friend and humble servant.

LEWIS CONDICT

*Two Morristown ladies were married to Presidents but neither lived in the White House. Mrs. Harrison delayed joining her husband until after his inauguration on March 4, 1841. However, he died April 4 before she could reach him. Caroline Carmichael, born in Morristown to Charles and Temperance Blachley Carmichael, married Millard Fillmore in 1858, five years after he left the presidency.

Courtesy of The Woman's Club of Morristown

Hon. Lewis Condict, M.D. (1772-1862)

He was a versatile man — doctor, politician, historian, founder and first president of the Morris County Medical Society and first president of the Morris and Essex Railroad. This is the only portrait known to exist, an undated daguerreotype.

The horsehead penny (right), which was minted by Walter Mould, 1786-1788, at Solitude. Dr. Condict's memorandum about the penny is on the opposite page (see box).

Congratulations for the new Dr. Hedges (opposite, far right), written by Dr. William A. Whelpley, who was for a time principal of the Morris Academy. Other signers were Dr. Condict; Dr. John B. Johnes, son of Dr. Timothy Johnes, who had taught Condict medicine — all of Morristown; and Dr. Jephthah B. Munn of Chatham. All were prominent men and the last three were also active in politics.

new British vaccine against smallpox to be sent free through the mail. There is a story that he vaccinated his own two-year-old daughter on the front steps of his house to prove its safety to the skeptical townfolks. He inoculated her with smallpox in one hand and vaccinated her against it in the other. The child showed no sign of the disease.

The good doctor had many other interests as the partial list of his awesome accomplishments reveals: charter member of the Morris Aqueduct (1799); sheriff of Morris County for the maximum three-year term (1801-04); member of the commission that settled the boundaries between New York and New Jersey (1804); assemblyman (1805-10 and 1837-38, and in the speaker's chair in 1808-09 and 1837-38), congressman (1811-17 and 1819-33) and Speaker of the House, two terms; president of the Medical Society of New Jersey (1816-19); county judge and justice of the peace (1818); trustee of the College of New Jersey, later Princeton (1827-61) — having received an honorary A.M. degree from the college in 1816; president of the first national convention of the decennial revision of the U.S. Pharmacopoeia in Washington, D.C., (1830 and 1840) and the society president for 20 years (1830-50); communicant member of the Presbyterian Church (1834); first president of the Morris and Essex Railroad (1835); chairman of the commission which led to the building of New Jersey's first insane asylum in Trenton (1843-45), and then a commissioner of the asylum; an original member of the New Jersey Historical Society (1845) and second vice president of the American Medical Association (1853).

Dr. Condict died at the age of 89, leaving his house to his daughter, Martina Louise Brandagee. Later Dr. Kinsley Twining, editor of the *New York Independent,* lived there making it a literary center in Morristown.

During World War I, the Morristown Chapter of the Red Cross took over the house and surgical dressings for military hospitals were made there. Later the Misses Mary and Grace Thomas of the Seth Thomas clock family purchased it from the Condict family and organized the Women's Community Club for working women of the post-war era. In World War II, the Red Cross again used it for making dressings, and it was the headquarters for Bundles for Britain.

In 1936, the Community Club disbanded and offered the building to The Woman's Club of Morristown for $1 and the assumption of a large mortgage. At various times, the house has provided office space for the Junior League, Girl Scout Council, Women's Republican Club, Visiting Nurses Association and the Social Planning Council. Many meetings, plays, festivals, weddings and so forth have taken place within its historic walls. □

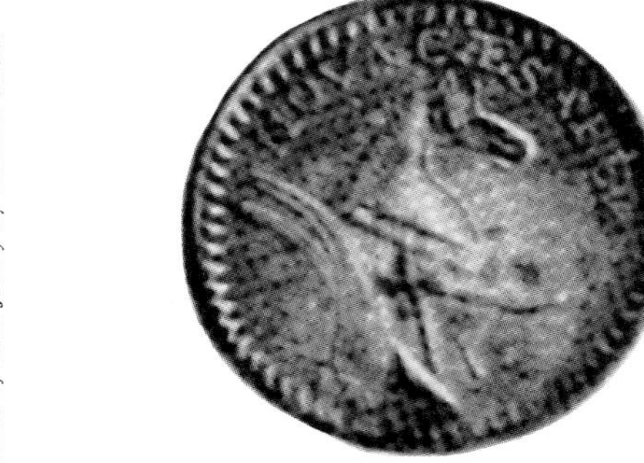

No Mint Then Existed

Memorandum from Hon. Lewis Condict, M.D., to the New Jersey Historical Society, January 17, 1856

An Englishmen, named Mould, in or about the year 1781, came to Morristown with his family, and occupied the premises called "Solitude," owned by John Cleves Symmes, Esq., who had just gone to take possession of a large purchase on the Ohio river, then called the Miami Country.

Mr. Mould had been an artisan in some of the shops in Birmingham, and had brought to this country the tools and implements of his trade.

Coin of any kind, was very scarce, and especially copper coin. No mint then existed in any of the States of the Union. The United States, under the articles of the confederation, could exercise no power over the currency, nor in any way supply the deficiency. Mould suggested to some of his neighbors, his knowledge of the process of coining, and his willingness to undertake it, if permission could be had.

Silas Condict, then and for some years previous, a member of the Legislative Council of the State, and the next door neighbor of Mould, was consulted by him, who advised to apply to the Legislative authority. He soon had his machinery in operation at Solitude, about two miles west of Morristown, on the Turnpike leading to Sussex Court House, where he sold his "Horseheads" as *merchandize*, to all who desired to purchase and issue on their own responsibility. They were, in weight and purity, about equal to the copper emission of Queen Anne, a few of which were then in circulation — the principal difference consisting in the substitution of a horse's head, for the head of her Majesty, a change not highly offensive in the nostrils of "rebellious" Colonists, so recently under the ban of her successors.

Mr. Condict subsequently added that he had been informed the manufacture of "Horseheads" was also carried on at Elizabeth-town, and, it was thought, by Mr. Robert Ogden, Jr. under the auspices of Colonel Matthias Ogden. But it was very certain that Mould's first enterprise was at Solitude, near Morristown.

Morristown, January 16th 1820.

We, the undersigned, as Censors of the District Medical Society, were concerned in the examination of Dr. Stephen Hedges, for his License and we have much pleasure, and much confidence in recommending him, as a physician to those among whom he may settle.

His examination was not merely satisfactory; it was interesting and gratifying to the Society in a very unusual degree. His medical reading appeared to have been extensive and discriminating; but what gave us uncommon pleasure were his judicious answers to an unusually wide range of Practical questions, into which his intelligence led the Members of the Society. In one word, we do but express the unanimous sentiment of the Society in saying he was one of the most accomplished Candidates, that has ever come before us.

Jephthah B. Munn
Wm. A. Whelpley
Lewis Condict. M. D.
John K. Johnes M.D.

TJFPLMMT

Curtiss Collection/TJFPLMMT

Photograph by Merrill Harvey

The 1786 Moses Estey House

The garden or rear view (above) is shown from Spring Street in May 1933. The Estey House and the early 19th-century L'Hommedieu-Gwinnup House (left) as they are about to be moved to Historic Speedwell, 333 Speedwell Avenue, Morristown, on December 9, 1969, where it is awaiting restoration.

Moses Estey

Moses Estey was one of the successful businessmen who moved to Morristown after the Revolution. Perhaps he heard about it from Alexander Hamilton. Certainly they knew each other during the war.

"Are you the son of Captain Estey?" Hamilton had asked young David, the oldest child. "I saved your father's life after the Battle of Monmouth, when I found him left for dead." In June 1778, when the battle took place, Moses Estey had been serving as captain with New Jersey troops in Hunterdon County.

About 1783, Moses and his second wife, Anna Kirkpatrick, moved to Morristown and they "renewed covenant" with the Presbyterian Church on December 18, 1783, when David was baptised. The other children — Elizabeth, Charles, William, Sarah, Hannah, Mary McEwen, Alfred, Edward Eugene and John — were all born in the big house at the corner of Spring and Water Streets. The house has a typical Georgian plan — similar to the Ford Mansion — a wide center hall with a boxed staircase at one side, four rooms on each floor, a high-ceilinged attic and a basement with dirt floor. There are large chimneys on the two end walls.

Like most successful merchant men of his day, Estey dealt in numerous wares. On November 5, 1782, he advertised the sale of leather britches, "a very neat assortment made in the newest fashion." Another time he offered "a fresh assortment of dry goods and groceries which will be disposed of on the most reasonable terms for cash, bar iron, flax seed, cider, spirits, and other kinds of country produce. He has for sale fine hair sieves." This last advertisement reminds us that barter was a common practice of the day, when money was generally scarce. He also made riding chairs and bought and sold land. According to the census report of 1786, he owned 11 acres of improved land, 30 acres in all, 2 horses, 2 cows and one riding chair.

On January 20, 1786, the 1770 house he had bought burned almost to the ground. As Joseph Lewis wrote in his diary: "About an hour before day this morning we were alarmed by the ringing of the bell & cry of fire. We ran & found Mr. Esty's house on fire, which broke out in the storeroom at the east end of the house. A considerable quantity of his furniture & goods were taken out of the west end of the house, but his shop goods and stock & trade were chiefly consumed & it is computed that his loss amounts to 1500 pounds; but this fire appeared more dreadful in the end because one of the chimnies fell on & killed George Phillips, the only son of Mr. Jonas Phillips and grandson of Jacob Ford, Esqr.; he was a young gentleman much respected & his death is much lamented. The chimney also fell on Jack, a negro belonging to Mr. Israel Campfield. He lived (tho much bruised) about four hours, then expired." Within a week, friends of Moses Estey had collected a subscription and the house was rebuilt within the year. Even the Town Committee offered to lend him money. It is not surprising to learn that Estey was a founder and member of the executive board of the first fire department.

He was also a district tax collector and a member of the Board of Proprietors of the Morris Academy, which his children David and Elizabeth attended.

The Estey children were bright and adventurous. Only Sarah, who married the prominent lawyer Lewis Mills, stayed in Morristown. David studied law with Judge Gabriel Ford, son of Jacob Ford, but before 1810 he moved to the new city of Cincinnati, where he married Lucy Anne Harrison, daughter of President William Henry Harrison (making him a relative of Anna Symmes), and became an Ohio supreme court judge. A younger sister and brother moved to Ohio also. Mary married an attorney and became chief matron of the Female Seminary of Cincinnati. Charles studied medicine and then became an army surgeon in the War of 1812. Elizabeth married and moved to Philadelphia, where John joined her. William, called "The Rover," served in the Napoleonic War with the French in Russia. Alfred resided in New York; Edward Eugene went with Hannah to Texas.

Hannah Estey deserves a special place in the history of American women. She married David G. Burnett, the first president of Texas when that territory broke away from Mexico in 1836 and declared itself an independent republic. Texas was not a peaceful place. During his first months as president, Hannah accompanied her husband on his trips around Texas, often cooking for her family in front of a tent and in constant danger of raids. They once narrowly escaped being captured by a band of Mexican soldiers, but when Burnett tried to send Hannah and his young family to relatives in the United States for safety, she stoutly refused; "No man should leave Texas at this juncture." Later, when a mob invaded their house, enraged by Burnett's refusal to assassinate the Mexican dictator, Santa Ana — she sat by an open window with a loaded pistol. Although she was only first lady of Texas for six months (Sam Houston replacing Burnett after a quarrel), her courage and steadfastness surely represent the pioneer women on the western frontier.

When Moses Estey left Morristown in 1829, the house passed to Lewis Mills, his son-in-law, but after some years went out of the family. On August 21, 1967, Mabel Heslin and Florence Leslie Meeker O'Brien sold it to the Town of Morristown to make way for the garage section of Headquarters Plaza. In 1969, the house was moved to Historic Speedwell. □

Congregation elected a committee of 3 persons to employ workmen, provide materials and superintend the building of a new meeting house: Moses Estey, Joseph Lewis, and Daniel Phoenix, Jr.
Minutes of the Presbyterian Church Session, December 11, 1789

Courtesy of Historic Speedwell

Moses Estey (1752-1836)

He was recalled as a very small but venerable-looking man often walking the streets of Morristown. Painter and date are unknown.

Curtiss Collection/TJFPLMMT

The Sansay House, Scene of Lafayette's Reception, July 14, 1825

This house at 17 DeHart Street, Morristown, was built in 1807 by the dancing master Monsieur Louis Sansay, an emigré from Santo Domingo, who had lost his fortune in the French Revolution. In the second-floor ballroom happy young people practiced the "feather step" and "spring step" and the minuet. Although much appreciated by a certain segment of the town, he ran afoul of several of the ministers — in particular, the Rev. Albert Barnes, who preached a fiery sermon against the sin of dancing. Discouraged and suffering a loss of business, he quietly slipped away one day to Elizabeth, where his fate is unknown. The house was later owned by Joseph Warren Revere, grandson of Paul Revere.

This undated photograph shows the house as it looked in the 1930s; it is now used for business offices.

Lafayette Returns

Early in the afternoon of Thursday, July 14, 1825, booming cannons announced Lafayette's arrival in Morristown to the huge crowd lining both sides of Morris Street and assembled on the Green.

Lafayette had left New York at 8:30 that morning by ferry to Hoboken and then traveled by carriage through Hackensack and Paterson to Whippany. He arrived on the Green accompanied by Governor Williamson, Colonel Ogden and William Halsey, a joint committee from Paterson and Morris County, a deputation from Morristown and a military escort of the Morris Cavalry which joined him at the county line.

Twenty-four of the foremost men of the town and township formed the committee of arrangements. General John Doughty was the chairman. Dr. Lewis Condict gave the welcoming address. Standing on a special "arch" erected in front of Mr. Ogden's house on the corner of the Green and Market Street, Lafayette gave his reply (box, following page).

In Monsieur Sansay's upstairs "long room," he enjoyed a sumptuous men-only dinner, for which tickets had cost three dollars. Later, while bells rang and rockets flared over the Green, he was introduced to the ladies at the Ogden house. There were more Morristownians to meet at the home of James Wood, on South Street at the corner of Pine Street, where he spent the night. On the following morning, he was off in his handsome carriage toward Philadelphia and Virginia. □

My Happy Visit

Lafayette's reply on the Green to speeches welcoming him to Morristown, July 14, 1825

Since the time when an honorable and affectionate invitation from the representatives of the people in congress, with congenial to my own feelings, has begun the series of inexpressible gratifications which I have had to enjoy at every progress of this, my happy visit to the United States, I did fondly anticipate the pleasure to recognize this interesting part of the country. Here, Sir, early in the war, has been completed a military movement, which alone would have sufficed to mark Washington's generalship on a very high rank. Here, sir, as you observe, security has been found against a superior enemy, and from here we have marched to check the devastations and cruelties to which you allude; nor can I refrain from emotions of reverence, affection, and regret when I see the tombs of many of my companions in arms, a sentiment in which the beloved survivors who surround us, heartily sympathetic with me.

I am highly honoured, Sir, by the testimonies of approbation, which in behalf of the citizens of Morristown and county you are pleased to give to my conduct in those trying times, and for my perseverance on another hemisphere in the principles and the feelings of American freedom — I beg them, and you accept a tribute of my affectionate and respectful gratitude.

This address, printed through the courtesy of The Woman's Club of Morristown, was sent by Lafayette to Lewis Condict in Philadelphia, where he was attending Congress. The copy was accompanied by the following interesting memorandum, although its meaning is not clear: "My Dear Sir, I hardly remember what I had the honor to tempore to answer your so very kind words, it seems to me however the few lines here enclosed are not far from my [indecipherable] on that day. Receive the best thanks and wishes of a sincere obliged friend. — Lafayette, Philadelphia, July 24th, 1825. Be pleased to forward the papers to Washington as they relate to my visit to you."

Morris Town, a name conspicuous in our Revolutionary War. May it ever be conspicuous in the enjoyment of the blessings which have been the object and result of our glorious contest.
General Lafayette to the people of the town, July 14, 1825

Courtesy of the City of New York

"Marquis de La Fayette"

Samuel Finley Breese Morse painted this portrait for the City of New York in 1824, shortly after Lafayette returned to the United States as the Nation's Guest.

"Farm Map of Morris Township, Morris County, N.J.," 1861/TJFPLMMT

The Cutler Homestead

This shows the house at 21 Cutler Street, Morristown, after it was transformed into rural Gothic style by Augustus Cutler for his bride, Julia Walker.

The house was doubled in size, a bay window and verandas were added and the front door was moved to the south, or street side. The house now had 14 rooms and nine fireplaces, with slave quarters over the kitchen. (Jenny Ader, one of the last slaves in Morris County, lived with the Cutlers until her death in 1892 at age 106.) Perhaps the most important change was the installation of a water system. This house may have been the first in the county to have basins with running water in every major bedroom. The system was based on a large spring house or reservoir on the hill in the neighborhood of the present Ralph Place, with a hydraulic ram system to keep the tank filled.

Three of Augustus and Julia's sons grew up at the Homestead — Willard, who followed in his father's footsteps as lawyer, county prosecutor and banker, and was also a judge of the Court of Common Pleas and later of the State Circuit Court of Appeals; Condict W., who practiced medicine in New York; and Frederick, a minister who was the last Cutler to live in the house.

It is unchanged in exterior appearance today and inside the original Dutch oven, fireplace and flooring can be seen. It is now owned by the Montessori Children's House of Morristown.

The Cutlers of the Homestead (opposite, clockwise from upper left): **Gen. Joseph Cutler** (1775-1854), builder of the original house for Silas Condict; **Elizabeth Phebe Cook Cutler** (1782-1846), his wife and Condict's granddaughter; and **Augustus W. Cutler** (1827-1897).

The Cutler Homestead

From 1799 through 1945, and perhaps much farther back into colonial times, the Condict and Cutler families have owned the land on which the Cutler Homestead is built.

Near the end of his life, the patriot Silas Condict decided to move from the house off Sussex Avenue, so well-known to the Council of Safety. In 1799, Joseph Cutler built him a Federal style farmhouse with the narrow end facing the street and the front door facing west. However, in 1801, Condict died and left the Homestead to his granddaughter, Elizabeth Phoebe Cook Cutler, who was married to Joseph.

Joseph Cutler was a man of great personal achievements also. In addition to being a successful farmer, he was president of the State Bank on the Green and one of nine directors of the Morris Turnpike Company, a toll road that ran from Elizabeth through Morristown to Newton. He was also a cavalry officer in the New Jersey state militia, rising to the rank of brigadier general.

Throughout the 19th century, the Homestead land was operated as a working farm. Near the kitchen door on the west side was a 60-foot well for water and an ice house filled every winter from nearby Speedwell Lake.

Joseph left the house to his youngest son, Augustus, his other sons having predeceased him. Augustus Cutler continued the family tradition of serving the county, state and nation. After graduating from the Morris Academy and Yale College, he studied law with former governor Haines and became a prominent lawyer. He was president of the Morristown Board of Education , county prosecutor (1856-61), state senator (1871-74), U.S. congressman (1875-79). In Congress, he introduced the first bill to create the Department of Agriculture. In New Jersey, he was the first public figure to call for integration of black children into the public school system and secured passage of the state's first civil rights bill. He also introduced the bill to make women eligible to be school trustees. He led the fight against the powerful railroads to control the state's riparian lands and to reserve the proceeds from their sale or rental for the public schools. While he lived, the Homestead was known as the unofficial headquarters of the Democratic Party in the state.

After Julia Cutler's death in 1908, the land around the house was deeded to the Cutler Land Company, which planned the residential area known as Cutler Park, whose streets are named after family members. □

Courtesy of Mr. and Mrs. Ralph H. Cutler, Jr.

TJFPLMMT

Speedwell Iron Works

Speedwell Iron Works about 1855 (above), corner of Speedwell Avenue and Corey Road, as painted by Edward Kranich. The triple-arched stone bridge over the Whippany River was built by Stephen Vail, owner of the Iron Works, and his men in 1848.

The building in the left foreground was the pattern shop, and the boxy white building across Speedwell Avenue was the office. Other buildings include a foundry, casting shop, blacksmith shop and sawmill. The houses on the right were rented to master craftsmen and machinists and their families, who were allowed to farm a small plot of land.

The Cutler Homestead began on the other side of the hill on the left. Sarah Davis Vail, Stephen's younger daughter and fourth child, married Dr. Silas C. Cutler, Gen. Cutler's oldest son.

Speedwell Bridge from Corey Road (opposite, above), similar view as the painting, and the **Iron Works from Speedwell Lake** (opposite, below).

J. Cummings Vail, grandson of Stephen and son of Alfred, commissioned a number of photographs of Speedwell after the Iron Works had closed in 1873, but, fortunately, before it burned in 1908.

The Vails of Speedwell

Perhaps no day at Speedwell has more historic significance than January 6, 1838, when Alfred Vail and Samuel F. B. Morse demonstrated the electromagnetic telegraph to Judge Stephen Vail on the upper floor of what is now called the Telegraph Factory. Stephen gave the secret message to Alfred who transmitted it over two miles of copper wire to Morse, thus proving the success of the machine that had been perfected at Speedwell. That message, "A patient waiter is no loser," must have had special meaning for Stephen, since he had been far from patient in the previous months when work had fallen behind schedule and he had harbored dark thoughts of canceling the project. But now the way was open for a triumphant public demonstration on January 11. An enthusiastic local paper, *The Jerseyman*, observed prophetically, "Time and distance are annihilated and the most distant points of the country are by its means brought into the nearest neighborhood." Sad to say, however, Alfred, who spent most of the rest of his life working on the telegraph, never received full public credit for his many brilliant contributions.

The Whippany River narrowed and deepened in its flow from Speedwell Lake into Pocohontas Lake, creating a natural source of water power that had been harnessed there since colonial days. Zachariah Fairchild operated a sawmill there in 1767 and John Johnson, Jr., had a forge "adjoining Zachariah Fairchild's pond" which appears on Revolutionary War maps.

In 1788, tavernkeeper Jacob Arnold and Sheriff Thomas Kinney took over the site and built a slitting mill there designed to roll iron into thin sheets to be cut into nails, hinges and barrel hoops and other essentials of farm life.

In 1793, James C. Canfield bought one-half interest in the mill from Thomas Kinney's estate. Two years later, Dr. Timothy Johnes, son of the Parson, bought the other half because Arnold had financial difficulties. In 1807, Stephen Vail, Dr. William Campfield and Isaac Canfield bought Johnes's half and began to operate the Speedwell Iron Works, but it failed after only two years. A determined Stephen would not accept defeat, however, and in 1815 became sole owner.

From then on, the ringing and thundering sounds of hammer blows, sizzling fireworks in the furnace, rumbling turns of the wheels, and the scent of burning cedar and pine were all a part of Speedwell Iron Works. It seemed there was nothing made of iron Stephen would not tackle, from the small machine parts to pumps and presses for large mills. Speedwell, whose business often came from out of state, made parts for the Baldwin Locomotive Works in Philadelphia and for places as far away as Brazil and Cuba. The commission that won the Iron Works national fame, however, was the building of the engine and other heavy machinery for the *S. S. Savannah*, the first steam-powered ship that crossed and recrossed the Atlantic in 1819, dealing a severe blow to British naval pride.

In 1830, George Vail became a partner — something Alfred had steadfastly refused to do — and in 1844, the firm became George Vail & Company, with his nephew, Isaac Augustus Canfield, and later stepbrother, John Lidgerwood, as partners. Stephen Vail still kept an eagle eye on things, for although George Vail lived across the street at Willow Hall, he was often away from the business. Like his father, George was a judge and deeply interested in Democratic politics. He served in the state legislature (1843-44), in Congress (1853-57) and as U.S. consul to Glasgow (1858-60).

TJFPLMMT

TJFPLMMT

Photograph by George Goodwin/TJFPLMMT

TJFPLMMT

In 1873, Speedwell Iron Works closed and George Vail died two years later. That year the machinery was sent to Scotland. This was probably because of William van Vleck Lidgerwood, who had represented Speedwell Iron Works first in Rio de Janeiro and then in London, where he imported machinery from Scotland and Morristown and sold it to coffee growers in Brazil. (This is the same man who joined with three others to buy the Ford Mansion and establish the Washington Association.) His brother, John, opened the Lidgerwood Manufacturing Company in Brooklyn but continued to live at the Vail House, preserving the site and Alfred's historic records.

Speedwell's days of glory were over. The sawmill was rented as a broom factory. In 1897, Robert D. Foote bought the property and rented it to the Morris County Traction Com-

The Telegraph Factory (left, above) where Alfred Vail and Samuel F. B. Morse perfected the electromagnetic telegraph. The first public demonstration took place here on January 11, 1838. In 1850, the grist mill at right was added, its huge wheel made at Speedwell Iron Works.

The Vail House (left, below) faced south, like the telegraph factory. Both had been bought by Stephen Vail in 1830 from his son-in-law, Dayton I. Canfield, husband of his oldest daughter, Harriet, who lived there with her four children until her untimely death in 1828. Sarah and Silas Cutler also lived there for a time. In 1841, Stephen and Bethiah moved in after extensive renovations, and both died there. Both buildings are at Historic Speedwell, 333 Speedwell Avenue, Morristown.

Our audience are astonished and delighted. See papers tomorrow.
Letter from Alfred Vail to his brother, George, after a demonstration of the telegraph in New York City, January 23, 1838

pany to store its machinery while the trolley line to Morristown was built.

In 1908, the buildings were destroyed by fire, leaving one factory wall standing in the present Speedwell. Fortunately, the Vail House, the telegraph factory, two carriage houses and a granary survived and are the nucleus of Historic Speedwell, a restoration open to the public. □

History of Morris County, N.J., 1739-1882, by W. W. Munsell & Co. /TJFPLMMT

Three photographs courtesy of Historic Speedwell

The Vails of Speedwell (clockwise from upper left): **Alfred Vail** (1807-1859) about the time of the telegraph demonstration; **Judge Stephen Vail** (1780-1864) at 81 with his month-old great-granddaughter Mary Vail Lidgerwood "taken August 21, 1861 at Davis Daguerreotype" in Morristown; **Bethiah Vail** (1778-1847), as painted by Samuel F. B. Morse in 1837, Stephen's beloved and pious first wife and mother of his four children; and **Hon. George Vail** (1809-1875), younger son, partner and eventual owner of the Iron Works.

Academy at Morris-Town, N. J.

JAMES D. JOHNSON,

PERMANENT SUPERINTENDENT.

In the classical department, the winter session commences the 1st Monday in November; the summer session the 1st Monday in May—each session continues 22 weeks. In the English Department, each session will commence a week earlier, and continue 23 weeks.

Quarterly Prices of Tuition.

Reading, Writing *and* English Grammar, *by rote, or any one of them*	\$2 50
The elementary rules *of* Arithmetic *and* Parsing, *or either of them*	\$3 00
Arithmetic -	\$4 00
Geography, *with* the use of the Globes, - - - - - - - - - - - - - - -	\$5 00
Greek, Latin, French, Rhetoric, Logic, Philosophy, Higher branches of Mathematics *and* Book-keeping, *or any one of them* - - - - - -	\$7 50

Scholars, studying any one of the above mentioned branches, will be entitled to instruction in all the inferior branches, without any additional charge.

All who enter the Classical Department, *will pay the same price, \$7 50 per Qr.*

BOARD, *with* WASHING *and* MENDING, *in respectable families, from \$2 50, to \$3 per week.*

Students may be boarded in the family of the Clergyman, *or in the family with the Teacher.*

October 5th., 1818.

TJFPLMMT

Important Firsts

Before the beginning of the 19th century, Morristown's enterprising citizens had formed several private organizations that added greatly to the town's reputation.

In 1791, a meeting was held "in order to establish and maintain a permanent school for the education of youth in the different branches of literature." There had been schools before, of course, since colonial times, but this was the first to offer a classical education for college entrance. The Morris Academy was organized November 28, 1791, by 24 gentlemen who each subscribed £25 for the purpose.

The first board of proprietors consisted of Jabez Campfield, president; Caleb Russell, first director; Gabriel H. Ford, second director; Nathan Ford, third director; Daniel Phoenix, Jr., treasurer; and Joseph Lewis, clerk. In February 1792, Mr. Campfield resigned and was succeeded by Caleb Russell, a lawyer, who was a graduate of Princeton in the class of 1770, which included Frederick Frelinghuysen. Dr. Johnes became first director. The place chosen was a "parsonage lot" on South Street "100 feet in front opposite Connor's land and 130 feet" deep for which the Trustees of the Presbyterian Church were paid £30. Caleb Russell gave his obligation for that sum and also contracted to build the academy for £520.

After the building was completed, Russell — although he was the county clerk and had a variety of other business to attend to — became principal and held that position until August 1797, when the Reverend Samuel Whelpley took charge until 1805.

On November 5, 1792, the school opened with 33 scholars; by January 1793, there were 67; and between opening day and April 1795,

Curtiss Collection/TJFPLMMT

The Morris Academy

This building was erected in 1792 in the vicinity of 52-56 South Street, Morristown. It was 60 feet long and the full cellar had a clearance of seven feet. For many years, plays were given during the fall vacation to raise money for the maintenance of the building. In 1869, the academy closed when the public Maple Avenue School began, but reopened in 1878 in the Library and Lyceum Building (page 236), which was built on the site. It remained open until the new building burned in 1914.

Prospectus of the Morris Academy (left), showing both a summer and winter session. The tuition was charged quarterly and provision was made for boarders. James D. Johnson resigned as principal in 1821, but it is not known when he began.

A Morris Academy Scholar's Week

Diary of Daniel Mulford, July 1804

Born September 17, 1781, graduated from Yale College in 1806, died October 26, 1811

1 Sunday — Read Pope's Homer. Went to Church afternoon. Aft. meeting read Homer again. Evening *Mariacum de re agenda loquebam.*

2 M. — Forenoon read Xenophon — 62 lines — Afternoon read Homer and evening rehearsed till 9 o'clock.

3 T. — Forenoon read 55 lines. Afternoon worked at a Map of Troy and the Grecian encampment, which is in the 2nd volume of Pope's Homer. Spent the evening in looking for clothes for the Exhibition.

4 W. — Spent the day at Mr. Sylvester Russell's — assisted Mrs. Russell and Eliza, in preparing my dress for the Exhibition. We began the play at 8 o'clock and ended at 12, before a very respectable audience.

5 T. — Worked at my Map, and committed to memory a historical prologue to our play, to speak tomorrow evening.

6 F. — Read 30 lines in Xenophon, and prepared for the play. Evening played — the Audience quite thin.

7 S. — Distributed my clothes which I had in the Play, went to Mr. Bull's and got my coat which he had mended — pay'd his bill amt'g. to £1-13-6 — paid it by a Credit at Canf'd. & Wood's Store. Ret. 2nd Volume of Pope's Homer and Bor'd. the 3rd. Borrowed the Tragedy of Cato, and read part of it. It is in contemplation to play this next Fall. Spent an hour at Mr. Esty's in the evening.

Daniel Mulford (1781-1811) moved to Morristown from "Turkey" (New Providence). From May 1801, he was a student and, as late as 1807, a teacher at the Morris Academy. He was a good friend of Moses Estey's children, David and Betsy, who were among the first students there. Mulford died of tuberculosis.

there was a total of 269, 196 boys and 73 girls. Another indication of the school's excellent reputation was the number of enrolled "strangers from New York, Philadelphia, Charleston, S.C., from Trenton, New Brunswick, Amboy, Pompton, Newton, Sussex County, and other places of lesser note in the State of New Jersey."

In 1792, the first library in Morris County was established. On September 21, 11 inhabitants of the county met at the house of Benjamin Freeman, at Morristown, and "advised and consulted" on the organization of "The Morris County Society for the Promotion of Agriculture and Domestic Manufactures." On October 1, 1792, the officers elected were Samuel Tuthill, president; Joseph Lewis, vice president; Dr. William Campfield, secretary; W. Canfield, librarian; Israel Canfield, treasurer. It was resolved that the society purchase three books and a stamp for marking them. "They then adjourned." The next meeting was April 1, 1795, when the bylaws were read and adopted, from which we learn that the librarian was to be at the library to deliver books "on all days, Sundays excepted, from 6 A.M. to 9 P.M.," and "that he shall collect all dues in specie." The society started with 96 volumes. At the end of the year the treasurer reported $35.47 on hand and 20 additional volumes in the library.

Things seem to have gone on well enough, but on February 3, 1812, the Morris Library Company was formed with Gabriel H. Ford as president and secretary. The old organization sold its library and transferred 123 names.

The first printing press and newspaper in Morristown were also the work of Caleb Russell. In 1797, he became owner and proprietor of a printing company and employed "Elijah Cooper, a practical printer to attend to its details." On May 24, 1797, the first number of the *Morris County Gazette* was issued by E. Cooper & Co. However, Cooper left in November and Mr. Russell continued alone. In the early part of 1798, he persuaded Jacob Mann — who had learned the printing business in Elizabethtown with Shepard Kollock, printer of New Jersey's first newspaper — to take charge. The *Gazette* was continued until May 15, 1798, when the name was changed to the *Genius of Liberty*. This paper was edited by Jacob Mann until May 14, 1801, when Russell gave the press and newspaper to his son, Henry P. Russell, who continued it for several years. The *Genius of Liberty* was succeeded by the *Morristown Herald*, which Russell edited and published from 1813 to 1820, when he moved to Savannah.

In 1808, Jacob Mann was again publishing in Morristown. This first issue of the new paper, called the *Palladium of Liberty*, came out on March 31 of that year. He continued to edit the *Palladium* until January 1832, when N. H. White succeeded him. White probably proved a failure, since Mann resumed charge of the paper in a few months and toward the close of the year made room for E. Cole and J. R. Eyers. Early in 1833, Cole retired, leaving Eyers sole editor and proprietor. On June 4, 1834, Eyers changed the name of the paper to the *Morris County Whig*.

The Jerseyman made its first appearance October 4, 1826, under the editorship of Samuel P. Hull. It continued as the leading Republican paper in the county until bought by the *Daily Record* in 1931.

No. 16

These Presents certify, that Gabriel H. Ford is a Proprietor of one Share of Eight Dollars, being No. Sixteen in the Morris Library Company; which Share is transferable only on the Company's Book of Transfers—and that in person or by lawful attorney....In witness whereof, the President of said Company, by their order, has hereunto affixed their common seal, and subscribed his name, this tenth day of April in the year of our Lord one thousand eight hundred and twelve

Gab H Ford, President.

Jabez Campfield Librarian.

The *True Democratic Banner,* established in 1838 by Louis C. Vogt, was the leading Democratic organ in the county and was published until 1945.

The first Fire Association of Morristown was organized July 26, 1797. Its officers were Samuel Tuthill, moderator; Joseph Lewis, clerk; and an executive committee including Alexander Carmichael, Caleb Russell, Colonel Benoni Hathaway, Moses Estey, Captain David Ford, and Dr. William Campfield. At the same meeting, according to Israel Russell, "all the streets and highways through the Town were given the names they now bear."

It is not known how efficient or long-lasting the first association was. However, they kept trying. A second company was formed. This note appeared in the *Palladium of Liberty* on August 16, 1815: "The Morris Fire Company will please recollect that their annual meeting is the first Monday in September; they will please to meet at N. Bull's [tavern] in the afternoon at 6 o'clock. It is hoped that there will be a general attendance of the inhabitants of the town, and that the committee appointed to

Share in the Morris Library Association (opposite, left), which merged with the 1792 Association for the Promotion of Agriculture and Domestic Manufactures in 1812. Both Gabriel Ford and Jabez Campfield had been active in the older organization.

The 1798 fire engine (opposite, right), called the "coffee mill" or "coffee grinder." The engine was filled with water emptied from buckets. The force pump provided with a leather hose supplied a continuous stream of water as men worked the handles.

Notices (right) in the *Genius of Liberty* that reveal local news in 1798.

Notice.

WHEREAS a certain *Writ of Attachment* hath iſſued out of the Inferior Court of Common Plea, in and for the County of Morris, to the ſheriff of the ſaid County of Morris directed, and returnable to July term, 1798, at the ſuit of John Yeomans, againſt the goods and chattels, rights, credits, and effects, Lands and tenements of Ralph Burnet, for *ſix hundred pounds.*—And whereas the ſaid ſheriff hath by virtue of ſaid writ, attached the defendant by a judgment in the Supreme Court of New-Jerſey, againſt Matthias Winans, and Martin Ryerſon, Executors of Joſiah Stagg, deceaſed, at the ſuit of the ſaid Ralph Burnet; alſo, a debt due on a note from Philip Farber, aſſigned by John Farber to the ſaid Ralph Burnet, for *eighteen pounds,* proc. dated 4th April, 1792, and payable on the 4th April, 1794.

Notice is therefore given, to the ſaid Ralph Burnet, that unleſs he appear and give ſpecial bail to the ſaid action and receive a declaration at the ſuit of the plaintiff, judgment will be entered againſt him by default, agreeably to the ſtatute in ſuch caſe made.

By order of the Court.

July 9, 1798. CALEB RUSSELL, *Clerk.*

Notice.

WHEREAS a certain *Writ of Attachment* hath iſſued out of the Inferior Court of Common Pleas, in and for the County of Morris, to the ſheriff of the ſaid County of Morris directed, and returnable to the term of July, 1798, at the ſuit of William Dixon, and Anthony Anderſon, againſt the goods and chattles, rights and credits, lands and tenements, of Reuben Chadwick, for *thirty pounds:* And whereas the ſaid ſheriff by virtue of ſaid writ, hath attached the defendant by all the debt due from Elias Bonnel to the ſaid defendant, the amount unknown, it being on an unſettled account.—

Notice is therefore given, to the ſaid Reuben Chadwick, that unleſs he appear, give ſpecial bail to the ſaid action, and receive a declaration therein at the ſuit of the plaintiffs, judgment will be entered againſt him by default agreeably to the ſtatute in ſuch caſe made and provided.

By order of the Court.

CALEB RUSSELL, *Clerk.*

July 9, 1798.

Notice.

WHEREAS a certain *Writ of Attachment,* hath iſſued out of the Inferior Court of Common Pleas in and for the County of Morris, to the Sheriff of the ſaid County of Morris directed, and returnable to the term of July, 1798, at the ſuit of Chriſtopher Gardner, againſt the goods and chattels, rights and credits, lands and tenements of Jacob Morriſon, for *twenty-ſix pounds.*—And whereas the ſaid ſheriff hath, by virtue of ſaid writ, attached the defendant by a horſe ſold by the ſaid defendant to Dan Hurd, for twenty-eight pounds, as is ſaid.

Notice is therefore given, to the ſaid Jacob Morriſon, that unleſs he appear, give ſpecial bail to the ſaid action, and receive a declaration therein at the

For Sale,

A QUANTITY OF

RED PERUVIAN BARK,

IN POWDER,

And warranted Genuine,

To be ſold cheap, for caſh, by the quantity or otherwiſe.—Apply to

LEWIS CONDICT.

Morris-Town, June 7, 1798. (3, tf.)

Good Paſture

TO BE HAD AT THE FARM

Late of ABRAHAM OGDEN, *Eſq. Deceaſed*

ENQUIRE OF

JAMES FORD,

On the Premiſes,

Hanover, May 8, 1798. (52, tf.)

A Negro Wench

FOR SALE, ſeventeen years old; ſhe is healthy and of a good diſpoſition, with a child 8 months old; ſold for want of employ, on reaſonable terms. Enquire of the Printer.

Morris-Town, July 4, 1798. (7, 3w.)

An Apprentice

WANTED, to the *Carpenter* and *Houſe-Joiner's* buſineſs; a Boy of 16 or 17 years of age. Enquire of the Printer.

Morris-Town, July 4, 1798. (7, 3w.)

For Sale,

A Healthy induſtrious Negro Wench, with a Young Child.—She is to be diſpoſed of on no other account, but for want of employ.—For further information enquire of the Printer.

Morris-Town, June 1, 1798. (3 tf.)

Wanted,

A few tons of firſt quality English

H A Y,

For which Caſh will be paid on delivery.—Apply to the Printer.

Advertiſement.

THE ſubſcriber begs leave to inform the public in Morris Town and its vicinity, that he ſpares no expenſe to render Hobuck Houſe and Ferry moſt commodious for the reception of the public, as he has the beſt boats upon the river, managed by excellent ſteady hands; his ſtables, hoſtlers and provender ſhall be equally pleaſing to them.

JOHN TOWN.

April 13, 1798. (48, tf.)

N. B. Mr. Elias Haines keeps the New York ſide for Hobuck.

Public Notice

IS hereby given, that the Subſcribers will attend at the late dwelling houſe of SAMUEL WILLS, Eſquire, deceaſed, on every Thurſday in the months of July and Auguſt next, for the purpoſe of adjuſting the accounts of the Eſtate.—Thoſe who are

THIS INDENTURE, *made this* Fifteenth day of April in the year of our Lord one thousand eight hundred and Fifteen Between the Proprietors of the *Morris Aqueduct*, of one part, and Daniel Phoenix of the other part, Witnesseth, That the said Company have demised and let, and do hereby demise and let, unto Daniel Phoenix one share of water in the Morris Aqueduct ; to have and to hold the same, unto the said Daniel Phoenix from the date hereof, for one year and no longer ; in consideration of Ten dollars, for the same :—And the said Proprietors promise to open the said share of water, for the said D Phoenix within two days from the date hereof, at such place on the Premises, and near or in the Dwelling-House of the said D Phoenix as the Proprietors deem convenient to him, and safe for them ; but as, by reason of risks, accidents, and unknown remediless causes, the Proprietors themselves are sometimes destitute of water from their shares, they do not warrant a constant supply for the aforesaid rent ; and, therefore, no abatement, or apportionment of rent, or claim of damages, shall be made by the said D Phoenix for any deficiency of water, at the said share, during the said term, unless the times of such deficiency, if taken all together, shall amount to one quarter of a year ; in which

In witness whereof, the President of the Proprietors of the Morris Aqueduct, by their order, hath hereunto set the Seal of the said Proprietors, and subscribed his name ; and the said D Phoenix hath set his Hand and Seal the day and year first above written.

SEALED, AND DELIVERED IN THE PRESENCE OF— } Israel Canfield Prest

TJFPL.MMT

Renewal of a one-year contract from the Morris Aqueduct. Both Daniel Phoenix, Jr., and Israel Canfield were original proprietors.

procure ladders, hooks, &c., &c., will be able to make a full report."

Still another fire company was formed at Speedwell in 1826 that lasted at least through 1828, but its history after that is not known.

It may seem strange that a town so full of inflammable wooden buildings and barns could not keep a permanent fire department, but this was often the case in early 19th-century America. However, in 1836, when still another company was organized, it purchased a hand engine for $250. A year later a second company was formed and bought an engine. On February 27, 1837, an act was passed incorporating the Morristown Fire Association with power to raise taxes to meet annual expenses. It took charge also of the two engines. This association lasted until the present Morristown Fire Department was organized, August 7, 1867. This fire department, it should be noted, served all the township also until the Pruddentown Fire Department (later Mount Kemble Fire Company) was organized in 1907.

On November 16, 1799, a charter of incorporation was granted to the "Proprietors of the Morris Aqueduct" for conveying water through the town from a spring on Mount Kemble. It was commenced on February 21, 1790, and completed in November. Its officers were John Doughty, president; Caleb Russell, Aaron Pierson, William Campfield, directors.

An editorial in the *Genius of Liberty*, November 21, 1799, reported: "An aqueduct, four miles in length including its various branches, has been laid and completed in this town since the 20th of June last. The fountain is 100 feet above the town, on the north side of a small mountain covered with wood [on Western Avenue about one mile away]. The pipe has been laid 3 feet under ground, at an expense of between $2,000 & $3,000. The work was executed by Pelatiah Ashley, of West Springfield, Mass."

The water was conducted into town through brick tile. However, after a few years, the system went dry and the town was again dependent on wells. James Wood then purchased the chartered right, repaired the aqueduct by laying chestnut logs with two-inch holes to replace the brick, and built a small distributing reservoir on Western Avenue, a wooden cistern capable of holding 100 barrels.

In 1848, John F. Voorhees became the proprietor of the aqueduct, relaid it with cement pipe and built a new 18-foot-square reservoir behind the Morris County Court House.

In 1869, new proprietors — Henry C. Pitney, president — enlarged the aqueduct again and ran it successfully until it was bought by the Town of Morristown in 1923.

While men organized companies and societies beneficial to the town and township, some wives were showing concern for the truly unfortunate.

The Overseer of the Poor, an office existing since colonial times, had the right to farm out paupers to the highest bidder for what was often an existence worse than slavery, since slaves were considered valuable property, while indentured workers were merely temporary assets. The fate of the weak and feeble and mothers with small children might be the Poor House, where conditions resembled a jail.

The Female Charitable Society of Morristown was organized August 13, 1813, to aid families with food, fuel or clothing. Mrs. Samuel Fisher, wife of the Presbyterian church minister, was the first directress; Mrs. Israel Canfield, second directress; Mrs. Arden, treasurer; and Mrs. A. M. Smith, secretary. Eventually, this society evolved into the Family Service of Morris County. □

The Morristown Ghost, 1876 facsimile copy of the 1792 edition. Based on actual events in 1788-89, this bestseller told how Connecticut schoolmaster Ransford Rogers — who professed a "deep knowledge of Chymistry" and powers to dispel guardian spirits — persuaded some prominent citizens, including Col. Benoni Hathaway, to search for buried Tory gold and were instead relieved of their own. Eventually, Rogers was discovered and lodged in the Morris County jail. He later escaped with his money, and some people believe he wrote this book in retaliation for his treatment. Others believe the author was Shepard Kollock, publisher of the state's first newspaper, *New Jersey Journal*, who recognized a good story when he heard one.

The story was printed five times and made into a play to the delight of future generations who believe such goings-on would not have fooled them!

The Morris-Town Ghoft

DELINEATED.

A DIABOLICAL intrigue invaded the county of *Morris*, in the ftate of *New Jersey*, in the year 1788. This unequalled performance, has taken vent and is promulgated throughout the continent, and deferves the attention of every perfon. But before I proceed any further, I think it requifite to advert a few minutes to the general character of that place.

It is very confpicuous that many of the people in that county, are much attached to machinations, and will fpend much time in inveftigating curiofities. I don't fay whether fuch a turn of mind is to be imputed to indigence or owing to the operation of the climate: this I fubmit to the candor of every perfon to determine within himself——it is obvious to all who are acquainted with the county of Morris, that the phenomena and capricious notions of witchcraft, has engaged the attention of many of its inhabitants for a number of years, and the exiftence of witches is adopted by the generality of the people.

I was once in Morriftown, and happened to be in converfation with fome gentlemen, who had, as it were, the faith of affurance in witchcraft. They informed me that there were feveral young women who were bewitched; and they had been harrafed fo much by witches for a long time, and all their experiments proved abortive, and the young women were fo much debilitated they were fearful they would never recover

TJFPLMMT

New Morris County Court House

Within a block of the old courthouse, a new one was built in 1826-27 on land bought from James Wood for $100. Not everyone thought the move was necessary — "Went to town this evening to see Judge [Henry A.] Ford about beginning building of a Court Hous in the town by raising a sum of 2500 dollars for the purpos by private donations," wrote Judge Stephen Vail on August 24, 1825. "The Town has manny mean Spirits in it that will not contrebut one cent." However, the "mean spirits" did not prevail and the Judge not only served in the new courthouse two years later, but his Speedwell Iron Works built the iron fencing around the building and put up the steps.

On September 26, 1827, Judge Ford was the principal speaker at the dedication ceremonies which followed a procession from the Green in this order: "1, music; 2, Sheriff; 3, Board of Chosen Freeholders; 4, Building Committee; 5, Master Builders; 6, Clergy and Orator; 7, Gaoler and Crier; 8, Constables; 9, Coroners; 10, Justices of the Supreme Court; 11, Judges of the Common Pleas; 12, Justices of the Peace; 13, Clerk and Surrogate; 14, Attorney General and Prosecutor; 15, Members

The 1830 jail limits, extended in 1843, showing the location of the new court house. Within these limits, prisoners not considered dangerous — principally debtors — could walk freely during the day. Though not intended for the purpose, the map records the town's growth since 1819 (pages 70-71). Most striking is the number of new buildings on the Green, down South Street and on Bridge Street (Speedwell Avenue). Note the James Wood House on South Street not on the earlier map, the new Episcopal and Methodist churches and the Cutler and Vail properties, and two new turnpikes through the town.

Pilch Collection/TJFPLMMT

of the Bar; 16, Grand Jury; 17, Petit Jury; 18, County Collector and Assessors; 19, Citizens.

"Order of dedication: 1, open with prayer; 2, address; 3, prayer; 4, opening of the courts in due form of law; 5, calling and swearing the grand jury; 6, charge to the grand jury; 7, adjournment of court to the next day."

This building was 74½ feet long and 44½ feet wide and originally contained on the first floor the Clerk's, Surrogate's and Sheriff's offices, a fireproof room for records, a parlor and five rooms for debtors and criminals. In one end of the second story, the courtroom [the present Number One, east side], 42 feet square and 17½ feet high, was located. The opposite end of the building from the courtroom was divided into two stories, with rooms for the deliberations of the Grand Jury and Petit Jurors and family apartments. In the basement story or cellar were three cells, with family apartments and a furnace for heating the prisons. The final cost, according to the *Palladium of Liberty*, was $20,000.

Inside the belfry with its gold-leafed cupola, the bell announced the start of court. For a time, it also tolled the fires. This bell announced the town's most celebrated trial of the 19th century.

On the night of May 11, 1833, Antoine Le Blanc, a French immigrant, murdered his employers, Samuel and Sally Sayre, and their black servant girl, Phoebe. Employed only for two weeks, Le Blanc left the bodies of the husband and wife in a dung heap at the back of their house and bashed in Phoebe's head as she lay in her attic room. Feeling ran so high, wrote Judge Vail, that "to hear the summing up there will be three times as many persons as able to get in the Court Room," and on the day of the hanging he estimated "4 or 5 thousand people" passed by his home at Speedwell. The size of this mob persuaded officials there should be no more hangings on the Green. □

"Map of Morristown, Morris County, N.J.," 1850, by Marcus Smith/TJFPLMMT

The Morris County Court House of 1827

This is the central building of the present court house complex on Washington Street between Court Street and Western Avenue, Morristown. Designed and built by Joseph M. Lindsley of Morristown and Lewis Carter of Chatham, it is generally considered one of the finest buildings of that period in New Jersey. This red brick building was originally painted gray-white with brownstone trim, as it appears in this early sketch.

Over the front door is the wooden Statue of Justice, which is unusual because, unlike most of her counterparts, she is not blindfolded.

TJFPLMMT

The Sayre House (above), 217 South Street, Morristown, where the three murders took place. The house is shown after it was converted into the Turnpike Inn.

The Sayres' house was the two-and-a-half-story part on the right. The stables and a garden were in the back. Samuel Sayre also kept cows and oxen and had rye and potato fields on the property.

Antoine Le Blanc (right), a likeness from the cover of "The Report of the Trial and Conviction of Antoine Le Blanc for the murder of the Sayre Family," an 1833 pamphlet prepared by Samuel P. Hill, editor of *The Jerseyman.*

A second publication about the murders was printed in Morristown by Jacob Mann (see box).

The Town's Most Famous Murders

Testimony of Collin Robertson from the *Trial, Sentence and Confession of Antoine Le Blanc, Who Was Executed at Morristown, N.J. on Friday the 6th Sept. 1833 for the Murder of Mr. Sayre and Family**

The deponent lives in South street, about one quarter of a mile from Mr. Sayre's house nearest the green. On Sunday morning, the 12th of May last, immediately after he arose, about half past 6 o'clock, he was informed that something unusual had occured in the front of Mr. [William A.?] Halsey's house that goods had been found in the highway, having on them the names of Mr. Sayre and those of the members of his family; that upon this intelligence he went out but found that the people had dispersed and the articles were removed; that he thereupon proposed to Mr. Halsey to accompany him to the house of Mr. Sayre, and apprize him of the probable robbery that had been committed about his premises. That Mr. H. and himself had proceeded for that purpose, when their attention was attracted by the barn door of Mr. S. being wide open, his cattle near the door, and every thing around in confusion, thought this a very unusual occurrence with Mr. S. and proceeded on into the gate leading to the stable yard . . . .

[He] observed the horse of Mr. Sayre in a lot opposite the stable yard grazing with a rope around his neck, the large gate leading from the stable to the lot where the horse was, being open, passed on to the stable to see if the mare was there, found

*Samuel and Sarah Sayre were found murdered with a club and hatchet and buried in the manure heap by the stable door shortly after Phebe, their servant and probably slave, was found in the house. Le Blanc was arrested fleeing to New York City on May 12, 1833, at the Mosquito Tavern in the Hackensack Meadows. He was tried in the new Morris County Court House and the jury took only about ten minutes to reach a guilty verdict. Le Blanc admitted to the robbery but did not confess to the murders until after he was sentenced. On September 6, 1833, he was hung on the Green. "No less than twelve thousand persons were present, of which the majority were females" was printed on the cover of the pamphlet quoted above. The now repentent prisoner's last words, spoken in French, were translated: "O ye rising generation and gazing multitude take warning by me." There is a curious ending to this story. Le Blanc's skin was removed from his skeleton and made into wallets, pouches and other assorted souvenirs still in the possession of some Morristown families.

the stable door open and the mare gone, looked around for the saddle and bridle and ascertained them to be gone also. Upon this he supposed that the beast was stolen and the house robbed . . . .

Witness then thought it time to go to the house; in going towards the house, observed in the lane leading thereto, about half way to and commencing with the street, a number of articles of wearing apparrel lying upon the ground, also a paper of tobacco, a brush with a looking glass upon the back and a silk handkerchief, he picked up and placed upon the fence the coat which the prisoner wore in court, he also found a small hatchet and a dark mixed roundabout lying on a shaving horse in the stable yard, under a shed about 12 feet from the stable door; that he saw under this shed a barrel of plaster of Paris lying on its side, and part of its contents appeared to have been spilled or strewed along towards the manure heap in front of stable door.

[Eventually Colin Robertson and Jacob Wilson entered the house by the unlocked back door.] Mr. W. took a dung fork and entered with witness into the kitchen. [They then looked into the entry hall, upstairs hall and the three rooms each on the first and second floors.]

The first room they entered in [the second] story was the back room over the kitchen; in this room there was a bureau broken open, the contents of which lay in the entry; the entry appeared to be the place where the selections of the plunder appeared to have been made, and apparently the place of general deposit; a set of silver spoons were found there. Witness and Wilson then went towards the garret door, merely looking into the front room, where every thing was in confusion; they then proceeded up in the garret. As witness arrived on the chamber door, he discovered the feet of the black girl projecting from the bottom of the bed clothes; there was a large buffaloe skin over the bed, which he pulled down and saw the murdered body of Phebe the colored girl; her face had been covered with the skin; there was a large quantity of blood and froth around her mouth and nose; saw large gashes made in the forehead apparently with an instrument similar to a pitchfork, could not say if the side of her head was bruised. Concluding from appearances that all the family had been murdered, thought it best to go to town and make an alarm . . . .

S. P. HULL'S
REPORT OF THE
TRIAL AND CONVICTION
OF
ANTOINE LE BLANC,
FOR THE
MURDER
OF THE
SAYRE FAMILY,
AT MORRISTOWN, N. J.
ON THE NIGHT OF THE ELEVENTH OF MAY, 1833.

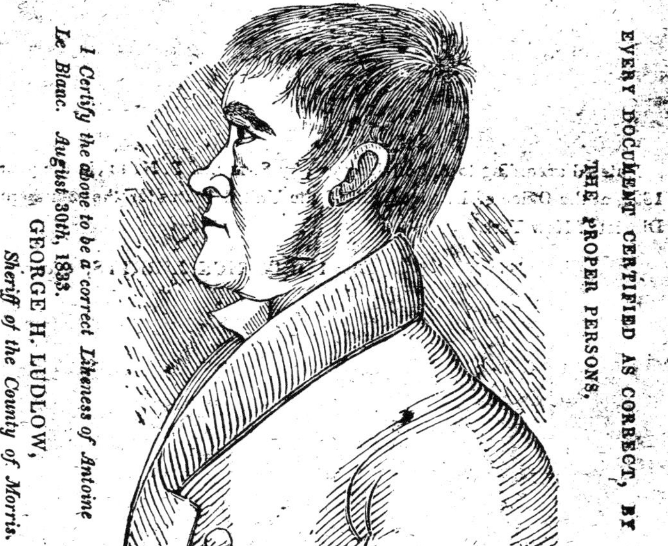

I Certify the above to be a correct Likeness of Antoine Le Blanc. August 30th, 1833.
GEORGE H. LUDLOW,
Sheriff of the County of Morris.

EVERY DOCUMENT CERTIFIED AS CORRECT, BY THE PROPER PERSONS.

WITH HIS
CONFESSION,
AS GIVEN TO MR. A. BOISAUBIN, THE INTERPRETER.

LEWIS NICHOLS, *Printer*,
Corner of Pearl and Beekman streets, New York.

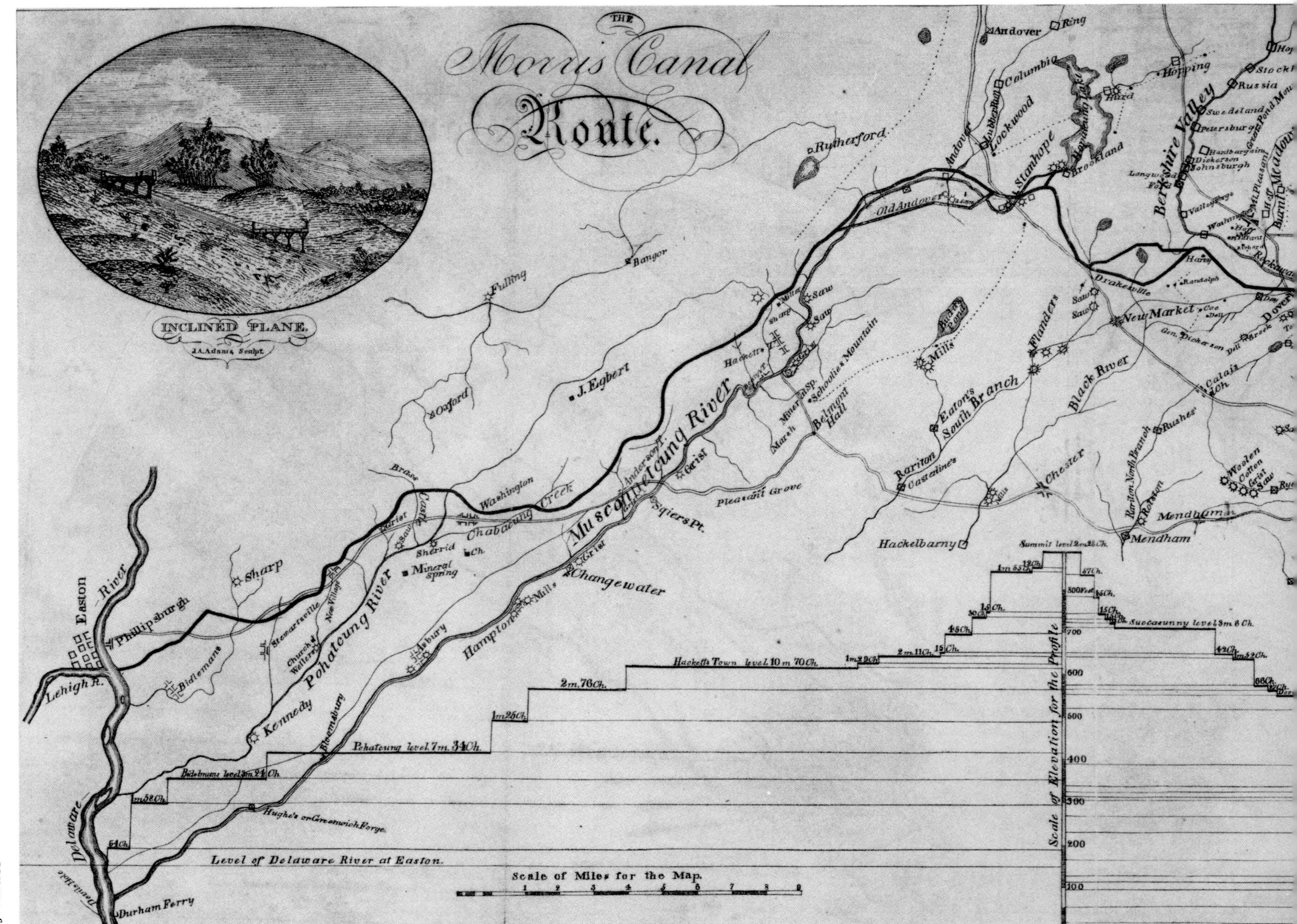
THE
Morris Canal
Route.
INCLINED PLANE.
J. A. Adams, Sculpt.
Andover
Ring
Columbia
Lockwood
Rutherford
Old Andover
Stanhope
Brookland
Hopping
Russia
Swedeland
Petersburgh
Dickerson
Johnsburgh
Berkshire Valley
Bangor
Fulling
Saw
Drakesville
Randolph
New Market
Dover
Mills
Flanders
South Branch
Black River
Eatons
Schoolie's Mountain
Mineral Sp.
Belmont Hall
Hacketts
J. Egbert
Oxford
Musconetcung River
Anderson
Grist
Pleasant Grove
Rariton
Castaline's
Chester
Calais
Rushes
Rariton North Branch
Mendham
Woolen
Cotton
Grist
Saw
Brass
Washington
Washington Creek
Chabaung
Sherrid
Mineral Spring
Sqiers Pt.
Hackelbarny
Changewater
Sharp
Easton
River
Phillipsburgh
Stewartsville
New Village
Church
Wellers
Pohatcung River
Hampton
Mills
Asbury
Bidlemans
Lehigh R.
Kennedy
Bloomsbury
Delaware
Hughe's or Greenwich Forge.
Durham Ferry
Summit level 2 m. 28 Ch.
Succasunny level 3 m. 6 Ch.
Hacketts Town level 10 m. 70 Ch.
2 m. 76 Ch.
1 m. 25 Ch.
Pohatcung level 7 m. 34 Ch.
Bidlemans level 3 m. 44 Ch.
64 Ch.
Level of Delaware River at Easton.
Scale of Miles for the Map.
1 2 3 4 5 6 7 8 9
Scale of Elevation for the Profile
700
600
500
400
300
200
100

TJFPLMMT

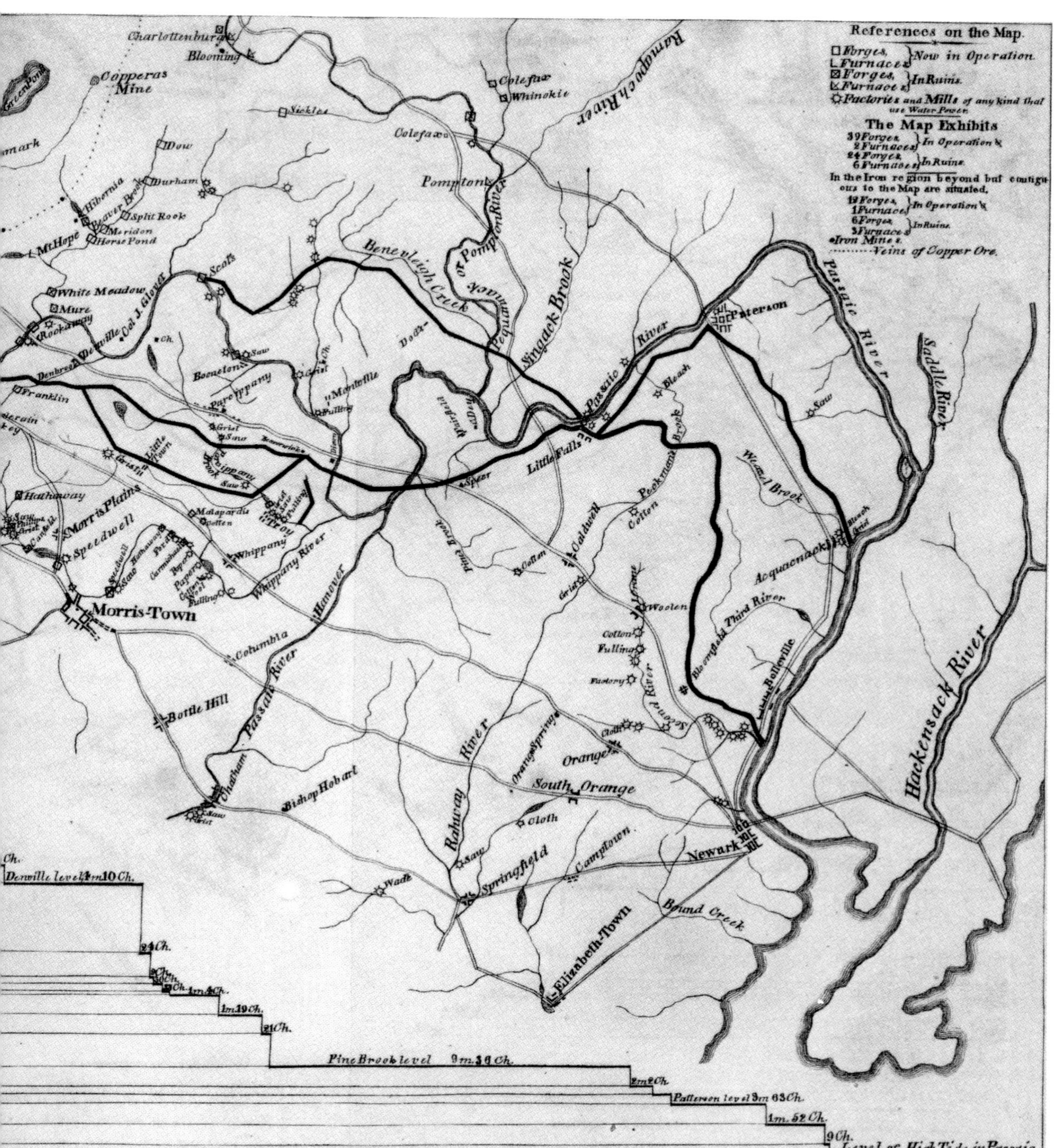

The Morris Canal, 1824-1924

This idea for the Morris Canal — an up-and-down marvel of 34 locks and 23 inclined planes — first came to George P. Macculloch on a fishing trip at Lake Hopatcong. The lake was 925 feet above sea level and then covered five square miles. If the lake's outlet were dammed and the water allowed to accumulate each winter, then in spring there would be plenty of water to release westward down the valley of the Musconetcong to the Delaware and eastward down the valleys of the Rockaway and Passaic Rivers to Newark. The canal could bring coal from Pennsylvania and provide an economical way to transport raw materials and finished goods in northern New Jersey. Macculloch interested the state in his project and, in November 1822, was appointed one of three commissioners to explore a practical route.

On December 31, 1824, an act was passed incorporating the Morris Canal and Banking Company.

The first trip from Newark to Phillipsburg was completed on November 4, 1831, and took about five days. Its most prosperous decade was 1860 to 1870, after which it began to suffer strong competition from the railroad. However, it was not abandoned until 1924 and several small sections are still visible. □

Possible routes for the Morris Canal, which accompanied the *Report of the Commissioners Appointed by the Legislature of the State of New Jersey, for the Purpose of Exploring the Route of a Canal to Unite River Delaware near Easton with the Passaic, near Newark, 1823.* The principal interest of this map today is the location of the forges, furnaces, factories and mills. The actual route of the canal was altered considerably east of Dover. Its final route went through Denville, Boonton and Montville to Little Falls; then from Paterson directly south to Bloomfield, East Orange, Newark and then Jersey City.

A MAP OF THE MORRIS AND ESSEX RAIL ROAD

Surveyed under the direction of

EPH^M. BEACH. ESQ. CIVIL ENGINEER

BY J. S. GREEN 1835

Littleton
Morris plains
Whippany
Monroe
Whippany River
MORRIS TOWN
Hanover
Columbia
Livingston
Bellville
Bloomfield
MORRIS CANAL
PASSAIC RIVER
Northfield
Spring Village
Passaic River
Orange
Madison
New Vernon
Union Hill
Green Village
Chatham
S. Orange
Jefferson Village
Millville
Camptown
Middleville
New Providence
Vauxhall
NEWARK
New Jersey Rail Road
Great Brook
Black Brook
Passaick River
Proposed Course of the Morris and Essex Rail Road
Springfield
Rahway River
Connecticut Farms
Elizabethtown River
New Jersey Rail Road
Westfield
Scotch plains
Elizabethtown
Elizabethtown Point
NEWARK BAY

Lith^d by W. Norris 1 Nassau St. N.Y.

The First Train

On January 1, 1838, the first train came to Morristown pulled by little "Orange," an engine painted that color.

In April, it was supplemented with the engine "Essex," making daily service possible in both directions.

Trains left Morristown at 6:30 in the morning and 1:30 in the afternoon, returning from Newark at 10 A.M. and 5 P.M.

The original route into town paralleled the Morris Turnpike (Route 124) in the Convent Station area of Morris Township. It crossed the road just above the Punchbowl about where the present Normandy Parkway joins Madison Avenue — what oldtimers call Sneeden's Crossing, the old path across John Sneeden's land. Then it paralleled the present Madison Avenue in Morristown, crossed over South Street about where Route 287 passes under it and ran down Maple Avenue to the station. □

We are at last safely housed in Morristown. The ride up by the railway was pleasant, we had a fine day. We had no difficulty with the baggage, they put nearly all of it in an apartment **under** *the car and none on top. We had a* **whole seat** *to ourselves. The car goes and returns three times each day except Sundays. You can be in town at 9 o'clock and stay until 5 in the evening and be here by dusk, we were precisely 3 hours from New York. They do not travel very swiftly, but just enough to view the country with pleasure. I think you will like it very much.*

Mrs. Colles, Morristown, to James Colles, New Orleans, June 10, 1838

TJFPLMMT

Proposed train routes (opposite) on *A Map of the Morris and Essex Rail Road, Surveyed Under the Direction of Ephraim Beach, Esq., Civil Engineer, By J. B. Green, 1835.* Ephraim Beach was also the chief engineer for the Morris Canal.

First railroad station (right), according to tradition in the Pitney family. It was at Maple Avenue and DeHart Street, from 1838 to 1848, on land donated by Lewis Condict.

TJFPLMMT

Early Developers

In 1837 a glowing prospectus raved about 45 parcels of land put up for sale on "South-Street, on which many of these lots front is the most elegant and improved street in the town: The lots are upon a beautiful level, and are the most desirable in the place, being immediately adjoined by some of the most valuable and highly improved property in the town. This property would have long since been built upon, could it have been procured in single lots." Somewhat coyly, the brochure noted that some of "the heaviest merchants of New-York have their residences in Morristown." Other attractions cited the railroad in the immediate vicinity, a forthcoming luxury hotel (page 107), the abundance of water power for businesses and the unusual healthiness of the climate. For "those unacquainted with Morristown" an endorsement was included from "gentlemen of the highest character." These were "Lewis Condict, late Member of Congress; James Cook, Member of Legislature; James James [whose land it had been]; and R. K. Tuttle, Surveyor and Assessor."

What is mysterious is the project's lack of success. The proposed James, Warren and Garden Streets were never put through. Franklin Street developed slowly. The present James Street is the old colonial road to New Vernon. No doubt the Panic of 1837 and the succeeding depression were factors. Perhaps such a large residential development was an idea before its time; none was proposed again until late in the century. □

Drawing and map, accompanying the prospectus, *For Sale, Forty-Five Parcels of Land, situated at Morristown, N.J., 1837.*

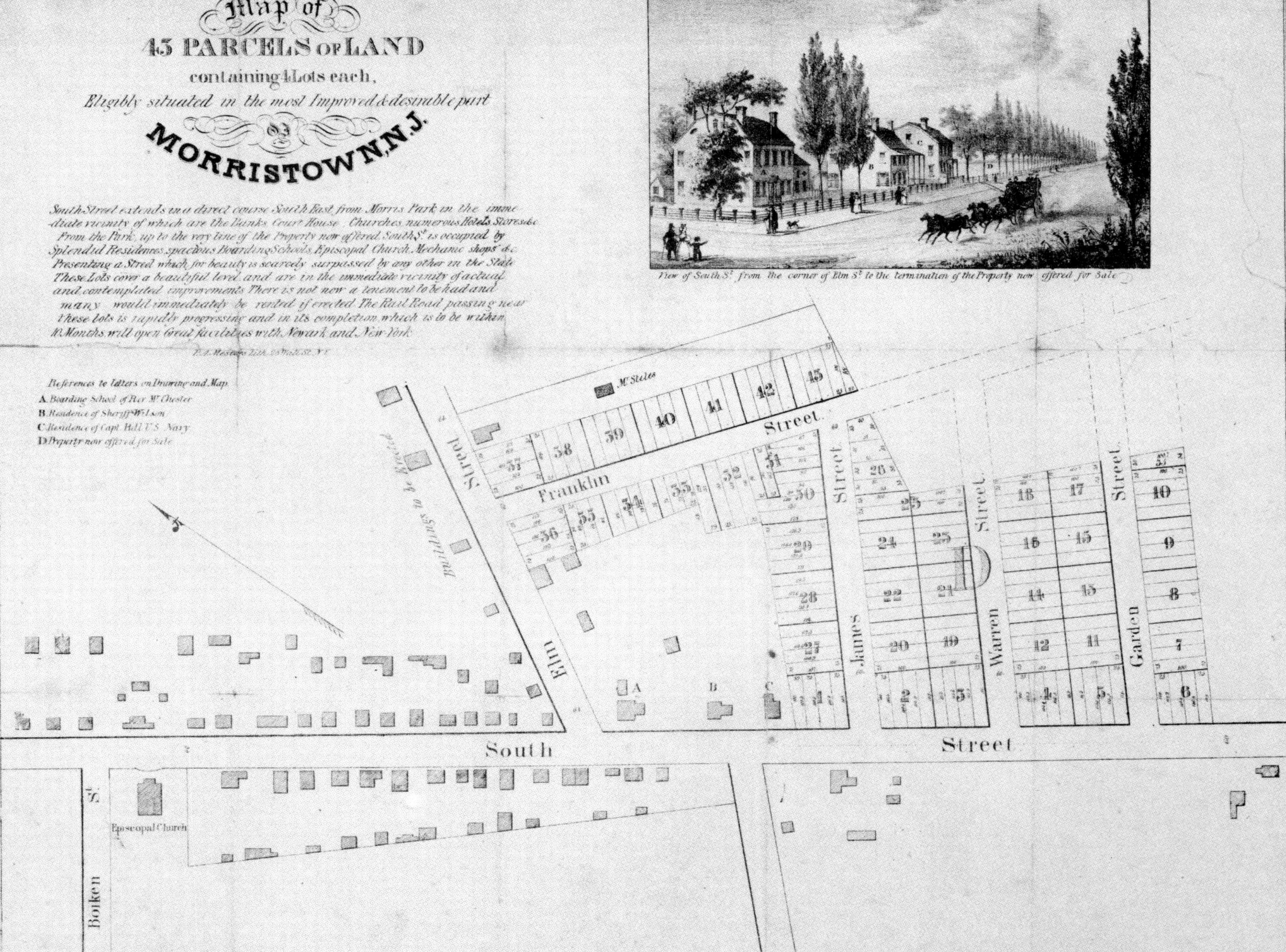
Map of
43 PARCELS OF LAND
containing 4 Lots each,
Eligibly situated in the most Improved & desirable part
of
MORRISTOWN, N.J.
South Street extends in a direct course South East from Morris Park in the imme-
-diate vicinity of which are the Banks Court House Churches numerous Hotels Stores &c
From the Park, up to the very line of the Property now offered, South St. is occupied by
Splendid Residences spacious Boarding Schools, Episcopal Church Mechanic shops &c
Presenting a Street which for beauty is scarcely surpassed by any other in the State
These Lots cover a beautiful level and are in the immediate vicinity of actual
and contemplated improvements There is not now a tenement to be had and
many would immediately be rented if erected The Rail Road passing near
these lots is rapidly progressing and in its completion which is to be within
10 Months will open Great facilities with Newark and New York
View of South St. from the corner of Elm St. to the termination of the Property now offered for Sale
References to letters on Drawing and Map
A. Boarding School of Rev. Mr. Chester
B. Residence of Sheriff Wilson
C. Residence of Capt. Hill U.S. Navy
D. Property now offered for Sale
Mr. Stiles
Franklin
Street
Elm
James
Warren
Garden
South
Street
Buildings to be Erected
Episcopal Church
Boiken
St.
A
B
C
1
2
3
4
5
6
7
8
9
10
11
12
13
14
15
16
17
18
19
20
21
22
23
24
25
26
27
28
29
30
31
32
33
34
35
36
37
38
39
40
41
42
43

TJFPLMMT

Historical Collections of the State of New Jersey by John Warner Barber and Henry Howe, 1844

Early Elegance

Morristown had never seen anything like it. Certain unnamed "gentlemen of New York" persuaded William Gibbons of Madison — whose handsome home is now Mead Hall at Drew University — to erect on the Morristown Green one of the most spacious and splendid hotels in the state.

About 1837, he bought a large property for $16,000 on West Park Place at the corner of Market Street (the present site of M. Epstein) extending back to Maple Avenue. From 1842 to 1844, he watched closely as the hotel costing $200,000 was erected. Huge carved mirrors, gilded furniture and velvet carpets were imported from Paris. There was a fireplace in every guest room and a servant to tend it. From its opening with a Grand Ball in 1844, people flocked to see it and came away full of praise.

However, on May 6, 1846, a tragic fire that began next door at Drake's Hotel (the old O'Hara's Tavern) burned this supposedly fireproof hotel to the ground. Amazingly, there was only one human casualty; a Mr. Bailey in the drugstore was never seen again. As the fire ate into the eaves, Morristown's little bucket fire engine became wedged in the stairway and the conductor of the only available train ran to Newark with two flat cars to bring back more apparatus. Although this trip took less than two hours both ways, it was to no avail. The financial loss was estimated at $120,000, according to one newspaper account, "plus a keg of applejack forty years old."

The appearance of the Green suffered for about 20 years. Gibbons, it was reported, would neither rebuild the hotel or sell the property, because he was (1) too heartbroken, or (2) furious with the ineffective fire department. □

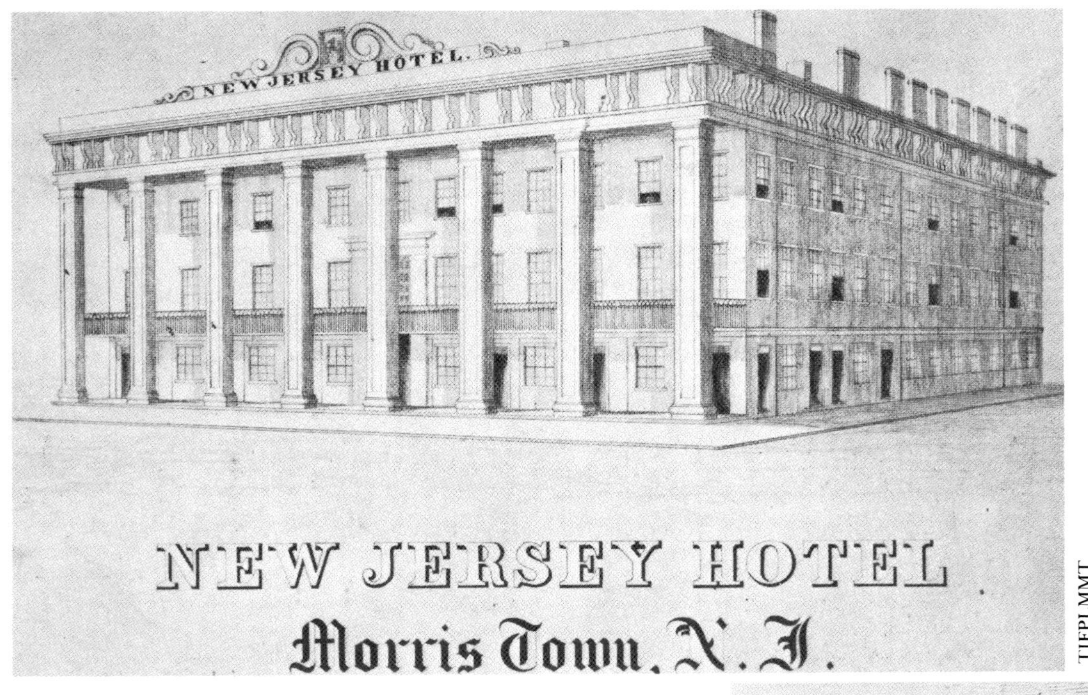

TJFPLMMT

Our new Hotel is now fairly under way. Sophia and myself with about 18 others dined there yesterday to see the style and give them a substantial indication of our good wishes . . . . So you must expect Morristown to be no longer the dull *place you once deemed it, but to find it grown into a regular full fashioned* airing *place, if not a* Watering *place.*

James Lovell, Morristown, to brother-in-law James Colles, Paris, July 14, 1844

TJFPLMMT

The new Morris County House (opposite) on the Green in 1844. It was built by Ashbel Bruen of Chatham.

Architect's Drawing by J. Frank Johnson (upper left), showing the three-story hotel with brownstone trim and eight pillars. It was first called the New Jersey Hotel.

The hole on West Park Place (lower right) in 1858 after the hotel burned.

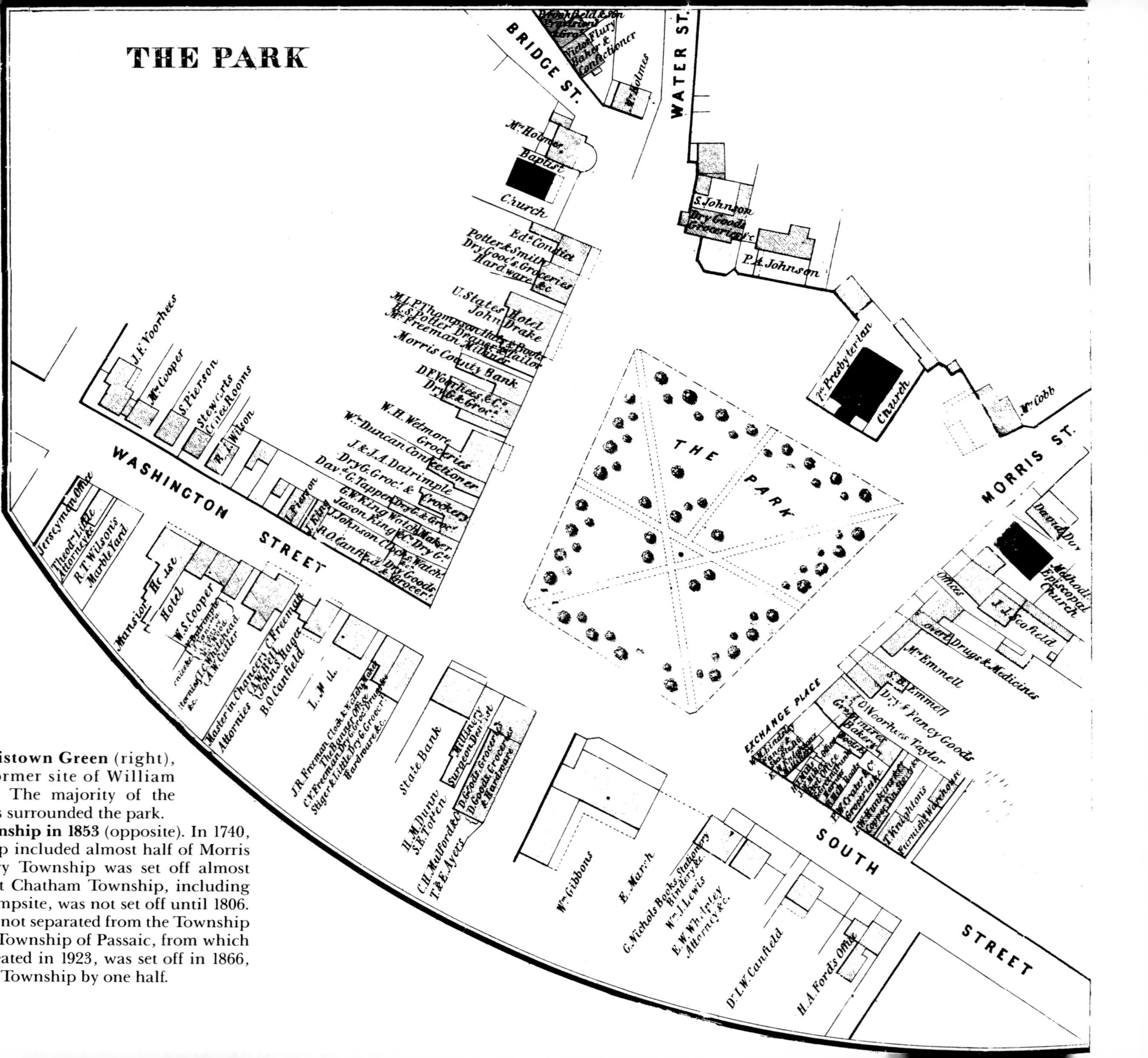

"Map of Morristown, Morris County, N.J.," 1850, by Marcus Smith/TJFPLMMT

The 1850 Morristown Green (right), showing the former site of William Gibbons' hotel. The majority of the town's businesses surrounded the park.

Morris Township in 1853 (opposite). In 1740, Morris Township included almost half of Morris County. Roxbury Township was set off almost immediately, but Chatham Township, including the Loantaka campsite, was not set off until 1806. Morristown was not separated from the Township until 1865. The Township of Passaic, from which Harding was created in 1923, was set off in 1866, reducing Morris Township by one half.

In the Mid-19th Century

In the 1840s and 1850s, the town and township followed the same pattern established 100 years before and would continue to follow for almost the next 100 years. Farms, meadows, and woodland completely encircled Morristown, the bustling center of businesses, town houses and churches.

On all sides of the irregular circle that is Morristown, there were open spaces with clusters of houses in addition to two villages — New Vernon, which had had its own Presbyterian Church since 1833, where the township committee met alternately with Morristown; and Pleasantville, now disappeared with only a street through the Great Swamp to commemorate it.

According to the 1850 census of Morristown, as reported in *The Jerseyman*, January 23, 1851, the Morristown fire limits — and thus the town limits — extended "one chain north of Speedwell Bridge to one chain south of the residence of Mr. Alexander Robertson [South Street a little below James Street], and from the bridge over a small stream near the residence of R. K. Tuttle, Esq. [Morris Street near the intersection with Ridgedale Avenue], to one chain west of Mr. Lovell's premises [formerly General Doughty's property, where Mount Kemble Avenue intersects with Doughty Street].

This census reported that there were within these fire limits "on the 1st day of June 2306 inhabitants, 462 dwelling houses, 503 families, 21 Dry Goods and Grocery Stores, 2 Book Stores, Apprentices Library and Circulating Library, 1 Bindery, 2 Printing Offices, 12 Lawyers, 8 Carriage Makers' Shops, 12 Blacksmith's Shops, 1 Foundry, 1 Extensive Machine Shop (Vail & Co's), 3 Bakers and

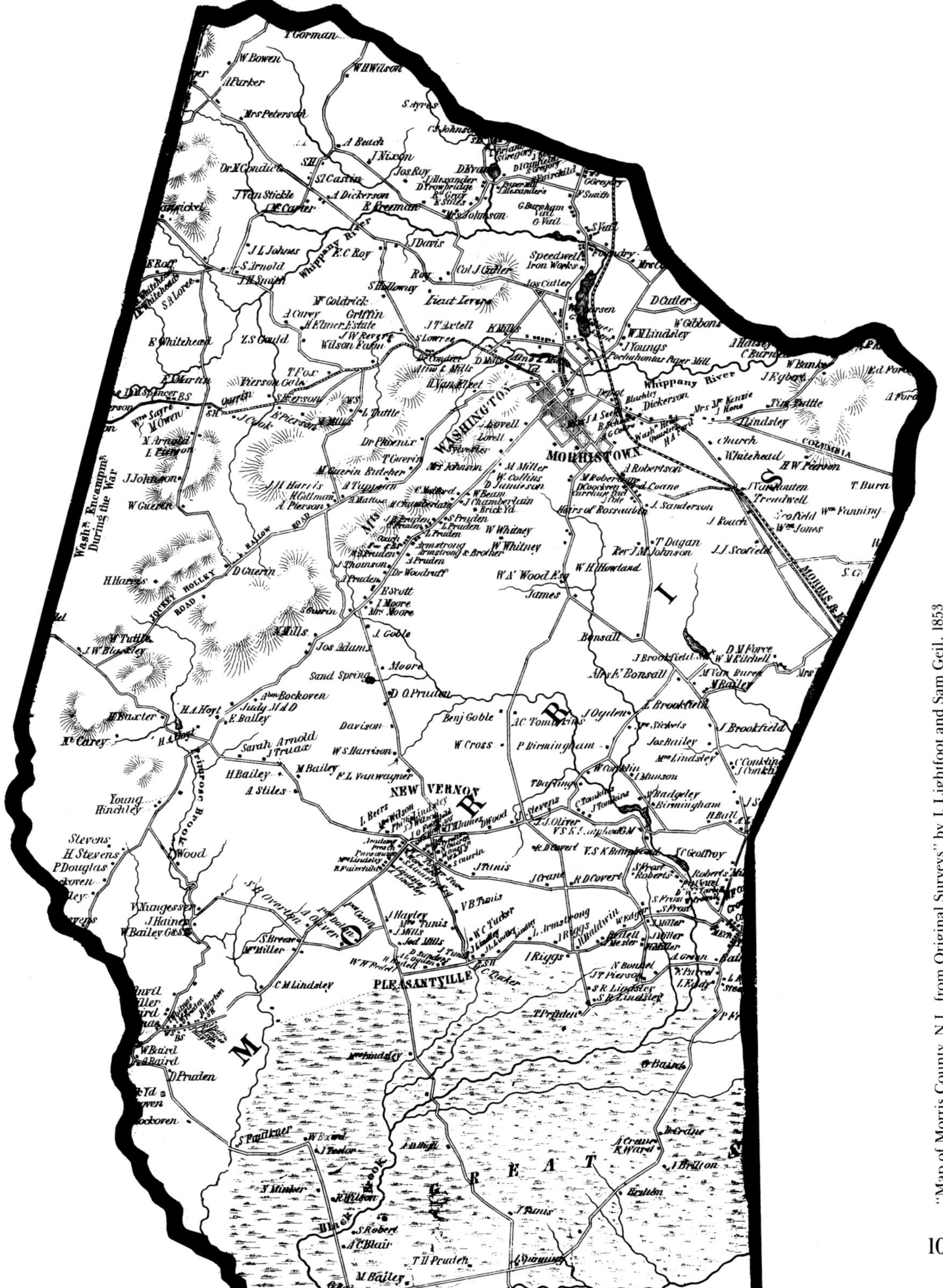

"Map of Morris County, N.J., from Original Surveys" by J. Lightfoot and Sam Geil, 1853

"Map of Morris County, N.J., from Original Surveys" by J. Lightfoot and Sam Geil, 1853

The Mansion House, 1853, Washington Street, one of the oldest in existence in the county at that time. It was owned by William Cooper, whose father was W. S. Cooper, a partner in the grocery firm of Troxell & Cooper. In 1864, it was bought and enlarged by B. C. Guerin, who owned it until 1878. In its heyday it could accommodate 80 to 100 guests and featured steam heat, gas lights and electric bells connected with each room. There was a large stable in the rear. The hotel was torn down in 1940. The site is now occupied by an office building, 3 Schuyler Place.

Confectioners, 7 Tailors, 4 Millineries, 5 Shoe Shops, 5 Jewelers and Watch Stores, 1 Clothing Store, 2 Harness Makers, 1 Hat and Cap Store, 1 Apothecary, 1 Varnish manufactory, 3 Hotels, 7 Churches, 1 Bank in good standing and 1 broken one, 7 schools, 1 Paper Mill, 2 Flour and 2 Saw Mills, 3 Butchers, 2 Cabinet Ware Houses, 2 Tanneries, 4 Stove and Tin Shops, and 3 Lumber Yards. Of adopted citizens, the Irish are the most numerous, these being 266; there are also 158 colored persons.

"Among the Societies are, one Lodge of Free and Accepted Masons, 2 of Odd Fellows, and 1 Division of the Sons of Temperance numbering one hundred and eighty-nine members in good standing — the largest Division in New Jersey, and one which has proved of lasting benefit to a large number of our citizens."

Most remarkable was the existence of seven churches and seven schools. Morristown was then, as now, a town of towers and spires.

In addition to the Presbyterian and Baptist Churches, located on the Green since before the Revolution, there was the Methodist Church (erected in 1827 on Market Street and in 1841 on the Green). Within a few blocks of each other were the 1828 St. Peter's Episcopal Church, South Street; the 1841 South Street Presbyterian Church; the 1843 African Methodist Episcopal Church, Spring Street; and the 1848 Catholic Church of the Assumption, Maple Avenue. In 1852, the eighth church was established when part of St. Peter's congregation withdrew to form the Church of the Redeemer, originally on Pine Street and later moved to South Street. Several others followed by century's end.

Privately run and of varying sizes, the schools included "dame schools" for children, academies and boarding schools. Although monies were appropriated for a public school beginning in the 1840s, town officials, perennially short of cash, were still diverting these funds to other purposes. In addition to the town's schools, the township had four district schools supported by local farm families.

Strong leaders with foresight guided the growth of town and township, but their success was helped greatly by the availability of cheap labor. By this time the slave population was significantly reduced or had been freed; however, the flow of immigrants provided a steady pool of workers who labored long hours at low wages. The 1850 census gives the following average figures:

Monthly wage for a farmhand, $10.
Weekly wage for a female domestic, with board, $1.

Daily wage for laborer, with board, 75¢.
Daily wage for laborer, without board, $1.
Weekly cost of laborer's board, $2.50.

Should a worker get into trouble with the law, prosecution and punishment were swift and sure, probably accounting for the low figures for convicted criminals in that year: foreigners, 14; native born, 37.

On April 6, 1865, Morristown was incorporated by the New Jersey State Legislature. The *True Democratic Banner* called it a Republican "monstrous scheme," but it survived repeal attempts in 1868 and 1869. (By this time, Morris Township had been reduced by more than half its size when Passaic — later Harding — Township was created.)

For 30 years the separation of Morristown and Morris Township remained fuzzy. The town provided the township's fire protection; the township assessor collected road, poor and school taxes for both. Not until February 18, 1895, the height of the Golden Years, did a complete separation of "City from the Township" take place. ☐

TJFPLMMT

Old St. Peter's Church (above), after the 1859 renovations. The rectory is on the left. The present stone church (page 230) was built to the right. **Church of the Redeemer** (below), first constructed in 1853 at the corner of Morris and Pine Streets. It was moved to South Street in 1886, this view, and replaced with the present stone building in 1917.

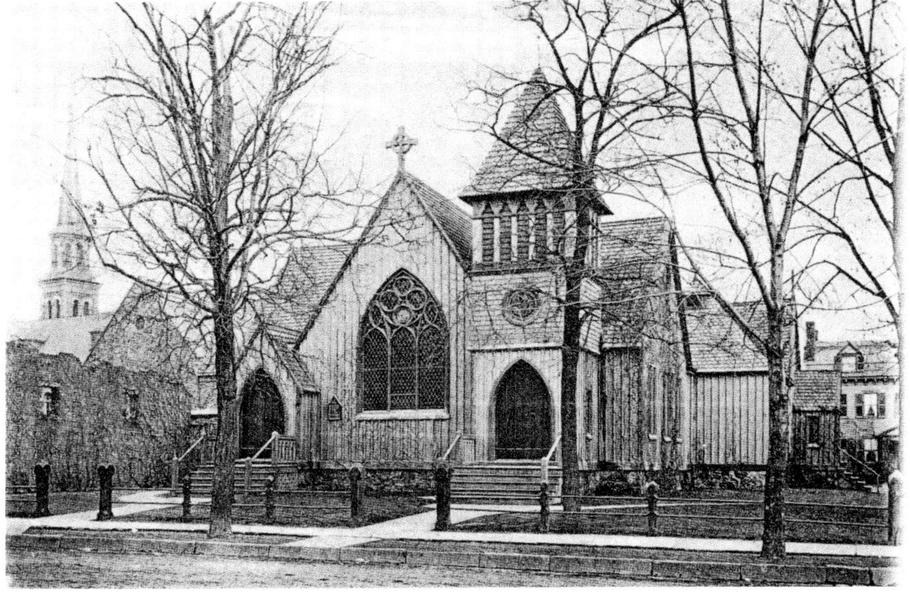

TJFPLMMT

TJFPLMMT

"View of Morristown from Fort Nonsense Hill"

In this Edward Kranich painting of about 1855, the 1827 Morris County Courthouse can be seen at the right. Washington Street is in the foreground, and Early Street is behind it. Speedwell Avenue is the road on the right. The newly renovated Homestead of Augustus Cutler can easily be identified in the center rear, and for many years this painting hung in the Cutlers' living room.

TJFPLMMT

"Morristown from the First Presbyterian Hill looking towards Water Street"

In this Edward Kranich painting of the late 1850s or early 1860s, a train is about to cross Water Street (Martin Luther King Avenue). In the foreground is Spring Street, and at the intersection of Spring and Water Streets can be seen the Moses Estey House on the northwest corner and the L'Hommedieu-Gwinnup House on the northeast. The Dickerson Tavern, rebuilt after a fire, is on the southeast corner.

Courtesy of George Shannon

The Golden Years

Overleaf Late 19th-century garden scene at "The Grove," Macculloch Avenue, Morristown.

THE MORRISTOWN AREA of the 19th century never lacked compliments. The lovely scenery, healthy air, pure water, and handsome mansions and villas were praised frequently in books thousands read. Self-promotion was hardly necessary. In 1844, John Warner Barber and Henry Howe — who traveled through all the United States, and should know — called Morristown "one of the most beautiful villages in the Union." They noted it was "situated on an elevated plain, 50 m from Trenton, 19 from Newark, and 26 from New York." Like all historians and writers, they dwelled on its place in the Revolution, but there were clearly contemporary reasons.

"The situation of a city could hardly be finer," wrote J. K. Hoyt about 1873 in *Pen and Pencil Pictures on the Delaware, Lackawanna and Western Railroad.* "In its surroundings of hills it somewhat resembles Florence in Italy . . . . The city itself occupies a plateau, not entirely a level plain, but with just enough of the 'rolling' quality to give variety to the scenery and afford architects of rural dwellings a chance to display their best points. Many of these residences erected by New York business men are very elegant and with fine surroundings."

In 1878, *The Daily Graphic*, a New York newspaper, focused on the "streets well flagged and well lighted throughout" and on its center, The Green, "being a fine park or square . . . to which, like Rome, all roads [of Morris County] lead." On the all-important matter of health, the article continued: "The atmosphere is cool and dry, grateful to weak lungs and pulmonary affections, and a destroyer of

TJFPLMMT

Scenes of Morristown and Morris Township about 1900: Whippany River; Ford Mansion; Garden of Mrs. Augustus Graves, 126 South Street; 1884 Levi Lathrop House, One Franklin Place.

chills and fever and the like. The best of water, and plenty of it, gushing from the sides of the mountains to the west of the town, follows the ducts through every street."

In 1879, another newspaper noted the steady growth of the town: "Twenty or thirty years ago the place was but a scattering village famed for the salubrity of its climate and the beauty of its surroundings . . . . Since then the village (now a city) has been quietly enlarging and beautifying its domain so that at the present time it can be compared not unfavorably with Newport in the beauty of its streets and the elegance of its private residences."

In Munsell's *History of Morris County,* published in 1882, Morristown was called "like Zion of old, beautiful for situation."

If comparisons of Italy, Newport and Zion and other extravagant praise did much to heighten Morristown's reputation, so did the seemingly endless number of postcard views. Since the picture on the first card — probably a sketch of old St. Peter's tower in the early 1870s — hundreds of scenes of peaceful streets, imposing public buildings and an inviting public Green have circled the world, sending a message stronger than words. Here was a very pleasant place to be.

It is not surprising, then, when New Yorkers who had amassed fortunes in banking, insurance, and private companies began looking for a cool escape in the summer, they looked at the beautiful country area, a short ride from New York. Their arrival between 1880 and 1929 became Morristown's Golden Years. □

A Most Pleasant Place to Live

TJFPLMMT

Maple Avenue, Morristown, near Church of the Assumption, 1900.

In 1884, a novelist, Miriam Coles Harris, describes the charms of Marrowfat (Morristown) in *Phoebe*. The author analyzes the town while the book's principal characters, Barry and Phoebe, newly married, walk to the old St. Peter's Church one Sunday morning.

"It was an old town, with ante-Revolutionary traditions; there was no mushroom crop allowed to spring up about it.... The climate of the place was dry and pure; it was the fashion for the city doctors to send their patients there; and many who came to cough, remained to build. The scenery was lovely; you looked down pretty streets and saw blue hills beyond; the sidewalks were paved and the town was lit by gas, but the pavements led you past charming homes to bits of view that reminded you of Switzerland, and the inoffensive lamp-posts were hidden under great trees by day, and by night you only thought how glad you were to see them. The drives were endless, and roads good; there were livery stables, hotels, skilled confectioners, shops of all kinds, a library, a pretty little theatre, churches of every shade of faith, schools of every degree of pretension; lectures in winter, concerts in summer, occasional plays all the year; two or three local journals, the morning papers from the city at your breakfast table; fast trains, telegraphs, telephones, all the modern amenities of life under your very hand; and yet it was the country, and there were peaceful hills and deep woods, and the nights were as still as Paradise. Can it be wondered at that, like St. Peter's at Rome, it had an atmosphere of its own, and defied the outer changes of the temperature."

Despite its small size in 1880 — a population of 5,446 in Morristown; 1,392 in all the surrounding Morris Township — there were many comforts, even luxuries, found in far larger places. Gaslight was introduced before the Civil War and, by 1880, there were 70 street lamps lit each night. A telegraph office was started at an early date. In 1882, a telephone exchange began with the requisite number of subscribers, 45, who paid $3 each a month. Most of these were businesses (number 1, the undertaker), but former Governor Theodore F. Randolph (number 2) led a small group of individuals who saw a future for the invention in private homes. In 1885, an electric light company was formed, only three years after Thomas Edison first installed incandescent light. And on October 1, 1888, free postal delivery and corner letter boxes were introduced. (The drop letter cost two cents.) There were at least two general deliveries daily, but double that number to the businesses around the Green. Although most of the deliveries were within the town line, Postmaster E. A. Quayle promised that the service would be enlarged as soon as possible.

Does this not seem a most pleasant place to live? □

Both photographs courtesy of Mr. and Mrs. James T. Yardley

The Christopher Raymond Perry Rodgers House

The future U.S. admiral was only a lieutenant when he built this house at 40 Macculloch Avenue, Morristown, about 1852, for himself and his wife, Jane Slidell. He was a nephew of Commodores John Rodgers, Oliver H. and Matthew C. Perry, officers with distinguished records beginning with the War of 1812. Commodore Matthew Perry, whose expedition to Japan in 1854 is famous, is credited with bringing back the wisteria that adorns this porch and a number of other houses in the area.

Rodgers was appointed midshipman in 1833 and served in the Mexican and Civil Wars. He was the Fleet Captain, commanding the "new Ironsides" in the attack on Charleston in April 1863. Promoted to Captain in 1866 and Rear Admiral in 1874, he was Chief of the Bureau of Yards and Docks (1871-74), Superintendent of Annapolis (1874-78) and Commander in Chief of the Pacific Squadron (1878-80).

According to the 1868 and 1887 maps, the Taylor family owned this house, and it is probably two members of that family on the porch. The house is still a private residence, but the painted stripes on the porch roof and decorations along the eaves are gone.

Portait of Commodore Perry that hangs in the Rodgers' house.

Courtesy of Mrs. Henry F. Hartmann

The William Bailey House

This house at 44 Macculloch Avenue was built about 1872 on land acquired from the neighboring Taylors. The porch on which the two maids stand and the front entrance have been changed, but the house remains a private residence. The roof of the Pitney House, 43 Maple Avenue, is in the background.

Historic Town Houses

The gracious buildings still standing on and near Macculloch Avenue demonstrate Morristown's appeal in the second half of the 19th century and reflected their owners' social position and comfortable affluence. Trees flourished in narrow strips between slate sidewalk and curb. Fences of iron or wood or low stone walls, piazzas and porches separated the bustle and mud of the street from the individual sanctity of the home. The deep lots provided ample room for flower and vegetable gardens and fruit trees.

Emily Johnston de Forest recalled in *Old Morristown Days* the bounty on the table when the James Colles family gathered for the Fourth of July, a holiday only slightly less important than Thanksgiving or Christmas. "All day long we children raced and ran, climbed trees and stuffed ourselves with cherries, or sneaked into the garden and robbed the currant bushes while Jamieson [the Scots-Irish gardener] had his back turned . . . . Or we went wading in the little stream at the foot of the hill . . . . At two o'clock came the family dinner and all my grandmother's sisters and their families made their appearance . . . . On the centre of the long table were three pyramids of flowers, each about two feet tall, made of successive rings growing smaller toward the top and each ring filled with wet sand. The flowers of all kinds were snipped down to about three inches in length and stuck in the wet sand in such a way as to give the greatest possible variety of color . . . . As to the vegetables and fruits served at this dinner, my grandmother would not say much about them (for very pride), but she would have been much mortified had she had less than eight or ten kinds of each to offer, and all of them produce of 'The Garden.' "

TJFPLMMT

The George E. Voorhees House

George Emmell Voorhees, Jr. (1838-1925) is shown on the porch of his house, 46 Macculloch Avenue, built before 1868. With him are his wife, Mary Gertrude Ditmars, and four children — George Emmell, James Ditmars, Cornelia Emmell and Gitty Remson, probably before 1880. Voorhees was the second generation to run a highly successful hardware store (2-4 Washington Street, still standing) and was the promoter of Morristown's first electric light company. The house no longer has the front porch and some of the trimming, but it is still a private residence.

Courtesy of George Shannon

It was not the thing to be very rich in Marrowfat [Morristown], it was only tolerated; it was the thing to be a little cultivated, a little clever, very well born, and very loyal to Marrowfat.
From *Phoebe* by Miriam Coles Harris, 1884

In the 20th century, however, the eager commercialization that hit other areas of Morristown also was felt in this totally residential district and parking lots and brick office buildings began to appear between private homes with no apparent effort to fit into the former homogeneous scene. In the 1970s a desperate attempt was made to halt this plundering of 100-year-old architecture by creating a Morristown Historic District while there were still 50 or so worthwhile structures still standing. Thanks to this designation, it is still possible to imagine the 19th-century town (on Sundays or keeping ears closed to traffic), walking from South Street to Ogden Place and from James Street to DeHart Street and its extension, Wetmore Avenue (endpaper map). □

Courtesy of Mrs. Thomas Turner Cooke

The Grove

The house (opposite, left), 71 Macculloch Avenue, built about 1865, shown as it appeared about 1885. It was bought by Mr. and Mrs. C. Wicliffe Throckmorton in 1901. The house is a surviving representative of the many mansions in Morristown that had the mansard roof, so popular in the middle of the 19th century. Frederick Law Olmsted created the original landscape design; Commodore Perry brought back from Japan the large ginko tree and the wisteria. A puddingstone wall replaced the fence when the street grade was made steeper. (An enlarged detail of the garden is on pages 114-115).

The Throckmorton children (above), in the beautiful grove that was at the rear of the house — Elizabeth (Mrs. Thomas Turner Cooke) and younger brothers, John Wicliffe, Edgerton Alvord and Alwyn Alvord.

Photograph by Barbara Beirne/TJFPLMMT

Photograph by Barbara Beirne/TJFPLMMT

Macculloch Hall

George Perrot Macculloch was an adventurer, merchant, scholar, linguist, agriculturist and dreamer of practical dreams. He may be best remembered as the man who conceived the Morris Canal, but he was so much more.

A Scotsman born in Bombay, he was educated in Edinburgh. At 24, he moved to London to become a partner in an export trading firm. He probably moved to America when the Napoleonic Wars ruined the trade between France and England.

On 25 acres of farmland bought from General John Doughty, he built Macculloch Hall. In 1810, he built the first of three sections on the foundations of a pre-Revolutionary stone cottage beside a creek. In 1812, he built the central hallway section and, in 1814, he added a large schoolroom wing on the western end to accommodate his Latin School for boys, which he operated for 14 years. In this schoolroom, Episcopalian services were held until St. Peter's Church was built.

George P. Macculloch married Louisa Edwina Saunderson in 1800 in London, where they had two children, Francis Law (1801-59) and Mary Louisa (1804-88), who made the 1819 map of Morristown (page 71). She married the Honorable Jacob Welch Miller (1800-62), who was a New Jersey assemblyman, state prosecutor and senator. Known as the last Whig Senator from New Jersey, he became one of the founders of the Republican Party.

Six generations of the Macculloch-Miller family lived at Macculloch Hall and several Macculloch grandchildren and one great-grandchild built houses around it. In 1867, Lieutenant Commander Henry William Miller (1836-1904) built The Moorings, 69 Miller Road, which originally faced Macculloch Avenue,

Photograph by Robert Scalera/Courtesy of Macculloch Hall Historical Museum

Photograph by Barbara Beirne/TJFPLMMT

Photograph by Barbara Beirne/TJFPLMMT

Macculloch Hall

The house (opposite), 45 Macculloch Avenue, front and garden views, built by George P. Macculloch in three sections between 1810 and 1814, in Federal style with a later portico. It is now Macculloch Hall Historical Museum. The house and garden are open to the public.

Entrance hall (above) with portrait of grandson George Macculloch Miller; **upper sitting room** and **dining room**.

Photograph by Wendy R. London/TJFPLMMT

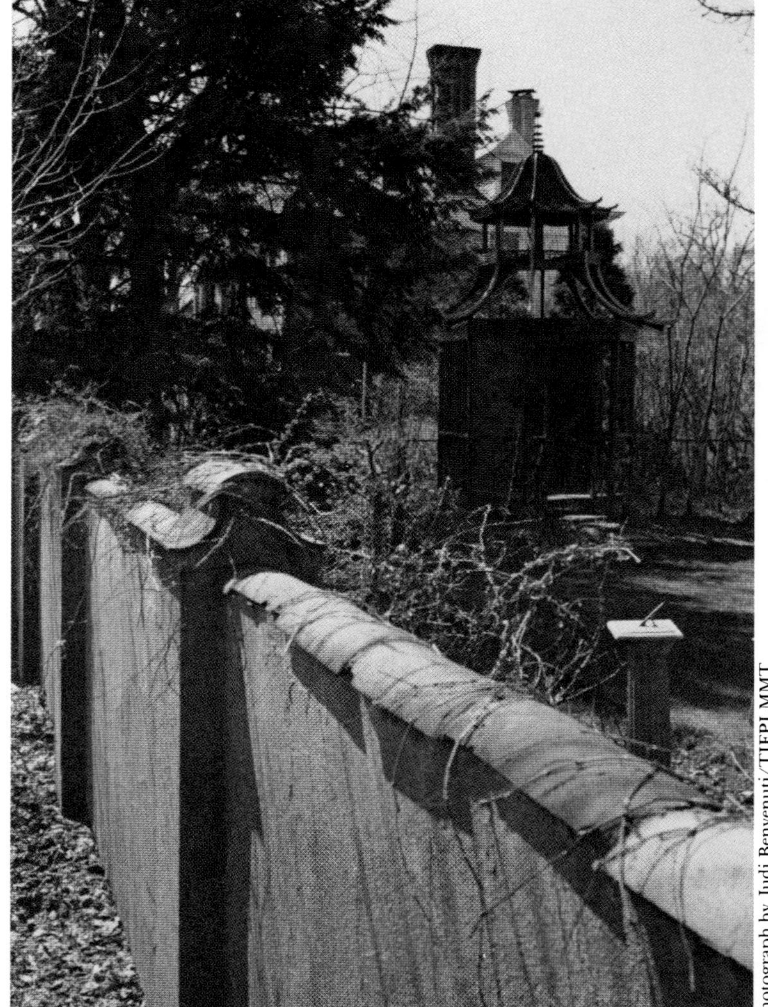

Photograph by Judi Benvenuti/TJFPLMMT

The Kedge

The house (left), 49 Macculloch Avenue, built 1870-80 by Henry Miller, grandson of George Macculloch and another of Morristown's distinguished naval officers. The first section of this brick-and-shingle house was only four rooms when it was built as a summer cottage facing Miller Road. It was later enlarged and the front door was moved to its present position when Henry Miller decided to live in it permanently.

The pagoda-style gazebo (above) seen over the garden wall. This is still a private residence, occupied by members of the family.

but was moved to its present location when the Miller Estate Association extended Boykin Street (Miller Road) to Ogden Place. Henry Miller had resigned the year before from the U.S. Navy after a distinguished career. In 1870, he built The Kedge, where he decided to live. The names of both houses reflect his naval background. In 1890, Edward Quinton Keasbey (1849-1925), a great-grandchild of George Macculloch, built Edgewood, 56 Miller Road, as a summer home. The following year his father, Anthony Quinton Keasbey (1824-95) — who had married two Miller daughters, Elizabeth (1828-52) and after her death Edwina Louisa (1826-88) — built Good Rest, 53 Miller Road. Two of his daughters lived there until their deaths at the beginning of World War II. Also in 1891, George Macculloch Miller (1832-1917) built The Knoll on Ogden Place.

Macculloch Hall was occupied by the same family for 139 years; but in 1947, after the death of Dorothea (Dolly) Miller Post, it was put up for sale. Most fortunately, there was a protector in the wings. The Honorable W. Parsons Todd, a Morristown mayor for six years and town alderman for many more and a noted philanthropist, had known the family well. His uncle, Henry Davis Todd, had been friends with Henry Miller since both were midshipmen serving on the *U.S.S. Mohican*. In 1947, Macculloch Hall was conveyed to the W. Parsons Todd Foundation, Inc., so that it could be preserved as a museum.

Macculloch Hall Historical Museum also has acquired a fine collection of the works of Thomas Nast through Mr. Todd's friendship with Nast's son, Cyril. In addition to original cartoons and cartoons in print, the collection includes family photographs and personal belongings such as Nast's walking stick. □

Courtesy of George Munson

Beautiful Homes of Northern New Jersey, c. 1910

The Knoll

The house (right), on Ogden Place, built in 1891 by George Macculloch Miller as a summer home. The house faced south into the valley where he owned considerable property. It was torn down after his death in 1917.

Orchards of the Macculloch Homestead (above), showing The Knoll and the corner of Colles Avenue and Miller Road from the roof of Good Rest, 53 Miller Road, another house occupied by George Macculloch's descendants.

TJFPLMMT

George Perrot Macculloch (1775-1858).

Louisa Edwina Saunderson Macculloch (1785-1863).

Hon. Jacob Welch Miller (1800-62).

Ever Dearest Louisa

George P. Macculloch to his wife, undated letter accompanying his will of August 22, 1856

As my last thoughts will be of you and my last earthward prayers be for your welfare I think that a suitable accompaniment to my Testament will be a few suggestions upon what seems to be the course most conducive to the happiness of your future days in the new position into which my decease will place you.

It seems clear beyond hesitation that you ought to pursue nearly the same plan of life which we have jointly followed. Your best, most congenial, most respectable home is undoubtedly with your son and daughter in your ancient abode surrounded by your good and affectionate descendants. I well know that monotony is constitutionally irksome to you. When you feel the want of temporary change, make an excursion to Francis and Charlotte, Anthony and Edwina or a *very short trip* to New York. Such visits will create sufficient variety and any other wandering would be at once both expensive and unrespectable, unless in company with some party of your own family.

Your income being now what has so long sufficed for us both is liberal. Dispense it liberally among our dear children and grandchildren, equally and impartially, for altho' it is impossible to feel an equal attachment to all yet suffer no preference to become visible. A parent must be not a little weak and somewhat wicked to cause domestic jealousies by an exhibition of favoritism.

The infirmities of old age increase & you will very soon require some attendant to yourself, some young girl whose board you will pay to Jacob. He is exempted from interest upon $10,000 in the purchase of the homestead as a part consideration for board but in this as in every other matter be as generous as your income & other duties will permit. The $2500 I have left in my will subject to your own disposal is not intended for expenditure but merely to give you the means of showing kindness to such of our descendants as may in your judgment require it. Do with that sum whatever you think I would do if still living.

Let me inculcate as a general maxim never to consider yourself to be a separate individual but as the member of a little community, whose common happiness depends upon banishing all selfish or clashing interests, feelings & views.

TJFPLMMT

Company scrip, April 1, 1840. E. R. Biddle was the president. William Pennington was New Jersey Governor.

Old age is prone to become captious & querulous. For several years I have felt this tendency growing upon me, have seldom passed a day without invoking the power to repress a snappish fault finding temper. Much I fear that yourself & all our dear ones have sometimes found this prayer to have been unavailing. Let me implore you as you value your own peace and the happiness of all you love to guard against this natural defect of advancing years. Where faults are glaring you cannot but see them, only never watch for opportunities to criticise and when constrained to reprove, let your animadversions be short, gentle & kind.

What so beautiful as placid, indulgent, cheerful old age, what so repulsive as a morose, sulky, snappish dotard?

I can foresee the possibility of no real difficulty in your future life. Should any such occur, *refer it without delay or hesitation* to the good sense and good feeling of Jacob, Francis, Anthony, George & Lindley who are in every and all cases your only safe & natural counsellors. Should you ever imagine yourself aggrieved by either of them lay your complaint candidly in an appeal to their own judgment. Temper will sometimes hastily effervesce but not one of your children will ever deliberately & intentionally give you cause of serious offence. Never for a moment forget that love, consolation, advice, aid, sympathy are nowhere to be found by you so generous, warm or active as at home in the bosoms of our own dear ones. It is a true maxim that man is happy in the exact degree in which he promotes the happiness of those around him. Be kind & indulgent, for your years demand a large return of kindness & indulgence.

The present is an appropriate and solemn occasion to declare my reverence and faith in religion. If I have habitually dissented from common place opinion, it was in order to counteract the tendency of the female mind to mistake formal observances for genuine piety, to surrender itself to plausible pretences, to crouch before pompous assumption. He must be a bigot & dupe who believes that any theological system monopolizes the Divine favor. My opinions are the result of thirty years of meditation and earnest prayer. I go with unwavering confidence to the Paternal & merciful tribunal where these opinions are to be judged.

Ever dear Louisa — Adieu — If ever I have seemed cold, careless or harsh, it has been in manner only, for my heart has always cherished an earnest solicitude for your welfare. Think of me with love and regret — forget my faults and failings; dwell upon our long, affectionate union, pray. I now pray that we may meet again in that future existence where all is bliss.

Farewell

Four photographs from *James Colles, 1788-1883: Life and Letters* by Emily Johnston De Forest

Photograph by Joan Bender

The Evergreens

The house (above) on Macculloch Avenue about 1874, and as it appears today (left) as The Kellogg Club, 25 Colles Avenue. It was built in 1836-37 to designs by Martin E. Thompson, architect for the Second Bank of the United States. James Colles is seated on the lawn on the left; George W. Colles leans against a column facing his wife, Julia Keese Colles, and daughter Gertrude. Others are members of Frances Colles Johnston's family. The gardener is Daniel Jamieson.

The Evergreens

James Colles had made a phenomenal success as an importer in New Orleans when he built his handsome house called The Evergreens, named for a splendid row of arborvitae in the back of the property. The house was originally on Macculloch Avenue, with the present Farragut Place as its driveway. Colles was married to Harriet Augusta Wetmore, whose family had many roots in Morristown, where the couple spent their summers.

In 1832, when General Doughty's house and farm went up for auction, James Colles and James Lovell — who had married Harriet's sister, Sophia — bought it jointly. This partnership lasted only a few years, however, after which the brothers-in-law divided the land. James Lovell kept the house and property on the west side of Mount Kemble Avenue; James Colles took the meadows on the east side, about 45 acres next to George Macculloch.

Construction of The Evergreens was supervised by Harriet's nephew, Benjamin Ogden Canfield, who took infinite care over every detail. In one letter, he proudly wrote "Aunt Colles" that he had made a fence along the neighbor's property in such a way that "Mr. Macculloch's hens" could do no more than "look through" at the Colles garden.

Five Colles children grew up here — Harriet Augusta (1822-1863), Frances (1826-1888), James, Jr. (1828-1898), John Henry (1831-1871) and George Wetmore, 2nd (1836-1911).

Even though James Colles built a mansion in New York City at 35 University Place and furnished it with French antiques acquired on a three-year grand tour of Europe with the family, Morristown remained the beloved home. In 1877, nine years after Harriet's death, James Colles moved to The Evergreens permanently, where he died at age 95.

The roses strongly reminded me of Morristown, and I thought of you and of everyone at home.
George Wetmore Colles, Naples, to his mother, Mrs. James Colles, May 8, 1859

James Colles (1788-1883).

Harriet Augusta Wetmore Colles (1795-1868).

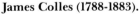

Paintings by John Wesley Jarvis, shortly after their 1821 marriage.

A few years later, George subdivided the homestead property he inherited and Wetmore and Colles Avenues, Doughty Street and Farragut Place came into being. The latter, in fact, followed the line of The Evergreens' driveway. (This was the same period that the Miller Estate Association was opening up Miller Road and Ogden Place.)

Colles Park was for "people to come here and locate permanently if eligible sites could be secured at reasonable prices," according to an unidentified newspaper article, probably in 1886, which also noted that "hills were cut away here and hollows built up there, avenues and streets were laid out and already curved, and water and gas pipes are being laid before the road beds are made."

George himself was proprietor of the gas company, which apparently operated smoothly. "I see no reason why this gas should not be entirely satisfactory," Charlton T. Lewis wrote to him, "indeed, for household purposes it seems to be preferable to that furnished by the Morristown Gaslight Company . . . . When it leaks, the odor is much the same as that of the watergas furnished by the city, certainly no worse, and it is not poisonous as city gas is."

In 1886, the house was moved south to its present location at 25 Colles Avenue and owned by several prominent families. Mr. and Mrs. Charlton T. Lewis owned it in the 1890s, followed by Mr. and Mrs. William A. Dell, who called it Dellenord. In 1916, it became the home of Mr. and Mrs. Frederick R. Kellogg. He was a prominent New York attorney, at one time a partner of Charles Evans Hughes. When the house and property were sold to a social club, theirs was the name adopted. □

John Henry and George Wetmore Colles, with their beloved nurse, Mary McBride.
By Edouart, 21 Broadway, N.Y., November 11, 1839.

Courtesy of Macculloch Hall Historical Museum

Photograph by Wendy R. London/TJFPLMMT

Villa Fontana

The house (above), 50 Macculloch Avenue, built before 1868, as it appeared after 1876 with the gate and fence Thomas Nast bought at the Centennial Exposition in Philadelphia.

The present house (left) after John Holme Maghee enlarged and remodeled it in 1910. Designated as a National Historic Landmark, the house is still a private residence.

Villa Fontana

One of the most creative illustrators of his time lived in Morristown. From the deeply talented mind and sure hand of Thomas Nast sprang the Republican Elephant, the Democratic Donkey, the Tammany Tiger, a tall rangy version of Uncle Sam, an alternately grieving and scolding Columbia and the roly-poly Santa Claus we all know today.

The Tiger got him into trouble. A friend of Thomas Nast's warned him in 1870 that his biting political cartoons infuriated "Boss Tweed" and his Tammany Ring, who ran New York City, where Nast lived. Soon after, a banker associated with that corrupt government was more blunt. He promised Nast $5,000 if he would take his family on an extended trip to Europe. When he refused this incredible offer — which would have paid the mortgage on his city home and provided a very comfortable income for life — the banker warned him quietly: "Only be careful, Mr. Nast, that you do not first put yourself in a coffin." Yet, only two years later, after the Tweed Ring was smashed, the same banker met him one day on the street and exclaimed admiringly, "My God, Nast, you did it after all!" Such was the tremendous power of Nast's cartoons.

Nast did move away — but only as far as Morristown, where he hoped the good air would improve his chronic asthma. With him came his wife, Sarah Edwards of New York City, whom he had married on the eve of his 21st birthday, and three children, Julia, Thomas Edward and Sarah Edith. Two more children, Mabel and Cyril, were born in Morristown. The family lived for a year in a boarding house, thinking the move to be temporary; but in 1872, Nast bought Villa Fontana from David Rockwell for $21,250, a not inconsiderable sum for those days. It was to be his last — and most precious — home.

Young Tommy Nast became a professional illustrator at the age of 15, earning $4 a week at *Frank Leslie's Weekly.* Later at *Harper's Weekly* — where he invented his popular symbols — he also drew many graphic illustrations of the Civil War. He met Lincoln during his presidential campaign and became fast friends with Grant on one of his visits to a battle zone. They admired his sense of compassion and family devotion as well. Both men recognized his passionate commitment to the Union cause and his genius in depicting the horrors of war and the dangers of a divided nation. Lincoln called him "my best recruiting sergeant."

Although his pen drew savage attacks on corruption and corrupters, he also sketched the most tender family scenes. On January 3, 1863, *Harper's Weekly* published his original drawings for Clement Moore's classic poem, *'Twas the Night Before Christmas.* A tremendous success, the series was to run each holiday season for more than 30 years. Santa Claus drawings featuring his children in the familiar scenes at the Villa Fontana and Morristown are still part of the Christmas tradition today.

Villa Fontana became an artistic and social center. Famous men came to call, including President Grant and Mark Twain. Success at last brought the money to allow him to indulge in many interests and he crowded the house with all manner of objects.

It was a true Victorian house. Mary Dean, writing for *Lippincott's Magazine* of March 1880, described the interior of Nast's house as "incomparable and filled not with articles to help furnish, but with works of art."

Grant visited Villa Fontana just before a trip around the world after he left the White House. According to Albert Bigelow Paine,

Let's stop them d—d pictures. I don't care so much what the papers write about me — my constituents can't read; but d—n it, they can see pictures!
"Boss" William Marcy Tweed of Tammany Hall, speaking of Thomas Nast's cartoons, 1871

Courtesy of Macculloch Hall Historical Museum

TJFPLMMT

Thomas Nast (1840-1902)

The "father of the political cartoon" is shown **on Banjo, June 25, 1884** (above), and as he looked **in 1901** (right), in a portrait by Morristown's Ensminger.

The earlier photograph was taken beside the front gate in front of the fountain that gave the house its name. Mrs. Nast reportedly gave the fountain to the Town of Morristown, but its fate is unknown. The present one is a recent addition.

Courtesy of Macculloch Hall Historical Museum

Nast's Victorian parlor (above) and three **Christmas drawings** (right and opposite), featuring his children, Santa Claus and interiors of Villa Fontana. The drawing on the lower right shows part of the mantelpiece in the photograph. The drawing on the upper right shows an adaptation of the mantelpiece in the photograph on page 136.

TJFPLMMT

Mrs. Nast with Family and Friends, Delaware Water Gap, August 1886

Mrs. Nast is in the center with eyes closed. Just below her are Mabel and Cyril Nast. Next to them is Julia Nast, for whom the unusual debutante party was given at Lyceum Hall (page 238). Edith Nast is second from left in the middle row with her arm around Anne Howland Ford, a founder of the Morris County Golf Club. Edith married Robert Porter, son of General Fitz John Porter, a neighbor at One Farragut Place. Henry C. Pitney, Jr., second from right, bottom row, was a neighbor at 43 Maple Avenue.

Nast's biographer: "The table was artistically arranged and decorated, the courses had been carefully chosen and came in due sequence, the coffee appeared at last to complete the successful round of refreshment." At this point, the host panicked. He had forgotten cigars! How many times had he depicted Grant puffing serenely on a cigar undisturbed while his enemies assailed him? The evening ended happily when Grant assured him he had remembered Nast did not smoke. "Besides," the ex-general observed, "I never go into action without ammunition."

In later years, however, disappointments crowded in. The public became apathetic toward his cartoon subjects; only Santa Claus was eagerly awaited. Financial investments in western mines proved disastrous. Nast sometimes paid the doctor, dentist and lawyer by painting their portraits. His grandson, Thomas Nast St. Hill, wrote that "I was told that he once paid a tax collector in this manner, although how the collector settled with the taxing authority is not quite clear."

He wrote his friend President Theodore Roosevelt requesting a consular position. Secretary of State John Hay replied with regret that the only one available was in far-off Ecuador. In July 1902, a discouraged and aging Nast left alone for Guayaquil, Ecuador's principal port; in December, he was dead of yellow fever. □

Courtesy of Macculloch Hall Historical Museum

My limbs get stiff and crampy. It must be the drafts one gets into after so hot and moist. I walk in the night with cramps and have some stiffness in shoulders and arms, but I must not forget I am getting old. It is funny though, no matter what you have, the natives all come to the conclusion that it is the yellow fever.

Thomas Nast in Ecuador to his wife, Sarah, in Morristown, November 21, 1902, 17 days before his death from this disease

Courtesy of Macculloch Hall Historical Museum

Nast's studio (above and right) in an upper floor suite at Villa Fontana. In the first photograph, note the heron, or flamingo, design on the mantelpiece, sketch books on the easels on casters and the skeleton Cyril and his playmates sometimes appropriated on Halloween.

In the second photograph, Nast is at work at his roll-top desk, on which is a statue of "The Gladiator." Two pet birds are nearby.

Four of Nast's famous political symbols (opposite): Democratic Donkey, Republican Elephant, Uncle Sam and the Tammany Tiger.

"Himself as a Fireman" (opposite, lower right, painted in 1897 to celebrate the 100th anniversary of Morristown's fire department. Nast was an enthusiastic member of the Independent Hose Company No. 1.

Four drawings from *Harper's Weekly*

Curtiss Collection/TJFPLMMT

Courtesy of Morris County Historical Society

Acorn Hall

The house, 68 Morris Street, built in 1853 by Ashbel Bruen, is now headquarters and museum of the Morris County Historical Society.

The Crane family, 1870 (above). On March 17, 1870, a Newark photographer took this picture. Mrs. Augustus Crane is in the sleigh; Mr. Crane is standing behind with the white beard. Either Mary or Julia is seated beside their mother; the other is on the porch. Benjamin stands near his father. Augustus, Jr., who was attending military school in Worchester, Massachusetts, could not get home. The coachman had been with the family many years.

On March 16, Augustus Crane wrote to his son, Augustus, Jr., "A photographer was engaged to take a view of our house and lawn at noon today — the snow has prevented him from doing it. It will be taken on the first pleasant day — I thought my children would be pleased to have picture of the home in which they have passed their earliest and happiest years . . . . Many changes take place in the score of years and it is delightful to have something to which one can look, to forcibly remind us of our 'boyhood home' when we ourselves are no longer young." On March 23, he wrote again to say: "The photographer came on Thursday — the snow still remained on the ground — the day was cloudy but the atmosphere very fine. He succeeded in getting a very fine negative and printing for us some beautiful pictures; one of them is for you . . . ."

The Crane family, about 1890 (right). Mr. and Mrs. Augustus Crane are on the lawn; Julia and Dr. Corning are on the porch. This view shows the Italianate features of the house. The tower and the dining room wing in the foreground were added in 1860.

Courtesy of Morris County Historical Society

Four photographs by Judi Benvenuti/TJFPL.MMT
Courtesy of Morris County Historical Society

Acorn Hall's summer bedroom (above), with charming painted cottage furniture. It overlooks the two-acre garden in the rear.

Augustus Crane (1817-1906) and **Mary Bolles Crane (1823-1913),** about 1850 (left).

Old rhododendron bushes (opposite, left).

Library (opposite, above), with handsome Italian marble fireplace. On the mantel are a French clock and figurines dating from about 1850. The mahogany Gothic Revival bookcase belonged to Augustus Crane and still contains his books. His marginal notes on Thomas Bridgeman's *The Young Gardener's Assistant* served as a guide for planting and restoring the grounds.

Music room (opposite, below), a popular room for this musical family, was adjacent to the parlor on one side and a picture gallery on the other. Augustus Crane purchased the rosewood Chickering parlor grand piano. The Gothic Revival piano stool, however, came from the Castleman family, as did other heirloom furniture in the room. The printed velvet rug was purchased by Dr. Schermerhorn from Crossley Brothers of Halifax, England, about 1850. It is similar to the rug in the parlor, which is identical to one exhibited at the Crystal Palace in London in 1851.

Acorn Hall

In 1853, Dr. John Schermerhorn and his wife, Louisa, moved from New York into a fine home on eight acres bought from a distant relative, John Hone III. They named it Acorn Hall, probably for the large black oak still standing near the present parking area.

Louisa Schermerhorn's death at age 24, following the birth of a daughter, was, no doubt, the reason her husband sold the house and contents in 1857 to Augustus Crane and returned to New York City.

In June of that year, Augustus Crane, a substantial New York merchant; Mary Bolles, his wife; and four children — Mary, Julia, Augustus, Jr., and Benjamin — moved into Acorn Hall. Soon Mr. and Mrs. Crane were very active in community affairs. He was a director and vice president of the First National Bank of Morristown, as well as an incorporator of the Library and Lyceum and of Miss Dana's School. Mrs. Crane was a leader in musical affairs, which, in fact, interested all the family.

Music promoted the romance of their older daughter, Mary, and the son of the man who had sold the land to Dr. Schermerhorn. Mary Crane, who played the organ, and John Hone IV, who sang in the choir at the Church of the Redeemer, were married on November 17, 1869. John Hone's maternal grandfather was Commodore Matthew Perry, whose expedition was largely responsible for opening Japan to western trade in the 1850s. He also was related to Philip Hone, society leader and mayor of New York, much admired for his diary illuminating the political, financial and social history of the city of his time and for the development of the Whig Party (1825-1851).

Julia Crane married the prominent New York doctor J. Leonard Corning, discoverer of spinal anesthesia. Augustus, Jr., and Benjamin became investment bankers in Washington, D.C.

After Augustus Crane died in 1906 at age 90, Julia and Dr. Corning moved into the house to care for her mother, as did Augustus, Jr., when he retired. All died there; Julia in 1935. Acorn Hall then passed to Julia's nephew, Augustus Crane Hone, who married Alice Castleman, whose distinguished Southern family was related to five United States presidents. They lived there with their daughter, Mary Crane Hone, who gave the house to the Morris County Historical Society in 1971. Although modern essentials have been added, the house remains very much as it looked after the 1860 additions.

In 1971, the Home Garden Club of Morristown undertook the Acorn Hall grounds as a civic project. Alice Dustan Kollar drew the design for the present garden, representing the period from 1853 to 1888. □

Photograph by Alice D. Kollar

Morristown's Victorian Architects

Barbara Hoskins

Morristown owes much of its charm to its Victorian architecture. Though an old colonial town, few structures survive from the 18th century. It is the architecture of the 1880s and 1890s, the years of the big building boom, that still predominates in the town.

These two decades were prosperous and exciting ones in Morristown. The population more than doubled within 20 years, from 5,446 in 1880 to 8,156 in 1890 and a huge leap to 11,267 in 1900. New streets were being laid out and real estate sales ran high as individuals and small developers scrambled for the best lots. Among the new streets were Abbett and Atno Avenues, Budd Street, Farragut Place, the extension of Boykin Street through the Miller property (now Miller Road), Harrison Street, Mechanic Street (now Cobb Place), and Ridgedale Avenue. Washington Avenue had very recently been given a name and it had only four houses and no sidewalks along its entire length in 1880 but this soon changed. "There is now building everywhere," *The Jersey-man* proclaimed in 1887 and so it seemed. Over 400 new houses were built in this small town in the 1880s alone.

Building slowed somewhat but not much in the 1890s despite the Depression of 1893 and the Spanish-American War. In this decade the Cutler Family was developing its large land holdings in the Speedwell Avenue area, beginning with Walker Street and continuing until eventually there would be a street named for nearly every member of the family. The Estate of Stephen Vail sold off land along Speedwell Avenue to form Thompson and Kinney Streets.

There was new building on nearly every street in town.

For the most part the townspeople turned to local architects to design their homes. These men were often carpenter builders who became known as "architects" though without formal

Photograph by Barbara Beirne/TJFPLMMT

Victorian Details

The houses (left) at 20, 24 and 28 Franklin Street, and examples of fine woodwork (right) at 10 Franklin Place and 28 Franklin Street.

training. Chief among them in terms of number of houses built was Collins B. Weir (1845-1930), a Civil War Veteran, enlisting when he was 16, who was first a carpenter and then a furniture salesman before becoming an architect. His own home was at 19 Hill Street and his office at 16 Washington Street. He was an architect for 40 years, retiring in 1918.

Collins Weir planned and designed over 160 of the smaller houses in the area in the 1880s and almost the same number in the 1890s. His houses for the most part were in the $1,500 to $3,000 range (equivalent to $40,000 to $70,000 today) and include those on Clinton Street which he designed for the hatter, Eugene Carroll. In addition to being the busiest architect in town, he served as town assessor for 21 years and when running as the Republican nominee for the Assembly was described as a man of "great capacity, integrity and industry."

George W. Bower (1836-1906) has left a legacy in Morristown in both residential and business buildings. He was born in Cincinnati, Ohio, but early in life came to Chatham, where he learned the carpenter's trade. His office in the 1880s was opposite the Depot in the Day and Ennis Building, later moving to the corner of Park Place and Market Street. He lived on Speedwell Avenue and examples of his work can be seen on Early and Elm Streets, among other places. He planned the Schmidt Building, the Salny Building on Speedwell Avenue, the Methodist Parsonage and a great number of residences.

Frank Colburn (1858-1898) first went into partnership with David H. Wilday in the building business, then opened an architectural office on the corner of Park Place and Market Street. He designed large houses both here and in Montclair, eventually moving his office to New York City. An accomplished organist, he had a pipe organ in his own home at 27 Ridgedale Avenue. His house was demolished years ago to make way for Route 287.

Frank W. Meeker, an architect, and his brother Ernest, a carpenter, together built a number of houses in town, in the

Photograph by Barbara Beirne/TJFPLMMT

Photograph by Barbara Beirne/TJFPLMMT

Water Street (now Martin Luther King) area. His own home, a "cottage," was on Linden Street. During the 1880s he built a lumber yard at the end of Willow Street where there was then a railroad siding.

Robert Corea Walsh (1856-1911) designed some of the larger homes in Morristown, including his own on Headley Road, built in 1899. Houses he planned were in the $7,000 to $10,000 range. He also planned the Mills Street and Liberty Street Schools, the Parker Building and other public structures, including the First National Bank. His office was in the Morris County Savings Bank Building, reportedly designed by the New York architects McKim, Mead and White.

Arthur S. Pierson (1866-1928), of 203 Speedwell Avenue, and William C. Van Doren (1868-1926), 60 Mills Street, also were practicing architects in the 1880s and 1890s.

A young man just getting started in the area in 1890 was Louis R. Hazeltine, well known to the residents of the time as the son of Chas. G. Hazeltine, Headmaster of the Morris Female Institute. He designed the residence that is now The Peck School, four houses on Farragut Place, including his own, and the Presbyterian Manse on the Green. He moved to Summit, then eventually to California, where he died in 1931.

Beautiful Homes of Northern New Jersey, c. 1910

Photograph by Wendy R. London/TJFPLMMT

Architects' Houses

Robert Corea Walsh designed houses for himself (upper and lower right), 10 Headley Road, and **General Fitz John Porter** (right), One Farragut Place. This was one of the first houses built in Colles Park, a subdivision of the property once owned by James Colles.

Collins B. Weir's house (upper right), 25 Hill Street, designed for himself.

Houses on Ridgedale Avenue (right), as seen from Washington's Headquarters, about 1895.

The Rev. William Todd Egbert (1843-1886), a cleric at the Church of the Redeemer, found architecture compatible with the ministry and designed a large house on Maple Avenue in 1879 of which it was said, "The marked style of architecture is a new departure for Morristown." He designed a house in Queen Anne style on Perry Street said to be "one of the prettiest in town," was architect for the Pumpelly house and the Roberts house, also the Dr. A. H. Flanders house on upper Court St., as well as his own house on Egbert Hill.

A word should be said about George A. Mills (1856-1928), master carpenter, who built a large and well-equipped steam-planing mill on Pine Street in 1893. Here he manufactured all kinds of cabinet worksash blinds, doors and moldings. There were over 100 men in his employ and it was these men who were often responsible for executing the plans of the foregoing architects. He built many of the beautiful homes in Normandy Park and his own home at 143 Washington Street.

It is, in part, to these little-known men that Morristown owes its architectural heritage. Many well-known architects designed houses and public buildings in the Morristown area, but the great majority of homes which survive are products of the often obscure men of the last century.

Photograph by George Goodwin/TJFPLMMT

Morristown, New Jersey, Photo-Gravures, by Wm. K. Muchmore

Photograph by Judi Benvenuti/TJFPLMMT

Curtiss Collection/TJFPLMMT

The John Smith House

This house on Washington Valley Road, Morris Township, was built between 1795 and 1812 on land bought from Jacob Arnold. The frame portion of the house is 18th century; the brick portion has the date 1812 on the chimney. About 1855, the house and homestead farm came into the possession of John H. Smith, who was called the area's first scientific farmer when he discovered that lime increased his wheat yield.

Mr. and Mrs. Zenas Smith (left), September 6, 1915. The house was in the Smith family until 1959.

Rural Life

On any road out of 19th-century Morristown, the scene changed dramatically. Meadows alternated with orchards, waves of grain rolled over gentle hills, a dense grove of woods would rise suddenly and just as suddenly give way to a clearing that revealed a farmhouse and cluster of barns. Seated on horseback or slow-moving wagon, there was always something peaceful or beautiful to see — the spring dogwoods, the laden peach and apple trees, the tall oaks and hickories, ducks preening on a tranquil pond, little brooks and meandering streams, grazing animals everywhere. The sounds of farmland reigned — a mooing, bleating, neighing, crowing, calling, singing world.

The last vestige of this early Morris Township is in Washington Valley. It is the one area where one can imagine the look and feel of rural life.

Washington Valley was settled early, probably first by "squatters" sometime between 1725 and 1750, but surely by 1749 when three families — Arnold, Condict and Loree — purchased land and made settlement.

The early settlers grew corn much as the Indians had before them, planting on hills with the same number of stalks on each, often with pumpkins between. As the number of settlers increased, so did the livestock and large dairy herds were established. The people of the Valley were soon almost self-sufficient with blacksmith shops, grist and sawmills and the brisk trade carried on by carpenters, cobblers, weavers, tailors, hatters and distillers.

On every farm, an orchard of apple trees was planted. Many of the apples found their way into cider, which when fermented produced the popular apple "spirits." Despite strong disapproval from local church ministers and an excise tax placed on spirits after the Revolution, the business thrived and large numbers of barrels were shipped to New York and then to the South. Peach orchards followed and the little Rockaway Valley ("Rock-a-bye Baby") Railroad from Watnong to Whitehouse spent its brief 30 years hauling fruit — and other freight, including humans — through the Valley.

In *Washington Valley: An Informal History*, published in 1960, there is a description of how the first homes were built: "Before a house could be built by these early settlers . . . it was necessary to make a clearing by cutting down the forest trees and leaving the stumps to decompose. This clearing was usually located at one corner of the farm, rather than in the center, and so the oldest houses were built in a corner near a road. A cellar was dug in order to provide a warmer house and a place for frost-free storage. The cellar floor was of dirt, but the walls were of stone brought in from the fields and laid together with mud or a clay and hair combination. Only one of the early houses in the Valley was built without a cellar. The house itself was built of wood or wood combined with stone. It was not until 60 years had passed after the settling of the Valley that the Smith house and the Schoolhouse were built of brick."

In the same excellent book, there is a recollection of life in the Valley in the late 19th and early 20th centuries by Caroline R. Foster, who lived 99 of her 102 years at Fosterfields:

"As I first remember it, this was a rural community, consisting of adjoining farms from here to Chester. Morristown was only a country village, where the stores remained open in the evenings for the convenience of the farmers who could not come to town until after

Photograph by Barbara Beirne/TJFPLMMT

TJFPLMMT

Meadows and Fields of the Township

The **high meadow of Fosterfields** (above). It is now maintained as a living historical farm by the Morris County Park Commission.

Rolling countryside (right), about 1900. This unidentified scene is typical of the western part of Morris Township at the turn of the century.

The last bell rang at 9 A.M., the pupils were all at their desks, two in a seat. Then came the busy hours of study and recitation . . . . During the noon hour many went off to find wildflowers, crabs, turtles and snakes.
Norman Gould, a former pupil at the Washington Valley School House

Courtesy of Morris County Heritage Commission

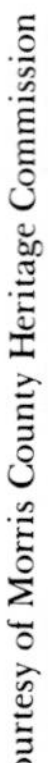

Washington Valley School House

This building, originally constructed in 1813, was rebuilt in 1869, as shown here. It could accommodate comfortably 52 pupils, although average attendance was much less. It was heated with one stove. Water was available after 1887 from an outside pump. Two privies were the required 35 feet away.

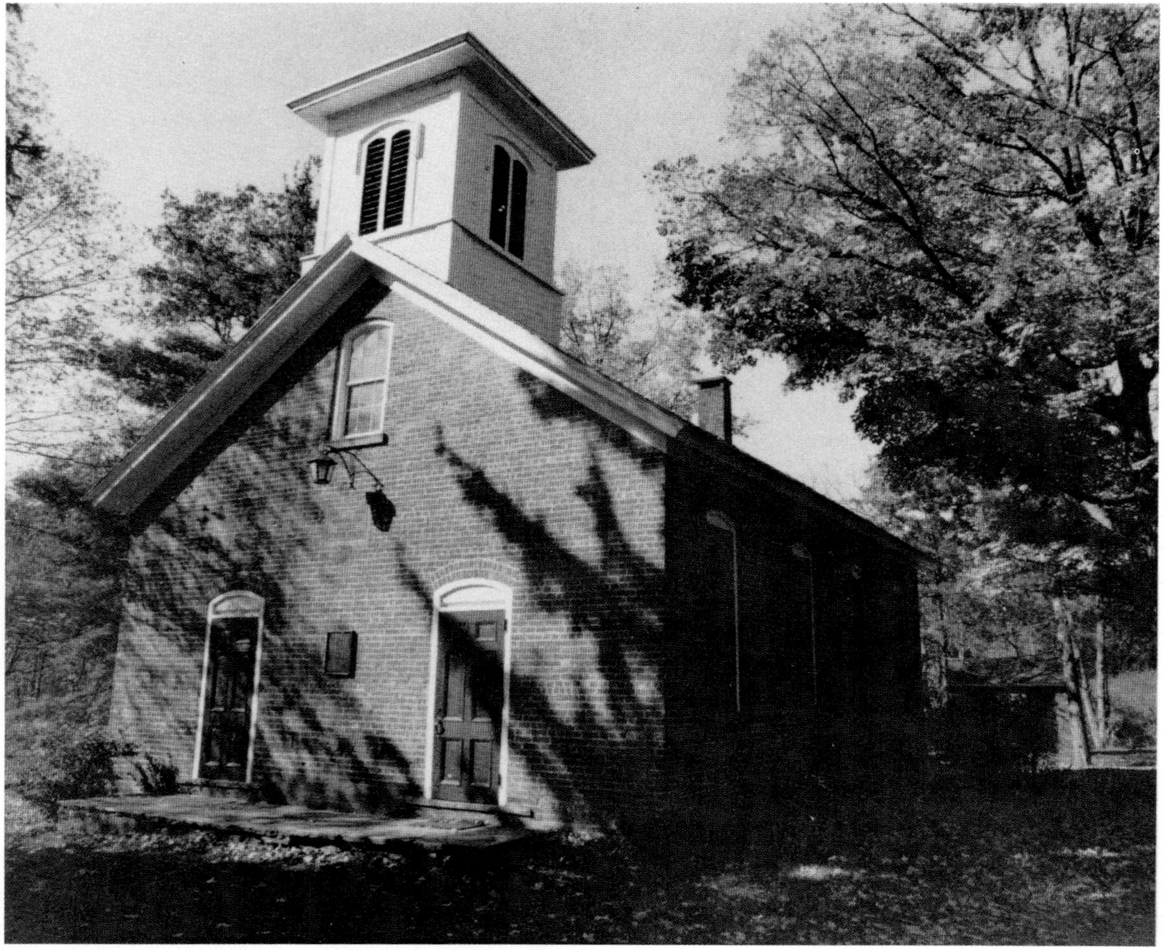

This was one of four township schools built between 1810 and 1814. The Mountain School, Mount Kemble Avenue, the oldest, was erected in 1810. The other two were the "Old Stone School" on Mendham Road and the "Board School House" on Hanover Avenue, both built in 1814.

In 1905, the Morris Township Board of Education was formed and one by one the little schools were abandoned. The Washington Valley School was closed in 1913 when the children were transported to Hillside School on Center Avenue (now condominiums) by horse-drawn carriage with boards for seats or by bobsled in winter until a bus was purchased in 1920.

the day's work was done. Going to market every day was an unheard-of procedure. Butcher wagons came around twice or three times a week from the Mendham-Chester district. Reaping grain by hand with a cradle is a far cry from the combine of today, which reaps, threshes and bags the grain in one operation . . . . The difference in the highway from here to Mendham is another evidence of drastic change. The road from Morristown to Mendham was a dirt road which was not surfaced until many years later. I remember riding in a box wagon, while the men of the farm drove a herd of twenty odd young heifers along Mendham Road, past the Hilltop Church to a farm beyond for summer pasture, and hardly a vehicle was seen on the way." □

Courtesy of Mr. and Mrs. Terrence D. Daniels/TJFPLMMT

The Jacob Arnold House

The Arnold House on Washington Valley Road, built about 1789, as it appeared November 11, 1870, when it was owned by Jacob's son, Silas H. Arnold, shown here with his family.

The Arnold family lived from 1747 to 1923 in Washington Valley, where they were large landowners and the most prominent citizens.

Jacob Arnold's father was Samuel Arnold, who was married to Phoebe Ford, the sister of Colonel Jacob Ford, Jr. By 1761, Samuel owned 380 acres, including a tract purchased from Thomas Penn, December 1, 1756. Samuel — who died in 1764 at 38 — is believed to have built Arnold Tavern (page 34).

Although there is no specific mention in his will, it is assumed he provided for someone to oversee the tavern until Jacob Arnold became 21, which happened shortly before the Revolution, when it became Washington's Headquarters in 1777.

Jacob first married Elizabeth Tuttle and they had ten children, five of whom died before maturity. After her death in 1803, he married Sarah H. Nixon — she was 24 to his 56 — and they had seven children. Not surprisingly, Arnold was one of the original subscribers to the Washington Valley Schoolhouse.

Silas H. Arnold (1813-90), third child of Jacob and Sarah, was born in the old homestead, where he later raised his own family. He held many county and city offices. He was married to Martha Louise Pierson and had eight children. He left the house to bachelor sons, Edwin and Willis, who were butchers. Sheep and cattle were driven on hoof from Pennsylvania and New York to the Arnold pastures where they were fattened, then slaughtered in the big barn and sold in this butcher shop on Market Street.

After their deaths, the homestead, reduced to 5.6 acres, was conveyed to unmarried sisters, Isabella and Emma, who sold it in 1923 to the Hurlburt B. Cuttings. The Cuttings remodeled and enlarged the house to its present size. There have been several more owners, but the house remains a private residence.

Four photographs courtesy of Morris County Park Commission/TJFPLMMT

Revere Family in front of The Willows, about 1867

The **house** (above), built 1853-54 in Gothic Revival style by Ashbel Bruen for Lt. Joseph Warren Revere, was named by him for a grove of trees in the meadow. **Interior views** (opposite) show the entrance hallway with the mantelpiece specially carved for the house and the dining room with murals painted by Revere.

In 1881, Charles Grant Foster bought the house and renamed it Fosterfields. In 1972, his daughter, Caroline Rose Foster, gave part of the property to the Morris County Park Commission to maintain as a "living historical farm." In 1979, she willed them the house and the rest of the land.

Fosterfields

Joseph Warren Revere was another military man who settled in Morristown after roaming the world. He wrote two books about his many romantic adventures: *A Tour of Duty in California* (1849), which became a handbook for pioneers and settlers in the Gold Rush years, and *Keel and Saddle* (1872), which summed up his career in both the Army and the Navy.

He was the grandson of the patriot Paul Revere and the son of Dr. John Revere, a noted New York physician. At age 14, he ran away to join the Navy, where he served with distinction for many years. He was later commissioned as Lieutenant Colonel in the Mexican Army, and upon retirement, he became the U.S. Government Timber Agent for the forests of Sonoma, California, where he stayed until 1852. That year, he bought the house and 88½-acre farm in Washington Valley, off Mendham Road, which had belonged in 1750 to Samuel Roberts and was later deeded to his son-in-law, Jonathan Ogden. The Ogden farmhouse was believed to have been the headquarters of General Henry Knox during the winter of 1779-80.

In 1853, Lieutenant Revere commissioned Ashbel Bruen of Chatham — also the builder of Acorn Hall that year — to erect a cruciform Gothic Revival house with an impressive two-story pointed-arch verandah. He lavished care and attention on every detail of the house.

The Willows was to have been his retirement home, but the Civil War prompted him to serve his country again, this time in the Army. He became a Colonel in the 7th Regiment of the New Jersey Volunteers and later, as Brigadier General, commanded the 2nd New Jersey brigade at Chancellorville. He is believed the only Union witness to the fateful wounding of Stonewall Jackson.

By 1872, suffering from numerous war wounds, Revere found running a large estate impossible, and he moved into the Sansay House on DeHart Street, where he died in 1880.

In 1881, Charles Grant Foster from Hartford, Connecticut, a member of the commodity exchange in New York City, purchased the farm and later enlarged it with two adjoining farms. His only daughter, Caroline Rose, inherited the property and lived there during her long life, which spanned many changes in Morristown — from rural haven to millionaires' playground to commuters' suburb to growing commercial center. Deeply interested in history, she found a way to preserve a rich heritage all but vanished in this area. □

Courtesy of Morris County Park Commission/TJFPLMMT

Courtesy of Morris County Park Commission/TJFPLMMT

Courtesy of Morris County Park Commission/TJFPLMMT

Caroline Rose Foster (1877-1979)

Miss Foster — Cara to her friends — was photographed in her sitting room about 1960. Her famous collection of Currier & Ives prints is on the walls.

Miss Foster's father did not believe in college for women, but she received an excellent education at Miss Dana's School in Morristown. She was interested in a wide variety of subjects, such as Greek mythology, philosophy and Shakespeare and could quote easily from poetry and the Bible. Her telescope was her particular delight, although she could no longer use it after she began to lose her eyesight. However, she was always interested in managing the farm, which she did even before her father's death. She wrote a chapter about Fosterfields in Washington Valley: *An Informal History*, which she also helped to finance. According to Barbara Hoskins, a co-author, "She was absolutely thrilled with that book. She said it was one of the first times that she had done anything that she could look at and hold in her hand."

Caroline Rose Foster Remembers

Mr. Ashbel Bruen of Chatham was to build the house for $7,128.15. The contract said that it must be finished within six months or said builder had to pay Lieutenant Revere $50 a month penalty until it was finished. And so I gather it was finished on time, and that was February of 1854, and considering all things, it is a very well-built house. Of course, it wasn't decorated inside for some time because Mr. Revere decorated it himself.

I have lived here since 1881 and it's exactly the same as it was.

When he moved into the house, he brought a wood carver and cabinetmaker with him from Germany who did most of the woodwork and carved the stairway, the dining table, sideboard and chairs along with other furniture.

Mr. Revere decorated the dining room with all sorts of animals, wild and tame, foods, vines and fruits — quite typical of what he considered the blessings of this world. He decorated the hall in a blue and brown pattern and the sitting room was much the same except only in lighter blue. The library was maroon and brown with black walnut trimming from bookcases to the doorways, making quite a Gothic scene. And this is still in the same condition as when he left it in 1872.

In 1881, my father bought this place, the 88½ acres, the house and barn and the Ogden farmhouse. We moved in, I think, in the spring. Of course, I don't remember too many details at five or six but I do remember a good many of the things that happened. I had a nurse with me until I was seven, and I remember long before she left to get married.

I remember wandering over the place with her and sitting under the trees and watching the vehicles go by on "the road from Jacob Arnold's" to Morristown. It came from the entrance of this place, the gateway, then over the hill and into the Washington

Adapted from an interview conducted by Marian Gerhart and Barbara Hoskins, February 1, 1968.

Valley Road at the foot of the Moody farm. Mr. Moody and Mr. Carey would come home late in a jovial mood and I would sit and wave at them as they came along. Of course, all the young people walked to school then and many used this road. It was a shortcut, really more or less a trail. I remember when the traffic began to slow up because of a good road from Mendham to Washington Valley.

When Pa bought the house he had only the central portion, the Revere property. Later he bought the Nathaniel Wilson farm on the south, about 76 acres, and the John Gribbon farm on the northeast. The road, as I've said, was a public road, but when he bought the land on both sides of it, he applied to the township for a vacation, and about 1886 it was closed to the public. We had to close the road at the gate once a year in order to establish that fact.

To return for a moment to the years after the Revere family moved to Morristown: The house was rented during the summer to many people, among them Mr. and Mrs. Bret Harte. It is said that he collected material here for his well-known novel, *Thankful Blossom*. He didn't write it while here, but took the material with him on a trip abroad and wrote the book there. It's very interesting reading for a winter's night, to go back to 1779 and 1780 and hear first-hand what was happening in the lives of the people during that time.

I found a letter in the library from Bret Harte around 1874 or 1875, saying that he hadn't quite settled in his new position in Glasgow, where he was appointed counsel. And in this letter I found a quotation that is quite interesting — although being a Morristonian I take it to heart somewhat:

"Since I wrote you from Scotland, I've received yours of the 15th of June. I am rejoiced to hear that you are out of town. Even if Morristown is the same old bigotted self-righteous, hypocritical place, it's better than being in a New York boarding house in summer. But will you not find some pleasanter place?"

Frederick H. Meserve Collection

Brigadier General, later Brevet-Major General, Joseph Warren Revere (1812-80)

Elizabeth Papps Remembers Miss Foster

Miss Foster's earliest memories were of sitting near Mendham Road with her nurse, Bridget, and watching the horse and carriages go by. She and her Irish nurse crept into a neighbor's yard to dig up day lillies. They then planted them along the ice house in the backyard of the Foster property. Today, there are still wild lillies growing in that spot. Miss Foster loved that ice house and nicknamed it "William Tell's Castle." She remembered watching the men cut ice from the reservoir on Western Avenue in Morristown.

She also used to love to climb the tall evergreen trees on her property. One time she had climbed very high and got caught on a branch with her red flannel petticoat. She hung in that tree until somebody came to rescue her.

Miss Foster was brought up by her father, or "Pa" as she called him, and her Aunt Carrie [Miss Caroline Elizabeth Thompson], who came to live at The Willows after Mrs. Foster [the former Emma Louise Thompson of Mendham] had died of tuberculosis when Miss Foster was three years old. This Aunt Carrie would try in vain to teach young Caroline domestic skills such as sewing and knitting but Miss Foster never wanted to learn. She hated sewing and wanted to work in the outdoors with tools instead. As a consequence, Caroline Foster never acquired any domestic skills and had always to rely on help. She and her father would go to Castle Gardens [now Battery Place, New York] to find servants and cooks. It was there that she found the "three Marys" who were Irish, taken right off the ship and stayed with the Fosters for years.

Miss Foster's favorite uncle was William Thompson, who was also surrogate of Morristown for many years. Miss Foster recalled one Christmas, when she was very young, her uncle gave her a special present. Set up in the library were the tree, trimmings, and gifts. When Miss Foster walked in Christmas morning, she saw a lovely doll's crib covered with dotted Swiss material with a beautiful blond curly-haired doll sleeping in the crib. Miss Foster was disappointed and disgusted, because she hated dolls. She wanted a toolbox and tools instead.

Miss Foster had two brothers who both died before she was born. One died of diptheria and the other, she believed, was dropped by his nurse. Whatever really happened, Miss Foster remembered that there was always some mystery surrounding the death of one of her brothers.

Aunt Carrie also tried in vain to have other children play with Miss Foster. On one occasion the son of a local minister came to play with her. Miss Foster had nicknamed him "milktoast." She decided to play the "French Revolution" with this boy and when his head was in the "guillotine," Aunt Carrie

Courtesy of Morris County Park Commission/TJFPLMMT

Miss Foster as a young woman with her father.

Adapted from an interview conducted by Sheila Sweeney Goeke, July 30, 1980. Mrs. Papps, of Bernardsville, N.J., was Miss Foster's nurse in her final years.

Courtesy of Morris County Park Commission/TJFPLMMT

Charles Grant Foster (1843-1927) with Chip.

Courtesy of Morris County Park Commission/TJFPLMMT

The sitting room in Mr. Foster's lifetime.

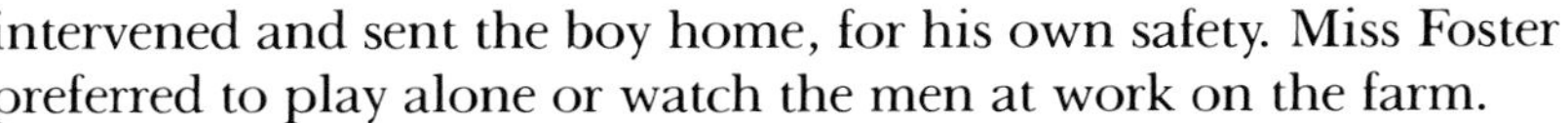

intervened and sent the boy home, for his own safety. Miss Foster preferred to play alone or watch the men at work on the farm.

Her father taught her to fish in the brook on their property. Later when she became older, she and her father would fish in streams farther from home to catch the good trout, but these places were kept secret. She also hunted on her property and later two rifles rested by her bedposts; rifles and fishing equipment were all over the house. She remembered walking into the kitchen on her property and seeing the farmers eat peas with their knives.

She and "Pa" would sit on their front porch and see who could spit tobacco the farthest. They would aim for a certain post or stone in the driveway or front yard. When Caroline Foster was in her late teens, she went to Washington, D.C., to visit some cousins, who were very sophisticated. Her cousins were smoking cigarettes at the time; when she returned, she, too, had started to smoke. One day "Pa" yelled up to her, "Cara, I can smell that smoke — you come down here and smoke with me." After that, Miss Foster ended up smoking cigars and pipes with her father.

Russell W. Myers Remembers Miss Foster

In the 1960s, we became fast friends. I would read various types of books to her once a week; many times they would be history books about Morristown and the area. You would be reading along and she would stop you and have very interesting comments about the people who lived in Morristown. For example, one anecdote she told me was about going to dinner at Florham, which belonged to Hamilton McK. Twombly and is now Fairleigh Dickinson University. She would go with her coachman in those days. You would be greeted at the door by the butler and Mrs. Twombly would be there. You would be introduced around and greet everybody and have a drink. Then, on to dinner, and she said, "I always put my hands over the soup bowl because the butler took it away too quick." After dinner, as usual in those days, the gentlemen would go to one room with the cigars and the ladies would go to another room. You would join again after that and Mrs. Twombly would come around and see each guest. When she got to the last person, she would say to the butler, "It is time." That meant time to go. People who had never been there before and did not realize what time to have their coachman return were left standing at the door. On occasion, Miss Foster said she took people home because on a cold night it would not be very pleasant to stay out there. That was just one of the many, many stories she told me about old Morristown around 1910. It was really a marvelous part of the world in which to live.

You have to understand she was a very thrifty person. She never spent money unless she had to. As a matter of fact, even in the early days when the porch had to be repaired, or whatever, she would always send her farmer to buy secondhand lumber. She would never buy new lumber.

I believe it was in 1922, or somewhere through there, that she did not own an automobile. When she would go to parties, she would go with a horse and buggy. All of her friends had cars in those days, but her father would not let her buy a car. So on Christmas Day, let's say in 1922, the chauffeur drove up from a nearby property and left a Model T Ford on the front of the driveway, which was given to her by her friends. She took off, she told me, and drove up to Connecticut because that was where her aunts lived. She said her Pa did not like that very much. To show you how thrifty she was, we still have that same car. She kept all her cars, probably six or eight of them. She never threw anything away. Everything was kept.

She was a very ardent farmer, and a very good farmer. As a matter of fact, she and her father traveled to the Isle of Jersey to bring back a thoroughbred dairy herd. I remember her telling me that her father wanted to go on the Cunard Line. In those days, the ships did not have ballasts on them and boats used to roll. She remembers that she hung on all the way over; she was sick from the time she got on the boat until the time she came home. They bought a good dairy herd and for many years they would sell milk and produce from the farm. I think you must understand that her farm was always a working farm. The quality of farming was of the best. I remember even when she was in her early nineties, when the grain was being harvested — she could not see well either — but she would pick up the grain in her hands after it had gone through the thresher and she would say, "Well, I guess we are going to get x number of bushels from this wheat today — that is very good."

Adapted from an interview conducted by Sheila Sweeney Goeke, April 8, 1980. Mr. Myers was secretary-director of the Morris County Park Commission when Miss Foster donated her land.

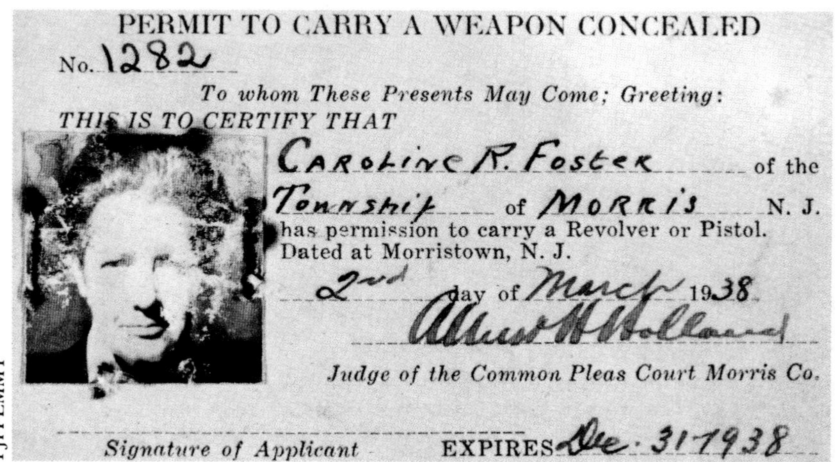
PERMIT TO CARRY A WEAPON CONCEALED

No. 1282

To whom These Presents May Come; Greeting:

THIS IS TO CERTIFY THAT

Caroline R. Foster of the Township of Morris N. J.

has permission to carry a Revolver or Pistol.

Dated at Morristown, N. J.

2nd day of March 1938

Albert H. Holland

Judge of the Common Pleas Court Morris Co.

Signature of Applicant EXPIRES Dec. 31 1938

TJFPLMMT

Gun permit. Miss Foster was a deputy sheriff and a good shot, as she occasionally demonstrated to trespassers on her property.

Earl Beach Remembers Miss Foster

When I first came here, she used to get up 6:00 every morning. We'd be down in the barn milkin' the cows and feeding the animals and down she'd come by 6:30 every morning to see how things were going, if everything was all right. And then she'd go out to the fields with us. I'd go out and cut hay and things and she'd come out to the field and watch me and then, when I got ready to bail the hay, she always drove the truck for me to load the hay in. And lots of times, she'd get off and even throw hay up in them days. In later years, of course, she got where she couldn't do any of that. But she used to go out to quite a few parties and things when I first came here. It was mostly afternoons and I'd take her to them; that's when I was chauffeur. But other than that, it was just normal 'round the place. She'd be out with me awhile. Then she'd be in the house and then she'd set in her chair and take her nap and then she'd be back out again. An you'd see her right up from daylight to dark, in and out all day long, workin' with you. Well, when I first came here, we had the ten milkin' cows and four or five calves — she told about her father having 50 or 60 milkers — and we had chickens and ducks. She always got young chickens every year. We had to raise those and then she used to have people come and buy the milk right here at the farm. They'd bring their own containers. And I think, if I remember right, when I first came here, she was gettin 12¢ a quart for the milk — the most it got to was 20¢ a quart over the years.

We used to plow in the spring, put in oats and corn, and then we had a big garden. We used to have fifty or sixty kinds of vegetables in the garden. Hayin' started around June 15th, and you tried to get it done as early as you could. Then you start combining your oat and your wheat and your barley. Then when that was all over with, you'd start plowin' in the fall to plant your winter wheat.

And in the wintertime, when I first came here, you always had to saw wood and split it for the furnaces and fireplaces. One man and myself is what I always had. Maybe for the last fifteen years there was nobody but myself. Had a man mow the lawn once in a while on a weekend.

Courtesy of Morris County Park Commission/TJFPL.MMT

Miss Foster and some friends.

But that's about all we did and then in winter, we helped paint the house and helped the maid when we had the time. And you had, of course, your barns to keep straightened up. We used to grind our own cow food — the wheat, oats and barley, mix it, and corn. You had to do that in the winter on good days.

Miss Foster told me what she wanted, and that's what would get done. She hired me to oversee the other man and she always said we'd have three or four but we never did get three or four men [laughing]. And that's the way we did it. Whatever she wanted done, I'd go and do.

Adapted from an interview conducted by Sheila Sweeney Goeke, March 18, 1980. Mr. Beach was her farmer and manager for 29 years. For the last ten of her life, he also did her housework, cooking and errands.

When Home Was a Mansion

TJFPLMMT

Bexley Hocombe on Lake Road, Morris Township.

THE PEOPLE WHO LIVED in the mansions didn't call them that. It was home or "in the country." It was never "living on the estate" and "growing up in a mansion." That was for other people to say.

In the Morristown area at the turn of the century, there were many who lived in a grand manner. It was a popular summering place of the wealthy; and at one time, it is said, more millionaires were in residence than any other place in the United States.

In 1902, the *New York Herald* noted that families worth a total of more than half a billion dollars were tucked away in the hills of Morristown — which, of course, included Morris Township. "The country town has only 12,000 inhabitants, and they are little known, but the wealthy people there have never sought lavish display. They have, instead, sought freedom from notoriety." The newspaper promised there were 15 tycoons with more than $10 million each and another 15 with more than $2 million. The other 30 or so trailed with only $1 million plus. Among those the newspaper named were John Claflin, Charles F. Cutler, Jesse L. Eddy, Benjamin F. Evans, George and Peter Frelinghuysen, L. C. Gillespie, Eugene Higgins, Otto H. Kahn, Gustav E. and Rudolph H. Kissel, Luther Kountze, Mrs. George Jenkins, Mrs. George McAlpin, Robert A. and Robert H. McCurdy, Charles H. Mellon and Louis A. Thebaud.

In 1913, *The Daily Record* published a map showing 122 sites "worth seeing." Of these, 94 were estates within the borders of Morristown and Morris Township.

An army of workers put up thick-walled stone and brick houses, mostly of European inspiration. Owners competed with each other to import the most skilled craftsmen to individualize their houses. Gardeners hauled tons of soil to rearrange slopes, build terraces and create gardens and flowerbeds. Magnificent full-grown bushes and trees were brought in by wagon and placed with loving care in clumps or rows or in long borders on either side of the entrance road, just as a prominent landscape gardener had decreed. Inside paneling, stained glass and furnishings were ordered specially to fill the often huge hallways and parlor rooms. Yearly trips to Europe were made to find just the right paintings, rugs, china and statuary.

Even the "smaller" estates — no deer herd, polo field or private gas plant — had numerous indoor and outdoor employees to maintain their special world of comfort and style. Butlers, housekeepers, parlormaids and upstairs maids; governesses, nannies and tutors; cooks and kitchen maids, coachmen, grooms and stable boys; managers, caretakers, watchmen; gardeners and assistants, all played their vital part in Morristown's Golden Age. □

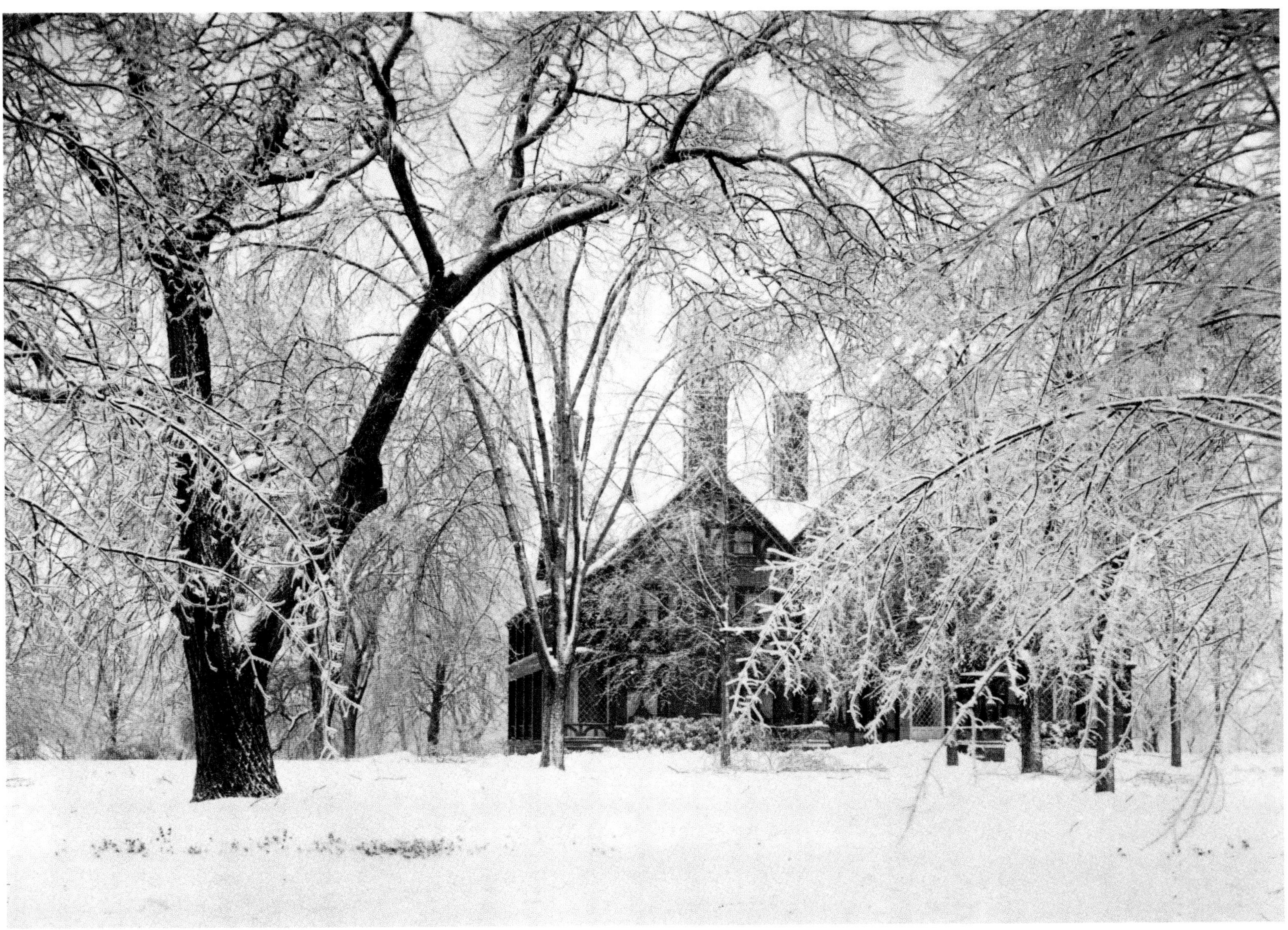

Courtesy of Malcolm McAlpin

Twin Oaks, 77 Madison Avenue, Morristown, Home of Mr. and Mrs. Benjamin Franklin Evans

The mansion is shown as it appeared in the blizzard of 1901-02.

The **entrance** (page 160) was opposite the home of Charles Henry Mellon, now the site of Morristown Memorial Hospital.

Wedding party (page 161) of Madelyn Evans and David H. McAlpin, June 17, 1905, on the porch of Twin Oaks. Mr. and Mrs. Evans are standing in front of the door. Caroline R. Foster, a bridesmaid, is seated on the bridegroom's right with a bouquet at her feet. The bride's parents built the couple a house next to theirs as a wedding present.

Twin Oaks was torn down in 1933; a nursing home is on the site.

Courtesy of Malcolm McAlpin

Courtesy of Malcolm McAlpin

Courtesy of Ralph H. Cutler, Jr.

Beautiful Homes of Northern New Jersey, c. 1910

Residence of Richard Aldrich McCurdy, president of Mutual Insurance Company, South Street side, which surprisingly was the back of the house. The front of the mansion was on Franklin Street where two stone posts are still standing; the driveway became Hamilton Road.

The building was an impressive sight in yellow brick trimmed with gray stone, costing an estimated $500,000 for 62 rooms and gold-plated fixtures.

Blair House is now on the site; however, the carriage house and stable still stands at the corner of Franklin Street and Ford Avenue.

Morristown's Millionaire Mile

Many beautiful and impressive houses were built in the lower — or southern end — of South Street and on Madison Avenue.

At first, a few old New York families made Morristown their summer quarters, but soon so many were coming out that the population in those months sometimes doubled. These families usually rented for a few years, then decided to build. Later, a number of older or retired couples made Morristown their permament address.

Eugene V. Welsh, a real estate agent for many years, had these recollections.

"Madison Avenue for many years, was the residential show area of Morristown and Morris County. The entire avenue was occupied by large residences of various types and designs, with broad lawns and mammoth trees. It was known generally as the 'Newport' of Morristown. The summer, strange to say, was popular for summer occupancy by out-of-town families, whereas the permanent residents of Madison Avenue would transport themselves to the seashore and mountains during their vacation.

"It was an interesting sight when a new family came to Morristown and rented one of the larger homes furnished and equipped for a three-month period. They would bring with them a staff of household servants, in addition to the stable help — a coachman, and one possibly two grooms, depending on the number of horses they would bring with them. Usually, there would be seven or eight carriages of various kinds and perhaps six or eight horses."

Most of the houses built on Morristown's Madison Avenue were on the old Randolph farm. The Honorable Theodore F. Randolph, former Governor of New Jersey, owned property running from the intersection of South Street and Madison Avenue to the intersection of Madison Avenue and Normandy Boulevard. His early 19th-century wooden farmhouse stood where Morristown Memorial Hospital now is located. In 1876, however, he built a house at 125 Madison Avenue for his daughter, Mrs. Stone, setting the high standard for the kind of mansions that were built on that street.

The Stone House is described by Elizabeth Lee Cutler. She and her husband, Ralph Cutler, Jr., a direct descendant of Silas Condict, were the last owners.

"This large house in Queen Anne style was built on two and one-half acres subdivided from the Randolph farm property. It sat on a knoll 20 feet above street level and set back about 200 feet. It had five plastered stories and slate roof. A large barn with horse stalls was at the rear of the property below the garden.

"The cellar was half above ground and had kitchen with dumb waiter, servants' dining room, laundry, and separate storage, furnace and coal rooms.

"The first floor had a piazza with a big glass front door and a wide hall with a staircase lighted by a skylight rising three stories. There was a library, front parlor with bay window, large dining room, and a ballroom in the rear with fireplaces and sliding glass doors. There was also a butler's pantry and china pantry.

"The second floor had a large hall with a 'picture window,' five bedrooms — four with fireplaces — and two baths.

"The third floor had a suite with a very large solarium and fireplace, three bedrooms and a dressing room-bath. In a rear wing were three maids' rooms with a bath.

"The fourth floor was the attic with three rooms around a central area with a skylight.

TJFPLMMT

South Street (above) and **Madison Avenue**, about 1910.

TJFPLMMT

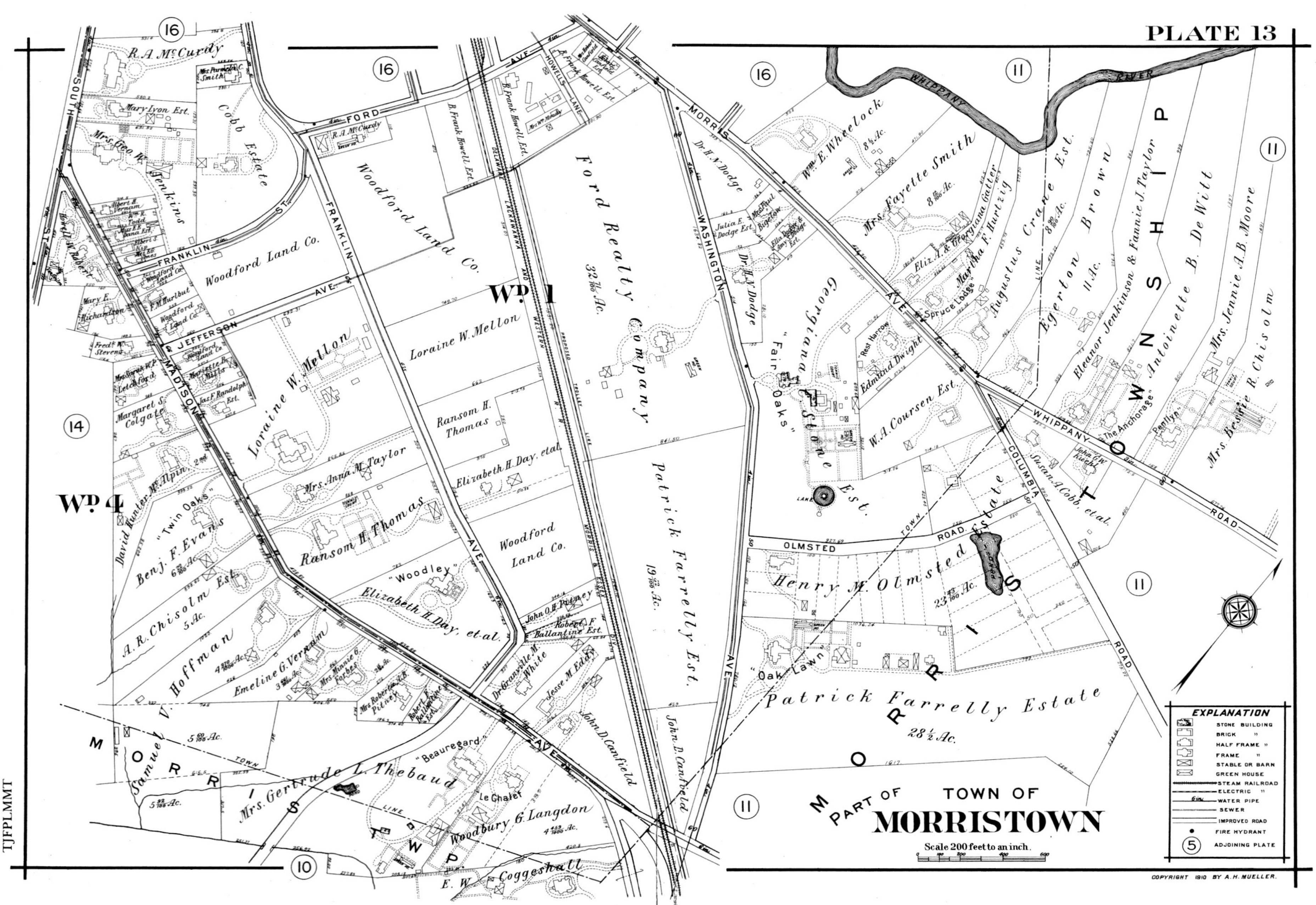

Morristown in 1910, Madison Avenue to Morris Avenue to the borders of Convent Station and Normandy Heights

"A rear wing, designed by local architect Fritz Baer, was added in 1910 when Mrs. Minnie G. Forbes owned the house [map]."

In 1927, Mrs. James Griswold, who was Mrs. Cutler's grandmother, bought the house from Mr. Forbes for $33,000. The Cutlers bought the house in 1959 from her estate and lived there until they sold it in 1964. It was vandalized before it was torn down, a sad but typical ending to a mansion on a street "paved with gold."

Morristown's Golden Age, of course, passed away in Mrs. Griswold's lifetime. The Cutlers held on much longer than most. The Depression and taxes took their toll and modern families simply did not want to live in huge houses that required such expensive upkeep. People moved "out in the country" to quieter places without so much traffic. □

Photograph by James L. Grabow/TJFPLMMT

Beauregard, Madison Avenue, Morristown

This Flemish brick mansion was built in 1905 on 30 acres by Louis A. Thebaud, son-in-law of Richard A. McCurdy. In the 1960s, it was converted into an office building, 151 Madison Avenue.

TJFPLMMT

The Stone House, Madison Avenue, Morristown

This mansion was built for Gov. Randolph's daughter. An office building, 111 Madison Avenue, is on the site.

Courtesy of Morristown-Beard School

Another Madison Avenue Mansion, Morristown

This was probably owned by Woodbury G. Langdon, N.Y. Rapid Transit Commissioner. An office building, 161-163 Madison Avenue, is on the site.

Courtesy of Mrs. E. Estey Stowell/TJFPL.MMT

Handsome Colonial Revival Mansions in Morristown

This popular architectural style reflected the English heritage.

Residence of Ransom H. Thomas (above), New York stockbroker, 98 Madison Avenue, built before 1910. It was later owned by Col. Franklin D'Olier, president of Prudential Insurance Company and first national commander of the American Legion. In the 1940s, it was torn down and became part of Morristown Memorial Hospital.

Residence of George W. Jenkins (opposite, above), banker, corner of South Street and Madison Avenue. Mrs. Jenkins, an heiress and philanthropist, was the aunt of Marcellus Hartley Dodge. The office building, 10 Madison Avenue, is on the site.

Residence of Charles Henry Mellon (opposite, lower left), investment broker and cousin of Andrew Mellon, Madison Avenue, built in 1901 on the site of Governor Theodore F. Randolph's house. It, in turn, was torn down some years after a bad fire in 1934 and became the site of the present Morristown Memorial Hospital.

Residence of J. O. H. Pitney (opposite, lower right), prominent lawyer, 127 Madison Avenue, built in 1899. Mr. Pitney was married to the daughter of Robert F. Ballantine, president of P. Ballantine & Sons Brewing Company, who also lived in the area. A new office building is on the site.

Beautiful Homes of Northern New Jersey, c. 1910

Morristown, N.J. is the Millionaire City of the Nation. It contains the richest and least known colony of wealthy people in the world.
From New York *Herald*, 1902

TJFPLMMT

Residence of Mr. Chas. H Mellon. MORRISTOWN, N. J.

TJFPLMMT

Madison Avenue, April 28, 1920

From *A Curious Childhood* by William E. Fiske

The trip, if one could call it such for it was only about a half mile, from Franklin Place to Madison Avenue, traversed more than distance, bridging as it did all that divided life in a simple, homely, white clapboard house from a far more formal style of living in a large, vaguely Tudor, black boarded and cream plastered house of some pretension which my grandfather Letchford had built in 1896 in Morristown. In short, my father, mother, and I were now, in 1920, when I was four years old, moving from our rented home to live with my widowed, maternal grandmother who had re-opened her Madison Avenue house and invited my parents to live with her.

It was, I recall, a cold, rainy day on that twenty-eighth of April when grandma's Cadillac town car waited for us on Franklin Place. This was the first time I had ever seen this car, and it bulks now, in memory, as large, or larger, than it was in life. It was painted in the old dark, Brewster-green, with black fenders, and had spare tires mounted on the side. Peter, the chauffeur, was almost entirely unprotected against the weather save for a skimpy flap of black leather, usually rolled back to the roof, but this day unrolled and attached to the top of the windshield. Mother and I got in, though "entered" would be more accurate, such were the attentions provided — Peter, umbrella in hand, held the door open, the dove-grey, wide, black-bordered and monogrammed lap robe spread upon our knees, the foot hassocks adjusted, the door closed, Peter then finally, slowly drove us off to an entirely new world which was to be mine for the next sixteen years.

The Madison Avenue house was large and handsome within and without, though by no means as grand as others on the four mile stretch from Morristown to Madison, an avenue of many fine, large houses built shortly before the turn of the century and among whose owners were members of the Harkness, Arthur Curtis James, Vanderbilt, Rockefeller, and Mellon families. Their homes, indeed estates, were far larger, far more imposing than my grandmother's which, when built, had actually been placed on what had once been the town trash dump.

However, no evidence of this lowly origin could even remotely have been surmised, the well planted grounds having been laid out by John R. Brinley, the landscape architect who had designed the New York Botanical Garden. The short, curving driveway ended in a carriage turn-around and a massive planting of hybrid rhododendrons, interspersed here and there with a peculiarly prickly variety of cypress, bordered the wide entrance steps and provided a sort of low, green forest from which the house, behind the tall-columned porch, rose to its considerable height.

The front door was opened by one of the Irish maids (North of Ireland, naturally), and there before us was the dark and impressive reception hall. The squarish room, about thirty by thirty feet with a ceiling of nearly twelve feet, was panelled to three quarters of its height by satin-polished walnut, the remainder of the walls being covered with mahogany-colored, gilt-tooled, Spanish leather. On either side two black bronze, half life-size, female figures in vaguely Grecian draperies held aloft torcheres fitted for gas (electricity had yet to be introduced to the house) and gave forth from frosted globes a pale yellow, slightly wavering light. Directly before us was a French Empire sofa upholstered in rich brown velvet. Behind this, framed by dark brown velvet portieres, was the opening to the oak-panelled dining room. To the left of the hall was a wide, also portiered, opening to the living room, while to the right a matching doorway gave into the drawing room filled with French furniture — a number of small and delicate, gilded side chairs with black tufted and buttoned seats, and also heavier pieces of

Selected from William Endicott Fiske's reminiscences of his Morristown childhood and reprinted with the permission of his wife, Sarah Pitney Fiske. The book was privately printed in 1975, the year before he died.

Mr. Fiske was a banker and active in many community affairs. At one time, he was treasurer and trustee of The Morristown Library, now The Joint Free Public Library of Morristown and Morris Township.

rosewood, all of which had been brought north from New Orleans, from whence my grandfather had come. In fact, all the furniture of the house had been his and was largely of massive black oak, dark, polished mahogany, or rosewood, for the most part richly carved in deep relief . . . .

Lunch that day was served almost at once, but not before I had been sent to the lavatory to "wash your hands." Why one's parents and grandmother had never to peform this ritual function I often wondered but did not question. Lunch, indeed "luncheon," proved to be a far cry from the scrambled eggs and bacon or chopped sirloin I had been accustomed to having with my nurse and the cook at noontime in the kitchen at Franklin Place. Properly announced, "Lunch is ready, Madam," it was promptly served at one in the large dining room, the walls of which were partly panelled in oak and thence to the ceiling covered with burlap cleverly painted to simulate gros point tapestry of scenes of castles, countryside and forest land, deer and mounted huntsmen. All this was an eye-opening and formal affair, commencing with a service plate setting, hot Parker House rolls folded within the napkins, and then, service plates removed, a concentrated beef bouillon was served in the thinest possible translucent, gilt-edged, two-handled cups and so moved slowly onward, interval to stately interval, of plate changing and silver platters and vegetable dishes passed with delicious creamed chicken, potato croquets, peas, and onions, followed by a tossed green salad for which a selection of olive oil and two kinds of vinegar was passed in a silver cruet with small, cut crystal bottles, all this being finally climaxed by a blanc mange with hot lemon sauce and finger bowls, in each of which floated a leaf of lemon verbena or rose geranium. All this was, for me, uncomfortably long and accompanied by that squirming restlessness common to small, captive children, and with admonitions to "sit still," "mind your manners," and, eventually, "Oh, all right, if you must go, say, 'Excuse me, please,' and leave as unobtrusively as possible."

When I got back, the dessert was gone, and grandma and mother were talking in the living room. I was put on the couch to nap in the "Little Room," a tiny alcove between the living room and dining room. Three windows overlooked the lawn. One small sofa, one wicker armchair, and a small mahogany drop-front desk and chair comprised its contents. It could not have held more. The walls, covered with a deep, pea green, pebbly-surfaced canvas, were hung with small water-color representations of a dozen or more renditions of various family coats-of-arms reaching back through generations of long gone Palmers, Phelpses, Slarks, Williamses, Fannings, Masons, Denisons, and others. English names, Connecticut Yankee names, with which, in my mind, grandma seemed intimately, almost daily, herself associated. But of their historical accomplishments and family connections, it was only in later years that I heard. Some few, indeed, did have accomplishments to their credit, of which one could be quietly proud ("One doesn't talk about such things, you know; it wouldn't do . . . .").

TJFPLMMT

Residence of William S. Letchford, 47 Madison Avenue, Morristown

Built in Tudor style in 1896, the house was torn down for Interstate Route 287. The Letchfords were William E. Fiske's grandparents.

Beautiful Homes of Northern New Jersey, c. 1910

Photograph by Timothy G. Cutler

Lindenwold, 247 South Street, Morristown

It was built in 1888 on the designs of local architect Louis R. Hazeltine for New York lawyer William B. Skidmore. The **mansion** (above, left) is shown as it appeared in 1910 when it was owned by New York drygoods merchant John Claflin and (above, right) after The Peck School bought it in 1947. The **vegetable garden and orchard** and the **lake** (below, left and right) are as they appeared in 1910.

Beautiful Homes of Northern New Jersey, c. 1910

Beautiful Homes of Northern New Jersey, c. 1910

Lindenwold

No guest could fail to be impressed on seeing this huge neo-Gothic mansion of dark ivy-covered stone, with its stepped Dutch gables reminiscent of early buildings in New Amsterdam. It was probably built in 1888, two years after an earlier wooden building on the property burned down. A history of the Morristown Field Club says the property was used by the club for tennis courts until the new mansion was built and the members were asked to remove themselves in keeping with the new dignity of the place. This they did — to the Lidgerwood property close by (map).

Sometime before 1868, the property was bought by George T. Cobb, a man prominent in Morristown history of the mid-19th century. Although orphaned at a very early age, he amassed a fortune in the iron business in New York; in or about 1853, he moved to Morristown, where he became known for his philanthropies and his business and political sense. In 1855, he gave 20 acres to the Evergreen Cemetery Association; in the late 1860s, he gave a lot and $10,000 for the Maple Avenue School; and during that same period he donated between $90,000 and $100,000 toward the building of the present Methodist Church on the Green (page 284). Through his efforts Morristown and Morris Township were separated in 1865 — though this was by no means unanimously acclaimed — and he served as first mayor of Morristown until May 1870. He was also a congressman (1861-63) and a state senator (1866-70). On August 6, 1870, he and his neighbor and close friend, J. Boyd Headley, were killed in a railroad accident near White Sulphur Springs, Virginia.

Lindenwold — although probably not so called at the time — passed to his only surviving child, Julia, who married William B. Skidmore on October 5, 1875. Like her father, he was a successful New York businessman who also associated himself with the interests of Morristown. He was, for example, an early founder of The Morristown Club (page 222), active in organizing the Library and Lyceum (page 236) and trustee of the Methodist Church.

On November 1, 1897, Julia Cobb Skidmore died and, in 1905, Lindenwold was sold to John Claflin, president of the H. B. Claflin Company, wholesale dry goods. He served at one time as rapid transit commissioner and as a director of the May Corporation. He was associated with J. P. Morgan in establishing the Jekyll Island Club, a millionaires' resort off the coast of Georgia.

The Claflins did extensive work on the grounds, which became well known for their horticultural displays.

The Peck School's addition of modern buildings now obscures the imposing entrance. □

Lindenwold in 1910, a detail from the Mueller Atlas, Plate 14, shows the front part of the estate. Interstate 287 goes through to the right of the house.

Morristown Topics

Spring Brook House, Morristown and Morris Township

The **rear view** (above) and **terrace view** (below) show the mansion in the early 1920s. It was built in Georgian Revival style in 1904-06 by New York architects Hasselman & Freeman for Robert D. Foote.

TJFPLMMT

Spring Brook Farm

One big difference between a mansion and a house is that the former looks as impressive from the front as from the rear. Spring Brook House, which Robert Dumont Foote (1862-1924) built on a commanding hill bordering the town and township, certainly qualified.

In 1865, John Tainter Foote (1818-1902) bought the property, some 750 acres of farmland and dairy pasture, after making his fortune in "high wines and rectifying spirits" and other commodities in the commission business in Cincinnati. After young Robert graduated from Harvard, he lived abroad for five years traveling and studying medicine. He returned to make his business and social mark in Morristown. He married Marie Gilmour Hopkins and they had three daughters and one son.

When Robert D. Foote inherited Spring Brook Farm in 1902, he took down the existing pre-Civil War farmhouse and erected his magnificent mansion of brick and Indiana limestone on the site. It cost him $400,000 and was worth more than $1 million at his death in 1924. (A real estate brochure said the mansion had 44 rooms, 36 of them bedrooms, with an additional 15 baths!) The interior woodwork was handsomely carved walnut; silk and velour hung on many of the walls. Many a reception and gala were held there — and, of course, the coming out parties. Older members of Morristown society still recall the blooming peach trees imported for the wedding of the Foote daughters. It took 15 Italian gardeners to tend the grounds.

Foote, a noted hunter, also owned a large hunting reserve in Hanover Township, and his own estate was well stocked with game. He brought some of the first Springer Spaniels to

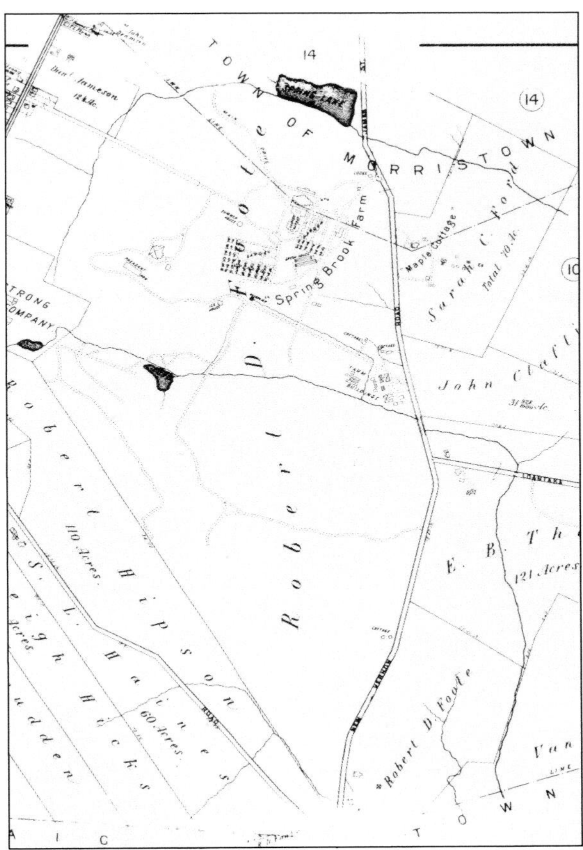

Spring Brook Farm in 1910 (map). The original estate ran from James Street to Mount Kemble Avenue and from Green Street to Harter Road. It had entrances on Ogden Place and James Street. It boasted its own pheasant pen, deer forest, orchards and greenhouses, and sunken gardens, as well as stables, ice house, farm buildings and a dairy.

Curtiss Collection/TJFPLMMT

All Souls Hospital, Mount Kemble Avenue, Morris Township, as it appeared in 1919 (above, right). As chairman of the building committees, Foote insisted the architects for his mansion produce a similar design for the Catholic hospital. This building was later enveloped in an expansion. It was acquired by Morristown Memorial Hospital in 1978.

America. A frequent visitor to Spring Brook Farm was Arthur Burdett Frost, the nationally known artist who lived on Treadwell Avenue in the old Boisaubin mansion. Frost enjoyed hunting with Foote and his friends and used the estate as a background for many of his hunting scenes using the owner as a model.

Foote became connected with the National Iron Bank as its vice president in 1897 and on the death of Henry C. Pitney became president. Under his direction, the new bank building at South Street opposite DeHart Street was erected, now Midlantic National Bank. He was also for a time president of the Morris County Traction (trolley) Company, a director of the New Jersey Corporation Railroad and, with John I. Waterbury of Madison Avenue and others, controlled the Morristown Gas Light Company, which later was sold to the Public Service Company of Newark.

Active in Democratic politics, he was a friend of Presidents Woodrow Wilson and Grover Cleveland.

In 1926, after her husband's death, Mrs. Foote sold the house and 125 acres to Charles W. Anderson of Montclair. The following year, on April 27, 1927, William W. Bender bought Spring Brook House with 20 acres and gave it to the Society of Jesus in memory of his mother. In her honor the hill was renamed Mount St. Katharine.

Within the estate's former borders are Spring Brook Country Club, which was developed in Foote's lifetime and of which he was a member; the Spring Brook residential area, begun in the Depression; the houses on and around Overlook Road; and Temple B'nai Or, built on that road in 1969 on five acres bought from the Loyola House of Retreat. In the 1980s, several housing and condominium developments have sprung up along James Street. □

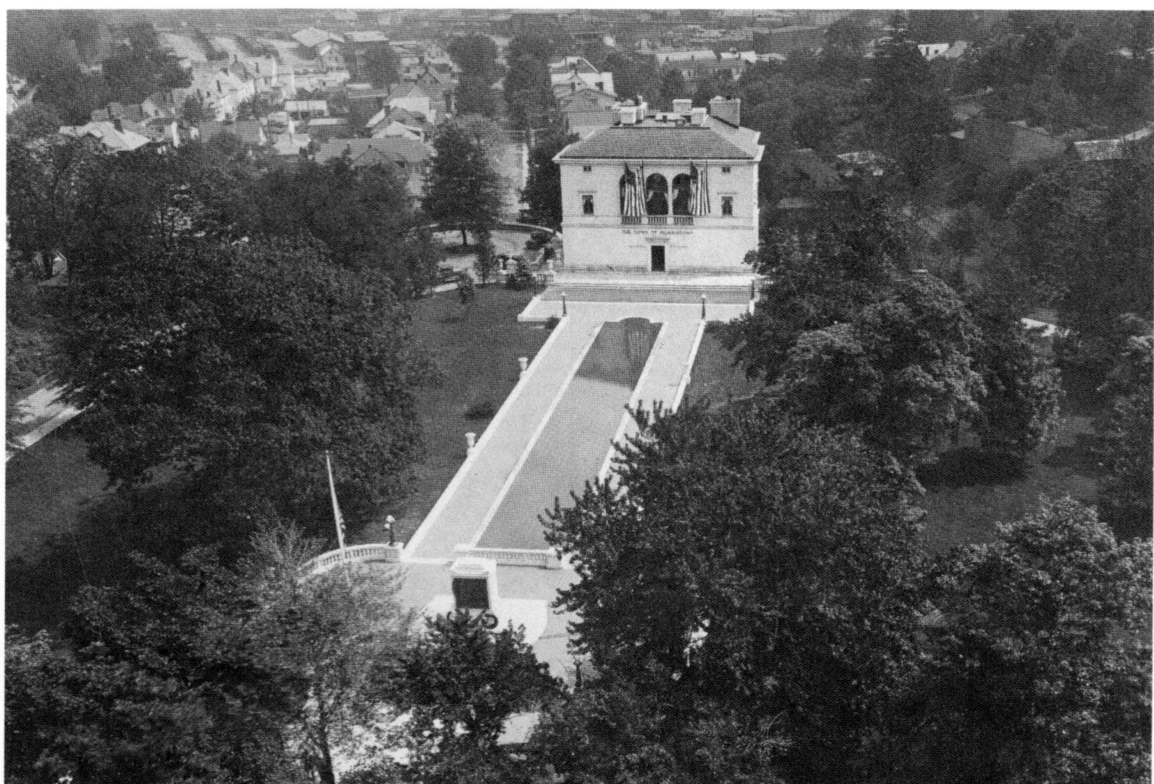

Curtiss Collection/TJFPL.MMT

Theodore Vail's Florentine Palazzo with Museum

This view is from the tower of St. Peter's Church on South Street, May 28, 1929, after it became the Morristown Municipal Building. It was built in 1916-18 of granite and Italian marble from a design by internationally known architect William Welles Bosworth, who worked on the restoration of Versailles and Fountainbleau and Rheims Cathedral after World War I.

The bronze doors of the mansion have eight panels executed in bas relief by Charles Keck, depicting (with one exception) scenes in Morristown's early history: (1) Ford Mansion; (2) Washington receiving communion with Reverend Johnes officiating; (3) two ladies greeting Martha Washington in their best finery astonished to find her simply dressed, knitting for the soldiers; (4) Alexander Graham Bell in conference with Professor Joseph Henry about developing the telephone; (5) Alfred Vail's father and mother taking their Sunday meal in the churchyard of the Presbyterian Church; (6) Lt. Col. Alexander Hamilton courting Betsey Schuyler; (7) Gen. George Washington and Martha Washington watching the skirmish at Springfield, June 1780 (actually Martha had already left New Jersey); (8) Alfred Vail and S. F. B. Morse working on the telegraphs at Speedwell Iron Works. In the foreground, at the base of the reflecting pool is the World War I memorial dedicated November 12, 1928. The cenotaph and its surroundings were designed by John R. Brinley and John S. Holbrook, civil engineers of Morristown, partners in a prominent landscape company. Erected by the people of Morristown, the cenotaph bears an inscription with 26 names of those who died for their country and are buried elsewhere.

Aerial view, 1928 (opposite), showing the mansion as the most imposing building in the neighborhood.

The Vail Mansion

Except for Alexander Graham Bell, no man did more than Theodore N. Vail to put the telephone in American homes and make sure it worked. He was born in Malvern, Ohio, but about 1847, his father brought him to Morristown. Davis Vail had come to work with his brother Stephen Vail at Speedwell Iron Works. Theodore attended local schools and the Morris Academy, but he was not college bound. Instead, he was fascinated by the telegraph his cousin Alfred had done so much to develop. At 17, Theodore became a telegrapher working in the office that was at that time part of a drug store on the south side of the Green. However, in 1866, he left Morristown for many years.

From telegraphy, Theodore became interested in the country's postal service, where he exhibited a genius for organization. However, his crowning accomplishment was joining all the long-distance telephone companies and, from 1885 to 1887, he was the first president of the American Telephone and Telegraph Company. Then, he resigned because of ill health. However, in 1907, he was recalled to the presidency and remained in that position until 1919, when he again resigned for health reasons. He remained chairman of the board. In 1911, he was elected first president of the Telephone Pioneers of America and held that office until his death.

On January 25, 1915, during the Panama Pacific Exposition in San Francisco, the first transcontinental telephone line was opened with a conversation among President Woodrow Wilson in Washington, D.C., Alexander Graham Bell in New York, Thomas A. Watson in San Francisco, and Theodore Vail at his vacation home on Jekyll Island.

TJFPLMMT

TJFPLMMT

Theodore Newton Vail (1845-1920)
Organizer and first president of the American Telephone and Telegraph Co.

Curtiss Collection/TJFPLMMT

Curtiss Collection/TJFPLMMT

During the intervening years between AT&T presidencies, Theodore Vail worked on public utility and water power projects in Argentina. He also had a large farm in Vermont.

He was married first, in 1869, to Emma L. Righter of Newark. The following year, they had a son, Davis. After both his wife and son died in Argentina, he returned to the United States and married Mabel R. Sanderson of Boston and adopted a niece, Katherine (Mrs. Arthur A. Marsters). When Theodore became president of AT&T a second time, he moved the headquarters from Boston to New York City, where he was residing when he commissioned his house with private museum in Morristown. However, death prevented him from ever living there, although he surely enjoyed watching its building progress from the Marsters' house on the property, which had once belonged to Alfred Vail and was where he died.

Theodore had never forgotten the celebrated Vail cousin. In 1918, he commissioned his first wife's brother, the Reverend S. Ward Righter, to review all of Alfred's papers in the Smithsonian Institution, where they had been unceremoniously dumped in uncatalogued boxes together with other materials such as magazine articles and court depositions. From these, Righter was able to assemble irrefutable evidence of Alfred Vail's many creative contributions in the development of the telegraph.

Theodore Vail died at Jekyll Island on April 16, 1920, and is buried in Parsippany. When no group or society stepped forward to operate Vail's mansion as a museum, which had been his wish, it became the Morristown Municipal Building. □

Curtiss Collection/TJFPLMMT

Interior views of the Vail Mansion, February 21, 1921, notable for its marble double staircase with iron balustrade: **upstairs hall** facing the organ room (opposite, above), **entrance hall** (opposite, below) and the **dining room** (above).

Residence of Mrs. A. A. Marsters (right), Vail's adopted daughter, and formerly Alfred Vail's home at 106 South Street, as it appeared February 6, 1923. The Vail Mansion is at the rear of the property.

TJFPLMMT

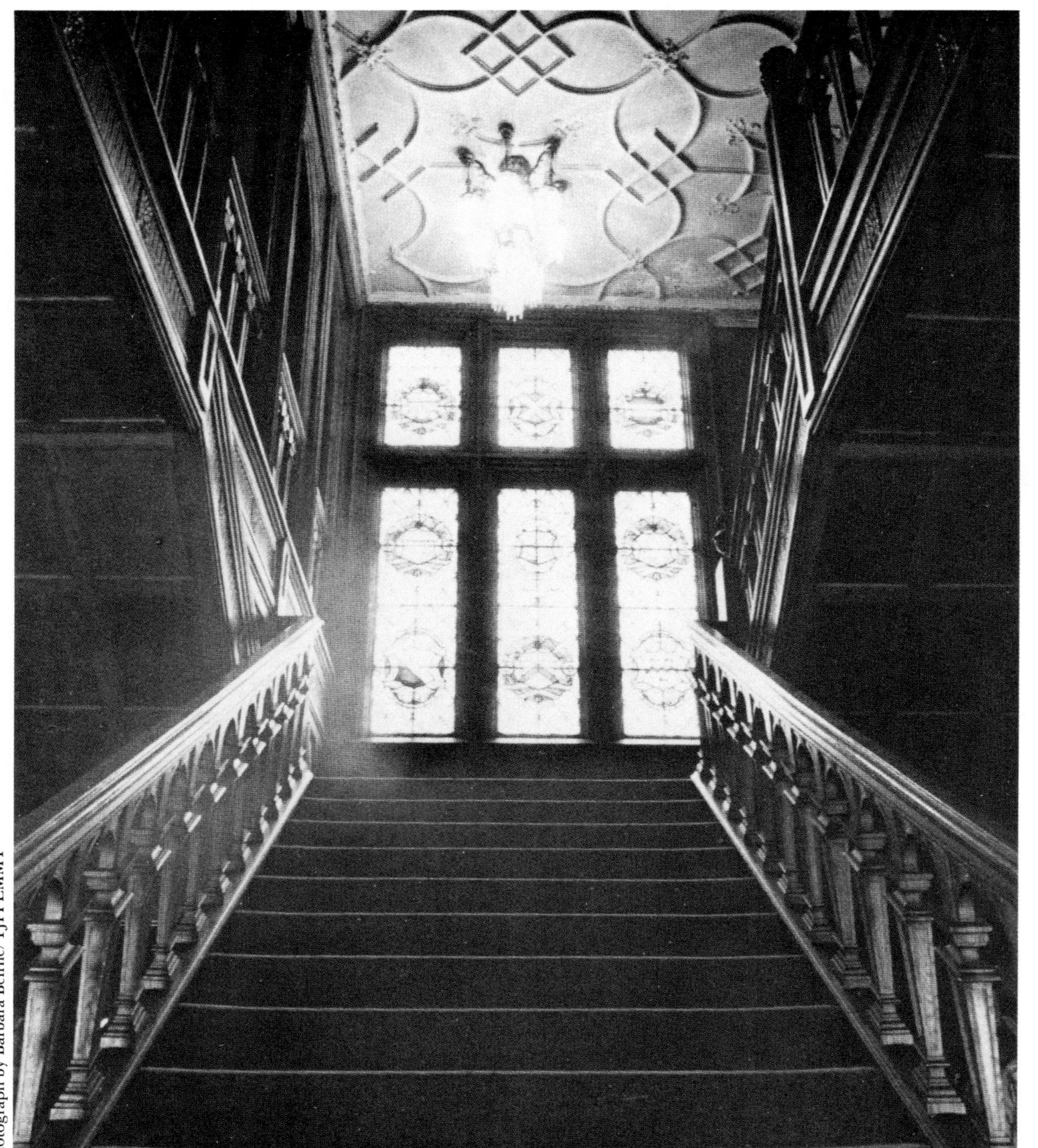
Photograph by Barbara Beirne/TJFPLMMT

Front staircase of Alnwick Hall, Morris Township.

Manor Houses of the Township

The English ideal is evident in much of the mansion-building — the desire for what Henry James called the "well appointed, well administered, well filled country house." Except for the Twomblys' Florham, none of the mansions in Morris County could rival a Duke's, but there were several in Morris Township that were very impressive indeed.

The township of the Golden Age was "real country" — sheep grazing by the side of the road, horseback riders on leisurely tour, and farm wagons swaying under heavy loads. There was ample open land on which to create an estate. In 1910, for example, Morris Township occupied 15.45 square miles with a population of only 3,161, while Morristown packed 12,507 residents in less than three square miles.

One by one wealthy men from Newark or New York purchased farms in this immediate area. Interestingly, although the builders of the township estates turned former meadows into manicured lawns and woodlands into sunken gardens, part of the property often remained as working farm. It was not unusual for an estate to include not only vegetable gardens and orchards but also a piggery, a chicken house, and perhaps a herd of milking cows or steer. If these estate farms were not particularly profitable, they paid the expenses. Perhaps more important, they provided the family with the freshest-of-the-fresh for the table, not only while in residence but also when back in the city, where wagons might make weekly trips with "something from the farm."

And what did the farmers whose families had lived on the land for generations think of all this? The realtor Eugene V. Welsh thought

Courtesy of Mrs. Godfrey Beresford

Garden at the rear of Glynallyn, Morris Township, 1920s.

Courtesy of the Sisters of Charity of St. Elizabeth/TJFPL.MMT

Convent Station, Morris Township

An 1880s view of the **motherhouse of the Sisters of Charity of Saint Elizabeth and Saint Elizabeth Academy** (above), as seen from the roof of the train station the nuns built. A wing on the left and the chapel are not yet built. This is now the Administration Building. **The Boisaubin House** (opposite, above), Treadwell Avenue, built by Vincent Boisaubin about 1790. The house was constructed on the former site of the Loantaka Campground (page 36). Boisaubin emigrated from Guadeloupe, French West Indies; he was a member of King Louis XVI's personal bodyguard and lost his fortune at the beginning of the French Revolution. He died here in June 1834. At the turn of the century, when Arthur Burdett Frost lived there, he gave it the nickname Moneysunk. **The Holt** (opposite, below), Kitchell Road, built in 1855 by Dr. William Kitchell, who made the first geological survey of New Jersey. He called it Tower House. President Theodore Roosevelt spent some months here as a little boy with his family about 1866. Some years later, in 1889, the writer Frank R. Stockton, a good friend of Frost's, purchased the house and renamed it The Holt, an old Saxon word for "wooded hills." Both houses were among the few in the area when the Sisters of Charity moved into the area. Both are still private residences, although The Holt has long since lost its tower.

they were ready to sell: "The prices these original farmers received for their farms were relatively high when compared to the prices these same farms would have gotten if sold for agricultural purposes." □

Convent Station

When Madison Avenue in Morristown curves to the right, or southeast, towards Madison and Chatham Township, it passes into Morris Township and enters the area called Convent Station. How the place got its name, as well as the only railroad station and post office in the township, is an interesting story, going far back before the commuter age.

In 1860, the Sisters of Charity of St. Elizabeth founded their motherhouse and established St. Elizabeth's Academy for girls on Madison Avenue. (The college came later, in 1899.) The nuns and the students formed the majority of the population of this sparsely settled area. Mother Mary Xavier Mehegan, the foundress, successfully petitioned the railroad to make a stop before Morristown to serve the community. In return, the Sisters donated the land and built a two-story wooden stationhouse in 1876. They paid the stationmaster, who was also the postmaster, for many years. The railroad named this stop Convent Station but did not build its own train station, the present one, until 1913. In 1900, some of the millionaires who had built homes in the area built a small separate post office (map, page 183), still standing but not in use, opposite the station on Convent Road. Charles Murphy, who had worked as stationmaster and postmaster for the convent since 1877, became the postmaster in the new building until 1912.

The growth of Convent Station as a summer retreat for the wealthy and well-connected was a dream come true for John Dodd Canfield

Courtesy of Mr. and Mrs. Robert H. Harvey

Beautiful Homes of Northern New Jersey, c. 1910

The development of Morristown and contiguous territory for residential purposes within the past decade has been remarkable . . . [and] on the lines of development fixed by the requirements of a cultured and for the most part wealthy people. The result is a substantial addition to the residence portion of the city . . . . The company will sell only to those who desire to improve the property and who will erect structures that will conform in dimensions and architecture to the standards established by the first purchasers.
Morristown Land and Improvement Company, 1894

Beautiful Homes of Northern New Jersey, c. 1910

Residence of A. Fillmore Hyde, Old Glen Road. A real-estate tycoon who was master of the Essex Fox Hounds, his wealth was estimated at $14 million. Although the 1910 map (opposite) calls the estate Seldomere, several issues of the Social List of Morristown gave its name as Seldomhere. If true, this was a humorous comment on the fact that most society families spent only a few months of the year in Morristown. The area called Bradwahl is now on the site.

(1845-1910), president of the Morristown Land and Improvement Company. This real-estate firm concentrated on selling generous-sized tracts of land to socially compatible buyers who would create the type of residence he envisioned. It is no accident that so many Convent Station mansions and gardens were photographed for *Beautiful Homes of Morris County and Northern New Jersey*, published locally about 1910.

Canfield, for whom the crescent-shaped road off Madison Avenue is named, had roots that went far back into 18th-century Morristown. His grandfather was Israel Canfield, a merchant, mentioned prominently in early town history. His father was Benjamin Ogden Canfield, also a successful merchant and, as you recall, the nephew who supervised the building of the Colles mansion, The Evergreens. After graduating from Williams College in 1866, John D. Canfield became a lawyer; however, his diverse interests led him to wear many hats, including historian, trustee of the Morristown Green, city clerk and shade tree commissioner. Nevertheless, his greatest legacy to the township was developing Convent Station and neighboring Normandy Heights and Normandy Park (page 194).

There is not much left of the Golden Age. Today's Convent Station has a decidedly modern look. As in Morristown, Madison Avenue (Route 124) has almost entirely succumbed to office buildings. Although beautiful older homes still exist between Madison Avenue and Woodland Avenue, the overall impression is of housing developed in the last 30 years. □

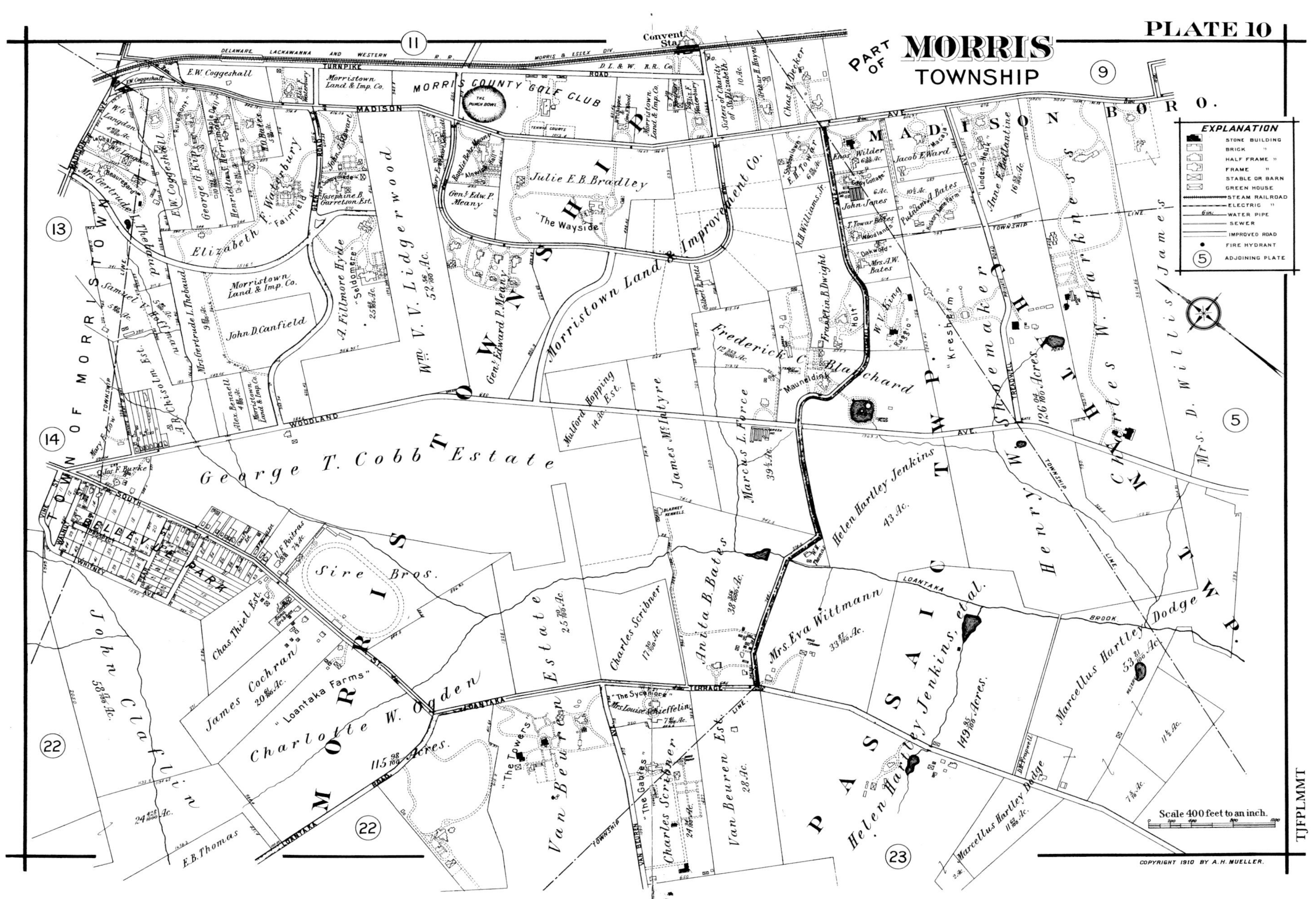

Morris Township in 1910, showing Madison Avenue and Convent Station.

TJFPLMMT

Photograph by Timothy G. Cutler

Alnwick Hall

Standing on the corner of Madison Avenue and Canfield Road, Convent Station, is this orange brick castle-like building with towers and turrets built in 1903-04 by General Edward P. Meany. It was inspired by Alnwick, the baronial manor of the Percy family in Northumberland, England.

Entranceway (left) was reached from a circular drive, where many carriages and later chauffeur-driven automobiles brought guests for lavish balls and musicales.

In 1926, the house was put up for sale. Mrs. Meany had died and the General had remarried and moved to New York. In 1960, it was converted into St. Mark's Lutheran Church and, in 1984, into an office building called The Abbey.

A "medieval" feature of the interior (opposite): a stained-glass panel, one of many throughout the house made specially by Heineke and Bowen of New York.

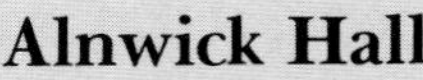

Alnwick Hall

General Edward P. Meany (1854-1938) did not have the tremendous wealth of the Dodges, Twombleys and Mellons, nor did he have the immediate social acceptance of his neighbors in Convent Station: John I. Waterbury, president of the Manhattan Trust Company; Charles F. Bradley, president of P. Ballantine of Newark; and John A. Stewart, president and chairman of the board of the United States Trust Company, who had been Assistant Secretary of the Treasury and valued adviser to President Abraham Lincoln. However, Meany had his credentials. He was the son of a distinguished Kentucky jurist and himself an attorney. He was one of the organizers of the American Bell Telephone Company and a director or officer of a number of railroads and financial and other institutions, including the local National Iron Bank of Morristown and the Carteret Trust Company. The title came from his position of Judge Advocate General of New Jersey, to which he was named in 1893 with the rank of brigadier general in the National Guard. He was very active in Democratic party politics in New Jersey and was familiar with political and social circles in New York and Washington.

In 1913, Meany resigned as Judge Advocate General and was mentioned for the post of Secretary of War in President-elect Woodrow Wilson's cabinet.

Mrs. Meany was Rosalie Behr of St. Louis. Considered a social upstart by some of Morristown society, Mrs. Meany — apparently — couldn't have cared less. She loved to give parties, for which she had the perfect house. Despite the rather forbidding exterior, the interior of Alnwick Hall was luxurious, with the very latest conveniences. Notable features were a Louis XVI drawing room; an octagonal, oak-paneled breakfast room; a dining room of Circassian walnut; a handsome library; marble fireplaces and parquet floors. A garage accommodated six "motors" and the coach barn had stalls for eight horses, quarters for the coachman, harness rooms and so forth.

The house had a central heating system with individual room controls, an electric washing machine and a built-in vacuum cleaning system, all innovations for the time.

Perhaps the most impressive room was the high-ceilinged and paneled Great Hall, seating 225 people. Here Mrs. Meany held her favorite musicales. On one occasion, the hall was transformed into a miniature opera house where Madame Alma Gluck, the legendary Metropolitan Opera diva, sang for 200 guests.

Unlike most of Morristown's society, who used the local caterer Wilbur F. Day, Mrs. Meany used only Delmonico's of New York.

On the 21st birthday of her only son, Shannon Lord Meany, the mansion's entire first floor was decorated with roses and palms for a dance for 150 young people.

Rosie Meany's actions caused a great deal of comment, though she must have been an individualist with a good sense of fun. For one Christmas party she wore a ball gown into which tiny flashing tree lights had been sewn. Another time she appeared as a rosebud.

She took her exercise in an unusual way. She liked walking, but not too far or fast, so she had her automobile follow closely behind her should she tire. The sight of the handsome foreign chauffeur sitting up high in his latest model French automobile crawling along Madison Avenue while attempting to keep a serious and dignified expression was too much for one little girl growing up in a nearby mansion. A favorite pastime was to bring her pony and wagon abreast of the Meany car and silently challenge the chauffeur to a race. □

Photograph by Barbara Beirne/TJFPLMMT

Both photographs courtesy of Mrs. Godfrey Beresford

Glynallyn

This mansion on Canfield Road, Convent Station, was designed in Tudor style by noted New York architect Charles I. Berg and built in 1913-17 for George Marshall Allen. The model was Compton Wynyates, a manor house in Warwickshire, completed in 1528. In May 1952, it was converted into offices for General Drafting Company.

The mansion was rushed to completion, despite World War I, for the wedding reception of **Loraine Allen** (left) in the Great Hall, August 21, 1917. Not all the furnishings were complete, however, and some were borrowed for the event from W. & J. Sloane!

Glynallyn

Glynallyn — spelled as the family preferred it — was named for the beautiful wooded glen on the property by George Marshall Allen (1863-1941). He was a man of many interests, a world traveler, yachtsman and empire builder. He owned property in Bermuda and was the founder of the Bermuda Electric Light Company. He traveled for years between London, New York and Bermuda as a representative for companies interested in building of The Bermudiana Hotel in Hamilton, Bermuda. For many years, he headed the George M. Allen Publishing Company, which pioneered color printing, and he made sure there was a darkroom in his new house.

The 1910 map of Convent Station (page 183) shows the Glynallyn property on the south curve of the as-yet-unnamed Canfield Road as lots owned by the Morristown Land and Improvement Company.

In 1913, after years of careful planning, the building of Glynallyn began. The first building erected was a lodge for the gardener and other servants and a garage for the Allen carriages and cars. However, the Allens themselves lived in this lodge, starting in September 1914, so that Mr. Allen could personally supervise the construction of the main building and watch the work on the property as terraces, pools and low walls were built and landscapers and gardeners brought in huge specimen trees and flowering bushes to complete a complex plan that would provide variety and color most of the year.

This handsome setting even made the movies. In 1919, Glynallyn was the backdrop for the film *Witness in the Case,* starring Elsie Ferguson. □

My Father's House

Loraine Allen Beresford, 1980

During his travels, my father, George Marshall Allen, always carried a notebook in which he would sketch anything and everything that interested him, from the design of an ornate ceiling to the brick pattern of a chimney. From these sketches, he planned Glynallyn. Next he engaged a well-known architect, Charles L. Berg, to draw up working plans and blueprints. A plastic model was made so every detail could be checked.

In 1913, construction commenced. The front entrance to Glynallyn, the windows in the Great Hall, the two-story bay window in the rear of the house and the 16 chimneys (no two alike) are copied from Compton Wynyates. Many other architectural designs were taken from my father's sketch book.

Because of World War I and the fear of governmental restrictions on building, all construction of Glynallyn was stopped in 1914 with only the cellar completed. A temporary roof was placed over the cellar with only a doorway appearing above ground. While awaiting the end of the war, my parents gave some famous parties in the unfinished cellar, guests having to descend underground.

In 1916, construction was resumed on the house at full speed. My father personally supervised the building of the house and left no doubt as to the details he wanted. When skilled masons [Sturgis Brothers] asked his approval of a sample, they were dumbfounded when he told the master builders that it was "not acceptable," due to the regularity with which the bricks had been laid, which did not convey a feeling of antiquity. In all the work he tried to create the impression of age.

The chimneys were set upon the ground brick by brick without cement in order to establish the individual patterns, and then again brick by brick cemented in place on the roof. When the front door was finished, he ordered a crack to be put across the face of the brick to convey age. My mother was Grace Fanshawe Allen and the coat-of-arms over the front entrance doorway is of the Fanshawe family. The two quotations are:

Dux Vitae Ratio — Reason, the Leader of Life
In Cruce Victoria — Victory in the Cross

My father had spent endless hours abroad searching for parts of old homes that he could buy or somehow wheedle from owners. He was fortunate enough at one time to arrive at Compton Wynyates where some remodeling was in progress and he was able to acquire the fine 400-year-old oak panelling that eventually was used in Little Hall, the entrance of Glynallyn.

Glynallyn was finished in 1917 and he once confided to his son-in-law that he had "invested" around $500,000 in the house and land. The cost alone of the stain glass in the windows of the Great Hall was over $15,000. To build Glynallyn today would cost at least one million dollars.

The Great and Little Halls of Glynallyn were smaller versions of the original English "Castle."

Above the Great Hall was the Minstrel Gallery, which extended the full length and across one end of the Great Hall and led to the bedrooms. Tucked away in a corner across from the Minstrel Gallery and reached by a narrow stairway from the Great Hall was a small balcony containing an organ console — an instrument my father enjoyed playing. On the panelled wall of the Minstrel Gallery hangs an old print found in an antique shop depicting a jousting tournament at Compton Wynyates.

Separated by sliding doors from the Great Hall was the Morning Room, used primarily by my mother to receive morning callers. So as not to detract from the appearance of antiquity in the Great Hall, my father concealed a fire hose in the wall, and covered the opening with the head of a very large carved oak beer barrel suspended on hinges.

Mrs. Beresford prepared this material for the Morris County Historical Society. Shortly before her death in 1984 at the age of 85, she kindly gave permission for its inclusion in this book along with the photographs of Glynallyn from her personal collection.

While traveling in England, my father visited Compton Wynyates, now the home of the Marquess of Northampton, and decided this was the manor house he would like to use as a model for a home he would build in America.
Loraine Allen Beresford, 1980

Elizabethan guest room.

Entered from the Great Hall was the large dining room, which had three secret panels: one opened onto the terrace, a second hid a linen closet and a third concealed a walk-in safe to protect the family silver.

Against the walls of a small chapel were four "Misericordia" seats above which, imbedded in the walls, were stone carvings depicting the murder of Sir Thomas à Becket.

The rest of the first floor consisted of butler's pantry, kitchen, laundry and servant's dining hall. Nine servants were needed inside the mansion, while eight maintained the grounds.

The second floor consisted of bedroom suites, guest rooms, a sitting room, a study, servants' quarters and sewing room. In my father's bathroom was a "peephole" through which he could see what was going on in the Great Hall below. He devised removable newel posts on the stairways leading to the second and third floors to facilitate in the carrying of large trunks or pieces of furniture.

The third floor contained a studio and darkroom used for his hobby — photography. The rest of the third floor consisted of guest rooms, servants' quarters and storage rooms.

Last, but not least, we must return to the original cellar, upon which the house now stands. The mansion having 42 rooms, required two heating systems. The 125 tons of coal consumed annually were conveyed from bin to furnaces over a narrow railroad track built in the cellar. (The tracks are still visible today.)

However, the cellar was not used entirely for utilitarian purposes, as a large area was given over to the creation of a "refectory" used in European monasteries as a dining hall for the monks. Here my parents continued to entertain informally with Halloween parties, amateur theatricals, and so forth, as they had done before Glynallyn was built.

Access to the refectory was by means of the original door as before, but now a part of the Great Hall with descent through a heavy oak door taken from Dannemore Prison and opened by depressing a foot pedal in the floor of the Great Hall. The stairs down were made uneven and to appear as if worn down by monks' feet. Heavy iron chain and shackles hung on the walls.

Little Hall (above), front entrance hall leading into Great Hall. **Refectory** (below), a cellar room that was scene of many parties and amateur theatricals.

All photographs courtesy of Mrs. Godfrey Beresford

Living room (page 190) in the mid-1920s, with a sculptured ceiling copied from Oxford University and old oak paneling imported from England by W. & J. Sloane, and **Great Hall** (page 191), prepared for Mr. and Mrs. Allen's 25th wedding anniversary dinner party in June 1921, attended by the cream of Morristown society.

Courtesy of Mrs. Godfrey Beresford

Courtesy of Mrs. Godfrey Beresford

Photograph by Judi Benvenuti/TJFPLMMT

Photograph by Judi Benvenuti/TJFPLMMT

Hollow Hill Farm

Hollow Hill Farm was an immediate neighbor of Glynallyn. It stretched from Canfield Road — the front entrance — to Woodland Avenue and ran along Kitchell Road. It included the farms of Frederick C. Blanchard and Marcus Force, and other land, approximately 67 acres in Morris Township and 17 in Harding Township. After Mrs. Moore's death in 1980, her heirs valued the land at $10 million.

Paul Moore (d. 1959) was a founder of Republic Aviation and a director of the National Biscuit Company (Nabisco), the American Can Company, the Delaware Lackawanna and Western Railroad and Bankers Trust Company. His wife, Fanny Hanna Moore, was a niece of Mark Hanna of Cleveland, the Republican party chairman who managed William McKinley's 1896 Presidential nomination.

Both Moores were philanthropists and many local institutions benefitted handsomely from their generosity.

Paul Moore was the son of Judge William Henry Moore (1848-1923), a highly successful specialist in mergers. In 1898, for example, he arranged the consolidation of 90% of the cracker and biscuit baking firms into the National Biscuit Company. His hobby, shared by his son and daughter-in-law, was horses, and he built a stable of hackneys second to none. In 1914, he brought up his prize-winning horses from Virginia and, with his son, leased the land they later bought from Joseph W. Ogden. In 1919, they acquired other adjoining parcels and established Seaton Hackney Farm, named after the judge's celebrated English-bred harness horse, "Lady Seaton." In 1958, their Seaton Hackney Farm with its race track, judges' stand and stables was donated to the Morris County Park Commission. ☐

You could always count on Fanny Moore to open her beautiful home and graciously entertain people we wanted to talk with privately or win over to our cause.
A fellow member of the Great Swamp Committee fighting the jetport proposed there in the 1960s

Photograph by Judi Benvenuti/TJFPLMMT

Hollow Hill Farm

Two views of the **brick mansion** (opposite) seen from Woodland Road, designed by New York architects Albro and Landaburg and built in 1913-14.

Garden terrace (right).

Seaton Pippin (lower left), hackney mare buried near the house, who won 203 blue ribbons and seven championships, always driven by Mrs. Moore.

Cow barns (lower right), for the prizewinning herd of Guernseys.

TJFPLMMT

Photograph by Judi Benvenuti/TJFPLMMT

Photograph by Judi Benvenuti/TJFPLMMT

Photograph by Judi Benvenuti/TJFPLMMT

Friends on Normandy Heights Road

Jesse Leeds Eddy and Joseph Dickson were partners in the firm of Eddy and Dickson, an anthracite coal company that made them both very wealthy. **Valley View** (above), Eddy's "summer cottage," was built on Normandy Heights Road in 1896. First called "Grey Stone" (map), it is an innovative mixture of hand-hewn Vermont granite and shingle. Its many fine features include 20 rooms anchored by a great central hall and classical decoration, as in the **music room** (left). **Wyndmoor** (opposite), Dickson's house across the street, was completed in 1892. Both houses are still private residences.

Normandy Heights and Normandy Park

Why this eastern part of Morris Township was named Normandy is not recorded — although since it was often spelled *Normandie* (into the late 1930s), perhaps someone thought the name recalled the beauties of the French province. That someone might have been John D. Canfield, who developed this area as well as Convent Station.

In 1894, Normandy Heights Road, Normandy Parkway and adjacent streets were lined with the newest type of lamppost and gas mantle light. Water supply being a problem, the private Normandy Water Company was started on property along Columbia Road in Hanover Township.

Later, in 1931 Morristown bought this land and turned it into Morristown Municipal Airport. Canfield would not have been pleased by the encroachment. When rumors surfaced in 1910 that the town and township might merge again, he was more than upset. If that happened, he promised, he would have the area declared a separate borough.

Canfield moved from his family's homestead on Madison Avenue, the site where Beauregard now stands, to a house he built on Normandy Parkway (map). His father, Benjamin O. Canfield, in fact, had owned all the land on either side of this new street.

In 1925, George Weldon moved from Rochester to Canfield's old house with his wife and daughter, Elinor. Shortly before she died in that house, Miss Weldon told me this amusing and revealing story related to her naming the house.

Newly arrived, Miss Weldon wanted to buy some things at Sears, Roebuck and Co., which then had a Morristown branch. Before opening a charge, the salesman made some inquiries:

"What is your address, Miss Weldon?"

"Normandy Parkway."

"Yes, but what is the name of the house?"

"It doesn't have one," she replied.

"But if you live on Normandy Parkway, you must have a name for your house."

She thought for a moment, and her mind rested on the eleven tall oak trees in front of the house. Then she remembered the name of a boarding house where she had stayed as a child.

"It's called 'Levenoaks,'" she said, recalling the unusual, abbreviated spelling.

The salesman looked pleased.

Not every house had a name, of course, but most did. (Street numbers were introduced about 1890 but were slow to be used for residences.) Normandy Heights had its share of interesting names, such as Onlya Farm, Cherrycroft and Wyndmoor, but the most formal sounding one, Cedar Court, belonged to the most formal family.

There is a 1909 account of the Kahn household by "Anonymous," undoubtedly a student at The Morristown School, who was invited with a friend to Sunday lunch at Cedar Court. The excerpt comes from *Morristown Parade, 1715-1965*, compiled by Jessica C. Schoeffler:

"The Kahn household was always a source of wonder. There seemed no limit to it. The immaculately raked carriage road sweeping majestically up to the high Villa was awesome enough, but there had to be two large flocks of imported sheep inching their way across the golf fairways with all the fanfare of dogs, shepherds, and shepherd's crooks. By the time we reached the front door and were arguing with each other whether fifty or sixty flunkeys were in residence in the high servant's wing

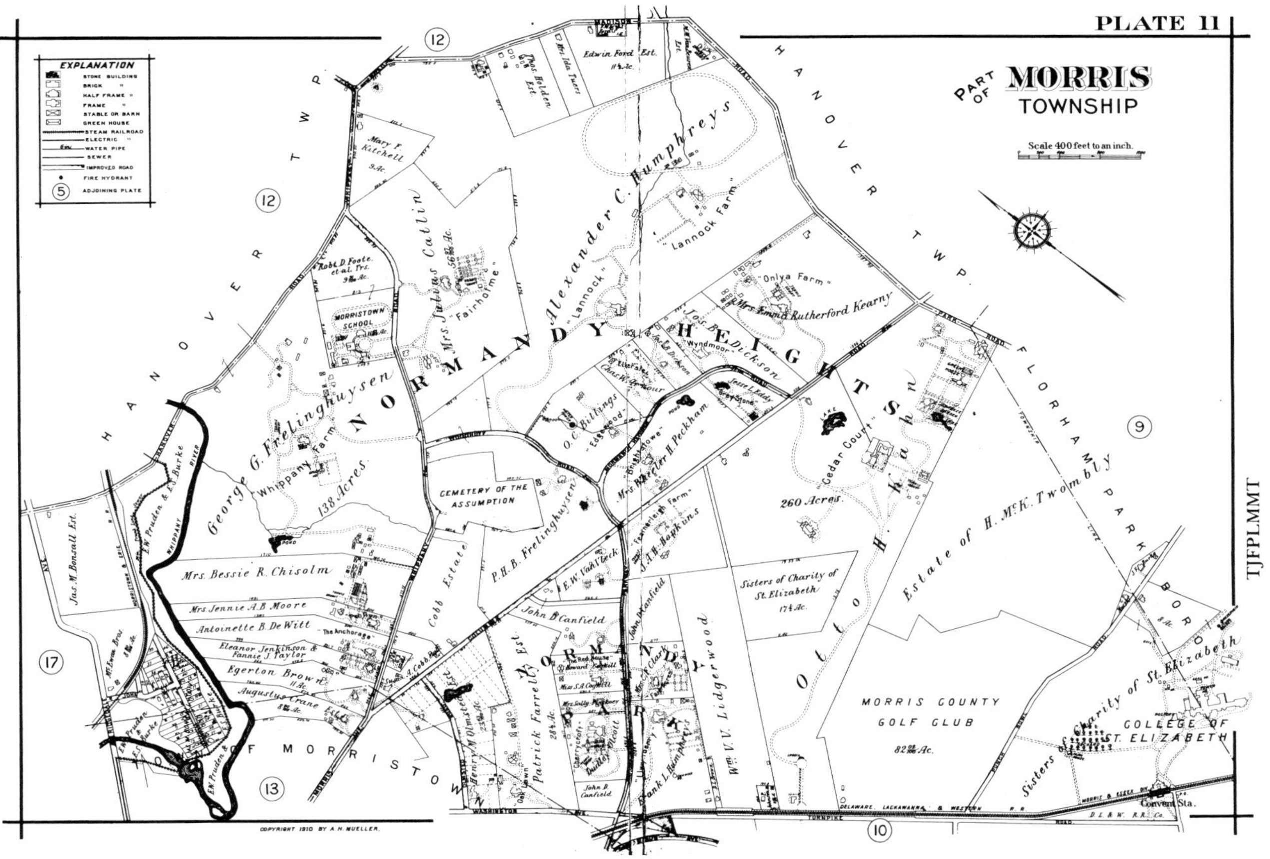

Morris Township in 1910, showing Normandy Heights and Park, Columbia and Whippany Roads.

Beautiful Homes of Northern New Jersey, c. 1910

Beautiful Homes of Northern New Jersey, c. 1910

Cedar Court

This residence of Otto H. Kahn, Columbia Road and Park Avenue, was built for Abraham Wolff, Kahn's father-in-law in 1897-99, one of two identical Italian villas by Carrere and Hastings, who also laid out the grounds. Allied-Signal Corporation now owns most of the property.

The view (below), as seen from Cedar Court at the top of the hill.

Beautiful Homes of Northern New Jersey, c. 1910

Jesse Eddy, of Normandie Heights, was thrown from his sleigh yesterday afternoon when it turned over on South Street near the park. He turned around in too short a space, causing the sleigh to go over on its side . . . . The frightened horse was stopped in front of the Mansion House [on Washington Street].
From the *Daily Record,* December 14, 1910

---

beyond the courtyard, my self-confidence began to droop."

The nervous author went into the dining room with Mrs. Kahn, three Kahn children, Maud, Margaret and Gilbert, and the head and second governesses. Mr. Kahn's seat was vacant.

"We stood waiting. The uniformed attendants took their positions as if for a kickoff. I imagined the Major Domo would blow a whistle, and I felt the same empty feeling that precedes the start of an important game. A door opened. The room froze to attention. Mr. Kahn, with commanding and precise movements, strode to the head of the table . . . . Even for this simple occasion he was immaculately groomed, as if for an important meeting with a Board or a Prime Minister."

The second half of the 20th century also has crept relentlessly into this formerly quiet, elegant section. Yet it seems easier somehow to imagine the Normandy Heights and Normandy Parkway of the Golden Age than it does in

The Normandie Park Estates has just sold to Ira J. Lindsley, local contractor, five lots through J. Raymond Prideaux, of the office of Stephen C. Griffith, Jr. It is Mr. Lindsley's intention to start building in the month of March and sell the houses for about $12,000.
Unidentified newspaper, February 9, 1931

Courtesy of Morristown-Beard School

Fairholme

At this residence of Mrs. Julius Catlin, Whippany Road, Rudyard Kipling was a guest in the spring of 1899. After Mrs. Catlin's death in 1913, it was purchased by Woodbury Langdon for The Morristown School (page 234) across the street; the students had enjoyed the pond and gardens. The house no longer exists. Although another private residence was built on the property, it too was razed.

Convent Station. A drive through Normandy Parkway, where the gaslights still cast their soft glow, reveals good-sized residences set far back from the road by manicured lawns. Long branches of old trees still sweep the ground. Curving into Normandy Heights Road, Peter H. B. Frelinghuysen's former mansion, now the Morris Museum, and William Thorne's Gateways, now the Morristown Unitarian Fellowship, still seem very much to belong on the street. Allied Corporation's buildings on Otto Kahn's Cedar Court are set far enough back from Columbia Road so they cannot be clearly seen.

There is no denying intrusions, such as the heavy traffic into this once quiet area. Columbia Road carries ever more traffic to and from Livingston and the Oranges. Normandy Parkway through part of Normandy Heights Road to Woodruff Road is a convenient short-cut between Madison Avenue and Whippany Road. Canfield's dream is not totally lost. □

TJFPLMMT

Gateways

This Georgian brick mansion was built in 1911 for William S. V. Thorne as a surprise for his wife. Designed by New York architects Belane and Aldrich, it had 25 rooms and baths and cost $400,000. It is now the Morristown Unitarian Fellowship. The house is on the site of Brightstowe (map, page 195), first one on Normandy Heights, built by Wheeler H. Peckham. It was razed after his death.

Photograph by Gottscho-Schleisner, Inc./TJFPLMMT

Frelinghuysen Farms: Whippany and Twin Oaks

The Frelinghuysen family has been prominent in New Jersey since the early 1700s.

George Griswold Frelinghuysen (1851-1936) chose for his country estate a property on the border of Morris and Hanover Townships in an area called Monroe, presumably for the fifth U.S. President. Known as the Reverend H. D. Hayden's farm "on Morris Avenue opposite the Catlin place," he renamed it Whippany Farm. At the center of the estate, he built his handsome 15-room summer home and commissioned a landscape designer, William McPherson of Trenton, to surround it with an English park-like setting of stately trees and rolling lawns. The ornamental plantings can still be enjoyed along with the imposing cut-leaf silver maple that shades the porte cochere and fine specimens of chestnuts, black and northern red oaks, American beeches, lindens and Austrian pines.

However, he continued to operate the rest of the property as a working farm. The family occupied the house from Memorial Day until fall, but dairy products and flowers from Whippany Farm were delivered twice weekly to the winter home at One Sutton Place South in New York.

The son of Frederick T. Frelinghuysen, a former Secretary of State under President Chester A. Arthur, George Frelinghuysen enjoyed a family fortune based on real estate, insurance and mining. A patent lawyer, he served as President of the Howard Savings Institution in Newark and as a member of the board of directors of the Mutual Life Insurance Company. With his marriage to Sarah L. Ballantine, granddaughter of the founder, he became president of P. Ballantine and

Company, also of Newark. There were two children: Peter H. B. Frelinghuysen (1883-1959) and Matilda E. (1888-1969).

Peter Frelinghuysen continued his father's interest in farming and established Twin Oaks Farm, a name recognized worldwide for its prize-winning cattle. Peter, Jr., was a longtime congressman and grandson, Rodney, is a New Jersey state assemblyman and former Morris County freeholder.

After the death of her parents, Miss Matilda E. Frelinghuysen remained at Whippany Farm and made it her home for life. In 1964, she began plans to donate Whippany Farm as an arboretum to be established upon her death, and in May 1971, 126 beautiful rolling acres, including her favorite rose garden, were dedicated in her parents' memory. She also donated the land for the Morris County Free Library as well as property along the Whippany River for Patriots Path, a walking and biking trail along the Whippany River linking historic sites and recreational facilities in six Morris County municipalities. □

TJFPLMMT

TJFPLMMT

Whippany Farm (opposite), Whippany Road and East Hanover Avenue, Morris Township. It was designed in Georgian Revival style by Rotch and Tilden of Boston for George Griswold Frelinghuysen. It is now an arboretum and headquarters of the Morris County Park Commission.

The barns (above right) along Whippany Road are now the site of office buildings.

Twin Oaks (right), rear view of the mansion of Peter H. B. Frelinghuysen, Sr., 6 Normandy Heights Road. The house is now The Morris Museum; the property in the foreground is now the site of Patriot's Plaza.

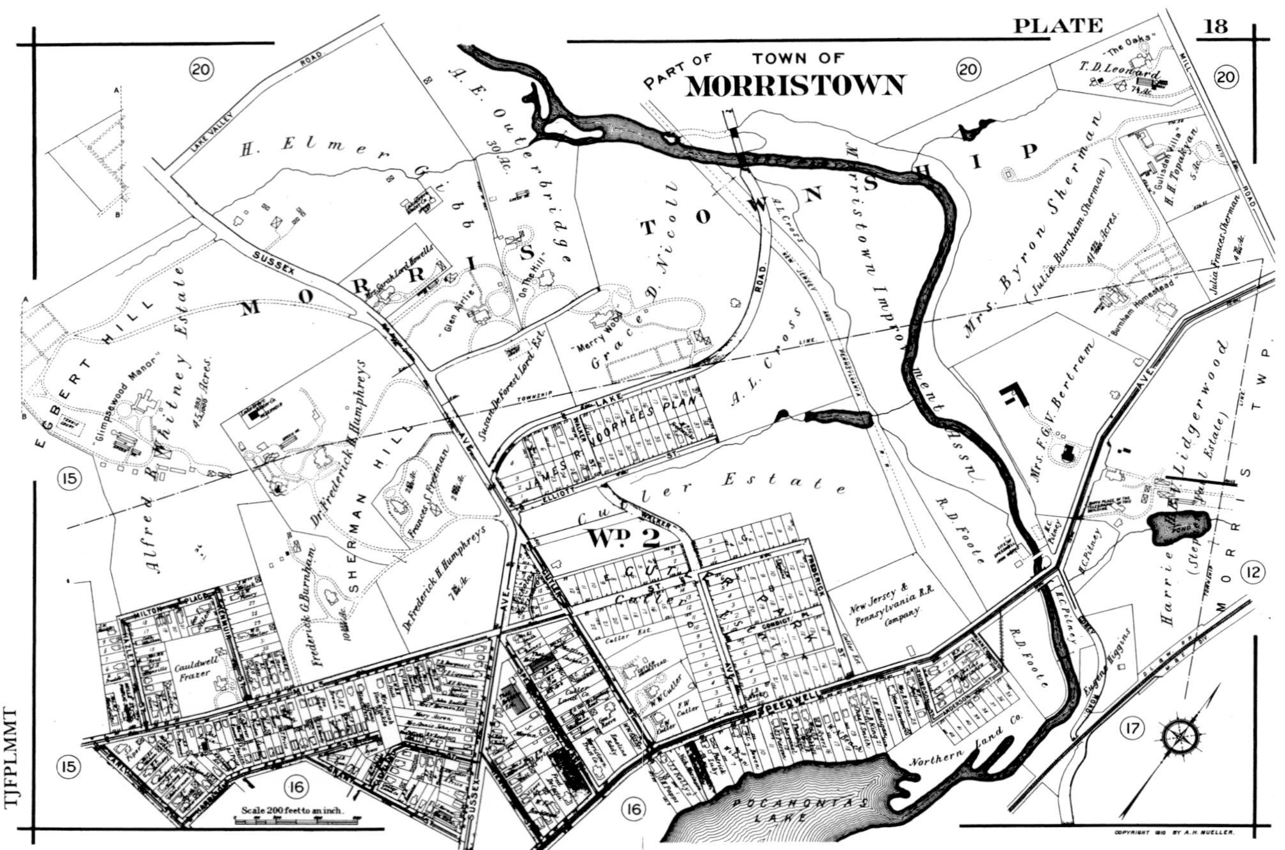

TJFPLMMT

Morristown and Morris Township in 1910, showing the estates off Sussex Avenue.

Glimpswood Manor (below) and the long **entrance driveway** curving up Egbert Hill from Sussex Avenue. It was built in 1891-2 by the millionaire iron and steel magnate Alfred Rutgers Whitney. The house was razed in the 1930s.

Beautiful Homes of Northern New Jersey, c. 1910

Western Morris Township

Morris Township divides approximately in half at Speedwell Avenue in the north and Route 202 in the south. This western part is hillier, was farmed longer and, to this day, is less densely populated than the eastern part, including Convent Station and Normandy Heights.

Grand mansions like Gustav E. Kissel's Wheatsheaf Farm, Louis C. Gillespie's Tower Hill and Luther Kountze's Delbarton were built to take advantage of commanding views of Washington Valley and the surrounding mountains. Substantial houses were constructed on Mount Kemble, Egbert Hill, Sherman Hill and Telephone Hill, located off the present Knox Hill Road and informally named for a private 70-acre compound owned by three New York and New Jersey Telephone Company executives.

All around the area was farmland. Although the soil was never particularly rich, it was well suited for livestock and the crops grown for their feed. Fosterfields, as noted earlier, kept a prize herd of milking cows imported from the Isle of Jersey and grew corn, wheat and rye. The cows on Inamere Farm, belonging to Rudolph H. Kissel, Gustav's brother and business partner, produced milk sold to New York's Walker Gordon Company.

Although, today, Inamere Farm is gone and houses spill over the hillsides, the area is still much less crowded than its eastern counterpart. Sussex Avenue is still mainly residential. Route 24 from Washington Street to the Mendham Township border has long stretches of woods, and houses, usually veiled by trees or shrubs, are set back off the road. This is in marked contrast to the eastern township's rapid commercial development on Route 24.

Beautiful Homes of Northern New Jersey, c. 1910

Ridgewood Hill, on Sherman Hill on the border of Morristown and Morris Township, belonged in 1910 to Dr. Frederick H. Humphreys. His fortune came from Humphreys' Homeopathic Medicine Company, whose "specifics" had a remedy "for nearly every disease." Sherman Park is now on the site.

One reason is surely the relative inconvenience for the commuter. The attraction to newcomers of having a railroad station nearby can't be underestimated.

At the turn of the century, this part of the township *did* have the Rockaway Valley ("Rock-a-Bye-Baby") Railroad, but it was more for the transportation of peaches than people (page 147). In 1892, the line reached Watnong at Speedwell Lake, one and one-half miles from its proposed destination, which would have linked it with the Morris and Essex Division of the Delaware, Lackawanna and Western Railroad and the New York market. Although there were two daily passenger trains, they were not devoted to a schedule, tending to stop for anyone who flagged them down. Never financially secure, the line, although later part of the New Jersey and Pennsylvania Railroad, was doomed when the 1905 scale virtually destroyed the peach orchards. Commuters would have to drive through Morristown or over Mount Kemble to reach a train station or a highway.

Another reason is the amount of land left in protected open space. Morris County Park System's Fosterfields and Lewis Morris Park, the Catholic institutions which preserved three of the grand mansions and zoning restrictions have helped to preserve some of the western township's Golden Age character. □

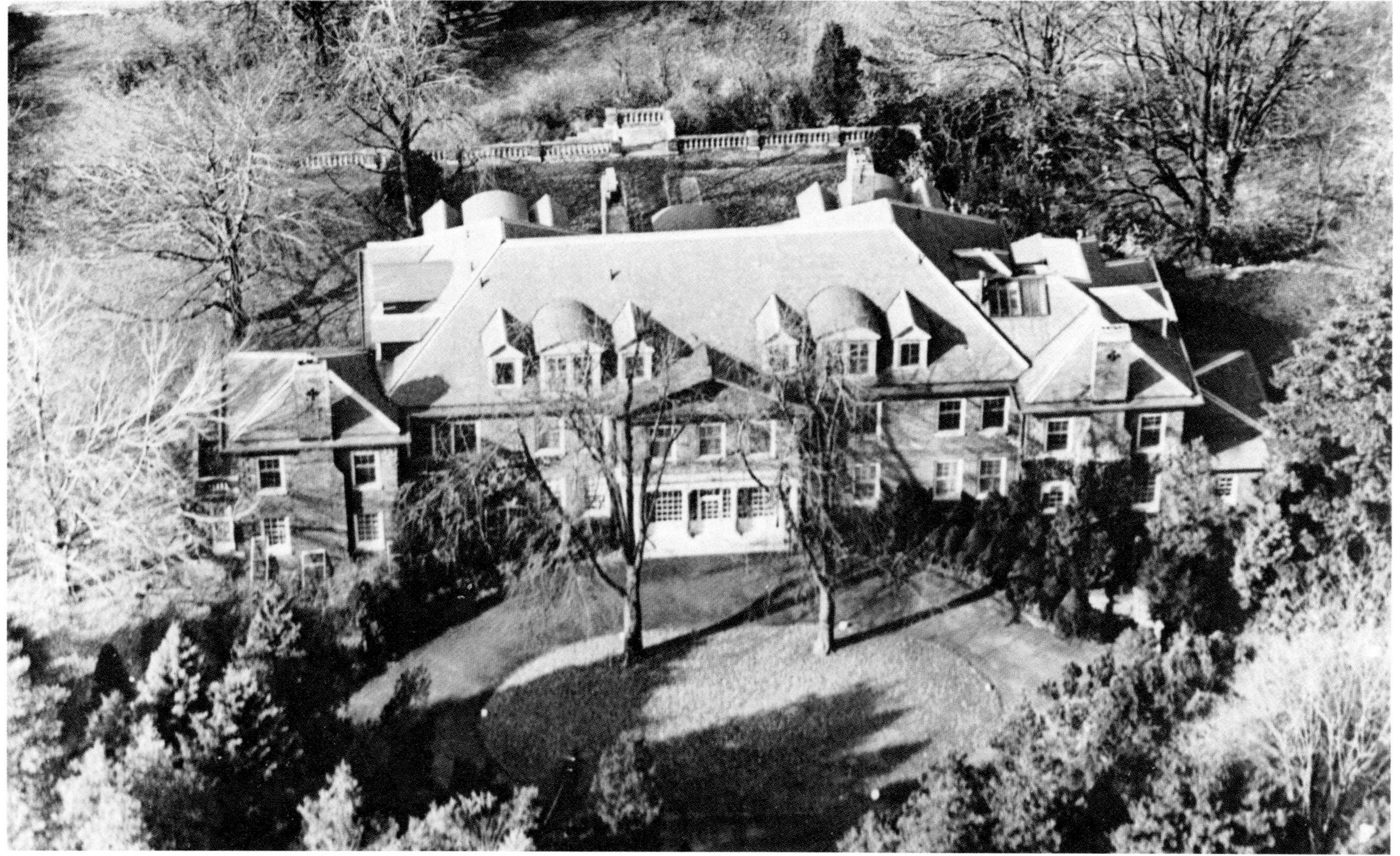

Courtesy of Sisters of the Good Shepherd

Wheatsheaf House, Kadhena Road and Sussex Avenue, Morris Township

From its commanding site, this brick manor house had a sweeping view of Washington Valley around to the Watnong Mountains. It was designed by New York's Hamilton Bell and built in 1904-05 for Gustav E. Kissel (d. 1911), a founder of Kissel, Kinnecutt, and Company, investment bankers, and Mrs. Kissel (d. July 1949), a granddaughter of Commodore Vanderbilt.

The house now is owned by the Sisters of the Good Shepherd, who use it as a retreat and counseling center. The rest of the property (map) is owned by the Rabbinical College of America, Sussex Avenue, or divided into the development called Wheatsheaf.

Girl Scout troop (right), terrace side, May 29, 1926. Mrs. Kissel is presumed to be one of the ladies on the left.

Wheatsheaf Farm

In 1887, Gustav Kissel bought the historic property called Solitude, once owned by John Cleves Symmes (page 74) and occupied by the coin minter Walter Mould (page 79). In the early 19th century, it became Wheatsheaf Inn, a successful tavern. The Kissels used it as a summer residence before building the mansion they called Wheatsheaf House to distinguish it from the rest of the property, Wheatsheaf Farm.

According to an article in *The Jerseyman*, August 26, 1904, the mansion was to be "144 feet in length by 50 feet in width, two and a half stories high." (By today's standards it was a full floor.) Other dimensions given were for the entrance hall, 22 by 30 feet, with a handsome freestanding staircase, 16 feet square; dining room, 21 by 26 feet; living room — which doubled as a ballroom and was called "Headlong Hall" — with a great fireplace, 38 by 37 feet; and an adjoining smoking room, also Mr. Kissel's library, 20 feet square. This latter room was, literally, the only room in the house where smoking was allowed. Headlong Hall and the smoking room were on the south, or left, end of the house; kitchen, pantries and servants' quarters were on the north end.

The second floor had nine bedrooms for the family and guests, with five bathrooms and additional servants' rooms. A private staircase went from Mr. Kissel's master suite to the smoking room/library below. The third floor had a suite of five rooms for the Kissel children, three girls and a boy, and more servants' rooms and trunk and storage rooms.

Mr. Kissel and his son, Thorn, were avid polo players, and the house was designed so that the private polo field, believed the first to be in Morris County, could be seen from the terrace. Mrs. Kissel, a founder and president of the Garden Club of New Jersey, created a marvelous sunken garden below the terrace on the left. Mrs. Kissel was also active in many charities and very interested in the Girl Scout movement of Morris County. She died at the house on July 30, 1949. □

Curtiss Collection/TJFPLMMT

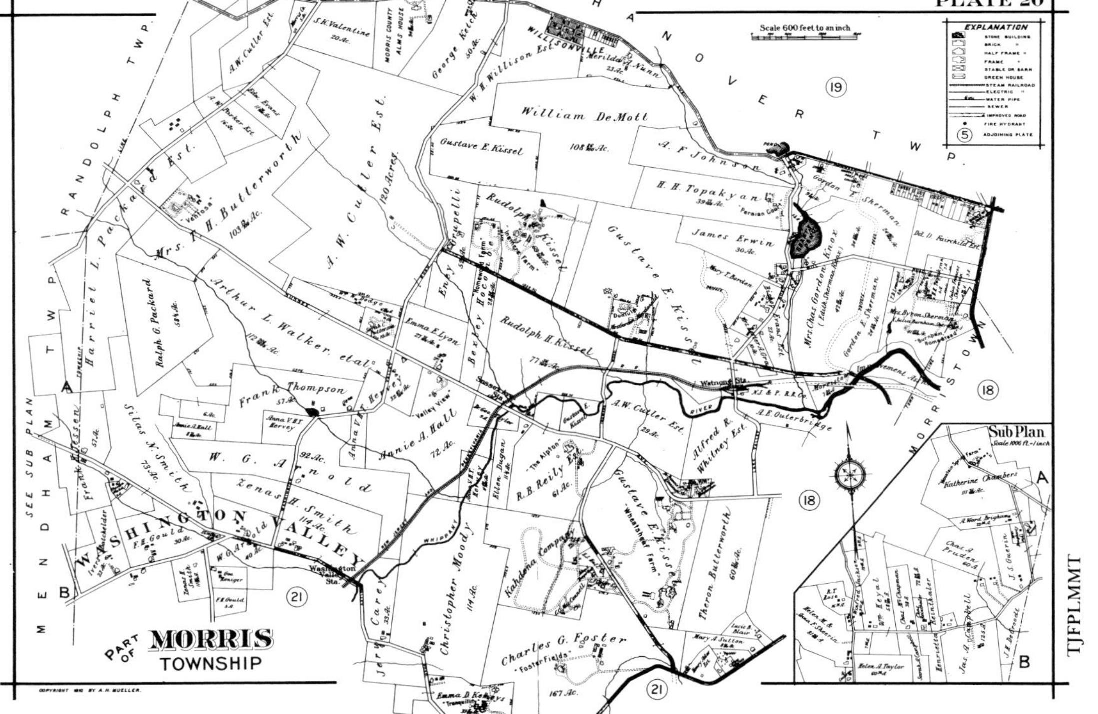

TJFPLMMT

Morris Township in 1910, from Sussex Avenue to Washington Valley.

TJFPLMMT

Tower Hill, Western Avenue and Picatinny Road, Morris Township

This Colonial Revival mansion was built in 1890 for Louis C. Gillespie of Philadelphia pressed brick with white marble trim and green-tiled roof. It is now Villa Walsh.

The view (below) toward Delbarton, Washington Valley and Mendham Township, 1983.

The 70-foot tower (opposite) that gave the estate its name.

Photograph by James L. Grabow/TJFPLMMT

Tower Hill

"Altogether, Tower Hill had much to offer in the way of diversion and pleasure for all members of the family and their guests, despite the relative isolation," recalled Louis Gillespie Erskine, grandson of the builder, in *Morris Township: A Glimpse Into the Past* by Barbara Hoskins. He mentions "stalls filled with driving horses for carriages and sleighs and Kentucky-bred saddle horses" and the pleasure of "driving and riding, tennis and croquet and, in wintertime, tobogganing on the steep slopes and skating."

In 1878, Louis Charles Gillespie (1835-1911) purchased 115 acres and built a summer home on Union Hill, where the elevation is 735 feet with an unsurpassed view of the valley below. The house had a furnace as well as fireplaces so that his large family — nine children — and their many friends also could enjoy it during the winter holidays.

His business was in New York where he imported chinawood oil from China on his company's own clipper ship, *Javery*.

In 1890, he decided to enlarge and remodel the house into a real Golden Age mansion. On the ground floor was a spacious hall, reception room, library, drawing room, billiard room, living room and dining room. The woodwork in each room was of highly finished quartered oak and mahogany with much hand carving. A beautiful divided staircase of carved oaks ascended to the third floor.

On July 6, 1894, *The Jerseyman* described the building of the tower: "Sturgis Brothers are erecting a huge stone tower for L. C. Gillespie on the hill near his residence on the Jockey Hollow Road [Western Avenue] which is 26 feet square at the base with walls 42 inches thick and tapering to the top where they are 20 inches through. The measurement in the clear will be 19 feet 4 inches. The tower will be six stories, in all 70 feet high with a chimney 12 feet higher, and on the second floor will be an open fireplace of red Potsdam sandstone. The structure is erected over a 417 foot deep well and on the ground floor will be a steam engine for pumping water into a tank on the fourth floor. There will be a lookout on the upper story, and the whole will be surmounted by a tile roof."

In 1929, Tower Hill was advertised for sale at $125,000. Fortunately, Bishop Walsh, Catholic Archbishop of Newark, decided to acquire the estate and keep the mansion as a mother house for the Religious Teachers Filippini, who started a school there the following year. Villa Walsh Academy remains a highly respected school for girls in grades 7 to 12. □

> ***If the old Tower Hill could speak out about the years from 1878 to 1919, it would tell of a full life lived there by three generations . . . . of the good spirit and the love that existed in that home.***
> **Louis G. Erskine to Barbara Hoskins**

Beautiful Homes of Northern New Jersey, c. 1910

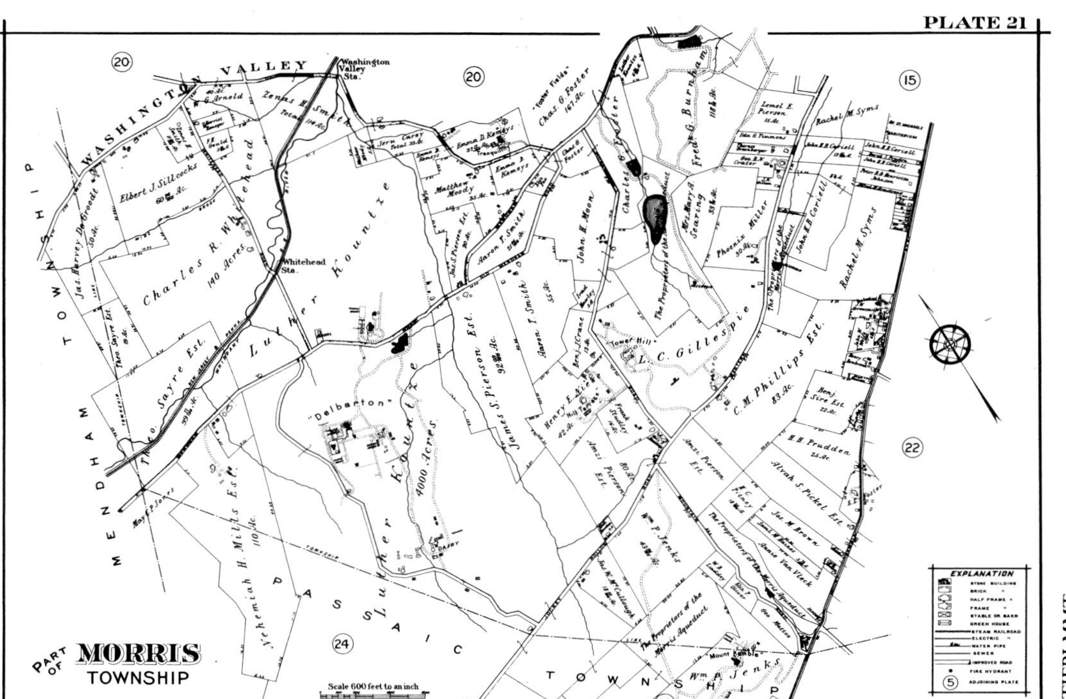

TJFPLMMT

Morris Township in 1910, showing Mendham Road, Western Avenue and Washington Valley. Tower Hill and Delbarton (following pages) are in the center.

TJFPLMMT

Delbarton, Mendham Road, Morris Township

This overview shows the Italian garden created on the west side of the mansion at the beginning of the 20th century by New York banker Luther Kountze on Mendham Road. A Greek garden, planned for the east side, was never completed. This photograph was taken after the estate was purchased by St. Mary's Abbey, which operates the Delbarton School; the white-granite mansion now is called "Old Main."

Delbarton

When Luther Kountze (1841-1918) moved into Delbarton in 1883, he was worth about $30 million, senior partner in the banking firm of Kountze Brothers, 14 Wall Street, New York, and had a large, comfortable house at 5 East 57th Street. He had been in the banking business since his teens.

In 1881, Luther Kountze began purchasing land on the southern border of Washington Valley, six farms in all totaling about 4,000 acres. The focal point of the Morris Township estate was the 50-acre farm of Nehemiah Mills, grandson of Timothy Mills, whose 1740 house still stands on Mills Street.

Nehemiah's farmhouse was moved about 100 yards southeast and became the superintendent's home. Kountze also purchased four adjacent farms. On Charles Leek's farm he found the gray granite used to build the two-foot-thick outside walls. He also owned a large part of Jockey Hollow, including Tempe Wick House and a portion of Lewis Morris Park.

Luther was born in Ohio, son of Christian and Margaret from Bakersdorf, Germany. About 1860 Christian Kountze took advantage of a financial boom in the new West, sold his retail store and moved to Omaha, Nebraska, where he established one of the first banks on the new frontier. His five sons joined together to create the firm of Kountze Brothers. Herman and Augustus remained in Omaha while Luther and Charles established banks in Denver and Central City, Colorado. They established the Colorado National Bank, which became the largest in the West. Later Luther went to study international banking in London with other sons of German-Jewish families making American financial history.

Pergola (above and right), covered with grapevines. The Italian sculptures represent mythological subjects. The vines are gone, but the pergola and statues remain.

These two photographs and the two on page 209 appeared in a real estate brochure in the early 1920s when the mansion was for sale.

Photographs courtesy of St. Mary's Abbey/TJFPLMMT

Photographs courtesy of St. Mary's Abbey/TJFPLMMT

He made a personally and socially advantageous marriage to Annie Parsons Ward, from a prominent Philadelphia family, who was also related to the DeLancey and Barclay families of New York. Two sons were given these names, and *Delbarton* is a combination of the first three letters of each. The *ton* comes from Livingston, both their daughter Helen's middle name and her married name. A second daughter was named Annie for her mother.

The mansion measured 150 by 125 feet and there were some 28 rooms on the first and second floors and 12 servants' rooms on the third. The first floor contained an armor room, music room and a Washington room devoted to Revolutionary artifacts, some of them found on his property, which he later gave to the Morristown National Historical Park. In addition to the essential carriage houses, outbuildings included a creamery, poultry plant, houses for the gardener and the dairy man, and a huge barn for cows, pigs, and other farm animals. Like most big estates in the country, it had its own water tower. In the 1890s, Mr. Kountze made Delbarton his permanent home, and he started to build an Italian garden on the west side. The great marble columns that form the pergola are believed to have come from the 5th Avenue mansion of A. T. Stewart, who owned the large and fashionable New York store that later was known as Wanamaker's. Two of the statues he imported from Italy are by the famous sculptor Bernini. Because there are so few examples of his work in the United States, the statues are on loan to the Metropolitan Museum.

In 1925, St. Mary's Abbey of the Order of St. Benedict purchased the estate for $155,000. In 1939, the monks founded there the Delbarton School, one of the finest preparatory schools in the state, serving about 500 boys. □

Delbarton's front hall (left), stretching from the front to the rear entrance. On the staircase landing is the dramatic 10-foot stained-glass window executed by Clayton and Bell of London. Called "The Twelve Immortals," it depicts famous painters, sculptors and authors, such as Michelangelo, da Vinci and Dante.

Dining room (below). The portrait of Luther Kountze and his horse, painted about 1876, can be seen faintly at the far, curved end. Across the room at the opposite end is a balcony where musicians could play during dinner.

Delbarton (opposite, above), as it appeared in the summer of 1893.

Kountze family and friends (opposite, below), from an 1891 album. From left to right, Luther Kountze, Amy Wagner, Annie W. Kountze, "Spottie," Helen L. Kountze, Annie P. Kountze, Barclay Rives, John Kane; on the grass, W. DeLancey Kountze and "Turks."

Photographs courtesy of St. Mary's Abbey/TJFPLMMT

Vital Problem in Morristown: Absorption of Farm Territory into Great Estates

From *Newark Evening News*, March 20, 1912

The recent purchase in Morristown of one hundred acres by Marcellus Hartley Dodge, from F. Hallet Lovell, is considered as another evidence of the rapid strides which have been made within the past year or so in the absorption of Morris County acreage into large estates. At the same time the acquirement of such large estates has raised complex problems in the town and this section of the county. Social, economic, religious and political factors are presented.

It is shown by the records that Mr. Dodge now owns about 500 acres of land, and he is said to be negotiating for more. He has extended his bounds as far toward Madison Avenue as it is possible to extend them. His immediate neighbors are Charles W. Harkness, Henry W. Shoemaker and the estate of D. Willis James. His recent purchase takes him nearly to the line of Madison borough. He has a force of men clearing brush from the land, grubbing out hedge rows, building roads and making other improvements.

To the holdings in Mr. Dodge's own name should be added those of Mrs. Helen Hartley Jenkins and George W. Jenkins, for their holdings interlock like the sections in a picture puzzle, and in one or two cases tracts are owned jointly by Mr. Dodge and Mrs. Jenkins [his aunt].

To the west of the Dodge holdings are the estates of Charles Scribner and the Van Beuren family. Then come Joseph W. Ogden and Eben B. Thomas, controlling the high lands to James Street on the road leading from Morristown to New Vernon. This thoroughfare has seen remarkable changes of ownership [and] is almost as strongly held as is Madison Avenue property. In Morristown proper the Lidgerwood lands bound James Street on the south from South Street almost to the town line. On the north side of the street Robert D. Foote has extended his estate from Green Street to Harter Road.

Mr. Foote purchased the Hipson farm of 110 acres last week and, with the exception of the brick yard property and a number of small lots, he controls the block bounded northerly by Mt. Kemble Avenue and southerly by James Street from Green Street and All Souls' Hospital to Harter Road.

The New Vernon section has for years been the chief source of supply for vegetables and small fruits, but within a few years Alexander H. Tiers has purchased two farms for a country place and since his death Mrs. Tiers has continued to buy adjoining property until her holdings approximate 350 acres and extend to the village church . . . .

Courtesy of Mrs. Marianne Foote Baker

Spring Brook Farm before 1904, when it was owned by John Taintor Foote. The lane in the foreground was known as the dairy entrance on James Street and is the present entrance of the Loyola House of Retreat.

THE GREAT KOUNTZE ESTATE

A number of large farms lie between the Foote and Tiers but there is not a great distance between this new "centre" and the country seat of the late David H. McAlpin and Mrs. J. Tolman Pyle. This large tract adjoins immediately the largest estate in this section owned by Luther Kountze, which is said to contain 4,000 acres. The Kountze land stretches across Morris to the Foster, Kahdena and Kissel properties and runs around the William P. Jenks and Gillespie estate properties, almost forming a junction with the Burnham tract.

From the old Skidmore place of about fifty acres, which John Claflin purchased some years ago, Mr. Claflin has extended his borders on nearly all sides, until at present he owns about 200 acres. His policy has differed from other buyers in that he has purchased land lying inside the block bounded by James and South Streets and Loantaka Terrace, leaving buffer lots between his property and the streets. Narrow strips give him access to the roads. In this block he has spent a large amount of money in ditching, clearing out brush and constructing bridle paths.

HOW PROBLEMS MULTIPLY

These developments, added to the former large estates, such as the Twombly, Leslie D. Ward and Normandie Park purchases, have caused a country problem near Morristown which is probably unique.

The farms are sold by the former owners for good prices, sometimes for very high prices. Some of the farmers purchased farms in other localities, but most of them go into the nearby towns, purchase houses and take up some new line of work, or live entirely upon the returns from the sale of their lands.

The new owner razes the poorer structures and erects a fine house. Many acres which formerly produced crops disposed of in the towns are turned into lawns. Drives are constructed, planting beautifies the place, and in most cases the tax valuation is increased. The estate requires more labor to keep it up than did the plain farm, and to get this work done the foreign-born laborer is employed. He lives with his family in the foreign quarters in Morristown, Madison or Bernardsville and every day goes to and from work on his bicycle or walks. In winter he is generally idle . . . .

In this way town and country social problems come together. The town has the problems of education, housing, recreation, etc., to deal with, as well as the block of voters, a large number of whom are influenced in their actions by a so-called leader.

The removal of the farmers is regarded as a blow to the country life in its social and religious aspects. The new owners, as a rule, with better means of transportation, seek their religious life, as well as their social relations, in the larger places, and the country church loses not only its support but its membership.

The products of gardening and small fruit raising by the change of ownership disappear from the market. The town deprived of them is forced more and more to depend on the commission merchant and prices for such commodities rise. There are a few exceptions, as, for instance, where a large owner conducts a dairy larger than is required for his own needs and sells his surplus.

The land taken for the larger estates is withdrawn from the market and city residents who desire to buy a small place are forced to look elsewhere. The local mechanic suffers from this, as he would be called up to build or remodel the necessary buildings and keep them in repair. With the great estates there are fewer buildings. Often the owner has financial or other connections with some of the large general contracting firms who do the work with their own men, sometimes brought from a long distance. In other cases the estate maintains its own force, with a skilled superintendent and abundant unskilled hands.

Beautiful Gardens in America, by Louise Shelton, 1915.

Gardens of Cherrycroft, residence of Dudley Olcott, Normandy Parkway, formerly farmland. Many annuals and perennials, "pink, dark red, blues and yellows," filled the broad beds.

All the Right People

TJFPLMMT

Special music commissioned for the Morris County Golf Club in 1896. An A. B. Frost illustration is on the cover.

MORRISTOWN MOVED IN THE TIGHT SOCIAL CIRCLES typical of Victorian times. The answers to three questions — "Who are they?" and "Where did they come from?" and "How did they make their money?" — determined a family's status in the community, not only of parents, children, relatives, but even houseguests. The correct answers — old name, old family, old money — guaranteed social acceptance, coveted invitations, and club memberships. The same people saw each other again and again, year after year. Many were connected by marriage, lifelong friendships and long-standing business associations.

Mention in the Social Register and connection with New York's "400," of course, promised immediate entrance into the top level of Morristown society. So were certain invitations, such as those to the annual five New Year's Day parties attended by the *crème de la crème.* The day began at 10:30 or 11:00 with breakfast at the South Street home of Grinnell Willis (coffee cake, scrambled eggs, Virginia ham) and then continued to the Madison Avenue home of Mrs. Ridley Watts (claret punch, delectable paper-thin sandwiches and numerous delicacies served from the table covered with a beautiful linen cloth embroidered to match the medallion design on the dining room ceiling). Then on to Morris Township to George Marshall Allen's Glynallyn (early afternoon eggnog and more delicacies) and the Charles Bradleys' The Wayside (afternoon tea). This hectic day, involving several changes of dress, ended at Seth Thomas's Red Gate Farm for a sumptuous dinner from 7:00 to 9:00.

For the social Morristownian, there was always plenty to do. For the younger set of both sexes, daytime sports, such as golf, tennis and bicycling, were the focus. Young ladies joined cooking classes and reading clubs or took courses with cultural emphasis, such as French history and architecture — taught in French, of course. Young men leaned towards polo and hunting. Every age group was interested in parties and games. The most exclusive group, however, read Shakespeare in evening dress on Monday nights, rotating among the members' homes. The Shakespeare Club — second oldest in the country and still existing — goes back to the late autumn of 1876. The membership was limited to 15 couples, six widows or bachelors, and relatives in residence, each of whom read a part from a play.

From the "outside" it looked like an exciting life of privilege. Social leaders' activities were followed like today's media stars. Whether it was really that thrilling is doubtful. "When I was growing up, life consisted pretty much of going from one tea party to one ball to one tennis match after another. We did not accomplish anything. Everybody was vying with one another to have a better party than the one before." □

Sports and Games in the Open, illustrated by A. B. Frost

A. B. Frost's "The Tourists" bicycling down a Morris Township lane

All a lady bicyclist needed was an escort of friends, the right hat, leg-o-mutton sleeves, a tightly cinched waist, a skirt with bloomers or knee britches, and she was ready for a carefree spin.

Arthur Burdett Frost (1851-1928) was one of the most popular illustrators and humorists in America. He must have viewed this carefree scene in Convent Station many times at the turn of the century.

How to Dress When Golfing

From *The New York Times*, c. 1894

The golf season is in full blast albeit the weather is even now too warm for the full enjoyment of the same. The women are very enthusiastic over the sport and while they may not perhaps have the strength sufficient to "drive" as far as can the men, many of them play capitally.

At Morristown, in particular, the women have evinced great skill, Mrs. Shippen, Miss Fanny Hopkins and Miss Howland play all the time and play well. The Hempstead women are most graceful and expert and at Tuxedo, Southampton and Newport the women play almost as much as the men.

How to dress when golfing has been almost as much of a puzzle as what to wear when bicycling. Bloomers and knee breeches have been seen on women when bicycling, but although some exceedingly short skirts have been seen in the golf field, the former hideous garments have fortunately been tabooed. Knickerbockers are an indispensable part of a proper golf outfit, but they are always covered by a skirt reaching to the ankles.

Every ounce of superfluous weight must be done away with, yet the skirt must be cut full enough to look well, a narrow skirt being unbecoming to the figure. The same length as for bicycle riding is the best — to the ankles — and about three yards wide, but the fullness must be differently arranged.

Mohair or alpaca is an excellent material for the summer golf costume, as it is so light. The skirt need not be lined but it is well to have it bound in velvet to give a certain weight. The prettiest of all fashions is to have a leather finish about two inches wide. This, however, looks best on tweed, cheviot, or serge; on mohair it is not so appropriate and seems more suited to the gowns that are worn in autumn and winter.

It is quite out of the question to play golf in a long skirt. Even on the most satisfactory links, the grass is long enough to retain a certain amount of moisture, which soon attaches itself to the bottom of a skirt that is of any length. Then there are the dust, the brambles and the thorns and the thousand and one things that are sure to fasten themselves on skirts and petticoats.

Petticoats are not to be worn with golf skirts. Knickerbockers or knee britches take their place. These can be made at home when money saving is an object. Satin is the best material but the same goods as the costume is also used, and even holland and linen in warm weather. Satin, however, is not a very warm fabric at any time and is particularly desirable, as it does not cling to the skirt as do any woollen goods.

The shoes should be carefully attended to. They must not be too thin, or the player will become foot sore, and should be made to order, not ready made. The soles must be broad, and the heels low and broad also, for there is a great deal of rough walking to be done even under the most favorable circumstances. Either low shoes or high boots can be worn. When the shoes are preferred, gaiters or leggings reaching to the knee are necessary. The leather leggings are very warm, but canvas or light cloth are to be had.

Some women who go in for ultra effects are wearing bicycle stockings for golf playing, but they are so extremely coarse and rough they will never be universally fashionable. Tan leather shoes or boots are the coolest, but it should be remembered that black are vastly more becoming unless a woman has a small and well shaped foot.

The Norfolk jacket is the favorite pattern for the waist of a golf costume, but until autumn the shirt waists will reign supreme and a golf cape will be kept at hand to don when stopping to rest. Something besides the shirt waist must be kept near by as one gets very warm while playing, and it is dangerous to cool off too suddenly.

A hat to shade the eyes is the best headgear. For this purpose either an Alpine or broad brimmed sailor will do, and this must be set squarely down on the forehead, not pushed back from the face as some women elect to wear it. If gloves are worn only rough ones, and extra large, are possible. Simply as a protection are they desirable — not for show.

Bicycling, riding and golfing are alike in one respect in that they demand a costume neat, trim and absolutely "fit." No trimming, nothing but severe effects, and the one that looks the best is the one that is most suitable for the game.

The Sporting Life

The leisure class was not the lazy class. Society's ideal young man was an athletic person devoted to the outdoors.

Few men filled this ideal better than handsome Eugene Higgins (1860-1948). One of America's wealthiest bachelors, he spent many summers at his Morris Township estate off Corey Road. The estate later became the Whippany River Club (page 220).

In 1898, a newspaper called Higgins "a devoted golfer, an expert cross country rider, a 'good gun,' a skillful fisherman and a yachtsman of no mean seamanship. Sartorially, he is all that can be desired." He was also a fencing champion and accomplished at "four-in-hand" coaching. Once, he was seen tooling around the Morristown Green atop his stage coach with all six members of the Flora Dora Sextette beside him. They were pulled by four matched horses, Dunder, Blitz, Blizzard and Bluster, while a green-liveried attendant tooted the "gabriel horn" to warn everyone to get out of the way — or stand back and watch.

Although Higgins was unusual because he excelled in a wide variety of sports, there were many sports enthusiasts — men and women — in the Morristown area. Gustav Kissel built the first polo field; Otto Kahn, among others, had practice golf courses; and a number of properties had private tennis courts. Although shooting was usually (though not exclusively) a man's pursuit, women participated enthusiastically in almost every other sport, from archery and badminton and croquet to fishing and fox hunting. For those with the time and money, there seemed an endless list of possible activities. □

Two of A. B. Frost's hunting scenes, "With Dog and Gun — Quail" and "With Dog and Gun — English Pheasant." Both drawings were copyrighted in 1897. The scenery probably represented views of his friend Robert D. Foote's property.

Both illustrations from Scribner's Magazine *Pictures by Popular American Artists, 1900*

Morris County Golf Club

Great interest was exhibited at the end of the nineteenth century for a game newly imported from Scotland, pronounced "gof" by those in the know. However, the Morris County Golf Club must be the only one founded by women.

On April 10, 1894, at the home of Mrs. Henry Hopkins, the first officers of the Morris County Golf Club were elected. Miss Nina Howland, president; Mrs. Hamilton McK. Twombly, vice president; Mrs. William Shippen, recording secretary; Miss Alice D. Fields, corresponding secretary; and Mrs. Charles Bradley, treasurer.

The charter announced that regular members, not less than 18 or more than 30, must be women. Men could join as associate members; either sex could be honorary.

The founders surely had drive — no pun intended. In 1894, the club had a seven hole course. In 1895, it had 18 holes and a clubhouse and the season was opened with a professional tournament between (alas) two men. In fact, female dominance was short-lived. In 1896, although Miss Howland is listed as honorary president (she resigned immediately) and Mrs. Twombly as honorary vice president, Paul Revere, a son of Joseph Revere, was president; J. B. Dickson, treasurer; and Arthur Berry, secretary. The women continued to play enthusiastically, of course — except, it is said, for Miss Howland — Miss Annie Howland Ford, Mrs.

"A Game of Golf — A Drive," showing the first Morris County clubhouse, Madison Avenue, by member A. B. Frost. The building was 70 by 32 feet, with inviting verandas front and back. Inside was an immense fireplace, huge paneled hall with yellow pine beams across the ceiling, dressing rooms and butler's quarters. It burned down November 8, 1903.

TJFPLMMT

William Shippen and Mrs. Henry P. Phipps went on to be top national competitors.

"All eyes on Morristown links," enthused *The New York Herald*, Sunday, September 11, 1898. "Golfdom is all agog with excitement. Tomorrow begins the National Amateur Championship game and the links at Morristown will during the week be the gayest, sparkling center in the Union." The event was the amateur championship golf competition. The prize was the Havemeyer Challenge Trophy, a $1,000 silver cup presented by the late Theodore A. Havemeyer, who had been first president of the U.S. Golf Association.

Golfing society turned out in force on the Morris County links. Non-golfing society watched from the veranda or followed the players at a discreet distance. Non-society pressed their noses against the fences to watch in fascination as the players waved sticks and pushed about a little ball, sometimes saying ungentlemanly things.

In the week of the competition, a brass band played continuously. Tents were set up for lunch, a separate restaurant tent for the ladies and a cafe tent for the men. Mr. and Mrs. Twombly returned from Newport specially for the week to entertain the visiting golfers. Guest players also were entertained by George G. Freylinghuysen, Ransom Thomas, Wynant D. Vanderpool and W. Alston Flagg. On Friday night, there was a dance at the club and, on the final evening, there were 62 dinner parties. A club and a game had been launched that became an important part of Morristown's Society. □

The Amateur Championship Golf Competition at the club, September 12-17, 1898: the first tee (top); Devil's Punch Bowl (middle); No. 5 Green (bottom) with Findlay S. Douglas, eventual winner, of the Fairfield Country Club, who had learned the game in Scotland, against Walter B. Smith of the Onwentsia Club, who was a golf champion at Yale.

TJFPLMMT

TJFPLMMT

Morristown Field Club's invitation-only horse show, next in importance to Madison Square Garden.

TJFPLMMT

Morristown Field Club

The Morristown Field Club was founded in 1881 and is the third oldest tennis club in New Jersey, predated by Seabright and Orange Lawn. It first operated as the Morristown Lawn Tennis Club with two courts — for men only — on a "lovely flat lawn" on the Skidmore (later Claflin) property on South Street. In May 1893, it organized formally as the Morristown Field Club and moved several hundred yards north to the Lidgerwood property. By 1895, women were allowed to join. A number of other sports and activities were introduced, including baseball, football, cricket, target shooting, croquet, pool and golf. A skating rink for a hockey team and an ice carnival was built on the James Street pond. Horse and dog shows were held annually, for which grandstands and horse sheds were built.

Without doubt, the most successful innovation was the annual horse show begun in 1897. Exhibitors came by invitation only and represented the whole metropolitan area and sometimes farther beyond. In three days of incomparable excitement, millions of dollars of horseflesh moved about nervously, harness bells jingling, waiting for race time. Mrs. Paul Moore, in a ladies' basket phaeton showed "Kara," Otto Kahn with "Starlight" and "Golight" in tandem, Walter Bliss with "Lady Whitefoot" and "Lady Lightfoot." There were classes for hunters, jumpers, saddle horses, road horses — even for ponies, which were judged partly for "good manners." There were competitions for fire horses and officers' mounts. Perhaps the biggest thrill, however, was watching the four-in-hands. The Twomblys and Otto Kahn always showed up. So did Bexley Hocombe who, as a poor boy in

The next improvement was in allowing the young women to become members of the club at the almost nominal due of $3 a year, and in electing two or three of them on the different committees. Always before, they had been merely invited to use the club and although they appreciated the compliment it was with a feeling of relief that they were allowed to pay their own dues, however small.

Alice Lavinia Day, writing about the Field Club in the *Morris County Chronicle*, December 1, 1896

England, watched the magnificent, cosseted horses and the supreme confidence of their owners and vowed that he, too, would master this skill. This he did in London and Brighton Beach on visits abroad and in Morristown at the Field Club.

Spectators were as interesting to watch as the competitions. Expensive private boxes were sold at auction. Some spectators jockeyed their carriages behind the field for a better position. Others leaned against the fence or walked about chatting, showing off the handsome and stylish cut of their clothes to the crowd.

Tennis, however, remained foremost for the members. In 1905, the first open New Jersey State Tennis Tournament was held at the Field Club, bringing such nationally known players as Bill Tilden. This event was held annually until 1916. In 1921 and 1923, the legendary Tilden returned to play tennis exhibitions for the benefit of the French War Relief. He returned again after World War II to play exhibition matches with Donald Budge in 1946 and 1947.

In 1941, the club moved to its present location on James Street, an 11-acre tract purchased from the Foote family, where it concentrates on tennis and paddle tennis. □

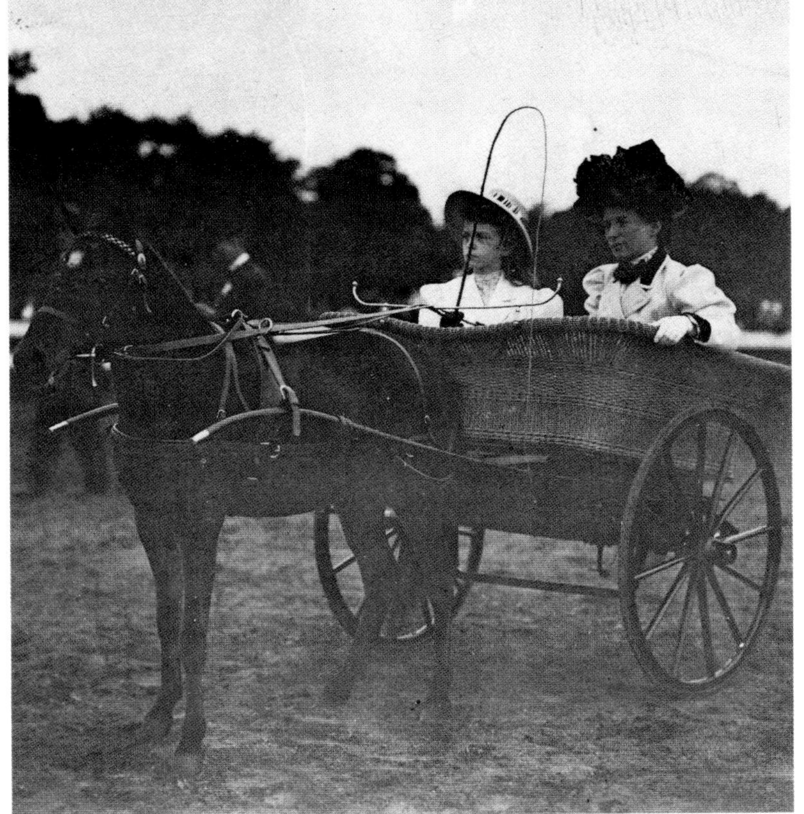

Courtesy of Mrs. Thomas Turner Cooke

Mother and daughter (right), Mrs. C. W. Throckmorton and Elizabeth (Mrs. Thomas Turner Cooke) at the Field Club, about 1904. **A smash at the net for Alice Day** (below), Field Club member who was New Jersey Open State Champion in 1905-1906 (singles) and 1909 (mixed doubles) and runner-up in 1907 (doubles). Kings Supermarket is on the site of the clubhouse.

TJFPLMMT

TJFPLMMT

TJFPLMMT

Whippany River Club (above), Corey Lane, Morris Township, as it appeared between 1904 and 1910. The clubhouse was the converted sports stable of **Eugene Higgins' estate** (map), which the club leased.

Coaching party (left), about to set out from the second clubhouse after the sports stable burned in 1910.

The entrance gate (opposite, top) of the Higgins estate after it became the club. The two posts still exist in greatly deteriorated condition.

The Mennen Company and the Morris County Park Commission now occupy most of the property.

Whippany River Club

The Whippany River Club, an exclusive men's sports club, emphasized horses — polo, steeplechase, coaching, races. But there were also such diversions as dances and receptions, vaudeville, a dog show and the more sedentary card parties. Although this famous club never seemed to have enough money, its members always had a wonderful time. Unfortunately, it did not survive long.

The club was organized by 12 millionaires on December 12, 1903, at 35 Wall Street. In 1904, Benjamin Nicoll, the noted polo player who headed his own iron, steel and coal firm, was elected president; Charles F. Cutler, president and chairman of the board of New York and New Jersey Telephone Company, vice president; Norman Henderson, another polo enthusiast with interests in the milk business, secretary; and Frederick O. Spedden, treasurer.

The club leased the estate of Eugene Higgins, who had moved away permanently to Europe (alternating his time between London and Paris) after his mansion burned in 1902. He had transformed his father's farm into a sportsman's paradise. The grounds included a polo field and a grandstand with a half-mile running track around it; tennis, racquetball and croquet courts; and a great sports stable with one huge wing for horses and another for carriages and other vehicles.

It was an ideal situation until tragedy struck again. In 1910, fire destroyed the clubhouse and stables as well as the new riding club and a squash court that had cost $10,000. The 41 horses and ponies were saved, but not much else. There was talk of joining with the Morris County Golf Club, but nothing came of it. The club almost dissolved, but somehow hung on until the Depression. ☐

The suitability of grounds and buildings led a number of society people of the vicinity to form the Whippany River Club . . . . Mr. Higgins had already erected a theatre and dance hall in connection with his stables and it made an admirable basis for a clubhouse.
From the *Daily Record*, July 21, 1910

The Polo Field

Grace Lord (Mrs. Benjamin) Nicoll

On the polo field when the skies are blue,
  And the summer day is dying,
How the merry shouts ring through the air,
As the ball goes flying everywhere,
  And the shadows soft are lying.

On the polo field where the ponies race,
  And the summer winds are blowing,
How the soft clouds smile on the sunlit scene,
While the sport runs high and the pace is keen
  With the steeds their mettle showing.

There is Mr. Kissel on the ball,
  And Mr. Thorn is turning,
While "Harges," "Headley" too, and "Flinsch,"
  The ground beneath them spurning.
Ride down the field, and ride so fast —
  And "Nicoll" comes like a stormy blast
With "Henderson," who won't be last,
  While the sunset's fires are burning.

On the polo field when the skies are blue,
  And the summer day is dying,
How fast the pace and how fair the scene,
And how soft the grass so rich and green,
  Where the merry ball goes flying.

TJFPLMMT

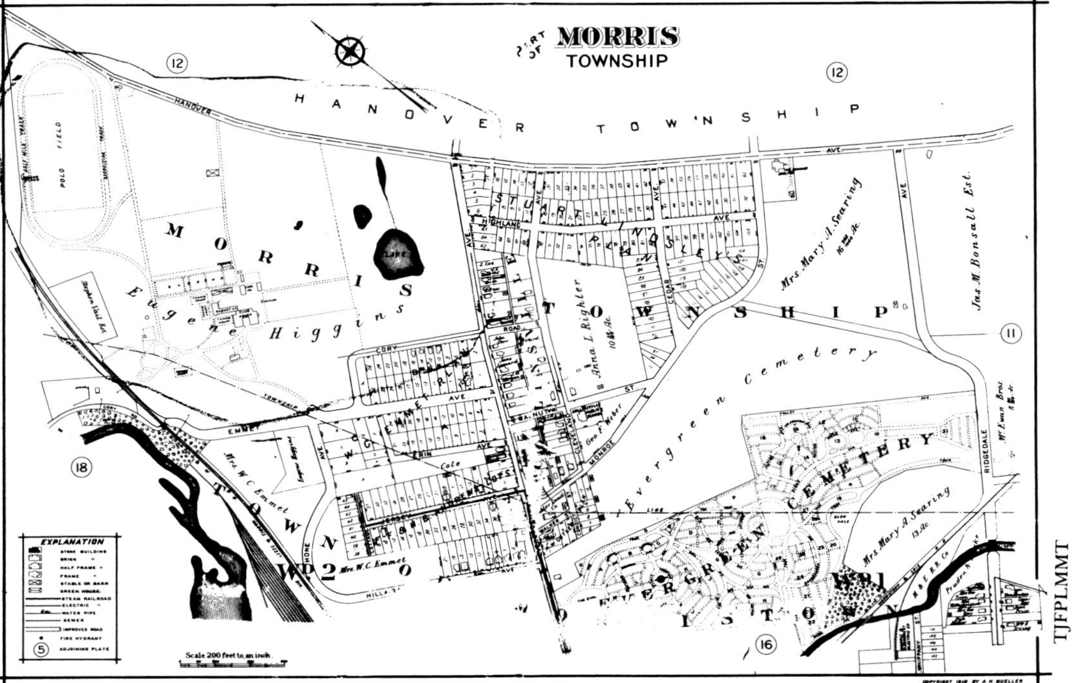

TJFPLMMT

Courtesy of The Morristown Club/TJFPL MMT

The Morristown Club's 25th Anniversary, June 22, 1909

President George Palmer is in the center foreground. Others in the photograph are (left to right) Elbert Kip, Elbert Hyde, Ledyard Thompson, Livingston Roe, Elmer Mills, John Brinley, Robert Foote, William Shippen, Charles Chapman, Leland Garretson, Palmer, Ridley Watts, George Dadmun, B. L. Chandler, Joe Willis, Henry Taylor, Peter Frelinghuysen, Ransom Thomas, Noah Rogers and Granville White. Two men are unidentified.

The clubhouse (opposite, left), from 1896 to 1929, in the former Stephen Guerin House, 126 South Street, later Lanterman's Funeral Home. The present one is at 27 Elm Street.

Millionaire's Express (opposite, right), February 24, 1898, so called for the wealthy men who sat in the club car, many of them Morristown Club members. This train left Morristown at 8:25 and returned from Hoboken at 5:07, making one stop in Madison. Dues were only $60 a year, but commuters had to be voted in to enjoy comfortable wicker easy chairs, bridge tables and a special attendant. For years this train was pulled by Engine No. 100, the "Centennial," built in 1876 for the Philadelphia Centennial.

The inscription on the back of this photograph is "Uncle Ben's [Engineer Day's] train, Morristown train station, February 24, 1898."

The Morristown Club

"Probably the most popular and luxurious resort for the gentlemen of Morristown," is how *The Morris County Chronicle* of December 1, 1896, described the Morristown Club. "The dignity of the position it holds as a place of social reunion places it rather outside the list of sporting clubs, and yet it offers as pastime billiards and pool, and as the center of all sporting gossip, it may well fill a place. The Club is supplied by all daily papers; and the various popular weekly and monthly magazines as well, are always found here."

The story is told of the little girl who learned forcefully this was a men's club. One day, her mother sent her to the clubhouse with a message. Called to the front porch, her enraged father bellowed at her, "Don't you *dare* come here again." Then he slammed the door, message unreceived.

For many members, the Morristown Club was a regular stopping-off place between the club car of the Millionaire's Express and home. In fact, it was two railroad men who received an honor never before given to nonmembers. On March 23, 1903, Benjamin Day, an engineer on the Lackawanna Railroad since 1862, and David Sanderson, conductor — both on the Millionaire's Express since its inception — were invited to the Morristown Club to celebrate the club car's 20th anniversary. Each was presented with a monogrammed gold watch and chain inscribed with a tribute to his "fidelity and unvarying courtesy" and $80 in gold.

The Morristown Club was founded in 1884 with Frederic Wood, first president; James S. Dunbar, vice president; Frank Turnbull, secretary; and George S. Wylie, treasurer. Mr. Wylie succeeded as president in 1885, followed by Joseph Bushnell, Albert H. Vernam and George

Courtesy of The Morristown Club/TJFPLMMT

TJFPLMMT

C. Kip, during whose presidency the club was incorporated (1897). Robert Foote was president 1904-1906, in 1909, the club's 25th year, George C. Palmer began a term that ran until 1934.

The first clubhouse was rented on the corner of Maple Avenue and Boykin Street (Miller Road). This was soon vacated because it was too large and expensive to maintain. In 1885, the club moved to the Judge Dalrymple House at 154 South Street. In 1887, obviously prospering, a country annex was opened at the Arthur Thompson cottage, "Brookbank" at Morris Plains, which featured two grass courts, a bowling alley and a pigeon shoot. However, in 1889, the annex abruptly closed. It is rumored that some members of this all-male bastion felt the presence of family members threatened to reduce the club operation to chaos. Once again, ladies were entertained only on New Year's Day. Later, women were welcomed regularly as guests, but they were not allowed to become members until October 1983.

In 1889, the same year the country annex was closed, the Stephen Guerin House was leased at 126 South Street. An addition was built in 1894 and a billiard room in 1901. The club might be there yet except for a disastrous fire in 1929. There is a tradition that President Palmer, mindful of the club's importance to its members as a way station, was so determined its services be uninterrupted he bought the present clubhouse at 27 Elm Street the same day.

Later that year, a place to retreat was certainly needed as momentous events occurred that would alter the lives of many of the members: On October 24, 1929, "Black Thursday," prices on the New York Stock Market, which speculation had driven to record levels, collapsed as 13 million shares were unloaded. Then, on October 29, "Black Tuesday," 16 million shares were sold. The Great Depression of the 1930s had begun. □

Courtesy of Macculloch Hall Historical Museum

The Morristown Train Station in the Golden Age

Both views show the Morris Street station from Blatchly Place. This 1881 station was built on the site of an earlier station; it is also the site of the present 1913 station.

Theodore Roosevelt campaigning (above) from the back of his train, 1912. Most of the town turned out to hear him, but New Jersey Governor Woodrow Wilson won.

Postcard scene (right), about 1905. C. W. Ennis owned the lumberyard next to the station, the building next door and the building on the far right, 63 Elm Street.

The First Ward Hose Company firehouse, built in 1899, was moved east to 155 Morris Street when work began on elevating the tracks in 1912-13.

TJFPLMMT

Courtesy of Mrs. Marianne Foote Baker

Social highlight, costume ball and supper (above), place and date unknown. **Roller skating party** (opposite, upper right) at the Morris County Golf Club. Marie Dumont Foote is in a white hat, third row, third from right; her husband, Robert D. Foote, is on her right; Rev. Philemon F. Sturges, D.D., rector of St. Peter's Church from 1903 to 1916, is on her left. **Annual fall dinner of the North Jersey Society for the Promotion of Agriculture** (opposite, lower right), also at the Morris County Golf Club, October 17, 1913. This second clubhouse burned on September 15, 1915.

In Pursuit of Perfection

As in the Golden Age of Greece, Morristown society believed that perfection was something to strive for and possible to attain. Nothing but the best.

Despite what must have been exhausting days, at least for the athletically inclined, the evenings were filled with dinners, balls, assemblies, house parties, receptions and other entertainment.

In that formal age, many regularly dressed for dinner in evening clothes, and when the occasion warranted — which could be frequently — they wore ballgowns with diamonds or white tie and tails.

In the absence of newspaper photographs to document the elegance of the ladies and the splendor of the setting, local social columnists vied with each other to report the guest lists, sometimes in the hundreds, and to describe the fabrics, colors and jewels: "effective costume of Turkish silk" or "pink silk with overdress of figures damasse-natural roses" or "Mrs. H. W. Miller, a superb costume of dove colored silk trimmed with pink — diamonds."

On Monday, January 2, 1892, for example, a newspaper described in detail two "beautiful receptions" among the "numberless entertainments" given that day:

"The house, always so charming, and with such a hospitable hostess, was more attractive even than usual. Superb plants of flowers were everywhere. Mrs. Catlin [of Fairholme], with her daughter, Miss Catlin, received at the entrance of the drawing room. Mrs. Park looked very charming at the tea table. The ballroom was most tempting, and although the young people had the evening of dancing before them, they could not resist the spirit of the delightful

Courtesy of Mrs. Marianne Foote Baker

Courtesy of The Morristown Club/TJFPLMMT

TJFPLMMT

music and all entered into it with enthusiasm.... The second reception, which was given by Mrs. E. W. Coggeshall [Madison Avenue, Convent Station], was an unusually beautiful affair. Mrs. Coggeshall, assisted by her daughter, Miss Coggeshall, and niece, received in the drawing room. The roses were simply superb — American beauties, in such profusion that one wondered if it could be the month of June, rather than January.... A delicious supper was served in the dining room. The table was exquisitely decorated with brilliant Poinsettas and greens, and the candelabra with their red shades, gave an unusual brightness and warmth to the table."

In the days before radio or television, the tradition of writing and acting in amateur plays (comedy spoofs or take-offs on society, for the most part) remained strong. What could be more amusing than acting with, or watching, your fellow townsfolks? Since most plays were performed to raise money for a local church or charity, *who* you were was less important than whether you had a talent, and these plays were one way different levels of society could meet and get to know each other, even if briefly. □

TJFPLMMT

Narranganset Pier (opposite) performed at Lyceum Hall for the benefit of St. Peter's Church organ fund, May 1909. A similar photograph was published in *Harper's Weekly,* which described the play, written by Morristown's van Tassel Sutphen with music by J. Sebastion Mathews, as a comedy about "the inanity of summer engagements at the seashore and the bartering of foreign titles for American gold." The cast included *Miss Diana Dashaway,* young lady cottager (Minnie Anita Parker); *Mrs. Rigidly Prim,* professional chaperone (Mrs. Clyde Potts); *Miss Vanilla Peachblow,* hotel boarder (Mrs. Harvey L. Williams); *Miss Imogene Marshmallow,* second young lady cottager (Clara K. Leek); *Mr. Fitzroy Plantagenet,* gentleman from England (Harold Myers); *Mr. Bob Sparkler,* sales-gentleman (Warren Carlyle Biggin); *Mr. Augustus Yardsticke,* second sales-gentleman (Homer G. Ayres); *Mr. Cholly Slimwaiste,* third sales-gentleman (Frederick P. Boniface); *Parks,* valet (P. Barton Myers) and the chorus of 20 young lady cottagers and 12 sales-gentlemen.

Seven Twenty-Eight (above), presented at Washington Hall for the benefit of the Italian Mission (Neighborhood House), February 29, 1908. Another home-grown comedy, this time written by Kingsley Twining and Charles Hull, the scenes took place in a country home and New York apartment of a Mr. Bargiss. Here, too, the description of the cast of characters gives some idea of the complications of the plot. From left to right: *Paul Hollyhock,* son-in-law of Mr. Bargiss, "devoted to potato beds" (Leon S. Freeman); *Senorina Palmiro Tamborini,* "late Mistress of the Ballet, Convent [sic] Garden, and now on a Mission and searching for an original" (Katherine Clarke, later Mrs. Michael Kernan); *Professor Gassleig,* "inventor and founder of a refuge for the outcasts of the pen" (Charles A. Hull); *Dora Hollyhock,* "at once her husband's tempter and victim" (Ethel Clark, later Mrs. Leon Freeman); *Mr. Launcelot Bargiss,* "a retired party who became a victim of the inevitable and is bound to his wife's hobby" (Kingsley Twining); *Jessie,* the maid, "with yearnings beyond her station" (Margaret Hoyt, later Mrs. Theodore T. White); Granville White; *Mrs. Hypatia Bargiss,* "a lady possessed of ancestors, aspirations and a hobby" (Elizabeth Caldwell, later Mrs. A. Heywood McAlpin); unidentified; *Courtney Corliss,* "a gentleman of leisure with a theory concerning boomerangs, employing his idle time in the pleasant pursuit of hunting a face" (Edward B. Hall, who was killed in World War I); A. Heywood McAlpin; *Floss,* the much sought-after "7-20-8" (Allita Emery, later Mrs. Paul Applegate); and *A Postman* "on his round" (Charles S. Dean). Marion Freeman Niles made the identifications.

Curtiss Collection/TJFPLMMT

TJFPLMMT

Curtiss Collection/TJFPLMMT

St. Peter's Church, South Street, Morristown

The church, as seen from Miller Road in 1926, was built in 1887-1911 in English parish style on the design of Charles McKim of the renowned New York architectural firm of McKim, Mead & White. The outside walls are stone from a quarry at Waterloo, Sussex County. The churchyard contains the graves of many prominent Morristonians, including members of the Macculloch-Miller, Mills, Canfield and Vail families.

The tower (upper right), as seen from South Street in 1925. The tower was finished in 1908 except for the turret that was completed in 1911. The cost had jumped from the original estimate of $48,000 to $70,000.

Interior view (left), from the nave toward the altar, 1931. Some of the fine stained glass windows can be seen as well as the brick walls and columns of Indiana limestone and the handsome 1893 wrought-iron rood screen.

St. Peter's Church

Whatever the pursuits and frivolities of Saturday night, Sunday morning was reserved for church — and the church most associated with society was St. Peter's. Its fashionable congregation was called jokingly the "Morris Country Club on its knees," which was partially true, but tends to obscure the church's long tradition.

The first recorded religious service for Anglicans was held in 1763 at the Morris County Court House. Thereafter, itinerant missionaries supplied the congregation until services were suspended during the American Revolution. However, as early as 1792, shortly after the organization of the Protestant Episcopal Church in the United States, visiting ministers were again conducting services from time to time. In the 1820s, the congregation met in the schoolroom at Macculloch Hall, and it was there, on January 1, 1827, that the parish of St. Peter's was organized. On December 4, 1828, the first edifice was consecrated, the first stone building of any consequence in Morristown.

In 1856, the building was altered and enlarged — despite the fact that two years before some of the congregation had left to form the Church of the Redeemer. However, by 1887, with the influx of summer visitors and the increase in residents, a new church edifice was needed.

On the first day of November 1887, All Saints Day, described as "slightly cold but a most beautiful day," Bishop Starkey conducted the service and laid the cornerstone with the assistance of Charles F. McKim, the architect, and Sturgis Brothers, the builders. The Reverend Wynant Vanderpool was in general charge in the absence of the Reverend Robert Merritt, D.D.S., who was in ill health. (His rectorship ran from 1853 until his death in 1895, the longest in parish history.)

Curtiss Collection/TJFPLMMT

Forty choristers from Newark were present, as well as visiting clergy and the invited clergymen of Morristown, the vestry of the Church of the Redeemer and the mayor and common council of Morristown. This mayor, George T. Werts (1846-1910), was soon to be the second governor of New Jersey (1893-95) from Morristown, the first being Theodore F. Randolph. Addresses also were given by the Bishop and Alfred Mills, the senior warden.

Since no stone was put in place until it was paid for, the church took 24 years to complete. The rectory was built in 1897-99 and the parish house in 1914-15.

The church has had many benefactors, but perhaps the most unexpected one was Sylvia Green, who was married there to Matthew Astor Wilks, great-grandson of the first John Jacob Astor. Mrs. Wilks was the daughter of Hetty Green, better known as "The Witch of Wall Street," the richest — and most frugal — woman in the world. Hetty Green was related to the Howland family and had spent summers in Morristown as a girl. On the wedding day, February 23, 1909, Mrs. Green, her daughter and a maid arrived in a hack from Hoboken, where they lived in a cheap apartment. As reported in *The Jerseyman*, "the bride wore a traveling gown of dark brown cloth, a white feather hat, white boa and a heavy veil." Although there were no bridesmaids, a Pullman car, "The Ivorydale," was chartered as a gift from her brother to bring a small number of guests. After the service, the visitors had a quiet luncheon at the Morristown Inn and left as quickly and quietly as they came. When Mrs. Wilks died in the 1950s, however, St. Peter's discovered that she had willed them $1,200,000 — $150,000 for church improvements, $300,000 for maintenance and endowment, and the interest from the rest divided among a number of worthy charities. □

Curtiss Collection/TJFPLMMT

Curtiss Collection/TJFPLMMT

John D. Rockefeller, Jr. (left), photographed for the *Newark News* in front of St. Peter's Church, May 28, 1924.

Uncrated bells (above), November 28, 1923, waiting to be put in place by **W. T. Bellinghurst** (top), English bell hanger, May 1, 1924. The original 37 memorial bells have increased to 47, including some marriage bells.

TJFPLMMT

Miss Dana's School for Young Ladies, Morristown, 1895

In 1862, the school opened on South Street near the intersection of Madison Avenue as the Morris Female Institute. The main building was built for $11,960 on a lot that cost $3,800. Many prominent Morristown daughters attended as day pupils; boarders came from throughout New Jersey and places as far away as Detroit, Michigan, and Savannah, Georgia.

There were about 70 students in 1910. Probably the most famous boarder was Dorothy Parker, the writer and humorist, who attended in the school's last year, 1911-12. The school reopened for a few years as the Randolph Military Academy.

A bank now stands on the site.

Little Ladies and Gentlemen

The training began with toddlers. (Say please and thank you, curtsy or bow, speak only when spoken to, and fidget not.) The school child absorbed a classical education that stressed the grand achievements of the European cultural heritage and the ways they could be copied. Thus, the adult emerged with a strong sense of how something should look, sound or feel and the desire to have it.

Miss Dana's was the undisputed queen of schools for young ladies who hoped to enter society.

It began as the Morris Female Institute, incorporated in August 1860. In 1862, it was leased to Charles G. Hazeltine, who ran it until it was leased on April 1, 1877, to Miss Elizabeth E. Dana, who later bought it and ran it until her death.

The collegiate curriculum at Miss Dana's included intellectual and moral philosophy, criticism and theology. Latin and Greek were taught as well as French, German, Spanish and Italian. "The mode of instruction is designed to be thorough and effective in the highest degree," says the catalog. "Unceasing effort is made to cultivate those habits of attention and of close application which lie at the foundation of all solid attainments.

"Special attention will be given to those branches (Reading, Spelling, Writing, etc.) which are too often neglected in schools for advanced pupils." Required drawing and music courses were obviously included to provide the "polite accomplishments" that were promised.

"Lectures, Shakespeare, and miscellaneous readings and other entertainment will be given during the school year." One of these lectures was given by Booker T. Washington on "Solving the Negro Problem in the Black Belt." This was probably only the second time he had come to this community.

Nor were athletics or practical matters neglected. "A large gymnasium is equipped with all necessary apparatus," says the school brochure. "Besides the usual wand and dumbbell exercises, aesthetic dancing forms are a conspicuous part of the work. Exercises are prescribed . . . and much attention is given to walking." In 1900, banking was introduced, "each pupil will open a bank account, draw her own checks and be required to balance and present her books each month. At the opening of school, a thorough explanation of the system will be given and this will be followed by occasional informal talks on other business matters."

In 1893, The Peck School began as Miss Sutphen's, a small "dame" school operating in a private house, where children of social peers learned the three R's while practicing manners and learning poise. In 1918, Lorain T. Peck, who had taught at the revived Morris Academy (page 236), became headmaster and owner and expanded into an elementary school. He ran it until his retirement in 1944 when he gave it to the parents. In 1948, the school moved to its present location at Lindenwold, 247 South Street, Morristown.

Perhaps because of Morris Academy's preference for preparing boys for Yale and Princeton, The Morristown School in Morris Township prepared for Harvard. A minister founded the school in 1891 as St. Bartholomew's School. However, after some financial difficulties a few years later — caused, it is whispered, by the minister's disappearance with the money — three Harvard graduates took over in 1898 and renamed it The Morristown School. In 1971, it became coeducational and merged with Miss Beard's School of Orange, which also was founded in 1891. □

TJFPLMMT

Miss Dana's girls (above), in the school hall, 1900. Possibly Miss Foster was the penciled-in "me."

A graduating class (right), in costumes that depict famous queens in history, the popular *tableau vivant*: Left, standing, Linda Philips (Mrs. Fred K. Lum, Jr., of Chatham). Right, standing, Eleanor Holden (Mrs. Ralph Stoddard, Madison). Next to left and seated, Nellie Van Orden (Mrs. Lawrance Da—?, Chatham), Alice Stinsbery (?), Helen Rogers, Catherine Barbery, Mary Vale Hendee and Paralee Pitts.

TJFPLMMT

Courtesy of The Peck School

Pupils of Miss Sutphen's School (left), later The Peck School, in costume for a play, about 1895. Left to right: Virginia Hunt, Margaret Brindley, Margery Ryerson, Margery Hoyt and Marie Letchford; on the grass, Gertrude Behr and Helen Colwell.

The old Peck School (lower left), 11 Elm Street, in 1878 when it was the residence of Josephine C. Tainter. It was torn down to make room for a supermarket and is now the site of an office building.

The Morristown School (lower right), now Morristown-Beard School, Whippany Road, Morris Township, about 1895. A young boarder wrote on a postcard like this one: "This is where the wealthy people send their boys. It is two miles from town. It is in a beautiful location." He might have added: The boys here all want to go to Harvard.

Morristown Select Classical School (opposite) on the Pitney House porch, 43 Maple Avenue, Morristown, photographed by "Alexander," June 1872. The seated top-hatted gentlemen are George L. Wright, Yale '67, principal, and Wilbert Warren Perry, Yale '71, assistant. Henry C. Pitney is before the open doorway. Three Pitney boys and three Pitney girls are in the photograph, along with his wife, Sarah Louisa. His son, Mahlon Pitney, who was appointed by President Taft in 1912 to the U.S. Supreme Court, is seated far left in a relaxed pose with his arm on a friend's chair.

Courtesy of Mrs. Alice Caulkins

TJFPLMMT

TJFPLMMT

TJFPL.MMT

Library and Lyceum, about 52-56 South Street, Morristown

This massive structure, 75 by 100 feet, was built in 1875-79 on the design of New York architect Colonel George B. Post. Its four outer walls were made of granite boulders from Jockey Hollow donated by the Morris Aqueduct Company. The first floor had rooms for the Morris Academy and a 50,000-volume library with public reading room. The second floor had a huge audience hall capable of seating 800 people with a stage and boxes. There was also a ballroom and dressing and retiring rooms.

A shareholder's certificate, 1906 (opposite, above). At first, the library was a private institution and only shareholders could borrow books, but after a $20,000 gift from William B. Skidmore, books were free to everyone.

The new Morris Academy (opposite, lower left), students and teachers, 1886, on the steps of the school's private entrance at the Lyceum.

The baseball team (opposite, lower right), about 1905. Lorain T. Peck, a teacher who later became headmaster of The Peck School, is seated at right in the middle row.

Commercial buildings are now on the site, which is opposite Community Place.

Library and Lyceum

Many notables performed or lectured there — Mark Twain, Lillian Russell, Lillie Langtry, Alma Gluck, Efrem Zimbalist, the pianist Paderewski and conductor Fritz Kreisler, Dr. Henry Ward Beecher and Woodrow Wilson, among many others. Some of Morristown's most unusual or fabulous parties were given there. The opening reception was only the beginning.

On Wednesday, August 14, 1878, an open house was held in the almost completed Library and Lyceum.

The Jerseyman proudly noted that it was "built almost entirely by Morristown mechanics in a thorough manner, cost a little over $50,000 and is unencumbered by mortgage." It also admired "the apartments of the Morris Academy, a commodious, well-lighted room furnished with desks for twenty-four scholars. On each side is a recitation room shut off from the main room by sliding glass doors."

The *True Democratic Banner* noted that from 9:00 A.M. to 10 P.M. "a labyrinth of carriages, embracing the finest establishments" crowded in front of the building on South Street. All day the librarian, Mr. Edwards, and the principal of the Morris Academy, Mr. Spaulding, "devoted their attentions to a smiling crowd [over 1,000 persons] who wandered through the cool rooms and spacious halls which were decorated with colorful and fragrant flowers and trailing vines amid numerous American flags. In the public reading room adjacent to the five thousand volume library, chandeliers and powerful reflectors hung over spacious tables. The floor was covered with triple thick linoleum, noiseless to the tread of the heaviest cowhide. In the corner was a fireplace of black walnut corresponding to the trimmings in the rest of the building. Modern methods of heating, however, were not neglected, and four large Boynton furnaces had been installed."

In the evening, Voss's band from Newark entertained a large audience in Lyceum Hall with the ladies in full evening costume.

The Lyceum became immediately popular for social entertainments on a grand and sometimes unusual scale. A Gentlemen's Assembly, for example, begun in 1878 and held several times thereafter, was given by the most distinguished young men of the community — such as T.M.F. Randolph, Paul Revere, Augustus Crane, H. P. Clarke, F. A. Woodruff and W. M. Wood — to thank the ladies of Morristown for their frequent hospitality. The guests stepped from their carriages under an awning reaching from the curb to the door, then into a Lyceum Hall transformed into a ballroom of flowers

Number 489 — Shares 2

MORRISTOWN
Library and Lyceum.

This Certifies that Joseph [illegible] entitled to Two (2) Shares of Twenty five Dollars each in the Capital Stock of the Morristown Library and Lyceum transferable in person or by Attorney on surrender of this Certificate

Morristown, N.J. April 23 1906.

Secretary — President

TJFPLMMT

TJFPLMMT

TJFPLMMT

TJFPLMMT

and tropical plants tucked in and about all of the boxes and around the floor. Dance cards quickly were filled for lanciers, waltzes, gallops and an occasional polka. Supper was served in two rooms "to avoid all difficulties," but since these were on separate floors, service must have been a bit complicated even for the experienced caterer W. F. Day, who kept the tables laden with delicacies for more than two hours.

On Friday evening, June 17, 1881, Thomas Nast gave a coming out party there for his daughter, Julia. "The Members of the Young Maiden's Cooking Association Request the Pleasure of Your Company," read the invitation, and the debutante and her friends received in frilly Swiss muslin frocks with aprons and cooking caps, wearing badges made out of small pans. This unusual debut was the outcome of the cooking school begun at Nast's house on Macculloch Avenue to teach fine cuisine to 12 of Julia's friends. The girls, later numbering as many as 35, ate each other's efforts at parties after class, sharing the hilarity of melted eclairs and fallen cream cakes.

In 1900, it was Richard A. McCurdy's turn to create a memorable evening, on which he spent between $50,000 and $75,000, more than the cost of the building. The three stories were transformed into a palace of pleasure. The ballroom's fluted columns "were disguised with grapevines containing taps [barrels] from which eight different imported wines flowed at the press of a button." An extra dance floor was constructed over the seats in the audience hall. The entire front of the building was covered with tiny electric lights. Strings of bulbs were draped across South Street to flash numbers to signal when a waiting coach was required at the Lyceum door. From the gold engraved invitations to the brilliance of the guest list, there may never have been another party like this in Morristown. □

TJFPLMMT

The burning Library and Lyceum (opposite), February 22, 1914. The fire, discovered by a watchman about 5:30 in the morning, burned out of control for hours. By 7:30, the beams supporting the slate roof gave way, causing it to cave in and send shooting embers high in the air and starting a fire across the street. One half of the books and other contents and many valuable papers and irreplaceable old newspapers were lost. The Morris Academy closed its doors forever. Although the fire's cause was not known, an explosion in one of the "modern" heating furnaces was suspected.

The old building as a new armory (above). Through the philanthropy of Grinnell Willis and persuasive powers of Samuel H. Gillespie, the neglected building became the armory for the Morristown Infantry Battalion, a home guard unit organized during World War I. The names of all those who served in the war are shown on either side of the door. In the 1920s, the eagle was given to The Morristown Library (page 241), where it hangs in the tower hall. The building was torn down when the present armory was built on Western Avenue in Morris Township in 1938-40.

TJFPLMMT

The Morristown Library, now The Joint Free Public Library of Morristown and Morris Township

Built in 1917, it is shown as it appeared on August 17, 1921, with the main entrance at One Miller Road. It was designed by Edward L. Tilton, one of the foremost library architects of the period, in Gothic Revival style to harmonize with St. Peter's Church across the street.

The tall windows at either end of the building feature central medallions of colored glass. In the Great Hall, at the west end on the left, the medallions represent Columbus's caravel, *Santa Maria*, and four famous printer's marks dating from the early part of the 16th century. In the Reference Room on the opposite end, the medallions are monograms of five great American poets — Oliver Wendell Holmes, William Cullen Bryant, Henry Wadsworth Longfellow, James Russell Lowell and John Greenleaf Whittier — representing the golden age of American literature.

In 1930, a Children's Wing in matching stone was added to the South Street side. The window medallions there depict epic heroes — Hiawatha, Roland, King Arthur, Siegfried, El Cid, Sorab, David and Odysseus — and were designed by Clara Bryant, an art teacher at Morristown High School.

In 1986, a second wing was completed on South Street. The main library entrance moves to that side.

A Little Jewel of a Library

What would Morristown do? Since February 1914, there had been no library building. Within two years of the Library and Lyceum fire, the board of directors decided to build again on a vacant lot at Miller Road and South Street. They consulted Edward L. Tilton, an accomplished library architect, formerly associated with McKim, Mead and White, who created a handsome design in stone similar to a small college library. The problem was, Where would the money come from? That remarkable philanthropist, Grinnell Willis, stepped forward. From his own resources, he built the library building on Tilton's plan, improved the grounds, added to the endowment, increased the number of books and employed additional librarians. This magnificent gift he dedicated to his deceased wife, Mary Baker Haydock Willis.

Grinnell Willis inherited his love of books from his father, Nathaniel Parker Willis, essayist, poet and journalist, who constantly entertained literary celebrities at his home on the Hudson. After graduating from Harvard in 1870, Willis entered the wholesale dry goods business. Influenced by his grandfather, Joseph Grinnell, the organizer of Wamsutta Mills in New Bedford, he subsequently established his own successful firm in New York City and became one of the best-known commission merchants of his day. On retiring in 1916, he gave his constant attention and support to The Morristown Library, which for many years operated from the income of an endowment left in his will, supplemented by gifts and public support.

On August 5, 1916, the cornerstone of The Morristown Library was laid in which there is a copper box containing photographs of Mr. and Mrs. Willis; Franklin B. Dwight, president; and Henry C. Pitney, Jr., secretary; photographs of Morristown streets and buildings, *The Morris County Press* and *True Democratic Banner* of August 3; *The Jerseyman* and *Daily Record* of August 4; the *New York Herald Tribune* and *The Times*, August 5, 1916; and U.S. coins, one cent to half dollar. The building was dedicated on October 20, 1917. The principal addresses were given by Mr. Willis and the Honorable Mahlon Pitney of the United States Supreme Court, whose family had long been identified with Morristown and the old library.

From 1917 to 1924, Miss Mary Prescott Parsons was the librarian of the new library. In 1924, Katherine Tappert took over. She established training classes for girls interested in library work and began the local history collection, which she made her particular concern. She enlarged the service that made weekly book visits to Memorial and All Souls Hospitals. She started a reading hour at the Neighborhood House and she arranged for regular visits of a

TJFPLMMT

Grinnell Willis (1848-1930)
He gave The 1917 Morristown Library in memory of his deceased first wife, Mary Baker Haydock Willis, and the 1930 Children's Wing after his marriage to Katherine H. Tappert, the second librarian.

Traveling book car (right) on Western Avenue, about 1924-26. Mr. Willis is on the far right; Miss Tappert is next to him. This tradition continues today with the Moby Dick bookmobile.

TJFPLMMT

TJFPLMMT

For nearly two years . . . while our hearts have been torn by the stress of war, we had before us this beautiful ideal.
Grinnell Willis at the dedication, 1917

TJFPLMMT

The Great Hall, West Wing, adult reading room (above), and East Wing, children's reading room, 1922.

A good library, like a good man or a good woman, is a creature of happy birth, slow growth and gradual development.
Henry C. Pitney, Jr., about 1919

"book car" to six stations in Morris Township. In 1927, she resigned to marry Mr. Willis, who in 1930 donated the wing of the library that contained the children's room until 1986. The opening reception was held on April 28, 1930, his 82nd birthday. In December, he died.

In 1967, this popular private library became The Joint Free Public Library of Morristown and Morris Township. By 1980, it was clear more room was needed; in 1982, voters in both municipalities strongly approved the necessary bond issue to provide another wing. On November 17, 1984, a ground-breaking ceremony was held for the large new addition that doubled the size of the library. The new wing was opened to the public in 1986. □

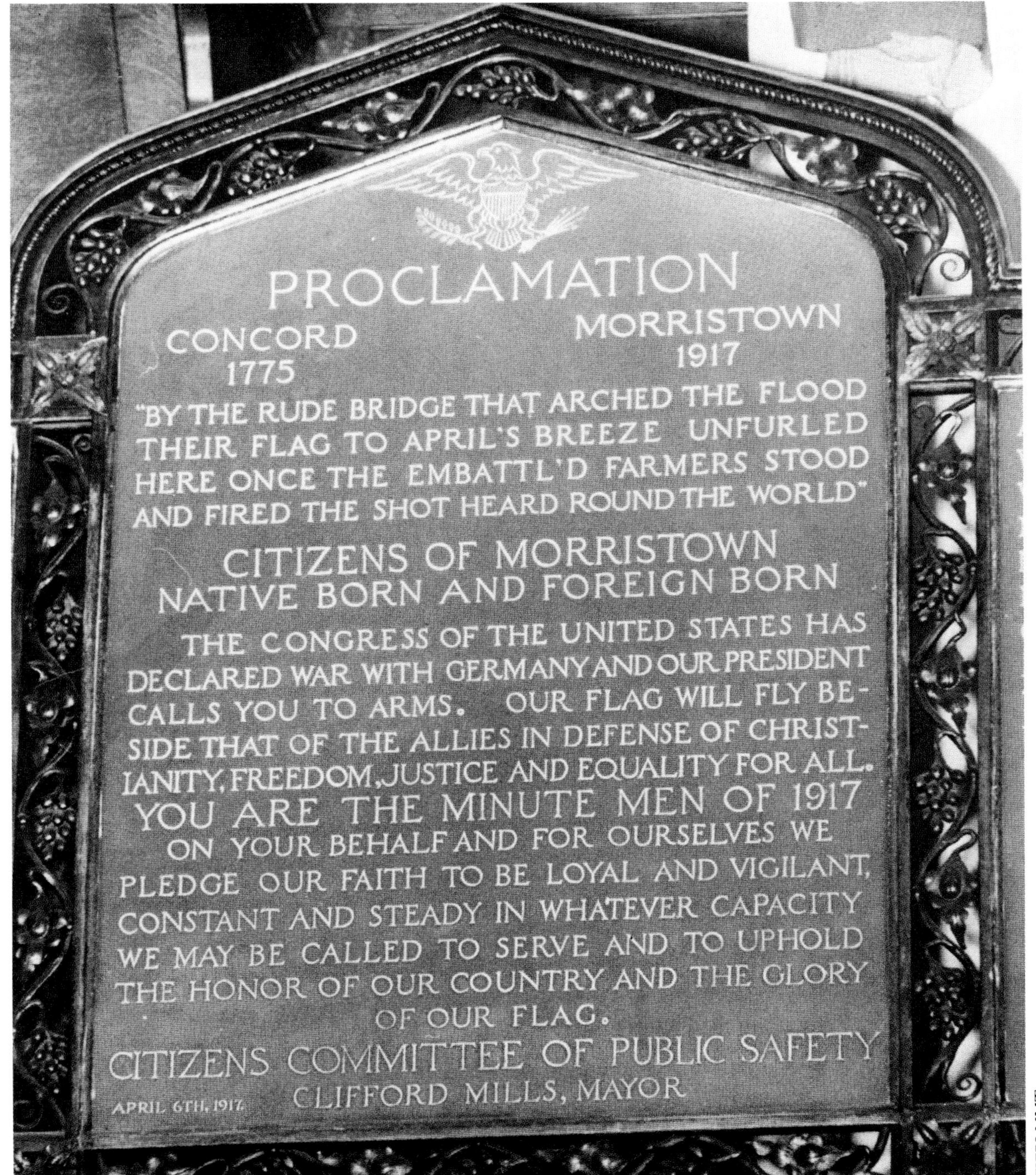

PROCLAMATION
CONCORD
1775
MORRISTOWN
1917
"BY THE RUDE BRIDGE THAT ARCHED THE FLOOD
THEIR FLAG TO APRIL'S BREEZE UNFURLED
HERE ONCE THE EMBATTL'D FARMERS STOOD
AND FIRED THE SHOT HEARD ROUND THE WORLD"
CITIZENS OF MORRISTOWN
NATIVE BORN AND FOREIGN BORN
THE CONGRESS OF THE UNITED STATES HAS
DECLARED WAR WITH GERMANY AND OUR PRESIDENT
CALLS YOU TO ARMS. OUR FLAG WILL FLY BE-
SIDE THAT OF THE ALLIES IN DEFENSE OF CHRIST-
IANITY, FREEDOM, JUSTICE AND EQUALITY FOR ALL.
YOU ARE THE MINUTE MEN OF 1917
ON YOUR BEHALF AND FOR OURSELVES WE
PLEDGE OUR FAITH TO BE LOYAL AND VIGILANT,
CONSTANT AND STEADY IN WHATEVER CAPACITY
WE MAY BE CALLED TO SERVE AND TO UPHOLD
THE HONOR OF OUR COUNTRY AND THE GLORY
OF OUR FLAG.
CITIZENS COMMITTEE OF PUBLIC SAFETY
APRIL 6TH, 1917.
CLIFFORD MILLS, MAYOR

TJFPLMMT

World War I Memorial, central tablet, in The Great Hall, West Wing, by Samuel Yellin, noted Philadelphia metal worker. There are 23 brass panels stretching along the balcony rail.

Mostly Just the Folks

Curtiss Collection/TJFPLMMT

Crowd inspecting Louis Bamberger's department-store airplane at the Morristown Field Club, July 29, 1919.

ALTHOUGH THE WEALTHY and privileged were the ones talked and written about, they were a small, mostly seasonal minority of the population of Morristown and Morris Township. Nevertheless, these Golden Age families greatly benefited the majority of the population by directly or indirectly creating jobs.

The first group of employees who come to mind, of course, are those in the mansions or on the estates. Not every family had 50 or 60 servants, as did Otto Kahn, but most mansions were run with far larger staffs than can easily be imagined today. Some did not travel with their masters and mistresses but stayed on the property year round. Furthermore, as in England's aristocratic households, servants in managerial positions — butlers and chefs, head coachmen and gardeners, and sometimes housekeepers — were given considerable discretion in making purchases and carrying out their duties. In one or two generations, descendants of these usually well-paid servants entered the mainstream of Morristown's middle class and became significant employers and consumers as well.

Skilled craftsmen and artists, carriage makers and blacksmiths, masons and carpenters, and small businesses, stores, and services of all kinds existed to carry out the often demanding requirements of the rich.

Society's presence, no doubt, encouraged summer visitors and accounted for the number of thriving small hotels and boarding houses.

To provide for the expected comforts and convenience, there were two rival gas companies. There were also two rival electric light companies and two ice plants, telephone and telegraph companies (the latter used much more than today). The companies provided a large variety of jobs — plant employees, operators, technicians, wagon drivers, lamplighters, messengers, and so forth.

A steady flow of immigrants filled the poorer, heavier, dirtier jobs in construction, landscaping and railroading. Women made overalls at the Rosevear Bros. factory on Water Street, one of several industries employing cheap labor. Although these workers had little use for banks or store charge accounts, their children and grandchildren grew up to seek and enjoy a comfortable living.

Great diversity of population enriched Morristown by the end of the Golden Age. Within its tiny 2.86 miles, there were foreign-born immigrants from Austria, Belgium, Canada, China, Czechoslovakia, Denmark, England, Finland, France, Germany, Greece, Hungary, Italy, Ireland, India, Japan, Lithuania, Netherlands, Norway, Poland, Portugal, Rumania, Russia, Scotland, Spain, Sweden, Switzerland, Turkey, Wales, Yugoslavia, Central and South America. □

TJFPLMMT

The Chambers family, June 20, 1915. George Chambers, a Morristown blacksmith and farrier, with his wife, Anna Connors, and the children, from left to right, Robert in his mother's arms, David and Ella May.

TJFPL.MMT

Morristown High School, Class of 1906, with Superintendent William L. R. Haven at the graduating ceremonies on June 22 at the Maple Avenue School. This was the largest class so far to graduate from the school. Mr. Haven served as its superintendent from 1869, the year the school was built, until 1908. Raymond P. Heath is "in the center" (bottom row?) according to information on the back of this photograph given by Mrs. Heath.

Look at the Birdie

Being photographed was popular, judging from the number of photographers. Ensminger Studio, Merritt and Charles Gregory, the Klinedinst family, W. K. Muchmore, The Parker Studio and The Sandrian Studio were among those who left an irreplaceable visual record of Morristown and Morris Township.

The largest surviving collection belongs to Frederick Fenton Curtiss, who photographed from 1903 until his death in 1938, carefully labeling and dating each camera view. A staggering 6,000 glass plate negatives, together with corresponding prints made in 1941 by G. D. Spinning, various subject indices and the original business records, were given after Curtiss's death to the Morristown National Historical Park. Because of its 20th-century subjects, this Curtiss Collection was deposited, in turn, with The Joint Free Public Library of Morristown and Morris Township, where it is widely consulted and reproduced.

Curtiss was born December 25, 1865, a son of Jesse L. and Mary Panghorn Curtiss. A Morristown resident for 50 years, he later moved to neighboring Morris Plains. He worked as a bookkeeper for the Morris Aquaduct Company until it was sold to the Morristown Water Company and then left to concentrate on commercial photography. His commissions came not only from families and business owners, but also from the town and township's many charities, clubs and organizations, the police department and insurance companies. Curtiss was not a society photographer. His subjects were ordinary people and things. His photographs might show a young couple on their porch, a mother with a baby, a girl in her first-communion dress, a proud black gardener,

Curtiss Collection/TJFPLMMT

Irish girls in a dance (above), May 19, 1918, and **boys on Lake Pocahontas** (below) from a 1920s postcard.

TJFPLMMT

Curtiss Collection/TJFPLMMT

Curtiss Collection/TJFPLMMT

Morristown Travel Club (above) on its way to Yellowstone Park, July 8, 1926. Members are standing on the elevated platform of the new **Railroad Station** (upper right), opened in 1913, the front of which is shown on December 2, 1916, and the parking lot side on November 27, 1913.

Members of the Union Baptist Church (right), on the corner of Spring and Water Streets (now Martin Luther King Avenue), waiting for transportation to a picnic at Grand View Park, August 5, 1926. The church, on the left, was the third black church in Morristown (1919) after the Bethel African Methodist Episcopal (1843) and the Calvary Baptist (1889).

Children's outing to Lake Hopatcong (opposite, above), corner of Speedwell and Sussex Avenues, August 3, 1927. The flatiron building, recognizable today, once housed a garage and chauffeur's school.

Ladies auxiliary of the Jewish Community Center (opposite, below) on Speedwell Avenue before an outing, August 23, 1932. Members of the Jewish congregation worshipped at a house on nearby Race Street before they built the first synagogue in Morristown. Its cornerstone was laid on March 3, 1929.

Curtiss Collection/TJFPLMMT

or an automobile after an accident, a house after a fire or the hospital's new X-ray equipment. Some photographs showed new or newly renovated buildings, store display windows or shop interiors. Some of his photographs, like those of historical buildings, local events or the new train station, were made into postcards.

During the years Curtiss was photographing, census data revealed important changes among Morristown's middle class and working people. In 1910, the town's population was 12,507. (Morris Township's 3,161 was too small for census analysis.) The Irish, who began arriving in the 1840s, were the largest immigrant group, 1,959 foreign-born and children of foreign-born. The Italians in this category numbered 1,177. There were 991 blacks and nine "Indian, Chinese and Japanese." The census also noted 5,892 first- and second-generation immigrants as opposed to 5,615 native whites of native-born parentage, proving the town's English and Scottish dominance had ended.

The 1930 census showed Morristown's population had risen to 15, 197. There were now 2,162 Irish — 1,884 Irish Free State, 278 from Northern Ireland — and 2,006 Italians. The black population had grown to 1,377, a dramatic increase of 54.5 percent over 1920. The number of Russians — 168 foreign-born and 221 of foreign-born parents — together with immigrants from neighboring European countries were creating a significant Jewish population. Several successful businesses existing today trace their roots to Jewish peddlers pushing their carts through Morristown's streets.

The group photographs Curtiss and others were taking have a particular historic value because they bring alive the flavor of life among "the ordinary folks" for the first third of the 20th century. □

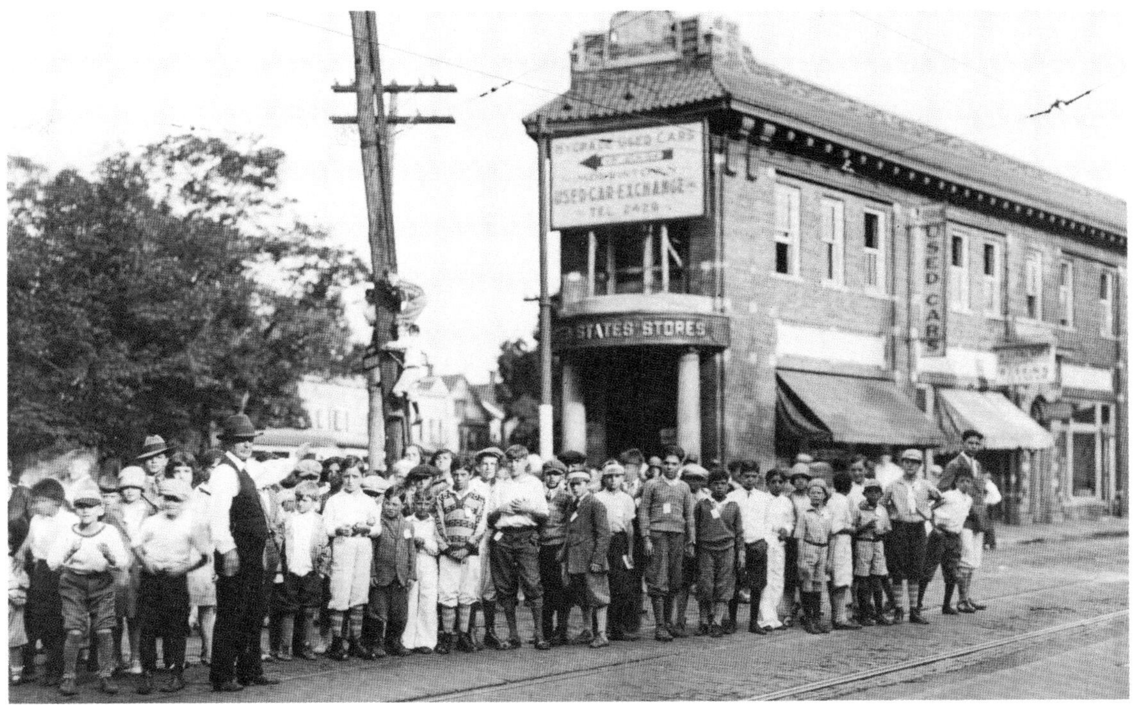

Curtiss Collection/TJFPLMMT

Curtiss Collection/TJFPLMMT

Curtiss Collection/TJFPLMMT

Decoration Day Parade, Speedwell Avenue, Morristown, May 30, 1917.

Curtiss Collection/TJFPLMMT

Baby Parade, South Street near the Morristown Green, 1918.

Morristown Chapter of the American Red Cross, May 30, 1917. Members are proudly displaying an award banner on the Green in a panoramic view that shows a background that stretches from the United States Hotel, North Park Place, to the Methodist Church, East Park Place. The Presbyterian Church, third edifice, and the Civil War Monument are in the center background. Founded on March 10, 1917, this Red Cross

TJFPLMMT

Chapter was one of 3,700 chartered by Congress at the onset of World War I. A motor corps with headquarters at the Armory on South Street provided transportation for military and hospital personnel, supplies and surgical dressings. In 1918, recalled Grace J. Vogt, local historian and newspaperwoman, "Many of these Red Cross volunteers met the terrible emergency imposed by the dread influenza."

Curtiss Collection/TJFPLMMT

Morristown's Battery F (above) of the 1st N.J. Field Artillery on Morris Street at the corner of Pine Street as it was about to entrain for Camp Edge at Sea Girt, July 25, 1917. This local unit of the National Guard was recruited as the Morristown Infantry Battalion. The original roster included 174 officers and enlisted men, many shown here. Later, 26 more were added for war strength. Battery F became the 104th T.M.B., the first infantry trench artillery battery in the U.S. Army. The men never saw actual combat as a unit, but approximately 30 percent saw combat due to

TJFPLMMT

transfers. On February 23, 1919, the outfit returned on the transport *Mongolia,* arriving in Hoboken on March 9; the men were mustered out by June 1.

Photographing photographers (opposite, left). William C. Parker, on the left, and Charles S. Gregory are photographed by Frederick Curtiss as they prepare to photograph Battery F.

Morristown train station, Morris Street (right). The departure of the boys was accompanied by a parade, band and huge crowd. The three-story brick building still stands.

TJFPLMMT

Patriotic rally, World War I era, probably in Burnham Park.

TJFPLMMT

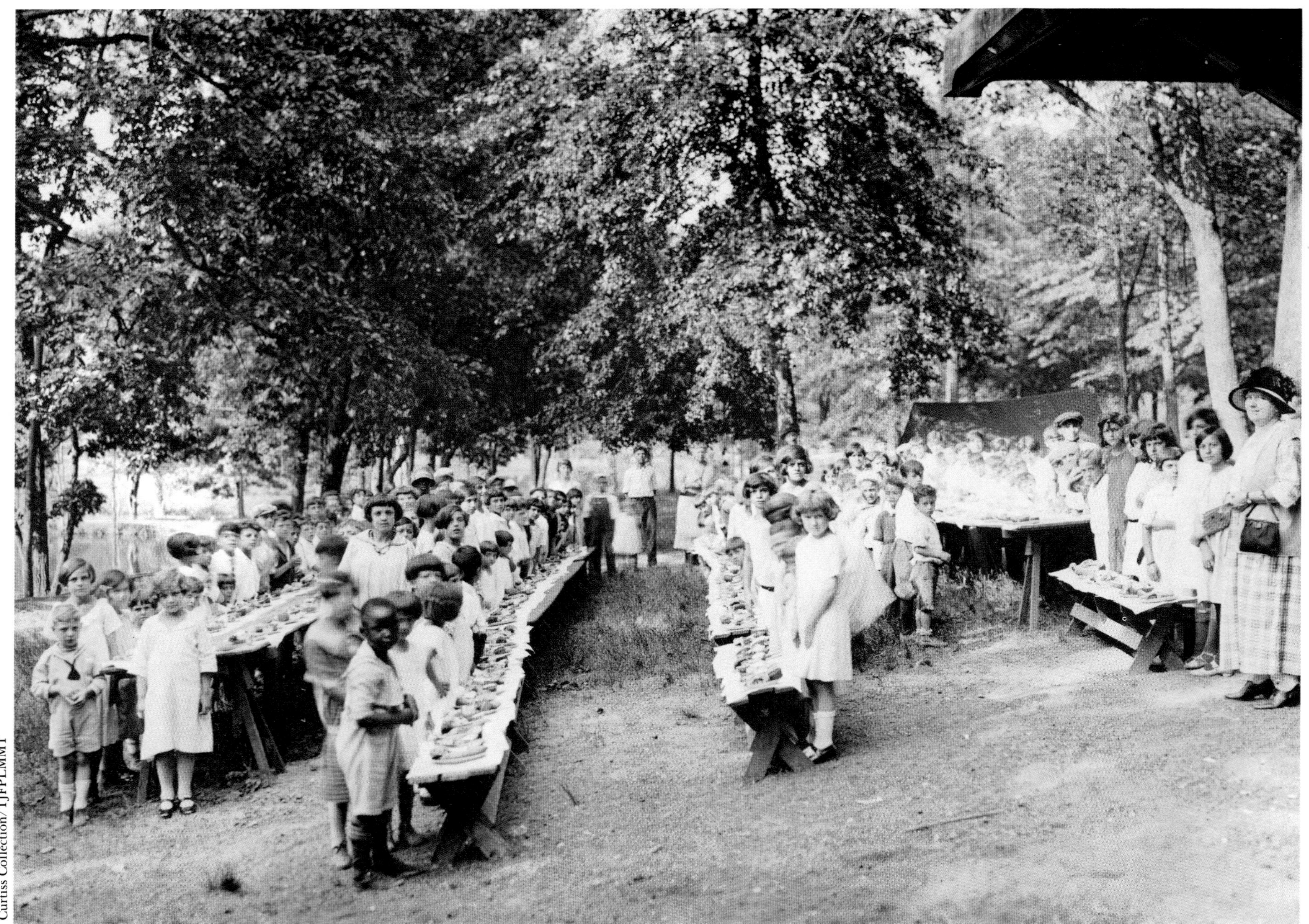

Curtiss Collection/TJFPLMMT

Neighborhood House picnic, Burnham Park, July 14, 1925. Neighborhood House, begun as the Association of Work Among the Italians in 1898, changed its name in 1912 when it began to serve more than Italian families.

Curtiss Collection/TJFPLMMT

Children's dance, Cauldwell playground, Race Street, August 18, 1925. The dance was presented by Miss Carr. This area became part of the Pocahontas apartment complex along the Whippany River.

Curtiss Collection/TJFPLMMT

St. Margaret's Church picnic, June 10, 1934. The church building on the left at Speedwell and Sussex Avenues replaced the 1885 wood chapel. The present church was finished in 1968. The present brick school building is on the right.

Curtiss Collection/TJFPLMMT

Swimming at Burnham Park, July, 1934. This pool was built in 1928 on the site of a pond and was hailed for having the "most recent style," a sandy beach. The present pool was opened in 1980.

Curtiss Collection/TJFPLMMT

Remembered Still

Even with the varying, often conflicting impulses of a growing population, Morristown's proud history remained a common bond. Dedications, parades and holiday celebrations brought out large crowds.

Thanks to the Washington Association and the Morristown National Historical Park, visitors in ever-increasing numbers have walked on the same ground as George Washington and his troops and the early patriots. Washington's statue stands guard over his old headquarters, the Ford Mansion, while a few feet away is a bronze plaque on a boulder marking the location where Washington's Life Guards built their huts. Another boulder with bronze plaque and a Morris County Heritage Commission marker commemorate the location of the Park of the Artillery. A memorial stone, erected by the Washington Association, commemorates Fort Nonsense. In Burnham Park sits a bronze statue of a pensive Thomas Paine surrounded by some of the inflammatory words that fanned enthusiasm for the American Revolution. This is one of the very few statues of Paine in the country which rejected him as an 18th-century hero because of his atheistic views.

Men from Morristown and Morris Township have answered this country's call in every war. There is a statue to the memory of the dead in every conflict except the War of 1812 and the Vietnam War. "Soldier at Rest," commemorating those lost in the Civil War, 1861-65, has stood on the Green since 1871. Stalwart-looking, carbine in hand, "The Hiker" honors the five Morristown dead in the Spanish-American War, 1898-1902, in the triangle at the intersection of Morris Avenue and Elm Street. In front of the Vail Mansion on South Street (page 174), the World War I memorial cenotaph, featuring a Winged Victory, honors the 26 Morristown residents who died fighting the "war to end all wars," 1914-18. And a monument to the 94 Morristown men who gave their lives in World War II, 1941-45, and the Korean Conflict, 1950-53, stands in tiny Veteran's Park at the junction of South Street and Madison Avenue. Throughout the area, there are plaques and memorials to remind old-timers and newcomers alike of Morristown's glorious past. □

Curtiss Collection/TJFPLMMT

Unveiling (opposite) of the bronze equestrian statue of George Washington, opposite Washington's Headquarters at the corner of Morris and Washington Avenues, October 19, 1928. The date commemorated Cornwallis's surrender at Yorktown in 1781. The sculptor was Frederick George Richard Roth of Brooklyn, New York. Dr. Henry N. Dodge donated the land and Miss Ellen Mabel Clark the statue. The speaker is Judge Charles W. Parker, credited with leading the drive to save the 1827 Morris County Court House when some proposed to replace it with a more modern facility.

Dedication (above) of tablet and monument at Gen. Knox's Park of the Artillery, Mendham Road (Route 24), by Morristown Post Number 59 of the American Legion, November 11, 1932.

Recollections of Morristown in the Golden Age

John Elliott

I was born on March 28, 1896. It was my good fortune to grow up in Morristown, New Jersey, then a town of some 12,000 souls, during its "Golden Age" in the first two decades of this century. It was called the Golden Age because it was widely known as a town of millionaires. Some 100 of them with estimated combined assets of half a billion dollars lived within three miles of the Green. The Twomblys, the Footes, the McAlpins, the Scribners and their ilk dwelled in large and luxurious mansions set in the midst of beautiful estates.

But Morristown was not only a beautiful community but, more important, it was a town with a great history. So it was an inspiration for any child to be a resident of Morristown. A schoolboy studying Latin could proudly say, paraphrasing the Romans, "Civus Morristowniensis sum."

Victorian morals and values prevailed. They were fostered by the many churches in the town — two Presbyterian, two Episcopalian, two Catholic, a Methodist, an African Methodist, and a Baptist — headed by eminent ministers.

People walked to church, for automobiles were few and owned mostly by the rich. When the automobiles broke down, as they often did, passersby would shout derisively, "Get a horse!" Gradually, however, cars became more common. I can remember an uncle of mine viewing the passing automobiles from the Green in 1910, saying portentously, "I believe that the automobile has come to stay!"

The Republican Party dominated Morristown. In my boyhood I can recall only one Democrat being elected mayor, and that was Charlton Reed, who held that office early in the twentieth century. My father and all his four brothers and one sister were die-hard Republicans. Only once did Father vote for a Democrat, and that was for Woodrow Wilson as Governor of New Jersey in 1910.

Selected from an interview conducted by Ruth Grimm at Mr. Elliott's home in Bethesda, Maryland, October 1982. He graduated from the Maple Avenue High School (1914), Princeton University (1920) and Columbia School of Journalism (1921) and served in both World Wars. He worked briefly for *The Jerseyman* but a major portion of his career was spent overseas for the *New York Herald Tribune.*

Father had a distant cousin who was a Democrat. Consequently we looked upon him as a maverick. Genial and well-liked (even by the Elliotts), he often dropped in Father's flower store to chat and engage in political arguments.

Life in Morristown tended to be tranquil and peaceful, but the monotony was broken from time to time by notable events:

The Parade of the Grand Army of the Republic on Memorial Day. The veterans of the Civil War, becoming smaller year by year, marched down South Street to the Green where, in front of the monument commemorating that conflict, patriotic speeches were delivered. This was the most stirring spectacle of my youth.

The Firemen's Parade in October. The annual parade of the town's fire companies was climaxed by the Independent Hose Company rushing to extinguish with its chemicals a roaring fire in a shack that had been packed with combustibles and erected near the five-storey Babbitt Building — the town's "skyscraper." In another exhibition the Resolute Hook and Ladder Company's truck drawn by "Tom" and "Jerry" would rush to the Babbitt Building, from which "smoke" was pouring from a window. The firemen would put up a ladder and rescue a dummy.

The Horse Shows at the Morristown Field Club. These were held every autumn at the clubhouse on South Street. There were competitions for ponies, hunters, jumpers and saddle horses, but the outstanding event was the exhibition of the four-in-hands.

Big Fires. The biggest fires I have ever seen in my life occurred in Morristown, and there were quite a number of them. I remember the Trimmer Building blaze, the fire that gutted the Church of the Redeemer, the big fire near the Maple Avenue school that some of us hoped would spread to that building and level it to the ground, and the burning of the Lyceum on Washington's Birthday in 1914.

Political Rallies. Republicans and Democrats alike held their rallies in the Lyceum. They were invariably preceded by a band playing "The Stars and Stripes Forever." I used to go to these meetings with my father. The only time I ever heard Woodrow Wilson speak was when he addressed one of these gatherings in his campaign for Governor of New Jersey in 1910.

Teddy Roosevelt Comes to Town. The celebrated Rough Rider came to Morristown when he was running against President Taft in the Republican primary of 1912. It was a "whistle stop" speech. He talked briefly from the platform of a rear car at the Lackawanna railroad station. It was a great event in the town, and we high school students were excused from the classroom to hear him. That meant a lot to me, for "Teddy" was my boyhood hero.

The Advent of the Trolley in 1909. This was a triumph for the *Morristown Daily Record,* which had strongly campaigned for it. It linked Morristown with Dover to the north and Chatham to the south.

The Weekly Band Concerts. They were held on the Green in summer and were extremely popular, drawing big crowds.

Cultural Life. The Lyceum on South Street was the center of Morristown's cultural activities. It contained, firstly, the theater with the image of Shakespeare on the curtain. Minstrels and comedies were the most popular at a time when the movies were in their infancy and television was nonexistent. I saw my first play there with my mother. It was "Uncle Tom's Cabin," and I was thrilled with Eva's escape over the ice from the pursuing hounds.

The theater was also the scene of political rallies and the high school graduation ceremony in June.

The Library. I was a frequent patron of this book storehouse. One of my most prized possessions is the *Autobiography* of Edward Gibbon, the author of *The Decline and Fall of the Roman Empire,* which I happened to have borrowed just before the library was destroyed by fire.

The Morris Academy. It was an excellent preparatory school for Morristown boys. It had many fine teachers such as Harry Landfear, the headmaster; Peck, who later founded a school of his own in Morristown and was much liked by his students; and Barker, who taught Latin and Greek and had the reputation of being a strict disciplinarian. I was coached by him in Greek because I had to take an entrance examination to enter Princeton for a BA degree. Greek was a subject that was not offered by the Morristown High School. Under Barker I covered three years of Greek in 18 months and got a "B" in the entrance examinations. One bit of advice that he gave me was, "If you are not sure of an answer to a question, give it an educated guess, anyway," and I found this to be very helpful. The Morris Academy unfortunately did not long survive the destruction by fire of the Lyceum.

Then there was the Friday Evening Club, founded in 1900. It invited distinguished speakers to talk on such subjects as politics, literature, religion, art and science. Mark Twain, Theodore Roosevelt and Henry Ward Beecher were among the notables who addressed the club.

I was not a member, but occasionally my father would get a ticket from a customer and would pass it on to me. So I attended quite a few of these weekly talks and found them a great treat. The speaker I recall most vividly was Dr. Henry Van Dyke, professor of English at Princeton and author of *The Other Wise Man* and many other books.

The Movies. The first cinema I entered was on Washington Street, and the admission charge was a nickel. As the motion picture industry developed, the Palace Theatre on Speedwell Avenue became the town's main cinema.

I had a strange experience in connection with the Palace Theatre which illustrates the Victorian strictness of the age. I had invited Mary Caskey to go to the Palace Theatre on a Thursday evening. She was the daughter of Robert C. Caskey, the teller at the First National Bank, as I knew very well because I handed over Father's checks to him every Saturday morning. He was an elder of the First Presbyterian Church. It happened that a member of the church saw Mary going into the cinema, and he was shocked that an elder's daughter should be going to the movies on a Thursday night, which was the prayer meeting night at the church. He reported it to her father, who must have reprimanded her, for Mary told me that I was never to take her to the movies again on a Thursday night.

The Dance. Dancing was still frowned upon in some quarters. My classmate, Marian Chadwick, the pretty and petite daughter of the Methodist minister in Mendham, was never allowed to go to the school dances. For a long time the Board of Education banned dancing in the high school, but eventually this august body relaxed, and occasionally dances were held in the high school after classes were over.

My father made me go to a dancing class in Washington Hall to chaperon my sister Alice, who was eager to attend. It was a very proper class. The boys had to wear white cotton gloves and

TJFPLMMT

Views from the tower of the Presbyterian Church on the Green, third edifice (the present building), about 1900-10. Water, Spring and Morris Streets: The historic burying ground is in the foreground; part of the roofs of the church and manse are seen. In the center of the photograph is the old Morristown Memorial Hospital (former site of the Johnes parsonage), now the Midtown Shopping Mall.

to bow to a girl to ask her for the honor of a dance. The waltz and the polka were taught, but the most modern dance on the curriculum was the two-step. The Turkey Trot and the Bunny Hug were all the rage then, but of course no instruction in these dances was imparted in this school.

Sports. Baseball was played Saturday afternoons in summer on Speedwell Avenue Field. I used to sit in center field to watch the game. Morristown was in the Lackawanna League and Boonton was the arch rival. One year Morristown had a star pitcher by the name of Johnny Ensman, who won almost every game he pitched. He later had a trial with a major league club but did not make the grade.

The most famous game played while I lived in Morristown was the playoff game in 1908 between the New York Giants and the Chicago Cubs for the National League championship. This game was necessitated because "Bonehead" Merkle had failed to touch second base in a regular season game between these two

Speedwell Avenue, Water and Spring Streets: On the left, at the corner of the Green and Speedwell Avenue is the McAlpin Building. At the corner of Spring and Water Streets are the Estey and L'Hommedieu-

TJFPLMMT

South Park Place and beginning of Morris Street: The buildings close to South Street still stand. The Methodist parsonage and church had a disastrous fire in 1972. Only the church was rebuilt. The Scofield House, left of the church, was torn down to make a driveway. The *Daily Record* bought the next building and replaced it with their offices. The present post office was built where Elliott's Greenhouses are.

TJFPLMMT

Gwinnup Houses and Dickerson's Tavern (rebuilt after a fire). Also on Spring Street is the Bethel African Methodist Episcopal Church, oldest black congregation in town, having been organized in 1843.

clubs, depriving the Giants of a victory over the Cubs and the championship. I was in the big crowd that stood outside the Western Union office on South Street as the score was posted, inning by inning. To my great disappointment the Cubs won, 4 to 2, defeating my boyhood hero, Christy Mathewson, familiarly known as "Matty" or "Big Six."

I was a great baseball fan, but my father sternly forbade me to go to a game on Sunday.

The Morristown High School had no football team when I attended it. Football was banned in 1906 when a Morristown High School player had his neck broken while playing against the Morristown School. There were no professional teams in my boyhood. It was then exclusively a college sport.

End of an Era. With the Lyceum in ruins the Class of 1914 was forced to hold its graduation ceremony in the sanctuary of the First Presbyterian Church. It took place on June 19. Nine days later on Sunday, June 28, the Archduke Francis Ferdinand, the heir to the Austro-Hungarian throne, was assassinated at Sarajevo. I don't know whether I read about this crime at the time, but if I did, it wouldn't have meant anything to me. I never would have dreamed that a shot fired in a far-off Balkan country was going to affect me, or that the United States would become involved in a world war because of it. I remember President John Grier Hibben of Princeton telling us undergraduates in the opening service in Marquand Chapel how fortunate we were to be able to study and learn when our contemporaries in Europe were fighting and dying on the battlefield. Little did he foresee that within less than three years most of the students he was addressing would themselves be engaged in that conflict.

For Morristown Sarajevo marked the beginning of the end of the Golden Age. Many of the millionaires, hurt by mounting taxes and inflation, would be leaving the town. Their stately mansions would be torn down and their lovely estates would be carved up into small lots for small homes. The war, too, would end the Victorian era in Morristown. The Jazz Age with its revolution in morals was just around the corner. The world in which our generation grew up was vanishing.

Robert A. Elliott, my father, who had been a gardener at Bernardsville on the estate of George Browne Post, the noted architect, entered the florist business in Morristown in 1895 at the age of 26. Elliott's Flower Shoppe was located at 13 Morris Street, now occupied by the United States Post Office. This store was the first home that I recall, for we lived in the rooms over it. One of my earliest memories is seeing the building draped in black in honor of William McKinley, who had just been assassinated. He was not a great President (Theodore Roosevelt complained that he had the backbone of a chocolate eclair), but McKinley was greatly loved by the people.

There were during my boyhood three major flower shops in Morristown: Mrs. Holton's, strategically located on South Street; Holmes's at the corner of Pine and Morris Streets, and the Elliott store at 17 Pine Street.

Business was seasonable. Christmas and Easter were high tide, and the planting days of spring were also times of great activity. But the summer, beginning with Memorial Day, was a period of slack business, save for funerals, until Labor Day.

My father led a gruelling life. He arose at six o'clock every morning. The store was opened from seven o'clock until late at night. It was open for business on Sundays until noon, although business on the Sabbath was negligible. I never could understand why the three florists could not come to an understanding to close their shops on Sunday or at least in taking turns in doing business on "the day of rest," as the drug stores do now. In winter my father had to get up in the night to see that the furnaces were functioning so that the flowers and plants in the greenhouses didn't freeze.

Father's chief relaxation was taking his family for a ride around the countryside in his gig on Sunday afternoons. These outings became less pleasurable as the automobiles became more numerous. Father capitulated in 1915 when he bought a Ford.

Father seldom took a vacation while he was in business. Once he went fishing at Barnegat Bay and returned home so badly sunburned that he was hardly recognizable. In later years he would go on motoring trips to New England with his brother, John Elliott, who was a lawyer in New Haven, Connecticut.

Mother served as a clerk in the store a great part of the day, besides preparing three meals a day. An Irish-American girl came every day to clean the house and do the washing and laundry. My main job was to deliver flowers on foot, escorted by my collie. This gave me a lifelong fondness for walking. I was also occasionally sent to New York to buy cut flowers wholesale.

An Italian-American named "Mike" was Father's chief helper. He went to work for the Elliott Flower Store in 1907 and was taken over by my brother-in-law James M. Lindsley when he bought the business in 1923. Mike was reported to have become very well off by practicing the strictest economy at the expense of his family. He was indeed a very hard worker.

In the valley behind the flower shop on Morris Street was one of the worst slums in Morristown. Scores of poverty-stricken blacks lived in rundown and dilapidated houses in the area. It bore the appropriate name of "Tin Can Alley."

In 1907 the flower store was moved to Pine Street, as the United States Government had requisitioned the Morris Street lot for a post office. In its new quarters the store had the Wiss service station as its neighbor on the right, while on the other side was a lane [now Dumont Place] that connected Pine Street with Morris Street. The Mills Wood Working Shop was located on this street.

Two years previously we had moved to a new home across the street from where the flower shop was to be. It was a double house that Father had built. One part of the dwelling faced Pine Street while the other half, which we occupied, fronted on King Place. It was roomier and more comfortable than the cramped quarters on Morris Street. The front door opened directly on the sitting room. This had the upright piano on which my sister and I played for our parents on Sunday evenings. Adjoining this room was the parlor. It was rarely used, being reserved for special occasions as, for example, when rich and extremely snobbish relatives from Montclair came to honor us with a visit in a chauffeured automobile. Mother also used it to store Christmas presents until the time came to open them.

But although the new home was larger, enabling my sister and I to have our own rooms, I always thought the cramped quarters on Morris Street to be more exciting. It faced on Morris Street, one of the liveliest thoroughfares in Morristown. Opposite our home was the First Presbyterian Church, the tower of which was circled by swallows in the evening. Nearby was the Green, the center of the town. This was a repulsive sight on Saturday nights, when its benches were occupied by drunken, vomiting men. In winter I used to love to sit by the window and watch the sleighs with jingling bells go by on the snow-covered street, especially the sleigh buses of the United States Hotel near the Green and the Mansion House on Washington Street — the two main inns of the town.

In June 1923 Father sold his business to his son-in-law, James M. Lindsley, and retired to a more leisurely life.

Courtesy of Morris County Park Commission/TJFPLMMT

Charles F. Cutler's coach stopping at South Park Place on its way from the Whippany River Club to Bernardsville.

TJFPL.MMT

Continuity and Change

Overleaf The Green, west side, toward Fort Nonsense Hill, 1893, from the tower of the First Presbyterian Church, second edifice, just before it was taken down.

CONTINUITY AND CHANGE. Tradition and progress. Photographs record both the stuff of nostalgia and the challenge of the future. The great symbol of continuity is the Morristown Green linking the headlong rush of the present with the peaceful beginnings of the colonial town. Here is history in grass and trees and memories, thanks to those farsighted Presbyterian forefathers who secured protection for this land.

This is not the colonial Green, of course, where neighbors met and animals grazed, but it shares the same spirit of the commons the first settlers knew. And it is in the original location, something that can be said about very few places today.

Comparing the Green at the beginning of the 20th century (above) with the same scene near the end of the century (the following pages) shows 19th-century buildings still in evidence but the 20th century firmly taking hold. This is most dramatically seen at the northeast corner of Park Place and Speedwell Avenue, where a group of glass-and-concrete structures rise above the other buildings on the Green.

Similar changes have occurred throughout Morristown and Morris Township. The small town of the Golden Age that eager promoters called "the City" has indeed become just that. The rural and residential township now competes for business properties. Office buildings cover cow pastures; condominiums rest side by side on

TJFPLMMT

The Green, north, east and south sides, showing Washington Street to the Baptist Church on the left, and South Street to the Library and Lyceum on the right, about 1912.

swampland long protected. Sounds of bulldozers and chain saws come out of the woodlands.

Perhaps this was inevitable. Morristown has always been more important than its small size. A county seat grows with its county.

A crossroads since Indian days, the Green was a commercial center in colonial days when iron miners from the outlying hills came down for supplies. George Washington's two encampments during the Revolutionary War brought the area national and international fame. During the Golden Age, word-of-mouth brought many people to Morristown and Morris Township, changing an essentially agricultural community into a residential one. Morristonians hung together during the Depression when a family in a mansion one day might occupy the chauffeur's apartment the next and the breakup of the large households affected everyone down the line. When World War II roared in, its citizens were once again proud to support and serve. In the middle of the 20th century, the area became a "bedroom community" and suburb for those who worked for companies in Newark and New York. Beginning in the 1980s, big companies moved nearer their employees, bringing their own set of requirements, such as new roads, traffic lights and parking areas. The streetscape alters again.

Change is always in the wind. What will it keep tomorrow and what will it blow away? □

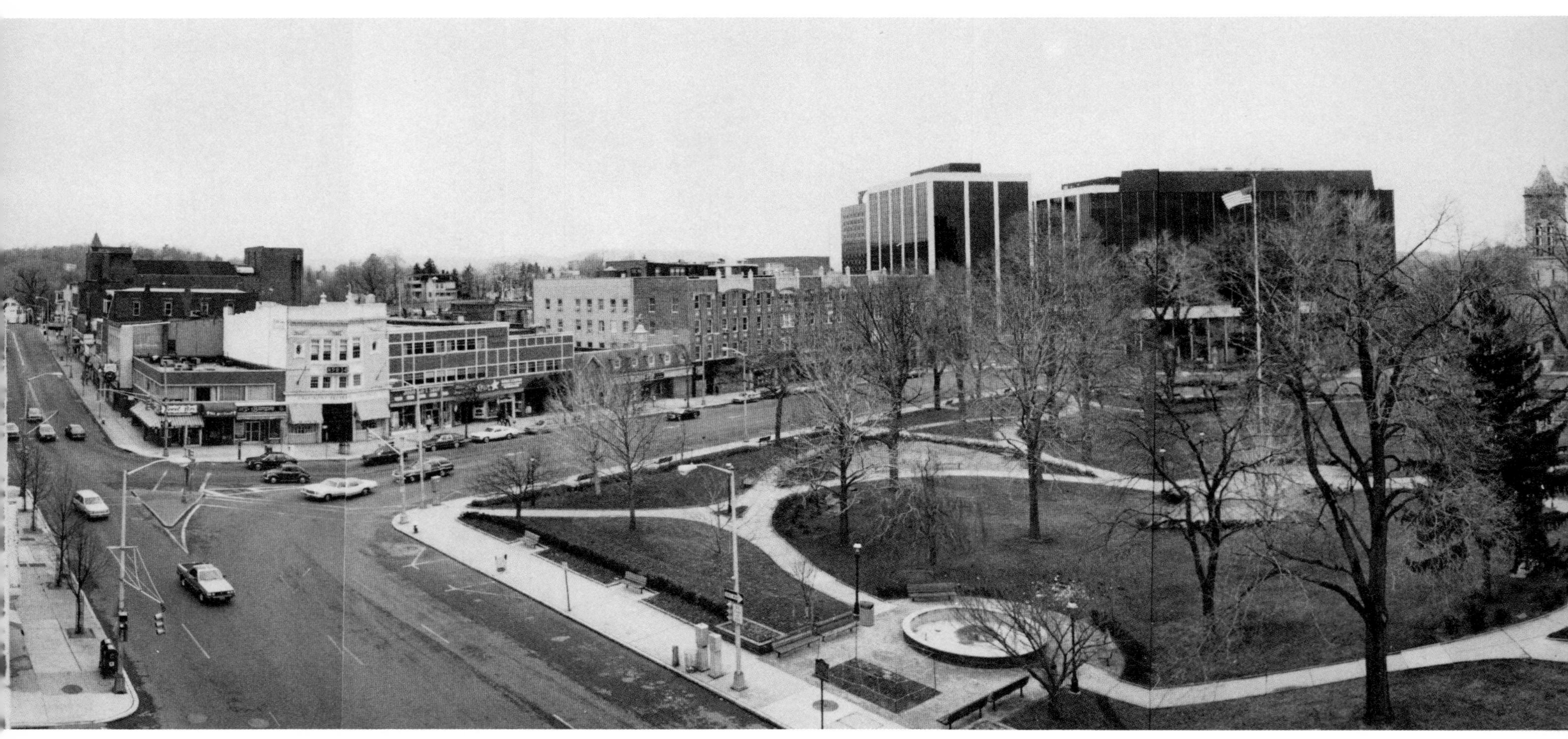

The Green, same view, April 14, 1984.

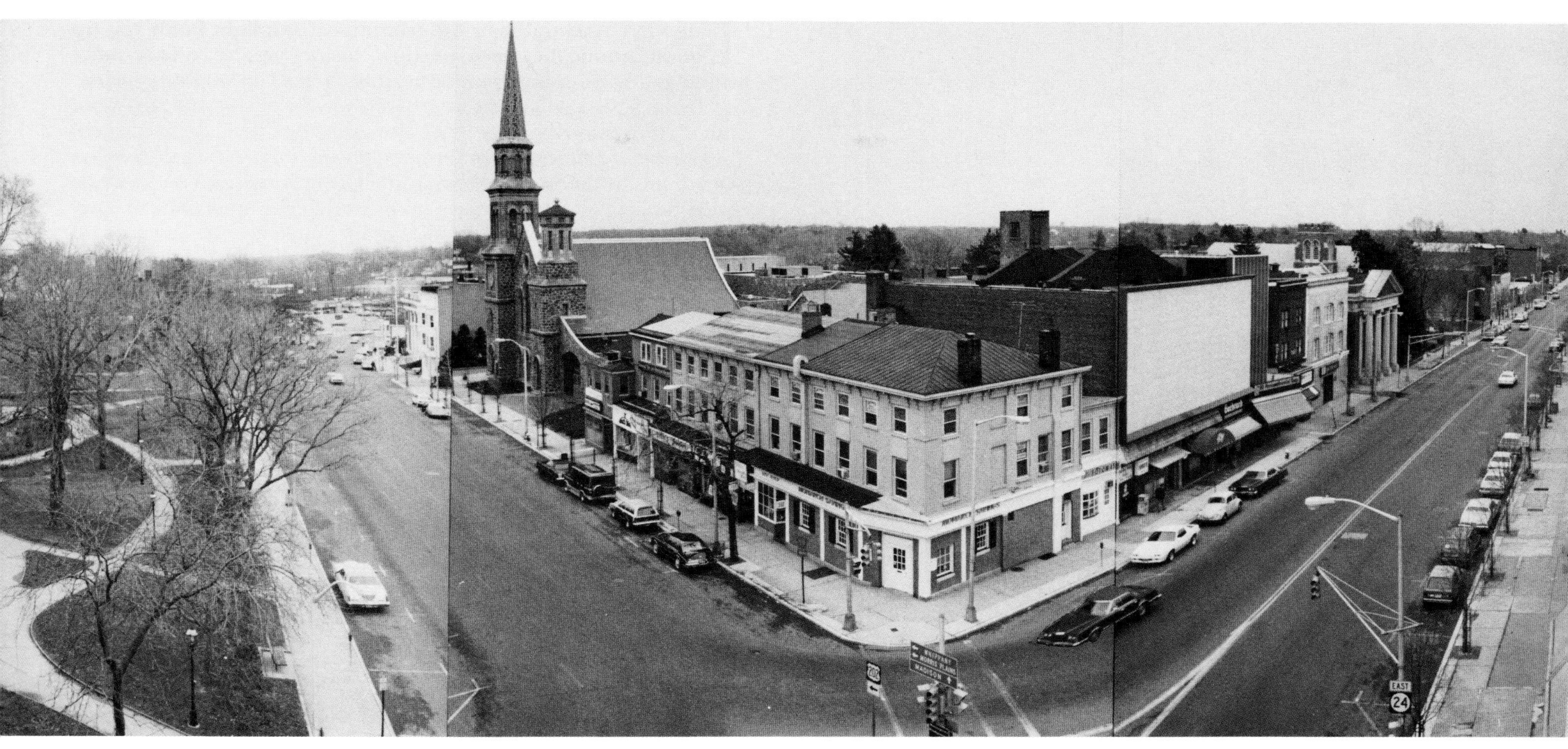

All photographs by James L. Grabow/TJFPLMMT

Passing Scenes

TJFPLMMT

Water pumper of the Independent Hose Company, 1884.

THE NEXT TIME traffic or the ever-present stoplight holds you up going around the Green, put on a "history cap," leave annoyance behind and let your imagination float back freely through the years.

Perhaps you will want to go way, way back. As you turn from Morris Street into East Park Place alongside the Presbyterian Church, imagine the wooden meeting house of long ago and the warm Sundays when families picnic and chat on the Green between services while children play among the stones in the burying ground and the long-time sexton, Moses Cherry, and later his son, shoos the chickens off the steps.

Or think about George Washington and his aides during those two crucial winters. Perhaps they are leaving Arnold Tavern after a morning conference, saluting a group of soldiers on the Green, and then leaping onto horses that gallop off towards Jockey Hollow.

You could imagine a handsome coach racing into town, lording over the middle of the road, the patent leather, brass and black enamel gleam in the sun, and there is no mistaking the feeling of superiority of the men wearing the house livery. Or do you see a hay wagon, whose horse is hitched peacefully at the side of the road for hours while the farmer waits for a customer. Only after the farmer has driven to the buyer's barn or stable and unloaded will the purchase be complete.

Or does your mind's eye see a graceful 19th-century carriage slowing to a stop in front of a favorite, awning-covered store? A hand leans out to ring the curb-side bell and an eager clerk dashes up with order pad in hand. The requirements understood, the clerk backs away with nods and smiles, then quickly moves inside to assemble the merchandise. Long after sunset that same clerk disappears into an unobtrusive doorway next to the shop and climbs steep, narrow stairs to a small apartment above.

If it is winter, no snow plow clears the early 20th-century road. Your carriage or an early model Ford follows the ruts others made and work crews use picks and shovels to make ditches for those vehicles wanting to turn. In summer, on the other hand, horse-drawn water tanks wet down the choking dust from the dirt roads.

When the motor car comes to stay — not just the rich man's toy as many people first thought — the speed is four miles an hour in town and considered fast at that. When the newfangled steam rollers are introduced to smooth the road, a man must walk ahead waving a flag to warn that something is coming that scares the horses.

There is lots to think about going around the Green — of carriages, carts and Model T's, of roller skates and bicycles, or races and parades in the days before the traffic jams. All you have to do is choose. □

TJFPLMMT

Turn-of-the-century scene at South Park Place and South Street.

The Green Left Free Forever

Judge John Whitehead's address at the unveiling of the monument on the Green erected by the Daughters of the American Revolution, Morristown Chapter, November 10, 1904

The first mention of the "Green" in the Trustees' book of the Presbyterian Church is found under date of January 12, 1767, when the Trustees "Gave Lieve that a School hous might be Built on the Green Near whair the old hous Now Standeth."

In May 1770 the Trustees met at the "County hous" and agreed "to Convey a Part of the meating hous Land to the freeholders of the County of Morris for the Benefit of the Court hous," and in June following a deed was given to "Three majestrets and the Freeholders" for "One acre of Land on which the Court hous Standeth." This "County hous" was probably the first court house, a log structure standing on the Green said to have been built in 1755.

On April 24, 1773, the Trustees of the church bought from Shadrach Hayward a large tract of land containing "Sixty one Acres and seventy two hundredths Acre" for the use and benefit of our community, the consideration being "one hundred and eighty five pounds, Three Shillings & two pence."

In 1774 an unsuccessful attempt was made to buy some land from Thomas Kinney, Esq., "to enlarge and accommodate the Public Parade, &c." Eleven years afterwards, in 1785, the same land was purchased "for the purpose of enlarging the Publick parade on the Green" from Capt. Silas Howell, to whom Thomas Kinney, in the meantime, had sold it.

At a meeting of the Trustees in April 1812, it was ordered "that Daniel Phoenix attend to the attempt made by Ezra Owen to lay a proprietor right on a part of the Green, or Commons, and to consult with Mr. Edward Condict, the Surveyor on the subject, and if necessary to attend the Annual Meeting of the Board of Proprietors at Amboy and to have a right laid on the vacant part of the Green, and to take a title for the same in the name of the Trustees, for the express purpose of a Green or Commons." A year later Mr. Condict "tendered his Deed to the Trustees for the Green or Commons in consequence of a deed he received from the Proprietor, which deed also contained an article of agreement mutually entered into between the said Edward Condict and the Trustees, stipulating that the land conveyed shall remain forever a Public Commons or Green, The Trustees having considered the same unanimously accepted it, and ordered the President to sign it in their behalf."

At a parish meeting in 1815, it was voted "that if any part of the congregation do by subscription or otherwise raise the sum of fifteen hundred dollars to add to the funds of the parish that the Trustees be instructed to sell no part of the parish land that now lieth common and called Morristown Green, that they relinquish the whole as a Common forever." A condition was affixed that "ground sufficient whereon to place a Session House should be reserved."

A year later, in 1816, at another parish meeting, the Trustees reported "that in consideration of the sum of sixteen hundred dollars they have conveyed all the right of the congregation to that part of the parish land which now lieth common and is called Morristown Green to remain as a common forever. And the lot now occupied by the county of Morris when the said county shall cease to use the same for a court and gaol to be considered as a part of said Common." The conveyance reported by the Trustees, at this parish meeting, was effected by a deed made to well known and influential citizens, and contained a condition that no buildings should be erected on the land except a meeting house, a court house, jail or market house, but, in 1868, this condition was annulled and the Green left free forever.

Corners of the Green

The first houses on the Green were surrounded by land, probably a combination of woods and pasture, orchard and garden — whatever the family needed. Fences, not buildings, marked off the corners of the Green. The house and place of business were usually in the same building or located next to each other. However, success brought the need for expansion. By the mid-19th century, land for new business in the center of Morristown was at a premium. Gradually the open space disappeared around the edges of the Green. Buildings were separated only by narrow strips of land or alleyways.

Many of the wooden buildings were destroyed by fire and the replacements were usually brick, or occasionally stone. By the 1880s, town fathers wanted to make constructing wooden buildings on the Green illegal.

With the increased confidence brought by the Golden Age, buildings became more elegant; plain walls and small windows were exchanged for fancier architectural details, such as decorative window treatments and turrets. Banks, organizations and businesses wanted their buildings to display their prosperity. Branch stores were attracted to Morristown of the Golden Age. Later chain stores — like the Great Atlantic & Pacific Tea Company (A&P), Woolworth's and National Shoe — moved into the area to compete with local merchants. With them came electric signs and lighted display windows.

By mid-20th century, the appearance around the Green was gradually altered again. Buildings in Victorian architecture were replaced or remodeled along plainer lines. Yet despite the individualism and variations of style on Park Place, a certain harmony persisted around the Green until the 1970s. □

TJFPLMMT

Early 20th-Century Green

This peaceful postcard view shows the Green from the southern corner, beginning of South Street, directly north to Speedwell Avenue. The fact that the sides of the Green do not align with the compass has caused confusion over the years. The side on the left is now called North Park Place, although some years ago it was called West Park Place (making the present West Park Place, South Park Place and so forth). On the far left of this photograph, on North Park Place, are the old Canfield houses dating to the beginning of the 19th century. Next to them is the 1840 United States Hotel with its long raised porch, a popular dining place and a stagecoach stop. When horses raced around the Green and down South Street, horse fanciers gathered here and at the Mansion House on Washington Street to exchange information and place bets. In the center background is the Municipal Building on the corner of Speedwell Avenue and Water Street. Built in 1907, it lost its main function when the Town of Morristown took over the Vail Mansion on South Street. To the right, on East Park Place, are the Becker Building, a combination of stores and apartments, and the partly obscured Park House, an early 19th-century landmark that served at various times as a school and a boardinghouse. At one time, J. Cummings Vail, Alfred's son, proposed it as a museum of Morristown history to include many photographs he had taken of the Speedwell Iron Works. All the buildings have been razed and Water Street has vanished. Only the Green remains.

TJFPLMMT

First Babbitt Building, North Park Place and Washington Street, 1882

At this corner, woodland during the Revolution, Washington and his men turned countless times to go to Jockey Hollow. The office building above stood from the 1850s until it burned in 1894. The owner, W. S. Babbitt, sold and cleaned carpets, and it was not unusual to see rugs hanging from upper windows. *The Jerseyman* served Morris County as a Republican paper from 1826 to 1931, when it was acquired by the *Daily Record*. The First National Bank, founded on April 4, 1865, merged in 1944 with the National Iron Bank and is now MidLantic Bank.

Hoffman Building, formerly Arnold Tavern, North Park Place, about 1886

This building remained a tavern into the first half of the 19th century, and it was visited by many American and foreign visitors who wanted to see Washington's 1777 headquarters. P. H. Hoffman may have owned it as early as 1849, when he opened a clothing store. The other tenant in this photograph was the leading grocery firm of Adams & Fairchild.

In 1886, the Hoffman firm replaced this wooden building with a red building named The Arnold, while this old tavern was moved to Mount Kemble Avenue and, much changed, converted to a boarding establishment, the Colonial House, and then to All Souls Hospital. It burned in 1918. The new Arnold, in turn, was replaced in the 1940s by the present office building at 20 Park Place.

Day Building, on the site of O'Hara's Tavern, West Park Place and South Street, constructed about 1850

On May 1, 1862, Wilbur F. Day, the first of three generations of that name to run Morristown's most famous bakery, confectionery and catering service, opened the Colonial Restaurant here. On December 5, 1982, Wilbur F. Day, Jr., talked about his grandfather's building:

"His store is in the left half; then comes a shoe store and a men's furnishing store, and the entrance to the upper floors. The Day apartment is over his store, and Lacey's Portrait and Photo Studio was over the shoe store and the furnishing store. The top floor was Washington Hall, the largest around, from which the Civil War soldiers were drafted, and where Tom Thumb and Major Tot entertained. Lacey did not use all of the back of his studio and, when Thomas Nast first came to Morristown, he rented it to him."

In 1895, Day sold half this building, 38 Park Place, to the First National Bank. In 1942, Childs Restaurant Corporation acquired the firm and operated the Townhouse on the Green at 40 Park Place.

M. Epstein department store is now on the site of these buildings.

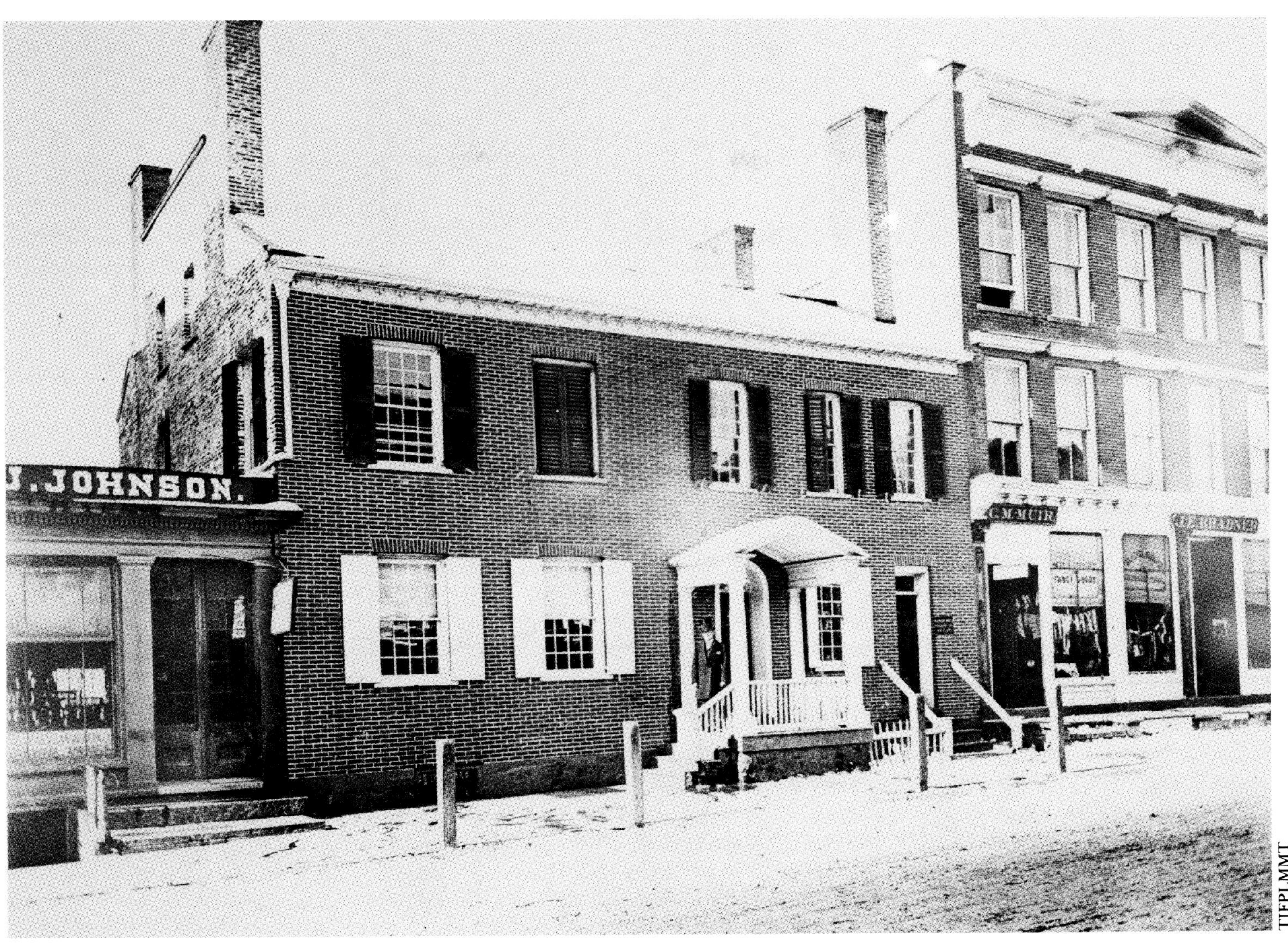

TJFPLMMT

Washington Street, 1869

In the early years of the 19th century, the Green area had many comfortable houses surrounded by gardens. However, by mid-century the houses began to disappear. An unknown person wrote the following information on the back of this photograph:

"Where the J. E. Bradner sign is, only a few years ago, Benjamin Ogden Canfield, nephew of Mrs. James Colles, had a dwelling house similar to the one shown in this photograph, which belonged to Judge Alfred Mills, standing on the front porch. John Bates, of Parsippany, bought the Canfield property and replaced the house and garden with the office building shown on the right." That building, 16-18 Washington Street, is still standing. Johnson's store became the site of 10 Washington Street (the part of the building with the iron steps).

Courtesy of The Methodist Church of Morristown/TJFPLMMT

The 1841 and 1870 Methodist Church on South Park Place about 1873

In this photograph, from left to right, are the 1841 or second Methodist Church building (the first was on Market Street), the second parsonage, the Scofield House, the third 1870 Methodist Church and the third parsonage.

In 1884-85, a fourth parsonage was built in the empty space on the right. Dumont Place cut through where the older church stood. The 1870 church building was rebuilt after a 1972 fire that left only the tower and front wall standing. (See also the caption on page 267.)

TJFPLMMT

South Park Place looking towards Morris Avenue, August 13, 1889

The occasion was the 21st anniversary parade of the Morristown Fire Department.

The Miller Building, Park Place, on the corner of South Street, still stands. For this part of South Park Place, the 1890 Sanborn Perris map listed, from the corner, a drugstore, millinery, boot and shoe shop, cigar store, telegraph office (extended awning), stove merchant with tin shop in back, harness shop, Methodist parsonage and the church.

TJFPLMMT

TJFPLMMT

The 1793 and 1893 Presbyterian Church on East Park Place

The second building (left) is shown, about the time of the final service, February 12, 1893. The Chapel on the left replaced the 1819 Session House in 1869; the Manse was built in 1885. Construction on the third building (above) began in 1893. The first service in the new church was held on September 9, 1894.

The architect, J. Cleveland Cady, designer of the original Metropolitan Opera House and the American Museum of Natural History, placed the new church 40 feet back from the old one. The Manse can be seen through a window on the right. (Photographs of the completed building are on pages 299-300.)

TJFPLMMT

West Park Place toward the corners of Market and Bank Streets, about 1912

The horses look insecure as the trolley goes by; indeed, hitching posts would soon become obsolete on the Green. The photograph above shows some buildings still recognizable in 1986. This is true of the buildings on either side of Bank Street — the old Voorhees Hardware Store, 2-8 Washington Street, now part of Schenck, Price, Smith and King law offices, 10 Washington Street; and the Bell Building, 26 Park Place. The narrow Runyon's Bookstore, 28 Park Place, is now Pottery International.

On the right side of Market Street is the Morristown Trust Company Building, 30 Park Place, now The Gap.

On the left side of Market Street is a large commercial building called Park Row, which replaced the Morris County House. Far left is the First National Bank, built in the 1890s out of half of the Day Building. Today, all the buildings are part of M. Epstein.

Jolting Through Morristown

Song written for the Independent Hose Company's Washington's Birthday Entertainment, 1908

Bring your fancy trotter out, if you
 would take a ride,
Hitch him to a wagonette, be sure
 the springs are wide,
Strap yourself upon the seat, if you
 would there abide,
While you go riding through Morristown.

CHORUS

Ha Ha Ha Ha we're jolting down
 the street,
Ho Ho Ho Ho we can't keep on
 the seat
So we put our arms around the
 girl who is so sweet,
While we go riding o'er Morristown.

Crank the Automobile up, we're going
 to take a spin,
See that all the street diggers are
 snugly packed within,
Take them over humps and bumps,
 and shake them up like sin,
While they go jolting through Morristown.

Soon you'll find on Speedwell way,
 the Trolley will go by,
That's what the owners tell us, but
 we think they tell a lie,
We hope the time will shortly come
 to navigate the sky,
Then we'll go riding o'er Morristown.

CHORUS

Ha Ha Ha Ha we're riding through
 the air,
Ho Ho Ho Ho it makes the people
 stare,
So we put our arm around the girl
 who does not care,
While we go riding o'er Morristown.

I loved trollies; I'd ride all day. One time I was in Perth Amboy, and I took the trolley to Elizabeth — mostly pathlines, no stops — and from there I went to Springfield on the Morris County Traction Company. From Springfield, I went to Morristown, got my bathing suit, and went to Lake Hopatcong.
Joseph Higgins, Morris Township resident, 1982

TJFPLMMT

First trolley, opposite the Resolute Hook & Ladder Company and the old Municipal Hall, August 27, 1909

On that Friday morning, prominent local men and officials of the Morris County Traction Company, which owned the trolley line, met at the United States Hotel on the Green and were taken by horse-drawn stage to Five Corners in Morris Plains (the intersection of Speedwell and Hanover Avenues and Mountain Way), where they boarded the trolley car to ride back to Morristown. The motorman was Edward Milburn and the conductor was Charles Robinson. Mayor Theodore Ayers, a trolley enthusiast, later rode the trolley on a temporary track to the Morris Street train station on December 31, 1910, to fulfill a campaign vow. However, the trolley line was not actually completed around the Green until February 1911. The line was abandoned in February 1928, primarily a victim of the rubber-tired bus.

TJFPLMMT

Changes on West Park Place

Both photographs were taken from the second Babbitt Building looking toward South Street. The Green is on the left and the corner of Market Street is on the right. The dark-looking building jutting out in the background as the street narrows is 31 South Street. Built for the Young Men's Christian Association, it later became The Parker Studio and is now an office building. Just in front of it, barely visible, is the former home of Col. William DeHart, the Revolutionary War hero, for whom the street was named. In the later photograph, a one-story storefront has been built on the sidewalk.

View in 1900 (above), photographed by Dr. Leonidas LeMay Mial. The paths through the Green are still in straight lines as seen on the 1850 Marcus Smith map (page 108). However, a fund drive begun that year collected $5,000 to beautify the Green with curved paths and new landscaping. The changes occurred in 1908 following the designs of Morristown's John R. Brinley.

View on June 21, 1934 (opposite). The horses and buggies and two-way traffic have disappeared. The traffic jam and corner policeman have arrived. Note the street sign reading "Park Pl. W." for what is now called North Park Place.

Morristown Trust Company and the First National Bank can still be seen, but Park Row and the smaller buildings (page 288) have been replaced.

Curtiss Collection/TJFPLMMT

Morristown and Its Points of Interest, 1894

Changes on North Park Place

This first side to be developed commercially, the old Court Street, has undergone many changes. Until recently, it was the only side with a five-story (the second Babbitt) building. **Looking west toward Bank Street, 1894** (above). The Arnold, or second Hoffman Building, has replaced the Arnold Tavern. To the left is a two-story building bought by jeweler John E. Parker and George A. Laurence in 1876. On the right is the Post Office and the new office of *The Jerseyman*. In the 1870s, this two-story building was remodeled by the James Wood Estate and became known as Post Office Row. Note the stores' call bells at the curb. **Looking east toward Water Street** (clockwise from lower left). **Early 1920s view.** From left, there are the enlarged and remodeled Parker Building (partly obscured), The Arnold Building, Post Office Row, two Canfield Houses, United States Hotel, unnamed building dating before 1868, McAlpin Building, and the 1907 Municipal Building. **The 1927 view.** The United States Hotel has been torn down. On the right of Water Street on East Park Place are the Becker Building and the Park Theater, which featured both vaudeville and movies. **The 1938 view.** On the left is the second Babbitt Building, built in 1896 and torn down in 1956. The Parker Building next door has been handsomely remodeled. The Park Square Building has replaced the United States Hotel.

TJFPLMMT

TJFPLMMT

Curtiss Collection/TJFPLMMT

Courtesy of George E. Nixon/TJFPLMMT

TJFPLMMT

Firemen's Day Parade

Harold A. Price

An annual event which the older residents of Morristown and vicinity will remember very well occurred on Firemen's Parade Day. It was probably the outstanding municipal celebration in Morristown. It was a day when, outside of the very substantial parade which took place, in which many companies from other parts of the state participated, there was a special contest arranged. A frame building about 15 feet in height was erected on Park Place, Morristown, at the corner of Park Place, Washington Street and Bank Street. As part of the entertainment on that day, after the parade a contest was held in which one of the companies with one of the pieces of horse-drawn apparatus would, on the sounding of a fire alarm, start from the corner of Madison Avenue and South Street in Morristown and, racing at full speed, come to the small wooden shack which had been erected on the street, as aforesaid. That shack had been ignited by pouring flammable material on it and setting it on fire. The test was to achieve the shortest elapsed time in which, from the time of the sounding of the alarm, the fire could be extinguished. It was an interesting contest. It was viewed by hundreds of persons from Morristown and vicinity. There was great rivalry among the various companies in attempting to extinguish the fire on respective occasions. They were really working against the clock. And the shortest possible time was the objective of the particular company then taking part in the event.

It is noted, of course, that this type of entertainment was one which had an added flavor because the fire engines were drawn by horses. These were very intelligent animals and it was not very long after a team had been selected and had gone through a

Selected from interviews conducted by Ruth Grimm at Judge Price's home in Morris Township, April and May 1982.

He was born in Morristown on July 13, 1893, and graduated from Morristown High School in 1910 and New York University Law School in 1916. That year he became associated with King & Vogt, later Schenck, Price, Smith and King, where he served as partner until retiring in 1985. From 1956 to 1963, he was a member of the Superior Court of New Jersey, serving as presiding judge from 1958 to 1963.

training period before the horses seemed to know the importance of the alarm and acted accordingly. For instance, in the fire station which housed the hook and ladder company and the horses drawing the hook and ladder, which company was known then and today is also known as the Resolute Hook and Ladder Company, the horses in the stalls, when an alarm sounded, would be released by the pressure of a button by the fireman on night duty or on day duty. The horses, usually dappled grays, always named "Tom" and "Jerry," would immediately run to the front of the truck. Another button would be pressed, and the harness would be released from the ceiling and land on the backs of the horses. So practically all the fireman in charge had to do was to fasten the strap by way of a girth and put the bits in the horses' mouths, and they were ready to travel. It always seemed to me that they were as excited and looking forward to the event as were the firemen in answering the fire alarm.

Over the years the firemen's parade, with the attendant entertainment, was viewed by persons who were not only, as I have indicated, residents of Morristown and Morris Township, but came from many surrounding areas in the state. In the parade it would be astounding to note the distance from which some pieces of apparatus of various types had been brought to the town for participation in the parade.

It also should be noted that one of the sidelights of the entertainment that day was for an extension ladder to be raised against the Babbitt building located at the corner of Washington Street and Park Place. It was called Morristown's skyscraper. It was five stories in height. It was razed many years ago and the two-story building now present was erected in its place. The five-story Babbitt building was the outstanding building in the Park Place area. As I have above noted, one of the events on Firemen's Day was the raising of a ladder up to the window on the fifth floor. A fireman would climb the ladder and go through the motions of rescuing a child from the fifth story. It was always a wooden doll, but he would climb the ladder into the window, grab the doll from what was supposed to be a room in flames, and climb down the ladder with the doll (assumed to be a baby) in his arms, indicating how the rescue could be accomplished.

Curtiss Collection/TJFPLMMT

Curtiss Collection/TJFPLMMT

Prince and Duke (opposite, above) pulling the Independent Hose Company's pumper in a fire-fighting demonstration at West Park Place and Bank Street on Inspection Day, October 13, 1903. **Tom and Jerry** (opposite, left) ready to race for Fire Chief F. A. Trowbridge on the Resolute Hook and Ladder truck. **Fire equipment demonstration** (above, right), showing a stream of water aimed over the flagpole on the Green and **rescue of a baby** (doll) from the second Babbitt Building, North Park Place, both on October 12, 1922.

TJFPLMMT

The Changing North Corner

The Speedwell Corner of the Green, about 1850. When Edward Kranich painted this scene, Speedwell Avenue was called Bridge Street. Not a colonial road, it was cut through in the early part of the 19th century and named for the bridge over the stream near Spring Street that filled the mill pond in the Hollow and flowed into the Whippany River (Macculloch Map, pages 70-71).

Water Street began to the right of the building marked L. D. Evans.

Between Speedwell Avenue and Spring Street, there was a deep ravine, whose steepness is seen behind the Flury (or Fleury) Bakery in the painting.

This corner went through a number of changes and is now part of Headquarters Plaza.

The Speedwell corner, about 1900 (above, opposite), showing the McAlpin Building on the left and the Becker Building on the right, and the **same scene in 1910** (below, opposite). Note the changes that have taken place in less than 10 years. In 1907, the tower-shaped Municipal Building was opened and the philanthropist D. Willis James donated the white Vermont granite water fountain with a generous-sized bowl for horses and, on the other side, a fountain for humans and a smaller basin for dogs. The carving was done by Morristown's Davis Granite Company, which also carved the Civil War Monument, and John R. Brinley and John S. Holbrook of Morristown were engaged to beautify the site with a small surrounding park. Handsome street lights have replaced the tall gangly poles.

The Most Dramatically Changing Corner

All the corners of Park Place have changed over the years, but none so dramatically as the north corner of the Green. Today, this is unquestionably the "city corner."

In 1893, the Baptist Church, which had occupied the northwest corner since 1771, was replaced by the elegant McAlpin Building. D. H. McAlpin, a wealthy New York tobacco manufacturer, erected the combination commercial and apartment building for approximately $100,000 on plans furnished by Morristown architect Robert C. Walsh. About 60 feet fronted on North Park Place and 210 feet on Speedwell.

The first story was Indiana limestone, and the upper three were buff brick and terra-cotta. Two large stores faced on Park Place with the building's main entrance between them. Nine large offices occupied the second floor. Above these was the second Washington Hall, which included a two-story ballroom, reception rooms, drawing rooms and kitchen facilities. McAlpin Hall became *the* place to give a social function, and the building was an excellent address to have. A curious omission was an elevator. Three years later the second Babbitt Building down the block had one.

On the Speedwell Avenue side were eleven street-level stores with eight sets of three-story apartments above. The parlor floor also contained a large hall, dining room, pantry and kitchen. For each apartment, backstairs and a dumbwaiter ran from the kitchen to the cellar. The upper floors contained bedrooms, up to seven, and — the latest thing in those days — one bathroom.

Unfortunately, the fate that struck many Morristown buildings also sealed that of the McAlpin Building. Despite thick brick walls

TJFPLMMT

TJFPLMMT

TJFPLMMT

Photograph by Barbara Beirne/TJFPLMMT

between sections, two serious fires occurred, one in the cellar in 1930 and a devastating one in September 1945. A lawyer, Edward LeClerc Vogt, whose family has long been associated with Morristown, recalled the second one in a 1984 interview:

"It's the only three-alarm fire that I can remember, and it's only by the merest chance that I happened to be home. Just about every fire company in Morristown and Morris Township was involved in that fire. In the early stages of it, the windows in the first floors blew out and severely injured several people standing on the far side of Speedwell Avenue."

The building was not rebuilt after this fire and instead was bought by Bamberger's of Newark, later Macy's, which opened its store in April of 1949.

The new store maintained closely the horizontal and vertical lines of the McAlpin Building. However, now across the street is a very different structure, the 12-story glass-and-steel "1776" Building, which has changed the face of the Green forever, just as the adjacent Headquarters Plaza complex — three 15-story office buildings, a hotel, mall and two multilevel parking garages — has transformed a triangle of land in the central business district. □

The Green in the 1920s. This aerial photograph is facing north toward Speedwell Avenue. Part of Lake Pocahontas is seen upper right. To make room for Headquarters Plaza, the Speedwell Avenue urban renewal project razed some 30 19th- and early 20th-century buildings on slightly more than 10 acres. The borders were Speedwell Avenue and East Park Place on the west, Spring Street on the north and east, and the Presbyterian Church on the south.

The 1960s hole (above). Note that the first building constructed for Headquarters Plaza was the 2,500-car garage approximately where the Estey house stood at the corner of Spring and Water Streets.

Courtesy of Edward L. C. Vogt/TJFPLMMT

Courtesy of League of Women Voters of the Morristown Area

Aerial view of East Park Place (above, left) looking toward North Park Place and Speedwell Avenue, March 8, 1966. Water Street is off to the right. The McAlpin Building has been replaced by Bamberger's department store, which opened officially at 1:00 p.m. on Friday, April 1, 1949. **The Green, early 1970s** (above, right). Water Street is in the right foreground. All the area from the old Municipal Building to the parking lot beside the Presbyterian Chapel, including Water

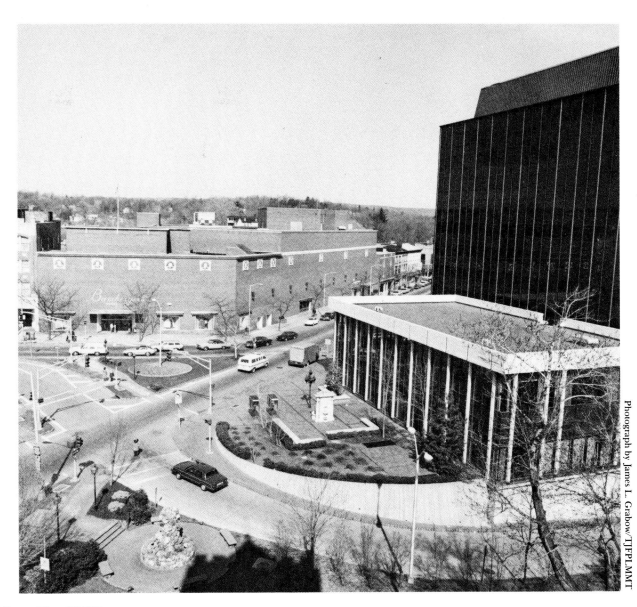

Photograph by James L. Grabow/TJFPLMMT

Street, is about to be razed for the "1776" Building. **The "1776" Building on the Green, 1983** (opposite). The road in the foreground connects the Green to the parking garage and Spring Street but does not follow the old line of Water Street. The building is connected by a mall to Headquarters Plaza on Speedwell Avenue. The Willis Fountain, although saved, looks out of place and is not connected to water.

Always Something New

Photograph by James L. Grabow/TJFPLMMT

Tree marking a former mansion's circular driveway at the construction site of the Shanley & Fisher offices, 131 Madison Avenue, Morristown, 1984.

PLACES, LIKE PEOPLE, change at varying rates. Just like a person, a place can go on for years looking more or less the same until suddenly something happens that alters appearances considerably. For Morristown and Morris Township, that "something" was Interstate Route 287. Even while the route of this highway was being hotly debated in the 1960s, plans were forming to transform the area into a leading commercial center. When the final route cut through near Morristown's center in late 1974 and early 1975, these plans went into action. First to change noticeably were the properties near highway exits and entrances. This was the death knell for a residential Madison Avenue. Then all the main roads began to show — not entirely, not uniformly, but unmistakably — a changing look to multi-story office buildings and city-style development. New roads have been cut through for office parks, not houses. Green areas turned to parking lots; old parking lots became parking garages.

The 1980 census counted a resident population of 16,614 in Morristown and 18,486 in Morris Township, but anyone caught in the clogged streets during morning and evening rush hours or the lunch break can well believe the unofficial estimates that the weekday population triples or quadruples.

Yet Morristown has had its building booms and its influxes of people before and retained its own identity. It is challenged again. □

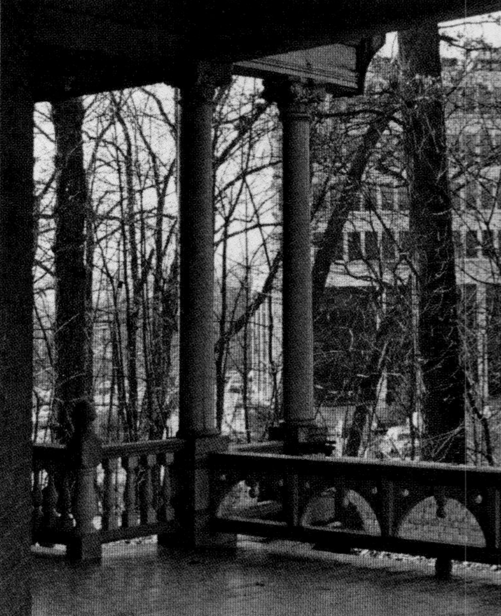

New 1980s offices (right) at 161-163 Madison Avenue, Morristown, as seen from the porch of the Edwin W. Coggeshall mansion, later State Police Headquarters, Madison Avenue, Morris Township, now demolished; and from the opposite side over the roof of **The Thebaud House** (opposite), 151 Madison Avenue, converted to offices.

Photograph by Barbara Beirne/TJFPLMMT

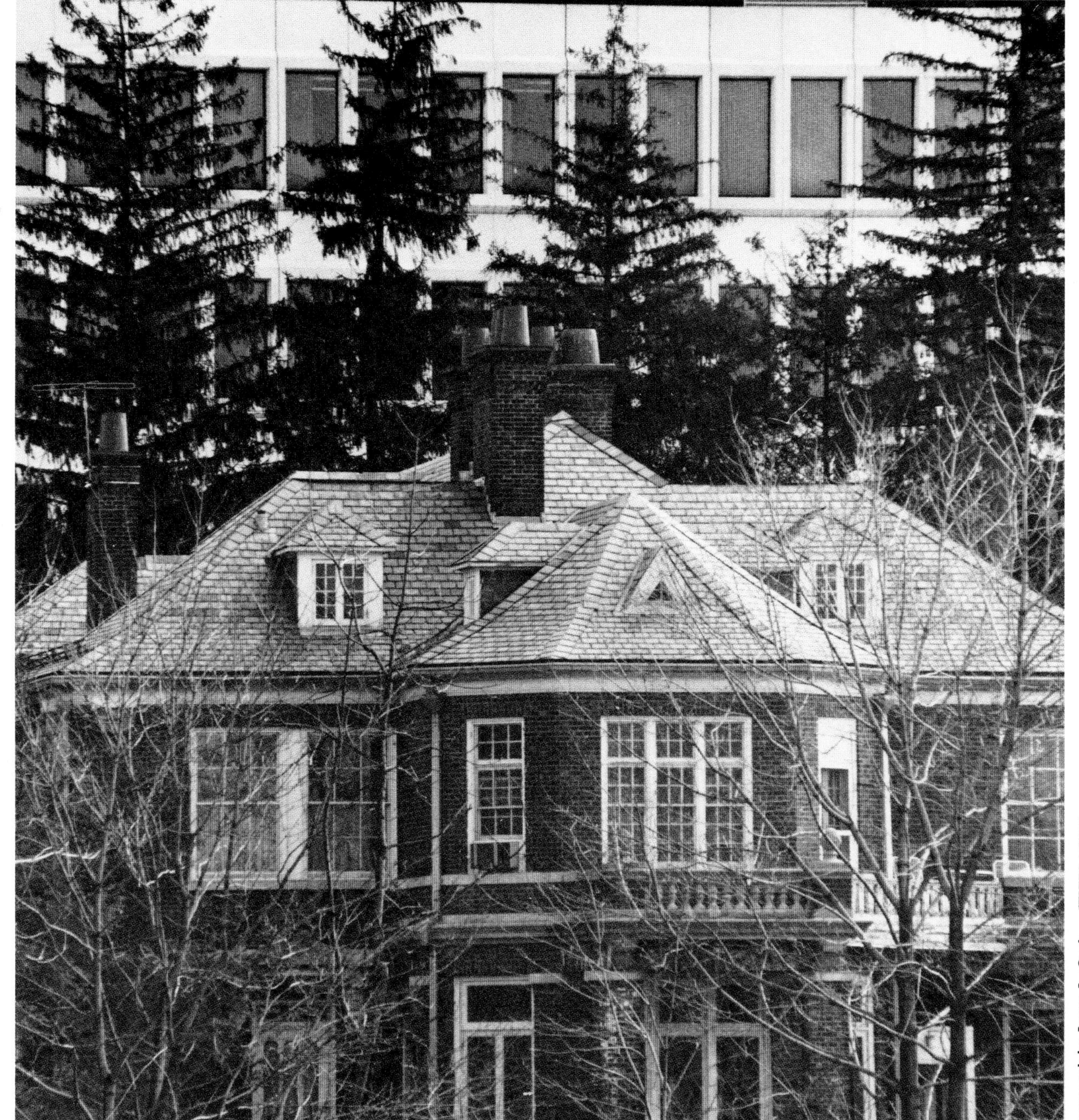

Photograph by James L. Grabow/TJFPLMMT

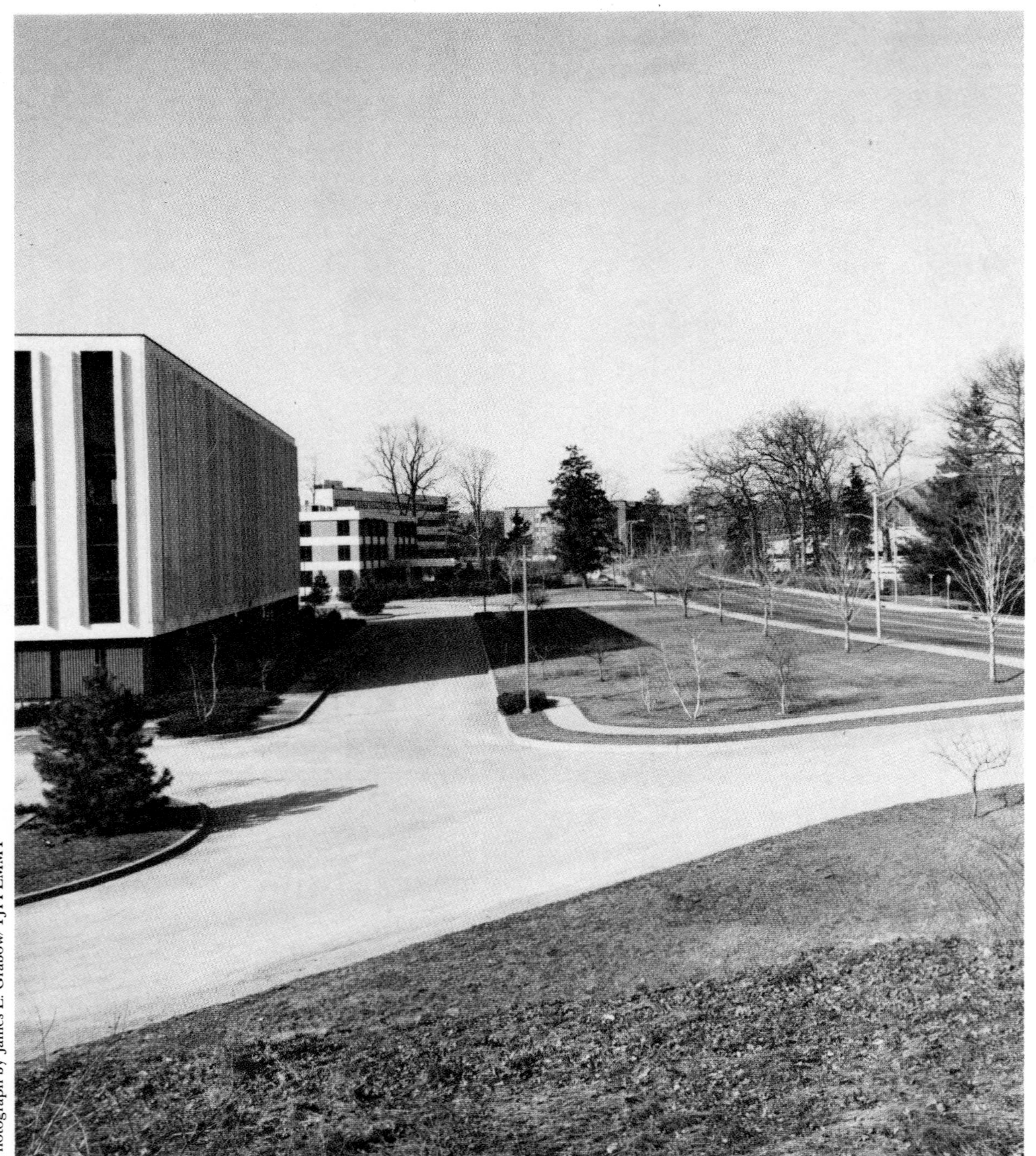

Photograph by James L. Grabow/TJFPLMMT

"Morristown's Golden Mile," 1984. Commercial buildings have replaced the mansions. Such a quiet scene was only possible by photographing early on a Sunday morning. The buildings are, beginning at the curve, The Morris Hills Multicare Center, 77 Madison Avenue; W. Parsons Todd Executive Office Building (formerly site of Airy Hall, the mansion he converted to his office), 95 Madison Avenue; Medical Arts Plaza, 101 Madison Avenue; and 111 Madison Avenue (site of the Stone House).

Photograph by James L. Grabow/TJFPLMMT

The new mix, 1984. Commercial and residential buildings are seen from the Route 287 overpass at James Street, Morris Township. The road in the middle is Southgate Parkway leading to a new office complex on South Street; in the foreground is 100 Southgate Parkway, presently occupied by AT&T. The old Blackberry Lane used to end here. Since this photograph was taken, new houses have been built in the wooded background, part of Rolling Hill at Blackberry. The natural area borders the overpass.

Photograph by Barbara Beirne/TJFPLMMT

Photograph by Barbara Beirne/TJFPLMMT

Photograph by Barbara Beirne/TJFPLMMT

Maple Avenue (above), near the corner of Miller Road, part of the Morristown Historic District. The residential look has been saved by commercial owners, mostly doctors and lawyers, who preserved buildings and maintained the lawns. **The 1827 Court House** (upper center) and its expanding complex, Western Avenue to Court Street, 1970s. The photograph was taken at the Baptist Church corner, High Street. **Washington Street** (lower center), from the High Street corner, 1970s. With the exception of the recent brick office building at 32 Washington Street at the corner of Schuyler Place, the buildings have a 19th-century look.

Photograph by James L. Grabow/TJFPLMMT

View from St. Peter's Church tower toward Egbert Hill (above). Market Street is in the foreground, with the old Washington Engine No. 1 and Independent Hose Company's firehouses in the center. In the middle is the 1827 Court House surrounded by county buildings and the jail. The number of houses is deceptive. There are many more homes than are visible in this photograph, and buildings are popping up in the narrow side lots at an astonishing rate.

In fact, something has been altered in each of the ten modern views in this section, reminding us that change never ceases in Morristown.

Author's Note — 1986

THIS IS THE BOOK I would like to have read when I moved to Morristown with my husband Cliff in May 1955. We lived in an apartment opposite George Washington's statue and always took visitors through the Ford Mansion across the street. I waited for the New York bus beside the stone commemorating the site of the Life Guard's huts. Another regular trip with visiting friends was down Madison Avenue, which still had a number of mansions on it, although they had obviously seen better days. It was hard to imagine what life had been like in those houses, but somehow you could still tell that they had seen sumptuous times. In researching this book, I kept in mind the questions that had occurred to us so many years ago.

I spent many, many pleasant hours delving through books, pamphlets, albums, maps, documents, the bulging "vertical files" of newspaper clippings and over 10,000 photographs and postcards in the Local History and Genealogy Department of The Joint Free Public Library of Morristown and Morris Township. I became more and more impressed with the library's resources and fascinated with Morristown history but confused about how to pack the interesting information I was learning into a reasonable-sized book. My research swelled into 14 notebooks, but the finished manuscript eluded me.

Finally, I decided on certain criteria and the book began to have life. I limited the book to Morristown and Morris Township and tried to convey the "look and feel" of this area by combining photographs, drawings, maps and original source materials. Although I am proud of the many excellent photographs in this book, I sometimes chose an old, faded photograph if it best illustrated a point I was making. In keeping with this search for capturing the flavor of a particular period, I retained original spelling and grammar in the quoted material, only lightly adding punctuation when necessary for modern comprehension.

In some areas, the library collection was incomplete — a natural outcome of photographs received as donations or through random acquisition — or it did not contain the exact view I wanted. When this occurred, I borrowed photographs from the organizations and individuals whose names are credited beside their photographs. Many of these photographs have now been added to the library collection, enriching it further.

The library has been a second home to me since Jeanne Will suggested this book in December 1981. I am also extremely grateful for the enthusiastic support of Barbara Hoskins and Marian Gerhart, then the library's director, and to the Caroline Rose Foster Fund, which agreed to publish this book. The members of the library staff have all been wonderful in many ways, but I want to thank particularly Diane M. Solomon and Lois R. Densky, as well as Wendy M. Beam, Diana Cheng, Sheila S. Goeke, Susan H. Gulick and Florence L. Many.

Many others gave me assistance and encouragement along the way. However, I doubt if this book would ever have been finished if it were not for Robert P. Guter, Frances D. Pingeon and Sybil Raiman, who read and commented on the manuscript, and Marion M. Wiss, who virtually adopted me while she was typing.

Author's Note — 1994

WHILE I BEGAN WRITING *In Lights and Shadows* more than a decade ago, The Joint Free Public Library of Morristown and Morris Township was planning a new addition that doubled its size. The two were related: a more modest version of this book was to be a thank-you present for the $1,000 donors to the building project. The Dowling Wing, dedicated on October 11, 1987, and named for major donors Edythe and Dean Dowling, provided a new Children's Room and Periodical Room on the main floor, a new and expanded Local History and Genealogy Department on the second floor, and a Meeting Room, a preservation laboratory and storage areas in the basement. Meanwhile, this book also grew and grew. Happily, the increase in scope greatly enlarged its potential audience. Now, mostly through word-of-mouth, the first printing is completely sold out, and this second printing is needed.

The important addition is the foreword by New Jersey's premier historian, John T. Cunningham, for which I am extremely grateful. It gives a broad perspective from one who grew up in Morris County and feels most comfortable here, changes and all.

In this edition there are few revisions except those required by the passage of time — Macy's corner, for example, "disappeared" as a helpful landmark when the store closed in June 1993 — and by the discovery of those pesky errors not caught earlier in proofreading. I am grateful to the Rev. James Elliott Lindsley and Lucille Mayo for sending letters that included corrections and suggestions and to Anne Yardley for informing me that the portrait in the Christopher Raymond Perry Rodgers House has turned out to be of Commodore Matthew C. Perry.

This is the fourth time I have counted on Jay Winslow at Birdlow Associates for typography and design advice and the second time on his partner, Arlene Hankowski. It is a great comfort in this fast-changing world to work with the familiar and dependable.

It cannot be a secret that The Joint Free Public Library of Morristown and Morris Township means a great deal to me. This printing was again funded by the Caroline Rose Foster Fund, and I thank Nancy B. Hammeke, former Library director, for enthusiastically initiating the process. Susan H. Gulick, new Library director, and Lesley Douthwaite, chairman of the Local History and Genealogy Department, have been highly supportive. Mrs. Douthwaite not only reread the book with her fine critical eye — something I felt too close to the pages to do — but also shepherded it through the reprinting process. All her department members have been very helpful as well, but I would like to mention in particular Deborah M. Smith, Cheryl C. Turkington and Claire Kissil.

Marion M. Wiss has again been completely indispensable. Long ago I learned I could never do a project without her, and this one is no exception.

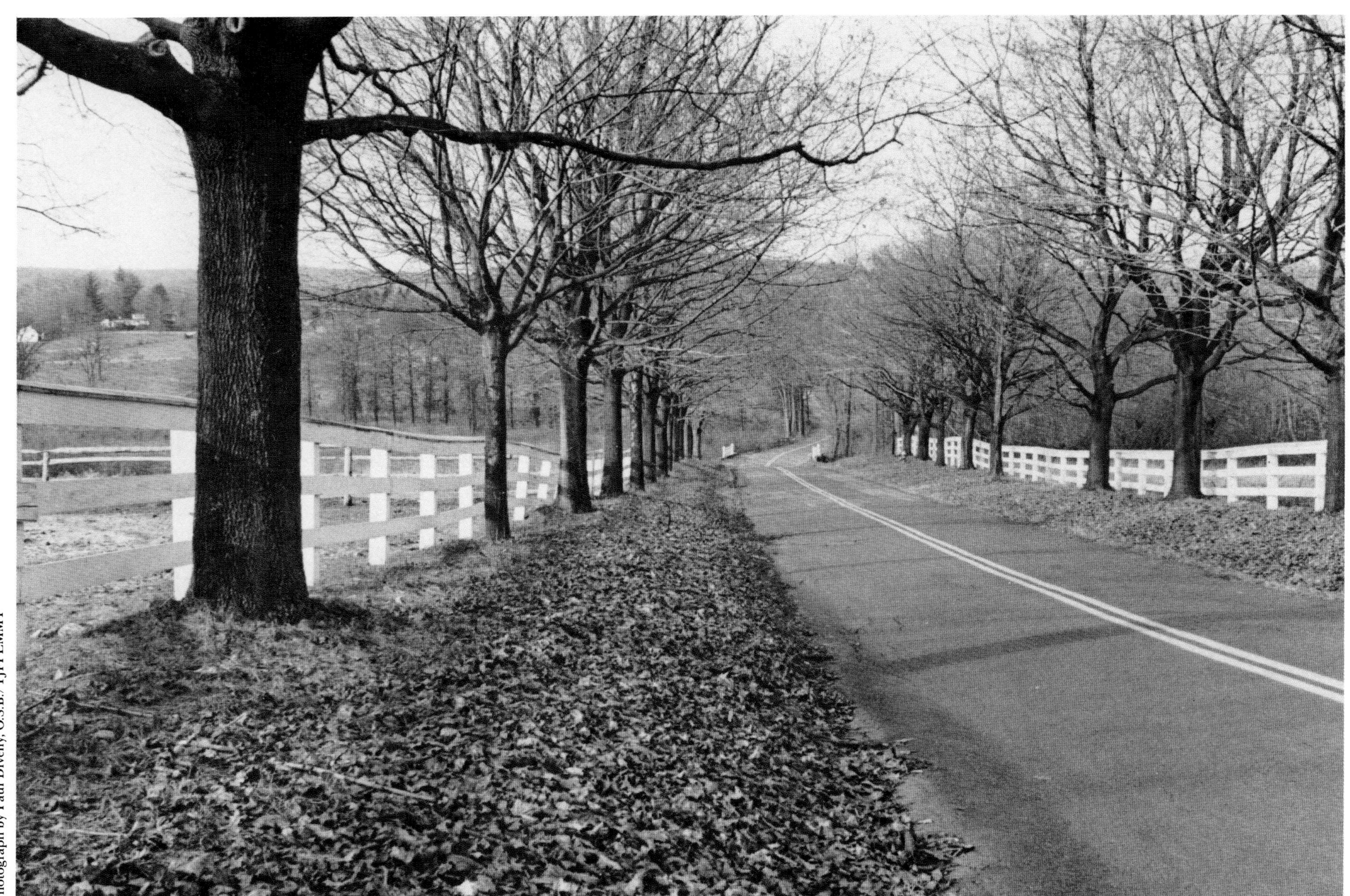

Photograph by Paul Diveny, O.S.B./TJFPLMMT

Whitehead Road, Washington Valley, Morris Township, early 1980s.

Bibliography

The Vivid Past

Introductory, General

Fitzpatrick, John C., ed. *The Writings of George Washington, 1745-1799*. Washington, D.C.: U.S. Government Printing Office, January 1931. (Includes Washington's letters from Morristown in 1777 and 1779-80.)

Flexner, James Thomas. *George Washington in the American Revolution (1775-1783)*. Boston: Little, Brown & Co., 1967.

Gerlach, Larry R. *New Jersey in the American Revolution, 1763-1783*. Trenton, N.J.: New Jersey Historical Commission, 1975. (Letters and documents helpfully introduced and footnoted.)

Gerlach, Larry R., ed. *New Jersey's Revolutionary Experience*. 28 vols. Trenton, N.J.: New Jersey Historical Commission, 1975. Volume 3: *Morristown, A Crucible of the American Revolution*, by Bruce W. Stewart.

London, Leonard. *Cockpit of the Revolution, The War for Independence in New Jersey*, 1940. Reprint. New York: Octagon Books, 1972, through special permission with Princeton University Press. (Good background material placing the Morristown encampments in perspective.)

Proceedings of the New Jersey Historical Society. First through New Series. Newark: By the Society, 1845-. (Morristown and Morris Township people appear throughout the indexes in this series.)

Sherman, Rev. Andrew M. *Historic Morristown, New Jersey, The Story of Its First Century.* Morristown, N.J.: The Jerseyman Press, 1905.

Thacher, James. *A Military Journal During the American Revolutionary War, from 1775 to 1783*. Boston: 1823.

Thayer, Theodore. *Colonial and Revolutionary Morris County.* Morristown, N.J. The Morris County Heritage Commission, 1975. (Published in honor of the nation's Bicentennial and authorized by the Morris County Board of Chosen Freeholders.)

Tuttle, Rev. Joseph F. *Annals of Morris County.* n.p., n.d. (Includes "Biographical Sketch of General William Winds of Morris County, New Jersey"; "Early History of Morris County"; "History of the Presbyterian Church of Rockaway"; "The Revolutionary Forefather of Morris County"; and "Washington in Morris County.")

________. *Revolutionary Fragments, Morris County, New Jersey.* Morristown, N.J.: *The Jerseyman*, 1896. Originally published in the *Newark Daily Advertiser*, 1850.

The Washington Association of New Jersey. *Publications.* 1887-. (Contain the yearly reports of the Superintendent of the Morristown National Historical Park to The Washington Association of New Jersey and the addresses given at the Washington's Birthday meeting.)

"Washington at Morristown During the Winters of 1776-77 and 1779-80." *Harper's New Monthly Magazine*, February, 1859. (A popular history for a national audience.)

Weig, Melvin J. *Morristown National Historical Park, A Military Capital of the Revolution.* Number 9 of the Historical Handbook Series, Washington, D.C.: National Park Service, 1950. (Concise account of Washington's two encampments.)

Special Interest

Archives of the State of New Jersey. Second Series, Newspaper Extracts. 5 vols. (Covers newspaper notices from January 1776 to July 1782.)

Bartenstein, Fred, and Bartenstein, Isabel. *New Jersey's Revolutionary War Powder Mill.* Morristown, N.J.: Morris County Historical Society, 1975.

Bartenstein, Fred, Jr. *The New Jersey Brigade Encampment Near Morristown, Winter of 1779-1780.* Mendham, N.J.: By the Author, October 1967.

Cataldo, Mary Ann, and Benvenuti, Judi. *Morristown, The War Years 1775-1783.* Philadelphia: Eastern National Park and Monument Association, 1979. (Quotations selected by Mary Ann Cataldo; four-color photographs, many taken during the Bicentennial year, by Judi Benvenuti.)

Chastellux, Francois Jean, marquis de. *Travels in North America in the years 1780, 1781 & 1782.* Translated from the French, 1787, 1828. Reprint. Chapel Hill, N.C.: For the Institute of Early American History and Culture at Williamsburg, VA, by the University of North Carolina Press, 1963.

Cherry, William. *Bill of Mortality: 1768-1806, Being a Register of all Deaths which have occurred in the Presbyterian and Baptist Congregations of Morris-Town New Jersey, For Thirty-Eight Years Past, containing (with but few exceptions) the Cause of Every Decease. This Register, for the first twenty-one years, was kept by the Rev. Doctor Johnes, since which time by William Cherry, The Present Sexton of the Presbyterian Church at Morris-Town,* 1806. Reprint. American Institute of Morristown, 1968.

Collections of The Joint Free Public Library of Morristown and Morris Township: Cutler Collection, Henry W. Pilch Collection.

Fleming, Thomas. *The Secret War in Morristown.* Morristown, N.J.: Morris County Historical Society, 1980. (Interesting account of Washington's spy network.)

Harte, Bret. *Thankful Blossom, a Romance of the Jerseys, 1779*, 1876. Reprint. Boston: Houghton Mifflin, 1891. (Novel set in Morristown and Morris Township.)

Hoffman, Philip H. *History of "The Arnold Tavern."* Morristown, N.J.: Chronicle Press, 1903.

Hoskins, Barbara, comp. *Men from Morris County Who Served in the American Revolution.* Morristown, N.J.: Friends of The Joint Free Public Library of Morristown and Morris Township, 1979.

Kelsey, Rayner Wickersham, Ph.D. *Cazenove Journal 1794, A Record of the Journal of Theophile Cazenove Through New Jersey and Pennsylvania.* Translated from the French, Haverford College Studies, Number 13. Haverford, Pa.: The Pennsylvania History Press, 1922.

Lindsley, James Elliott. *A Certain Splendid House. The Centennial History of the Washington Association of New Jersey.* Morristown, N.J.: The Washington Association of New Jersey, 1974.

McClintock, Emory. "Topography of Washington's Camp of 1780 and Its Neighborhood." The Washington Association of New Jersey Publications. Volume 1, 1897-1898. (Read at their meeting of February 22, 1894.)

Neighbors to the Winter Camp. Morristown, N.J.: Brookside Woman's Club, 1977.

"Orderly Book Kept by General George Washington at his Head Quarters in the Jacob Ford House, Morristown, N.J. from December 3, 1779 to May 29, 1780." Copies from the Original Manuscript on file in the Archives of The New-York Historical Society, 170 Central Park West, New York City. (General Orders during the second encampment.)

Scherzer, Carl B. *Washington's Forgotten Encampment.* Morristown, N.J.: Morris County Historical Society, 1977.

Smith, Samuel Stelle. *Winter at Morristown, 1779-1780, The Darkest Hour.* Monmouth Beach, N.J.: Philip Freneau Press, 1919. (Authoritative account of the second encampment, with emphasis on maps and military movements.)

Stryker, William S. *Official Register of the Officers and Men of New Jersey in the Revolutionary War.* Baltimore: Genealogical Publishing Company, 1967.

Stryker-Rodda, Harriet, ed. *Some Early Records of Morris County, New Jersey, 1740-1799.* (Published under the patronage of the Morris County Archives Publications Committee.)

Sunderland, Edwin S. S. *A History of Old Wheatsheaf Farm, formerly "Solitude," 1737, prior to, during and subsequent to the Continental Army and Washington's Headquarters being located, 1779-80, at Morristown, New Jersey, the Westernmost Colonial Puritan Churchtown and the Outpost of New England.* Morristown, N.J.: By the Author, October 21, 1955.

Thane, Elswyth. *Washington's Lady, the Life of Martha Washington.* New York: Dodd, Mead, 1960. (Excellent source on Martha Washington in Morristown.)

Youngs, Stephen. *Memorandum Book Begun In the Year of Our Lord One thousand Sevenhundred and Ninetty Three.* (Typewritten volumes containing examples of the original manuscript.)

Golden Years

Introductory, General

Cutler, Ralph H., Jr., and Scherzer, Carl B. *Morristown and Morris Township, A Guide to Historic Sites.* Morristown, N.J.: The Washington Association of New Jersey for The Morristown American Revolution Bicentennial Committee, November 1975.

History of Morris County, New Jersey, with Illustrations and Biographical Sketches of Prominent Citizens and Pioneers, 1739-1882. New York, W. W. Munsell & Co., 1882. (Interesting and invaluable source book with strong emphasis on names. The chapter on Morristown and Morris Township history was written by the Rev. Rufus S. Green.

Hoskins, Barbara. *Morris Township, a Glimpse into the Past.* Morristown, N.J.: American Revolution Bicentennial Committee, 1976. Reprint forthcoming. (The Township's historic houses and their owners up to the 1970s, organized geographically.)

Hoyt, J. K. *Pen and Pencil Pictures on the Delaware, Lackawanna, and Western Railroad.* New York: W. H. Cadwell, Publisher, n.d. (Morristown is covered in Part II.)

Kaschewski, Marjorie: *The Quiet Millionaires (The Morris County That Was).* Morristown, N.J.: Morris County *Daily Record*, 1970.

Rae, John W., and Rae, John W., Jr. *Morristown's Forgotten Past — The Gilded Age.* Morristown, N.J.: By the Authors, 1979.

Surdam, Charles E., and Osgoodby, William Gardner, compilers. *Beautiful Homes of Morris County and Northern New Jersey.* Morristown, N.J.: Pierce & Surdam, n.d.

Special Interest

Bell, Augustus W., ed. *A History of the Old Fire Association and the Present Fire Department of Morristown, New Jersey, Covering the Period from 1792 to 1926,* 1970. Mimeographed. (A handwritten history by year.)

Collection of The Joint Free Public Library of Morristown and Morris Township, Local History Department. Oral History. Day, Thomas, March 16, 1982; Day, Wilbur, Jr., December 5, 1982.

Colles, Julia Keese. *Authors and Writers Associated with Morristown, with a Chapter on Historic Morristown.* Morristown, N.J.: Vogt Bros., 1893. 2nd ed., 1895.

Costanzo, James V. *New Neighbors, Old Friends: Morristown's Italian Community, 1880-1980.* Morristown, N.J.: Morris County Historical Society, 1982.

Cutler, Elizabeth Lee. *Indeed a Happy Home, The Annals of The Mount Kemble Home, 1883-1983.* Morristown, N.J.: Hartline Printing, 1983.

Hoskins, Barbara. *Washington Valley Schoolhouse, 1869-1969.* Morristown, N.J.: n.p., 1969.

Jerseyman, The. (Weekly newspaper published from 1826 to 1931.)

Merrell, Lawrence, ed. *Morristown Topics.* (Bound copies available from December 31, 1920, to October 30, 1930. Society News.)

Morristown and Its Points of Interest, with Illustrations from Recent Photographs. New York, Mercantile Illustrating Co., 1894. (Contains description of many local businesses.)

Morristown, New Jersey, Photo-Gravures. Morristown, N.J.: Wm. K. Muchmore, Stationer, 1895. (Photographs of Morristown streets.)

Pitney, Henry C., Jr., ed. *A History of Morris County, New Jersey, Embracing Upwards of Two Centuries, 1710-1913.* 2 vols. New York, Chicago: Lewis Publishing Company, 1914. (Vol. 1, general history and articles by local writers; Vol. 2, biographies of prominent county residents with emphasis on the 19th century.)

Sherman, Rev. A. M. *Morristown, New Jersey, in the Spanish-American War.* Morristown, N.J.: Jerseyman Office, 1900.

Taber, Thomas T., III. *Morristown and Erie Railroad, People, Paper and Profits.* Morristown, N.J.: Railroadians of America, 1967.

Tomlinson, Norman Balderston, comp. *Fires of the Past in Morristown.* Morristown, N.J.: The Daily Record Print, 1926. (Description of fires from 1826 to 1926. Much of the material was secured from the scrapbooks kept by James R. Voorhees, volunteer of the Independent Hose Company.)

True Democratic Banner, The. (Weekly newspaper published from 1838 to 1917.)

Houses, Families

deForest, Emily Johnson. *James Colles, 1788-1883, Life & Letters.* New York: By the Author, 1926.

Fiske, William E. *A Curious Childhood.* Madison, N.J.: By the Author, 1975.

Foster, Caroline; Foster, Gladys; Hoskins, Barbara; and Roberts, Dorothea. *Washington Valley, An Informal History.* Ann Arbor, Mich.: By the Authors, 1960. (Caroline Foster wrote the chapter on Fosterfields.)

Matz, Mary Jane. *The Many Lives of Otto Kahn, A Biography.* New York: The Macmillan Company, 1963.

Morris County Historical Society. *Acorn Hall, The Families, The House, The Grounds.* Morristown, N.J.: By the Society, 1980.

Paine, Albert Bigelow. *In One Man's Life, Being Chapters from the Personal and Business Career of Theodore N. Vail.* New York: Harper & Brother, 1921.

Historic Speedwell

Braynard, Frank O. *S. S. Savannah, The Elegant Steam Ship.* Athens, Ga.: University of Georgia Press, 1963. (Much of the ship's engine was built at Speedwell Iron Works.)

Cavanaugh, Cam; Hoskins, Barbara; and Pingeon, Frances. *At Speedwell in the 19th Century.* Morristown, N.J.: The Speedwell Village, 1981.

Righter, S. Ward. *Smithsonian Alfred Vail Manuscript, Being the Description and Correspondence of the Conception and Invention of the Telegraph* (2 vols.), 1918. (Copy available at Historic Speedwell and The Joint Free Public Library of Morristown and Morris Township.)

Scott, Franklin D. "Three Weeks With This Serene and Hospitable People [Vail family]." *Baron Klinkowstrom's America, 1818-1820.* Evanston, Ill.: Northwestern University Press, 1952.

Vail, Stephen. *Diaries, 1825-1864.* Unpublished manuscript on microfilm.

Macculloch Hall

Foy, Sally Fairchild, and Winterberg, Linda Z. *Macculloch Hall, A Family Album.* Morristown, N.J.: The Junior League of Morristown, 1980.

Langstaff, John Brett. *New Jersey Generations, Macculloch Hall, Morristown.* New York: Vantage Press, 1964. (History of the Macculloch, Miller, Keasby and Post families.)

Villa Fontana

Rae, John W. *Thomas Nast — The Man Who Drew Santa Claus, and Other Artists, Writers and Publishers of the Golden Age of Illustration.* By the Author, December 1980.

Paine, Albert. *Th. Nast, His Period and His Pictures.* New York, Macmillan Publishing Co., Inc., 1904.

St. Hill, Thomas Nast. *Thomas Nast's Christmas Drawings for the Human Race.* New York, Harper & Row Publishers, 1971.

St. Hill, Thomas Nast. *Thomas Nast, Cartoons & Illustrations, 117 Works.* New York: Dover Publications, 1974.

Churches

Anderson, Diana Colehamer, and Anderson, John J., Jr., Ph.D., with assistance from the Publication Committee of the 250th Anniversary Committee. *Celebrate: A History of the Presbyterian Church in Morristown, New Jersey, 1733-1983.* Morristown, N.J.: The Presbyterian Church in Morristown, New Jersey, 1984. (Well illustrated chronological history interweaving church history with significant events in American history.)

Church of the Assumption. *The Church of the Assumption, Morristown, New Jersey.* Hackensack, N.J.: Custombook Inc., 1972.

Church of the Redeemer. *Centennial History of the Church of the Redeemer, 1852-1952.* n.p., 1952.

Eckman, Margaret. *Witness of the Spirit.* Morristown, N.J.: The Methodist Church, Morristown, New Jersey, 1968.

First Baptist Church. *One Hundred Seventy-fifth Anniversary of the Morristown Baptist Church, 1752-1927.* Morristown, N.J.: First Baptist Church, September 1927.

Flynn, Joseph Michael. *Story of a Parish, the First Catholic Church in Morristown, New Jersey, Its Foundation and Development, 1847-92.* Morristown, N.J.: By the Author, 1892. (Covers the early history of the Church of the Assumption, St. Virgil's Church and St. Margaret's Church; the church schools; All Souls' Hospital.)

History of the First Presbyterian Church, Morristown, New Jersey, Records of Trustees and Session. From 1742-1882. Two parts. Morristown, N.J.: First Presbyterian Church, n.d.

Lindsley, J. Elliott. *A History of St. Peter's Church.* Morristown, N.J.: By the Rector, Wardens and Vestrymen of St. Peter's Church in Morristown, 1952.

The Loyola House of Retreat at Mount St. Katharine, *Jubilee of Gratitude, 1927-1977.* Morristown, N.J., 1977.

Continuity & Change

Introductory, General

Perrucci, Dorianne R. *Morris County, The Progress of Its Legend.* "Partners in Progress" by Robert G. Geelan. Woodland Hills, Calif.: Windsor Publications, 1983. (Sponsored by the Morris County Historical Society. One of the few publications that updates Morristown and Morris Township history.)

League of Women Voters of Morristown Area. *This is Morristown and Morris Township.* Morristown, N.J.: By the League, 1984.

Special Interest

Bostock, Virginia. *The Public Monuments & Sculpture of Morristown, New Jersey.* Morristown, N.J.: By the Author, 1978. (Locations and descriptions with information on donors, sculptors and the "story behind.")

Cavanaugh, Cam. *Morris Township Times, 1740-1990.* Morris Township 250, 1990. (With E. R. Degginger.)

Cavanaugh, Cam. *Saving the Great Swamp, The People, The Power Brokers and an Urban Wilderness.* Frenchtown, N.J.: Columbia Publishing Company, Inc., 1978. (The 1960s fight to keep a 10,000-acre jetport out of the Great Swamp.)

Collection of The Joint Free Public Library of Morristown and Morris Township. Oral History: Beach, Earl, March 18, 1980; Elliott, John, October 1982; Foster, Caroline Rose, February 1, 1968; Mead, Mrs. Homer, May 3, 1974; Mutch, Dr. Thomas S., July 24, 1983; Myers, Russell, April 8, 1980; Papps, Elizabeth, July 30, 1980; Price, Judge Harold, April and May 1982; Schlosser, Milton, September 23, 1971; Vogt, Grace, April 13, 1973; Vogt, Edward L. C., October 1983.

Daily Record. (Publication began in 1900.)

Lowenthal, Larry, and Greenberg, William T. *Morris County Traction Company.* Conshohocken, Pa.: Crusader Printing, 1984.

Schoeffler, Jessica C. *Morristown Parade 1715-1965.* Morristown, N.J.: By the Author, 1967.

Taber, Thomas T., III. *The Rock-A-Bye-Baby.* Williamsport, Pa.: Lycoming Printing Company, 1972.

Index

Printed by Action Graphics, Lincoln Park, N.J.
Typography by Birdlow Associates, Inc., Millburn, N.J.

Bird's-Eye View of Morristown, Morris County, New Jersey, 1876.